Praise for *The Billionaire Who Wasn't*

"Chuck Feeney is a remarkable role model, and the ultimate example of giving while living." —Bill Gates

"Chuck Feeney's success in business, coupled with his commitment to philanthropy, stands as living proof that it is possible to do well and do good at the same time." —Bill Clinton

"Feeney's beneficence already ranks among the grandest of any living American and may someday make him the most generous American philanthropist of all time." —*Time* magazine

"You may never read a book as uplifting as Conor O'Clery's *The Billionaire Who Wasn't: How Chuck Feeney Secretly Made and Gave Away a Fortune*. In vivid, unvarnished prose, *The Billionaire Who Wasn't* recounts Feeney's meteoric rise from blue-collar beginnings in Elizabeth, N.J., to a perch as one of America's titans of commerce, head of Duty Free Shoppers, the largest liquor retailer in the world." — *Washington Post*'s Express

"A rollicking story of how, by stealth, an Irish American obsessed by secrecy built a business empire and revolutionised philanthropy." —*The Economist*, best books of 2007

"The riveting story of a billionaire who gave it all away disturbs deeply rooted assumptions about wealth and power. . . . What makes him so fascinating, and gives such richness to O'Clery's brilliantly engrossing account, is that Feeney both embodies and rebukes the American Dream. O'Clery turns his prodigious research and mastery of sometimes intricate detail into a tight, pacey, crystal-clear narrative. . . . An epic tale." —*Irish Times*

"An engrossing look at an unusual, influential philanthropist. . . . A superbly written, detailed look at Chuck Feeney, who gave away billions. Reads like fiction." —*BusinessWeek*, top ten business books, 2007

"An interesting and well-written book defining a man whom most of us have never heard of." —*Library Journal*

"If [Conor O'Clery's] compelling narrative becomes a blue-print for future efforts to record the life stories of philanthropists, then the reading public might become far more aware of the major donors who have existed in their midst. O'Clery's account of how Charles 'Chuck' Feeney rose from a blue-collar New Jersey neighbourhood to immense riches as founder of global retail enterprise Duty Free Shoppers, and then gave almost every cent away, reads like a cross between a whodunnit and an airport business guru book."   —*Philanthropy UK*

"Dublin-based journalist O'Clery presents an archetypal American success story, a rags-to-riches account with a twist. . . . A smart business book detailing some vicissitudes of retailing, wrapped in a vivid biography of an engaging tycoon."   —*Kirkus Reviews*

"For America's new generation of Internet and private equity billionaires, this is an exemplary tale."   —FT.com

"A gripping read."   —*Sunday Business Post*

ALSO BY CONOR O'CLERY

Phrases Make History Here (1986)

Melting Snow: An Irishman in Moscow (1991)

America, A Place Called Hope? (1993)

Daring Diplomacy (1997; published in Ireland
as *The Greening of the White House*)

Ireland in Quotes (1999)

Panic at the Bank (coauthor, 2004)

May You Live in Interesting Times (2008)

Moscow, December 25, 1991, The Last Day of the Soviet Union (2011)

THE
BILLIONAIRE
WHO WASN'T

How Chuck Feeney
Secretly Made and
Gave Away a Fortune

Conor O'Clery

PublicAffairs
New York

Library of Congress Cataloging-in-Publication Data
O'Clery, Conor.
    The billionaire who wasn't : how Chuck Feeney secretly made and
gave away a fortune / Conor O'Clery.—First edition.
        pages cm
    Includes bibliographical references and index.
ISBN 978-1-58648-391-3 (HC)—ISBN 978-1-61039-334-8 (PB)—
ISBN 978-1-61039-335-5 (EB)
    1. Feeney, Chuck, 1931–. 2. Atlantic Philanthropies (Organization).
3. DFS Galleria (Firm). 4. Businesspeople—United States—
Biography. 5. Billionaires—United States—Biography.
6. Philanthropists—United States. I. Title.

HC102.5.F44 O25 2007
361.74092
[BBS]
                                            2007299698
10 9 8 7 6 5 4 3 2

This, then, is held to be the duty of the man of wealth: first, to set an example of modest, unostentatious living, shunning display or extravagance; to provide moderately for the legitimate wants of those dependent upon him; and after doing so to consider all surplus revenues which come to him simply as trust funds which he is called upon to administer . . . to produce the most beneficial results for the community.

ANDREW CARNEGIE
(1835–1919)

CONTENTS

Photo insert between pages 146–147

AUTHOR'S NOTE AND ACKNOWLEDGMENTS

I first encountered Chuck Feeney at a White House party on March 17, 1994. I had been invited as a Washington-based journalist. Feeney was a guest because of his work to bring peace to Ireland. All I knew about him was that he was listed in *Forbes* magazine as a billionaire, and that he was wearing a cheap watch. But I didn't know, nor did anyone else in the East Room with Bill and Hillary Clinton that evening, that Chuck Feeney was the world's biggest secret philanthropist. Nor did anyone there have any idea that far from being a billionaire, he did not even own a house or a car.

I got to know Chuck Feeney in 2002 when I was assigned by my newspaper to Wall Street and we were introduced by a mutual friend. After several lunch meetings, mostly in his favorite saloon, P. J. Clarke's on Third Avenue, he agreed to cooperate on a book about his life to promote giving while living. He undertook to release family, friends, associates, and beneficiaries from long-standing vows of secrecy, and to allow me access to his archives. He did not seek any control over the final product. Nor did he or his philanthropy finance the biography in any way.

I subsequently received unstinting access. I traveled with him around the world on his never-ending quest to put his foundation's wealth to good use. I enjoyed lunches and dinners with him and his friends in locations as far apart as Honolulu and Ho Chi Minh City. Almost everyone who knew Feeney in his business and philanthropic life was enthusiastic about helping to tell his story, even those with whom he fell out during his business career. I traveled across the mainland United States and to Hawaii, the U.K., Ireland, France, Switzerland, Vietnam, Australia, Thailand, Hong Kong, and Bermuda to conduct interviews with scores of people from different phases of his life.

I am particularly grateful to Chuck Feeney for the patience and good humor with which he endured long interview sessions, and to Chuck and Helga for allowing me to visit them in San Francisco, Brisbane, and Dublin. Members of the Feeney family went out of their way to be helpful: Caroleen Feeney, Danielle Feeney, Diane Feeney, Leslie Feeney Baily, Juliette Feeney Timsit, Patrick Feeney, Jim and Arlene Fitzpatrick, and Ursula Healy. Their insight was invaluable.

The book would not have been possible without the enthusiastic cooperation of Professor Harvey Dale of New York University, founding president of the Atlantic Philanthropies, and John R. Healy, the chief executive from 2001 to 2007.

I am especially grateful to Chuck Feeney's business partners in Duty Free Shoppers—Bob Miller, Alan Parker, and Tony Pilaro—who graciously invited me into their homes in Geneva, Yorkshire, and Gstaad, respectively, to talk about their sometimes fractious relationship with the man who led them to unimaginable riches.

Thanks also to the following who gave interviews for the book: Gerry Adams, Harry Adler, Fred Antil, Adrian Bellamy, Padraig Berry, Gail Vincenzi Bianchi, Christine Bundeson, Jack Clark, Peter Coaldrake, Ron Clarke, Bob Cogan, Frank Connolly, Mark Conroy, Eamonn Cregan, Roger Downer, Francis "Skip" Downey, Jim Downey, Tass Dueland, Jim Dwyer, Joel Fleishman, Ken Fletcher, Phil Fong, John Ford, Howard Gardner, Jean Gentzbourger, John Green, Ray Handlan, Paul Hannon, Mark Hennessy, Ted Howell, Farid Khan, Hugh Lunn, Aine McCarthy, Vincent McGee, Jeff Mahlstedt, Colin McCrea, Michael McDowell, Michael Mann, Bob Matousek, Thomas Mitchell, John Monteiro, James Morrissey, Gerry Mullins, Frank Mutch, Niall O'Dowd, Chris Oechsli, Danny O'Hare, Pat Olyer, Le Nhan Phuong, Bernard Ploeger, Frank Rhodes, Chuck Rolles, David Rumsey, Dave Smith, Jim Soorley, Sam Smyth, Lee Sterling, Ernie Stern, Bonnie Suchet, Don Thornhill, Tom Tierney, Jiri Vidim, Ed Walsh, Sue Wesselkamper, Mike Windsor, and Cummings Zuill. Others who contributed to the project were Jonathan Anderson, Jane Berman, Loretta Brennan Glucksman, Mark Patrick Hederman, Chris Hewitt, Desmond Kinney and Esmeralda, Sylvia Severi, Paddy Smyth, and Walter Williams. Patrick O'Clery read the manuscript and made most helpful suggestions. Declan Kelly helped get the book under way. I am especially grateful for the encouragement of Esther Newberg, my agent, and the invaluable advice of

Clive Priddle, editorial director of PublicAffairs. And finally, my sharp-eyed and imaginative wife, Zhanna, put so much time and editing talent into shaping this book that it became in the end something of a joint effort. For both of us it was a labor of love. I of course am solely responsible for any shortcomings or errors.

All sources are identified in the text except in rare instances where someone requested anonymity or nonattribution.

I am grateful to all those who gave me interviews for the updated edition, in particular Bill Gates, Gara LaMarche, David Skorton, and Richard Kirsch, and to several senior figures in Atlantic Philanthropies and family members, friends, and associates of Chuck Feeney who gave generously of their time but would prefer not to be acknowledged because of the sensitivity of events in the Foundation in 2009-2012.

PROLOGUE

It was sunny and already hot at Nassau International Airport early on Friday, November 23, 1984, as passengers disembarked after the three-hour flight from New York. Most were American vacationers intent on partying in the Bahamas over Thanksgiving weekend. One rather deferential middle-aged man in blazer and open-neck shirt, unremarkable but for his penetrating blue eyes, emerged from economy class. He and his wife took a taxi to an office building on Cable Beach, a string of hotels and apartment blocks by the pale aquamarine ocean waters of the Atlantic, halfway between the airport and the city of Nassau. He was in familiar territory, as he had often used the subtropical island for the business dealings that made him one of the world's wealthiest men. This time, however, he had come to the Bahamas to conclude a deal unlike any he had made before, one that would change his life irrevocably.

Two attorneys were also bound for the Bahamas that morning to meet him. Frank Mutch flew into Nassau airport from Bermuda to act as a legal witness to the deal. Harvey Dale was expected to arrive simultaneously from Florida, where he was spending Thanksgiving with his parents. He was bringing all the necessary documentation. Dale had choreographed the event with meticulous attention to detail. The culmination of two years of planning, the transaction was taking place in the Bahamas to avoid the huge financial penalties that it would incur elsewhere. The Harvard-trained lawyer had secured a conference room from a trust company at Cable Beach where the papers would be signed, a complex process that would take up to three hours but would still allow time for everyone to catch evening flights back to their points of departure.

But when the time came for the signing session, Harvey Dale was nowhere to be seen. The one thing he could not control was the weather.

That morning all planes were grounded at Palm Beach airport because of a persistent thunderstorm overhead. His frustration grew as the hours passed and his flight was not called. In the Bahamas the others waited, going out for a fish and chips lunch before returning to the office and sitting around the conference table, making desultory conversation.

Dale was able to board the Nassau-bound flight at West Palm Beach in the early afternoon. The commuter jet flew straight into the still-rumbling storm cloud and took a heavy buffeting but quickly got clear and arrived in the Bahamas an hour later. He burst into the conference room, out of breath, sometime around 4:00 PM. There was only an hour before they had to vacate the building and return to the airport. He opened his briefcase and spread out agreements, power of attorney, corporate resolutions, and other legal documents on the table. "No time to talk, you sign here, you sign there," he said. Then he gathered up the papers, and they all hurried off to catch evening flights out of the island.

On the drive back to Nassau airport, the man in the blazer, Charles F. Feeney, felt a profound sense of relief. He had flown into the Bahamas that morning an extremely rich man; now he was flying out with little more to his name than when he had started out on his various business ventures three decades earlier. While millions of Americans gave thanks that Thanksgiving weekend for the material things with which they were blessed, he celebrated having divested himself personally of the vast wealth with which fate and his genius for making money had burdened him.

It was all done with the utmost secrecy. Few outside of the small group that gathered that day in the Bahamas would know what had taken place for a long time to come. As much as four years later, *Forbes* magazine listed Feeney as the twenty-third richest American alive, declaring him to be a billionaire worth $1.3 billion. But *Forbes* had got it wrong, and would continue to repeat the mistake for many years afterward. Chuck Feeney had gotten rid of it all. He was the billionaire who wasn't.

PART ONE

MAKING IT

The Umbrella Boy

In the spring of 1931, the Empire State Building was opened in New York as one of the last great triumphs of the economic boom of the Roaring Twenties. At the same time, a number of shocks began hitting the U.S. economy. The Great Depression settled over the United States, banks collapsed, and unemployment soared. It was precisely at this juncture of American history that Chuck Feeney was born, on April 23, 1931, into a struggling Irish American family in the blue-collar neighborhood of Elmora, New Jersey.

His parents, Leo and Madaline Feeney, had come to New Jersey from Philadelphia a few years earlier. The newly married couple had high hopes of a new life in the prosperous environs of New York City, only a few miles away on the other side of the Hudson River. Both their fathers worked on the railroad in Philadelphia and gave them wedding presents of railroad passes for the Pennsylvania–New Jersey line so they could keep in touch.

The pair set up home in Newark's Vailsburg section and later moved on to Elmora, a neighborhood that stretches over both Elizabeth and Union townships. Leo got a job as an insurance underwriter, and Madaline worked as a nurse. They had three children, all born in Orange Memorial Hospital in Elizabeth, New Jersey: two girls, Arlene and Ursula, and in between, their only son, Charles Francis Feeney.

The Feeneys survived the Depression better than many of their neighbors. Both were hardworking. Young Charles saw his mother take on double shifts at the Orange Memorial Hospital and his father setting off at dawn in suit and tie to commute to his job with Royal Globe Insurance Company in New York City. They lived first in rented houses, but when a grandfather died and the family inherited $2,000, they were able to put a down payment on a small, two-story red-brick house on Palisade Road, Elizabeth, in a neighborhood of Catholic Irish and Italian families. The house still stands, shaded by a spruce tree, in a quiet avenue of single-family homes amid a network of busy highways: the Garden State Parkway, Interstate 78, US Route 22, and State Route 82.

Money was tight in the Feeney household. Anyone who lived in working-class New Jersey in the 1930s knew the value of a dollar. Even with two jobs, they had little disposable income and struggled to pay their $32-per-month mortgage and maintain the family car, a green Hudson with worn floorboards and a horn that went off when rounding corners. Their old jalopy sometimes broke down on trips to Philadelphia—the railroad passes did not last for long—or the retread tires would get punctures. They would sometimes visit Madaline's relatives in Pottsville, who were considered rich because they owned a "pretzel factory," which in reality was no more than a large oven in the kitchen, and who reputedly hid their money around the house, though no one admitted to finding any after they died.

People looked after each other in those tough times. Madaline Feeney was a discreet Samaritan, doing favors without anyone knowing. When she noticed that Bill Fallon, a neighbor who had Lou Gehrig's disease, walked to the bus stop to go into New York every day, she would pick him up in the car as he passed the house on the way to the bus stop, pretending that she too was on her way somewhere. "He never knew that she wasn't going anywhere," recalled Ursula. During World War II, Madaline Feeney went off at night in a blue uniform to work as a volunteer Red Cross nurse. She could never understand how other Red Cross workers could take money for their "voluntary" service, which became something of a scandal when disclosed in the newspapers.

Leo Feeney was a daily Mass-goer and also spent much of his time helping others. He joined the Knights of Columbus, a Catholic men's fraternal society that rendered financial aid to members and their families. He was always conscious of getting value for money. When the children were big enough, he walked them to the library on Elmore Avenue. "We pay taxes," he would tell them, "so we must make use of it."

The young Feeney was a lively boy, and a bit mischievous, according to his sister Arlene. "He got thrown out of kindergarten in Bradley Beach for being cheeky. Not that he got into a lot of trouble or anything, but he was always funny. The highlight of my day was to sit with him and laugh. He was a clown. He had a quick wit. He was my mother's favorite. She would say, 'My Charles, my Charles. . . .'"

As early as ten years old, Feeney was displaying a talent for making money. "We didn't have anything," recalled his friend, Francis "Skip" Downey. "A dime was a dime in those days." His first entrepreneurial venture was selling Christmas cards door-to-door, provided by his pal Jack Blewitt's father. Blewitt had the local streets booked for himself, so Feeney went to another neighborhood. He earned a few dimes more helping the mailman post letters coming up to Christmas, and when it snowed he and a friend, Moose Foley, offered to clear people's driveways. "I would call and collect the 25 cents and Moose would dig the snow, and we would split the money," he said. Here he learned his first lesson in overextending a business. "If I got too far ahead collecting money, I had to help out with the shoveling!"

He was always thinking up new money-making schemes, however unrealistic. One summer afternoon, when he was eleven and hanging out at Skip Downey's house, he got a black crayon and wrote the words "Downey's Beer and Pretzels" on the porch, on the off chance that someone might come by and pay them to fetch an order. Skip's mother saw it and told the young Feeney, "Charles, if that is not gone by sundown, you will not see the sun come up." But she adored Chuck, said Skip, now a retired Exxon executive. "He was such a happy-go-lucky guy. She called him 'the mayor' because he knew everyone."

Charles Feeney went to St. Genevieve's Grammar School on Princeton Road, Elizabeth, and in eighth grade he became the only boy to win a scholarship to Regis High School on East Eighty-fourth Street in Manhattan. This was a Jesuit college for "Roman Catholic young men from New York metropolitan area who demonstrate superior intellectual and leadership potential" and who could not otherwise afford a Catholic education. He hated it. He had to get up every morning and walk forty minutes to the station to catch the 7:45 train to the boat pier and get a ferry across the Hudson River, then a subway to Eighty-sixth street. He often didn't get back until 7:00 PM, and then he had homework assignments to do. He couldn't make new friends in Manhattan when he had to commute so far, and all his boyhood pals had gone to St. Mary's of the Assumption High School in Elizabeth, at the top of a hill just at the end of the main street. After a year and a half of misery, and watching his parents scrimp and save to pay his fares, he got himself expelled from Regis High. "I got caught cribbing in a religion exam, but it was part of my plot. If you get caught cribbing in a religious exam they asked you to leave."

At St. Mary's, Feeney was much happier. Practically all the kids were Irish like himself. He was at the center of everything going on. He played Wayne in the school presentation of the comedy *The Divine Flora*, and wore the No. 38 jersey for the high school football squad. He was voted the "wittiest" in his class by the seniors in 1947. His peers voted him the class "cutup" because, said his friend Bob Cogan, "he was always fooling around and he made fun out of everything." He and his best friend, John "Jack" Costello, put on a comedy show. The school magazine for 1948 carried an advertisement: "For an Evening of Pleasant Entertainment Visit The Club Carefree Featuring America's New Comedy Sensation, CHARLIE FEENEY and JOHN COSTELLO." For teenage boys, St. Mary's was like heaven: There were 100 girls to only thirty-five boys in Feeney's year, and there was an all-girls' school across the road. Charlie Feeney had developed into a lean, good-looking youth and "they screamed at us like we were the Beatles," said Cogan.

Always on the make, Feeney made pocket money on weekends caddying at a golf course near Port Elizabeth. "It was nine holes for $1.00 with a tip of 25 cents, or eighteen holes for $1.75 and a tip of 25 cents," he recalled. "I would always look for two nine-hole players." During the summer holidays, when his mother took leave from nursing to rent a rooming house at Point Pleasant on the New Jersey shore and take in paying guests, he got jobs on the boardwalk renting beach towels and umbrellas, and allowing himself to be "dunked" in a tub by contestants throwing balls at him for a few cents. He got so good at winning cuddly toy prizes on the Skee-ball machines that he had to go to another district. In the end, the owner of the machines gave him a job giving out change.

In those days the beach was run by the junior branch of the New Jersey mafia. They had the concessions, including a 25-cent admission fee to parts of the sands. "If you came for a day's stay on the beach, they sold you a colored ribbon that you wore with a safety pin," said Feeney. "They had a bunch of guys who would say, 'Let me see your entrance ribbon, kid.'" His mother provided ribbons to her lodgers. A school friend figured out how to make an extra few cents by reusing ribbons or cutting them in two. "The mob was not pleased and let them know and they stopped," said Arlene.

As a teenager, Charlie Feeney would invite his friends to come for the weekend to the rooming house and bunk down with him in the attic. In the morning he took them for breakfast to a store where donuts were left in a box outside before it opened, allowing hungry boys to help themselves. In the evenings they roamed the boardwalk or went to the cinema. Skip Downey recalled driving Feeney, when they were sixteen, to the Paramount Theatre in Asbury Park, *the* place on the New Jersey shore to take a girl-friend on a date. The guy at the back door recognized Feeney and let them in free. They climbed a ladder behind the screen, crossed a catwalk and went down a ladder at the other side to get to the seats.

His friend Joe Cash years later remembered Feeney as "the type of guy who made you feel he was your best friend and whenever you talked to him he always seemed to be going down the road; he was always thinking ahead." Jack Costello would recall his friend as a hustler who sold umbrellas on the Point Pleasant boardwalk and who "was always working and always making money."

Four months after he graduated in June 1948, and still only seventeen, Feeney went with Costello to the recruiting office in Newark and signed up for the U.S. Air Force. "He volunteered," said his sister Ursula. "He didn't have to. He tried to go even earlier than that with Frankie Corrigan. One night they tried to sneak away from the house. They couldn't go anywhere. The car wouldn't start! They were going to join up and lie about their age, and they wanted me to come down and sign some papers that their mother had given them permission." At the time, three years after the end of World War II, there was still conscription and Feeney knew that he would be drafted anyway within a couple of years. "So I felt, well, I'll just be scratch-ing my ass, I may as well get it over with, so I signed up for three years."

Joining the military opened up new horizons for the New Jersey teenager. After training as a radio operator at Lackland Air Base in Texas, he was sent to serve with the American occupying force in Japan. It was his first time out of the United States. He now had a new life and a new first name—in the Air Force everyone started calling him Chuck. As an exceptionally bright recruit, he was assigned to the U.S. Fifth Air Force Radio Squadron's Mobile Detachment 12 at Ashiya Air Base, on the southern tip of Japan.

This was the nearest air base to the Korean Peninsula. His squadron was part of Signals Intelligence (SIGINT)—an arm of the National Security Agency that had broken the Japanese military code near the end of the war.

Japan was in ruins after the war, but life was not hard for a young serviceman. "Duty there was considered a sweet tour by American soldiers," wrote David Halberstam.* "American dollars went far, the Japanese women were friendly and ordinary enlisted men lived like aristocrats." Staff Sergeant Feeney, however, spent a lot of spare time learning Japanese to improve his intelligence skills. He took lessons at the U.S. military language school and read Japanese comic books, much to the amusement of Japanese children.

When the Korean War broke out on June 25, 1950, Ashiya Air Base became a staging post for F-80 fighter jets and C-119 planes that dropped supplies to U.S. soldiers on the front line. Feeney's tour was extended from three to four years. He wasn't sent to the fighting, but his desk job turned more serious. His squadron's task was to intercept radio communications used by the Russians flying sorties over the Sea of Japan. Soviet pilots would pick up the frequency of aircraft the United States sent up from Ashiya. The Cold War between the United States and the Soviet Union would become a local hot war if a line in the sky was crossed, and the American planes could only go so far before entering hostile air space. One new pilot, just out of his teens, flew across the line for five minutes, enough time for the Russians to scramble. His plane was shot down and he was killed, along with two Russian language specialists on the flight who had been on the shift with Feeney two nights before. He heard their screams in his earphones. When he returned to the United States, Feeney visited the family of one of his fallen comrades in the Bronx district of New York. He didn't know what to say. "They were dead because this guy didn't follow orders which were very clear—don't go over the line."

Throughout his four years of service in Japan, Feeney did not return home once. He was on the other side of the world, and there was a war on. "When he called at Christmas, we'd all sit in the kitchen and wait for the phone call," his sister Arlene remembered. They would accept charges. "We didn't have the money, so it was always—'Don't talk too long!'" His family never saw him in person wearing a uniform. However, the *Elizabeth*

*David Halberstam, *The Fifties* (Villard Books, 1993).

Daily Journal published a photograph of Sergeant Feeney and Corporal Costello, both in U.S. Air Force uniform, hair parted and Bryl-Creamed, enjoying a three-day furlough together in Tokyo. Costello was less fortunate than Feeney. He was sent into combat in Korea as a ground radio operator, though he survived the war and fathered a large family. The caption quoted Feeney saying, "It takes more than a war to keep Jack and me from getting together."

In his letters home, Feeney wrote that he was not allowed to disclose what he was doing. "Maybe that's where he got some of the secrecy from," said Arlene. "When he got out and came home he'd be sitting there doing that"—she rapidly tapped the kitchen table—"*tap, tap, tap:* then he'd say, 'I'm sorry, Morse code, used it in the service.' I don't know whether he 'thought' in it, but he kept on doing it every once in a while, going like this, *tap, tap, tap.*"

CHAPTER

The Sandwich Man

While still in Japan in the spring of 1952, Chuck Feeney began to think of how he might take advantage of the GI scholarship he was entitled to after his discharge. Under President Franklin D. Roosevelt's 1944 GI Bill of Rights, money was made available to returning World War II veterans to go on to higher education, and the scheme was renewed for Korean War veterans. It changed the lives of many Americans who served in the armed forces, such as Donald R. Keough, who went on to run Coca-Cola, and Bob Dole, who became a U.S. senator. Skip Downey suspected that his old school friend had his eye on a GI scholarship all along. The family didn't have the money to send him to college, but "in his mind he *knew* he was going to college and he went to the Air Force to be eligible for the GI Bill."

Feeney went to the base library and began to read up on universities. He found an article in the *Readers' Digest,* entitled "A School for Cooks," which featured Cornell University's School of Hotel Management. "I sort of thought, I could do that, I could look after people." The course offered an outlet for his entrepreneurial bent. Cornell, located in the town of Ithaca in the Finger Lakes region of upstate New York, was the first university in the world to establish a bachelor's degree in hotel management. Feeney had never set foot inside the two grand hotels in Elizabeth, the Winfield Scott and the Elizabeth Carteret, since defunct, but he liked the idea of "travel, elegant surroundings, people serving you." He applied for admission and was called for an interview in Tokyo with a Cornell recruiter. The woman who ran his Japanese language school knew the interviewer, and "she looked over the guy's shoulder to see he wrote only nice things about me!"

He was discharged from the U.S. Air Force on July 1, 1952, with $634.33 back pay and made his way home to New Jersey to await the result of his application to Cornell. He got a rapturous reception after such a long absence, but his parents weren't happy about his choice of university. In those days, Catholic boys from St. Mary's didn't go to Ivy League universities. His father's best friend, a Catholic high school principal, John Dwyer, suggested instead that they drive up one day and take a look at Seton Hall, a private Catholic university closer to home, where Dwyer had some connections. He was nervous that the young Feeney might be aspiring too high in seeking admission to a major Brahmin establishment. The next day, however, the acceptance letter to Cornell Hotel School came in the mail. Feeney was invited to enroll in September. From his class at St. Mary's, only two boys went to university. The other got a scholarship to Rutgers, the state university of New Jersey.

The letter of acceptance was a major event for the Feeneys. No one in the family had ever been to a university. But Feeney was already showing a trait that would assert itself throughout his life: thinking big and aiming to achieve the best result, even if it seemed unattainable. "He did not believe he was ever going to get admitted to Cornell," said John J. (Jack) Clark Jr., a past dean of the Hotel School from Boston, Massachusetts, who also had an Irish Catholic background and understood how big a thing it was for the young Feeney to cross the line. "Most of Chuck's generation and mine were the first generation that started going to college. There weren't a lot of Catholics at Cornell in the fifties or in the Ivy League."

Of all the colleges and schools at Cornell, the Hotel School accepted the lowest SAT (Scholastic Aptitude Test) scores, the standard used to judge a student's potential, but consistently produced the most successful entrepreneurs, such as James W. McLamore and David R. Edgerton, cofounders of Burger King, and Michael Egan, who built up the Alamo car rental business. "The rest of the university kind of looked down on us," said Clark. "One did not need to know the entire history of Greek culture to get accepted into the Hotel School, but it looked for a good combination of brains and physical energy."

At first Feeney felt he had strayed out of his social depth, his sisters believed. Everyone else seemed to come from prep schools and had cars. But he quickly adjusted to life in Ithaca. He found himself in the company of a lot of guys of like mind—budding entrepreneurs, eager to get an education, explore the world, and make their fortunes. "Once they let me in I was certainly capable of competing with the people who were in there," he recalled. "I had to get there to figure that out."

He soon showed just how talented an entrepreneur he was. He spotted a niche market right away. There was no Wendy's or McDonald's in Ithaca then. The students got hungry at night, and most were privileged, with cash in their pockets. Feeney began to make and sell sandwiches around the fraternities and sororities. He soon became known on the campus as the "Sandwich Man." He needed the extra income to survive at Cornell, as his GI scholarship provided only $110 a month during each term to cover tuition, leaving him with little disposable income. At the start, he paid for the ingredients at the store late on Friday so that his checks would not be cashed until Monday. "It was my first experience of deficit financing," he recalled. Feeney took the sandwiches to his customers in a basket, wearing an old army field jacket with big pockets for the change and blowing a whistle outside the fraternities to announce his presence. A contemporary in the Hotel School, Fred Antil, remembered Feeney coming around to his fraternity, and the running joke he had with him about how thin the sandwiches were.

Good-looking, crew-cut, and gregarious, Feeney made friends easily and was able to persuade helpers to come to his apartment to make and cut the sandwiches. "He was a hustler, he always had a smile. I figured out I made 16,000 sandwiches for him, working in the early evenings," said a former roommate, Tass Dueland. At his peak, he reckoned that he averaged 700 sandwich sales a week. Feeney had trouble getting dates because they had to be good sandwich makers, joked Chuck Rolles, a graduate of Binghamton Central High School in New York state who became Feeney's lifelong friend and later founded the Chuck's Steak House chain—another Cornell Hotel School success story. Retired and living in Aspen, Colorado, Rolles recalled that the Sandwich Man would tell his team to make sure there was only one slice of ham on the "baloney and cheese" sandwiches so as not to cut into his profits.

Feeney was in on every move. When Chuck Rolles got the concession to sell programs in the football stadium because of his sporting prowess—despite his small stature he had set a national school record in basketball in 1952—Feeney became one of his salesmen at the football stadium. "He always had a great wit," said Rolles. "I remember a guy from Princeton who we were playing that day came up to Chuck and joked, 'I don't need a program, I can't read,' and Chuck said, 'Oh you must be from Princeton!'"

As a sideline, Feeney sold Christmas cards on campus, and during vacation worked as a trainee at Industrial Food Crafts in Elizabeth, managed the Summer Club on Fire Island, New York, and acted as a taster and tester for Duncan Hines, the bread and cake maker.

On their last summer vacation in 1955, Chuck Feeney and Chuck Rolles took a working holiday together in Hawaii, so that Rolles could spend time with his classmate girlfriend, Jean Kelley, whose father, Roy C. Kelley, owned a chain of hotels there. "We got off the airplane and went to the hotel and checked in, and all of a sudden Chuck started speaking Japanese to the waitresses," said Rolles. "I didn't know he could speak Japanese." They lived in a rented cottage for the summer, and Feeney worked as a night clerk in the Edgeware Reef Hotel in Honolulu, where one of his jobs was security duty—letting guests back into their rooms who had locked themselves out. Then twenty-four years old, Feeney was getting his first experience of the hotel business outside the United States—Hawaii had not yet become a state—and he loved the exotic location. He had gotten the travel bug. And though he could not know it at the time, destiny would beckon him back to Hawaii.

Feeney graduated from Cornell in 1956 with a bachelor's degree in hotel administration. He had a number of job offers from hotel chains, but he didn't like the idea of working his way up inside a Marriott or a Statler. His mother wondered how he could turn down such fine offers, but he told her he was waiting for the right opportunity. He was impatient to see the world and make his own way as an entrepreneur. He and Chuck Rolles decided to drive across the United States from New Jersey to see what California offered.

Before they left, Rolles came to Elizabeth and Feeney introduced him to some of his old pals in a New Jersey tavern. One was a U.S. Navy veteran who boasted that he had a system to beat the roulette wheel in a casino. All they needed was to make sure the wheel had only one zero. They couldn't lose, he said. The two Cornell graduates decided to try out the system on their road journey. They headed for Reno, Nevada, where they discovered there was a single zero on the roulette wheels. Reno at the time was a fast-growing gambling town with several casinos, including Harold's Club and

Harrah's. They rented a room in a boardinghouse for construction workers and started hanging around the gaming rooms to see how things worked. "We'd sit there having a beer or something, taking down the numbers for an hour or so as they came up on the roulette wheel," said Rolles. Back in the rooming house, they studied the numbers.

After a couple of days they were ready. They figured they would need a stake of $500. Rolles had enough cash to put up half, but Feeney had to hock his portable typewriter and camera in a Reno pawn shop. Rolles took a picture of him going into the pawn shop dressed in shorts and an aloha shirt that he had picked up in Hawaii.

"We went to the casino and we started playing at 11 o'clock at night and we'd play all night, and, geez, the system worked," said Rolles. "We'd put ten cents on a group of six numbers. And if one of those six hit, we'd get 50 cents back. We covered all thirty-six numbers. The only thing that would hurt us was a zero. Otherwise we were making money on every roll."

Things went the way they were supposed to go, and they just kept making money. They would play for six hours, have breakfast with the construction workers, sleep a bit, play some basketball, then return at night and play six more hours. "We walked back to our apartment in the middle of the street afraid somebody would know how much money we had on us," said Rolles. "We'd have two or three hundred bucks in winnings. We thought we were wealthy."

In their enthusiasm, the two Cornellians fantasized about playing for a couple of years and retiring rich. "So we decided not to quit," said Rolles. "We kept playing. Then all of a sudden one morning, about 5:30, things started going not right. We got into our trouble zone, and covered our twelve numbers and put all the money on. We went twenty, twenty-five spins of the wheel without hitting one group of twelve numbers, and we thought that could never happen. Well, it happened. We put our last bets out and the twenty-fifth spin came and they didn't hit, and so I wanted to bet everything on the next one—I was ready to bet my life almost."

But Feeney wouldn't let him. "No," he said. "We're through." They cashed in their chips and left. They still ended up well ahead, by $1,600 apiece. Feeney got his typewriter and camera out of the pawn shop, and the pair drove on to California, where with two other friends they rented a cottage for the summer in Santa Monica, on the outskirts of Los Angeles. They spent some idle days playing volleyball on the sands. Rolles remembered

Chuck slipping off in the mornings to take a course at UCLA. "Three of us would kind of sleep in, but Chuck would go off to summer school in the morning to take lessons in Russian." At Cornell, Feeney had taken extra credit hours in French and Russian. At the time, he had half a notion that he might end up in intelligence. The National Security Agency had tried to recruit him at a debriefing on his discharge. An official told him, "People like you can continue to serve your country. Just sign here." He thought about it for a few seconds, then said, "No, thanks."

After a month, Chuck Rolles, who hadn't done his military service, got his draft notice to report to Pensacola, Florida, and the pair set off on the long car journey back to the East Coast. They drove through Nevada again and stopped at a little casino by a remote gas station. It was now Feeney who wanted to test the system a bit further. Rolles told him that he had had it, and he would wait in the car. He settled down to sleep as Feeney disappeared into the casino. He came back after thirty minutes and said, "Let's get the hell out of here." "He never told me how much he lost," said Rolles.

Feeney never played games of chance again. "I have always been down on gambling since then," he said. "We had the good fortune to make $3,200 divided by two before our system went belly-up, and to stop playing before we lost all of that."

The word went back to the tavern in New Jersey that Feeney and Rolles had made big money on the roulette wheel and that the system worked. The guys there put their money together and sent two representatives out to Nevada to cash in. They lost everything.

Banging the Ring

y midsummer of 1956, Chuck Feeney still had no idea what to do with his diploma. But after Cornell he felt confident he could go anywhere in the world. He had a bankroll of $2,000 based on his casino winnings, and he still had four months left of the thirty-six months of government money from his GI scholarship. To claim the remainder, however, he had to enroll in a course, either in the United States or abroad. Many hours spent in the Hotel School library reading books on tourism and travel had stimulated his urge to see the world. He had always wanted to go to Europe, and the bankroll was burning a hole in his pocket. He went to the French consulate on Fifth Avenue and Seventy-fourth Street in Manhattan to inquire about tuition fees in French colleges. To his surprise, he learned that university education in France was free. That was even better. He bought a cheap ticket for a Cunard liner and within a few weeks he was in Paris. After signing up for a month's intensive course in French at the Sorbonne, he wrote off to colleges in Grenoble and Strasbourg asking for admission.

In early September 1956, the secretary in the admissions office of Grenoble University in southeast France looked up to find the twenty-five-year-old crew-cut American in her office. "Here I am, I want to register for the school, for the political science department," said Feeney in heavily accented French. "The dean sees no one," she replied stiffly. "Well, I'm here," he said.

"I kept sitting there reading my magazine and this guy kept shuffling in and out of the room," recalled Feeney. Finally, in some exasperation, the secretary said, "The dean will see you." "*Naturellement*," replied Feeney. In his office the dean said, "Monsieur Feeney, you are an interesting candidate." "Yes, I appreciate that!" "You see, you are the first person to request admission to the political science school of Strasbourg and send the letter to Grenoble!" Feeney had put his application letters in the wrong envelopes. He shot back. "Yes, but it's evident I'm here and it's here I want to be. If I wanted to go to Strasbourg I would not be in Grenoble." The dean threw up his hands. "Why not!" he said. He admitted Feeney for a master's course in political science at the fourteenth-century university. The Cornell graduate was the only American in the department, something of which he was always proud.

Life was cheap in Grenoble, spectacularly sited in a broad valley surrounded by the snow-capped French Alps. Feeney's basic living costs came to about $15 a month. His French, tennis, and skiing improved considerably. The U.S. government inexplicably sent him $110 scholarship checks for six months rather than four. *Someone up there likes me*, thought Feeney.

At the end of his eight-month course, Feeney hitchhiked south with his kit and tennis racquet, looking for money-making opportunities. Getting rides was difficult as there were so many people on the roads holding up handwritten signs to show their destination. Outside Antibes, he displayed a notice in large letters on his tennis racket saying, "English conversations offered." He had no trouble getting a lift after that. On the Mediterranean Coast, Feeney met an American who was teaching children of naval officers from the U.S. fleet based at Villefranche-sur-Mer, a picturesque port of eighteenth-century houses and steep cobblestone alleyways. Villefranche was the home port of the USS *Salem*, a heavy cruiser serving as the flagship of the U.S. Sixth Fleet with a complement of nearly 2,000 officers and enlisted personnel. "I started to realize there were these naval dependents around," said Feeney. "I asked him [the American teacher] what they did in summertime and he said they were at a loose end, so I decided to start up a program like a summer camp for the navy kids." Feeney had seen a business opening, and a way of being helpful. He rented a room in a pension in Villefranche and organized a summer camp on the beach. Almost seventy American kids were delivered into his care by grateful navy parents, and Feeney had to hire four other Americans as staff.

In Villefranche, Feeney made a deal with the tennis club manager to sweep the courts in return for playing for free. On the courts he met André Morali-Daninos, a French Algerian psychiatrist on vacation who was intrigued by the young, educated American doing a job young French students would disdain. Morali-Daninos was a highly decorated war veteran who had joined the French Resistance during World War II and had brought his family to Paris in 1945. They came to Villefranche for their summer holidays, and in those days before mass tourism, the family usually had the beach to themselves. Morali-Daninos's twenty-three-year-old daughter, Danielle, a student at the Sorbonne in Paris, was somewhat disconcerted therefore at the invasion of the beach by dozens of screaming and whistling children with their American counselors. She was particularly struck, however, by the kindness and firmness with which the good-looking group leader treated the children. The vivacious French Algerian and the twenty-six-year-old Irish American got to talking, and a romance started up.

In Villefranche, Feeney came into contact with people making a living from the U.S. Sixth Fleet. Groups of pretty women and salesmen waylaid the sailors and hustled for orders to supply the ship's exchange store. He got to know a money changer named Sy Podolin who had bought up a row of old lockers and rented them to naval personnel so they could dump their uniforms and change into civvies when on shore leave. For a couple of weeks in August, Feeney made some extra money by managing the "navy locker club" for Pudlin in the evenings, opening up the lockers for sailors coming and going to the bars.

As the summer ended, Feeney planned to head north again. He loved the student life and "had enough money squirreled away that I could have gone to a German university." However, one night in a Villefranche bar he met an Englishman, Bob Edmonds, who was trying to start a business selling duty-free liquor to American sailors at ports around the Mediterranean. He asked Feeney to help him.

The U.S. Navy did not allow the consumption of alcohol on board, but Edmonds had established that sailors could buy up to five bottles of spirits duty free and have them shipped as unaccompanied baggage to their home port. It could be a big market: There were fifty ships in the U.S. Sixth Fleet in the Mediterranean and the crews were rotated three times a year. The savings for the military personnel were huge, and almost every seaman on board could afford to buy a five-pack for collection back in the United States. A five-pack bought duty free in Europe cost $10, including delivery, while the same five bottles in the United States would cost over $30. Edmonds had failed to convince a British military supplier, Saccone & Speed, to work with him and had gone out on his own. He desperately needed an American to help him.

"There's a big fleet movement, forty ships are coming in," he told Feeney. "I can only see twenty. I'm looking for a guy that can see the other twenty." "What do you mean?" asked Feeney. "Go and talk to them about buying booze."

Feeney and Edmonds started going on board ships to take orders from the crew members, mainly for Canadian Club whiskey and Seagram's VO. They then arranged for the liquor to be shipped to U.S. ports from warehouses in Antwerp and Rotterdam. There was no need for capital, as they did not have to pay for the merchandise in advance. For a period they had the market to themselves, but competitors were quick to arrive. Edmonds went to check out new opportunities in the Caribbean while Feeney went to Edmonds's home in Hythe in the south of England to process orders. Feeney returned to Villefranche in October and was told the U.S. Sixth Fleet was heading for Barcelona. He took the train to the Spanish port, only to discover that the ships had been delayed.

Feeney had read in a Cornell alumni bulletin that Robert Warren Miller, another graduate of the Hotel School, had started work at the Ritz Hotel in Barcelona. With time to kill, he made his way to the Ritz on the tree-lined Gran Via de les Cortes Catalanes. Entering the lobby, he saw the familiar figure of Miller, with a shock of brown hair and cheeky grin, behind the reception desk. They hadn't been friends at Cornell—Miller was a year ahead of Feeney—but Miller recognized the wiry blue-eyed American immediately. "Feeney," he said. "What are you doing here?" Replied Chuck, "What are you doing here?"

That casual exchange marked the start of one of the most profitable partnerships in international business history.

Miller's journey to Europe had been as haphazard as Feeney's. He was brought up in Quincy, south of Boston, where his father was a salesman for an industrial oil company. Miller got a draft deferment and went to Cornell from high school on a scholarship. Money was tight in his family, too, and he had to work part-time as a waiter and short order cook. A couple of months after graduating in 1956, when he was working as a line cook in Newport Beach, California, he got a message from his father in Quincy that his call-up papers had arrived. Miller drove to Santa Ana, signed up for the U.S. Marine Corps, and was sent to San Diego boot camp. However, a medical examination revealed a scar on his head from a childhood accident, and a marine captain asked him to sign a waiver releasing the U.S. Marine Corps from liability should he injure his head in combat, adding that if he didn't sign he would be honorably discharged. Miller took the honorable discharge. He was given $78 and put on a bus to San Diego.

Like Feeney, Bob Miller did not want a white-collar job. Having read a lot of Hemingway, the twenty-two-year-old Cornellian had romantic ideas of becoming a writer or a soldier of fortune. He signed on for a three-month trip on an ocean-going tuna boat and while waiting to sail, crossed the Mexican border into Tijuana for a weekend spree. There he got involved in a brawl and was badly beaten and thrown into jail. By the time he was released, with torn shirt and only one shoe, the tuna boat had sailed. It was the low point of his life, and he decided to sort himself out. Miller went back to hotel work in the United States, saved $3,000, and headed for Spain on a Greek ocean liner, the *Queen Fredericka*. He made his way to Madrid, and from there to Barcelona and the job at the Ritz reception desk.

When Miller finished his shift that day, he and Feeney went out for dinner. Miller still had his $3,000 bankroll and was already bored working "in a monkey suit" in the hotel. They decided to throw in their lot together and try to make money from doing business with the U.S. fleet. Miller told the Belgian hotel manager, Juan Vinke, what he was planning and handed in his notice. Vinke laughed and said, "There's no future in that. Stay with us at the Ritz. You could be a great hotel man one day."

While Miller was working out his notice, Feeney enrolled for Spanish lessons. "He was a hyperkinetic person always charging around, so he figured while he was there he might as well learn to speak Spanish," recalled Miller.

Miller had already gotten a glimpse of the duty-free rackets that were common in postwar Europe. He told Feeney about a Hong Kong priest in Barcelona who changed U.S. dollars at black-market rates. The priest had shown Miller a small assortment of watches, film, cameras, and cigarettes for sale in his back office that he had smuggled under his soutane from Andorra, a tiny tax haven in the Pyrenees. "Don't worry, all of the profits that I make go to the church," he said cheerfully, adding that Miller should go to Hong Kong, where almost everything was duty free.

Feeney and Miller made Villefranche their base and started taking orders for liquor from U.S. naval personnel. They needed cars, so Feeney got a little Renault Dauphine and Miller a Simca, and they started driving or taking trains to ports all along the Mediterranean where the fleet docked: Marseilles, Cannes, Barcelona, Valencia, Gibraltar, Genoa, and Naples. They would not see each other for weeks, then would meet back at Villefranche, agree on what to do next, and go off in different directions. Chuck designed a business envelope to give to people on the naval ships with a price list of whiskies. They found "bird dogs" on board, to whom they promised commission for getting sailors to sign up for the five-packs that they could pick up at their home ports. Receipts for duty-free liquor became so commonplace on board ships they were accepted as stakes in poker games.

The booze business in early 1958 had become very competitive, and the two Cornellians looked for other things to sell. In April, they went to the World's Fair in Brussels and got ideas for expanding their inventory, adding such items as perfumes, cameras, toy trains, transistor radios—the latest thing in technology—and German beer mugs, which they had inscribed with insignia such as the marine emblem, Semper Fideles.

The key to success was getting on board the U.S. ships, which were generally off limits to civilians. Feeney and Miller had to compete with salesmen from France, England, Holland, and Belgium, trying to flog everything from perfume to suits. Approaching a ship "cold" was difficult. But by dressing as respectable Americans and speaking "American," they could usually talk their way past the shore patrol to get on board and meet the supply officer, whose permission was necessary to sell items openly to the sailors. They sometimes "banged" the ring—the distinctive gold Cornell ring with azure stone engraved with the letter C—to make friends with Cornellians among the ships' officers, who would then invite them on board for lunch. They tried to find out from contacts in the United States if there were any Cornellians on board ships about to sail for the Mediterranean, especially supply officers who had trained at the Hotel School. In Naples, Feeney once got around a strict embargo on civilians boarding naval ships by climbing up the gangway with the garbage collector and telling the supply officer, "I'm here about the trash." "There were stories that Chuck would be on the beach and somehow he would be in a little boat and next thing in a bigger boat and next thing in the officers' quarters on a carrier selling to guys," recalled Chuck Rolles, who served in the navy. "He wasn't supposed to be there but nobody knew how he got there or how he got back." Cornell contemporary and ex-marine Fred Antil remembered hearing stories about Feeney turning up on the gangplank of an aircraft carrier and the admiral asking, "How the hell do you always know where we are?" and Chuck replying, "Admiral, who do you think sends you?"

Finding out where the ships were going was often the biggest problem. As a security measure, the U.S. Navy would schedule visits to Naples or Barcelona, then change the destination at the last minute. Often the best sources of information were the hookers in the ports. Miller courted a young woman in the U.S. consulate in Nice who tipped him off about movements of the Sixth Fleet. She told him once that an aircraft carrier and a destroyer were due to dock in Rhodes, Greece. Miller took the train to Naples, another train to Brindisi, then an Olympic Airways DC-3 to Corfu, Athens, and on to Rhodes. On the last leg, he found that he wasn't the only trader who possessed classified information about U.S. fleet movements. There was a "skinny Chinese guy" from Hong Kong named Smiley Chow, who sold bespoke (custom-tailored) suits to the navy. When they arrived in Rhodes, the two had to share a hotel bedroom. Miller saw that the tailor had a huge bundle of U.S. dollar bills sewn into his shorts. He also had an army knife, and said, "So don't get any ideas!" Smiley Chow told Miller he would make more money selling suits than liquor, and that there was a better place to make money. Like the priest in Barcelona, he told Miller, "You should go to Hong Kong."

The orders, and the money, piled up. Feeney boasted to Miller that they were on their way to making a million dollars. They called themselves the Young Turks. Out on the road the two American salesmen stuffed cash and U.S. Treasury checks into their pockets, and when they got a chance, lodged them in an account at Lloyds Bank in Geneva, Switzerland, where, said Miller, operating a U.S. dollar account was "less complicated" than in France. It also had tax advantages. Making money while paying minimal or no tax was part of winning in the game in which they were engaged. When Miller brought his parents to Villefranche, his father saw a pile of U.S. Treasury checks on a desk in the little garden house Miller had rented. "Heavens, how much money is in that pile of checks there? Must be thirty or forty thousand dollars," his father said. "He couldn't imagine it," said Miller. "I got quite a kick out of that."

Cockamamy Flyers

With World War II becoming a distant memory at the end of the 1950s, American tourists began turning up in Europe in large numbers. For the first time since before the Great Depression, members of America's growing middle class had disposable income and did not have to confine their purchases to necessities. The cocktail was their social lubricant and television advertising was pushing up the demand for liquor. Chuck Feeney discovered one day that these vacationers with their cameras and gaudy jackets could buy duty-free booze abroad and bring it home, as long as they resided in one of fifteen American states. They were permitted by U.S. Customs to import a five-pack of liquor—five one-fifth bottles amounting to one gallon—once every thirty-one days, without paying duty. "I all of a sudden realized, shit, you can sell this to anybody, anywhere," said Feeney. "It didn't matter where you bought it or where you shipped it from, as long as you declared it when you got back into the States."

The problem for Feeney was figuring out how to persuade the American tourists to buy five-packs of liquor from him and Miller, and then how to get it delivered to their homes. It had been relatively simple to ship liquor for the navy customers from bonded warehouses to American ports, where it was picked up by the incoming sailors. This was a bigger challenge. He took a flight to New York to figure out what to do.

He found the answer in the Railway Express Agency, the national small-parcel delivery service, since defunct, whose green trucks were a familiar

sight on U.S. roads. Railway Express was obliged by law to accept all shipments destined for anywhere in the United States. Feeney printed up tens of
thousands of brochures to tell American tourists traveling in Europe the
good news, that they could buy duty-free liquor from Tourists International—as he and Miller called their venture—and have it shipped to their
doorstep, as long as they lived in one of the fifteen states: New York, Connecticut, Rhode Island, Massachusetts, Pennsylvania, New Jersey, Delaware,
Washington, D.C., Ohio, Arizona, Idaho, Illinois, Missouri, West Virginia
and North Dakota. He organized for a ship chandler in Antwerp to take the
orders and transport the duty-free liquor in cardboard valises packed into
containers to the U.S. ports, where Railway Express picked them up.
Tourists who bought and paid for their liquor declared that they had unaccompanied baggage when passing through U.S. Customs, and when they
sent the receipt back to Feeney's office in Europe, the liquor was dispatched.
Those travelers who were prepared to cope with the form-filling and the
wait got good value. A five-pack of Seagram's VO costing $47.75 in New
York could be bought for $22.50 from Tourists International and delivered
to their door. There were similar savings on Jack Daniels, Tullamore Dew,
Jameson, Johnny Walker, Haig, and Bells.

The constant traveling did not leave Chuck Feeney much time for his
personal life, but he and Danielle Morali-Daninos met up again, a year after
their first encounter on the beach at Villefranche. Danielle came to New
York for a vacation while Chuck was setting up his five-pack postal scheme.
They later managed to spend some time together in England, and when
Chuck came to Paris in May 1959, they decided to get married.

Danielle's family was Jewish and she would have been expected to marry
a respectable Jewish Parisian working with her father. But like Chuck, she
had an adventurous spirit, and Feeney had opened up a whole new world for
her. Young, educated, and stylish, she brought to the relationship the so-
phistication of France. She had a vivaciousness that matched Feeney's restless energy. She and her family were in turn enchanted with the young
American, who by then spoke fluent French and always seemed keen to
help. They were married in Paris in October 1959, first in a civil ceremony
at the town hall of the Sixteenth Arrondissement Prefecture of the Seine,
and the next day in church, with Chuck Rolles as best man.

After their wedding, Chuck and Danielle drove to Switzerland in his
turquoise Renault Dauphine to establish a permanent European residence

there. He had to have what he described as a "perch" someplace in Europe. They found an unfurnished apartment in Ebikon, just north of the medieval town of Lucerne, took a yearlong lease, and put in a bed and a sofa. But they did not spend more than half a dozen nights there. They drove on to Liechtenstein, Feeney's real destination. The principality, barely as big as Washington, D.C., and landlocked between Switzerland and Austria, had strict residency laws that prevented them having an official perch there. "But it was a tax haven," said Feeney, "and people like us went there to do business." Banking and tax regulations were almost nonexistent. Chuck and Danielle checked into the four-story Waldhotel in Vaduz, the thirteenth-century capital on the banks of the Rhine dominated by a castle on a rocky outcrop. However, they found they had to pack their bags and check out again once every seven days, when the police called to ensure that people posing as tourists were not overstaying.

Feeney set up the first world headquarters of Tourists International in two small rooms in the hotel, which was located among fir trees overlooking the Rhine Valley, and hired two young resident Englishwomen to come every day to do the typing and paperwork. They got a brass plate made saying "Tourists International" and displayed it among dozens of shadowy "offshore" companies registered at Obera House, Altenbachstrasse 534, so they could have an official business address.

A year later, a letter arrived for Feeney at the Waldhotel from Leon P. Sterling, a fellow Cornellian from New York state who had been doing his military service in Germany as manager of officers' clubs in the Stuttgart area. Like Chuck, Lee Sterling had fallen in love with Europe and was looking for a job to keep him there after his discharge. He had seen from the Cornell Hotel School alumni newsletter that the Sandwich Man was in Liechtenstein. He inquired whether there were any good hotel jobs in Vaduz. Feeney invited him to join the company instead. Sterling arrived in Liechtenstein by train on October 24, 1960. Shortly afterward, Feeney asked him to take over the Vaduz office. "He said, 'This is what we are doing,' and then he left," said Sterling. "That was something I learned about Chuck. He was the kind of fellow that would give you responsibility and then let you do it. He didn't hover, he wasn't around; he was out making more deals."

Feeney was heading for Geneva to try to make a deal with an upstart American company that threatened his business. One of his salesmen had come across a full-color glossy catalog issued by a firm called Duty Free Shoppers with an office on Rue de Rhône in Geneva and trading under the name of Transocean. The twenty-eight-page brochure offered American tourists "fabulous values" for items such as Le Galion and Molyneux perfumes, cashmere, watches, and other luxury goods, many at half the U.S. retail price.

Feeney believed this company was way ahead of the game. But he thought they might agree to insert his liquor brochures into their next catalog if they weren't selling booze themselves. On December 19, 1960, he arrived in Geneva, booked into a modest hotel in Longemalle by the lake shore, then phoned Transocean and asked for the manager. He was surprised when the manager answered the telephone himself and invited him to come over right away. Feeney made his way through the Christmas shoppers to the address on Rue de Rhône.

Duty Free Shoppers was the brainchild of Stewart Damon, a U.S. Navy exchange officer who had been based in Naples. Its goal was to sell duty-free goods to American tourists abroad. He and another entrepreneurial American, Harry Adler, had persuaded seventeen investors in New York to put up $95,000 worth of shares, and they arranged for manufacturers to package and ship their products. They printed half a million catalogs and opened the office in Geneva to process what they expected would be an avalanche of orders. Only a trickle came in.

Damon had returned to the United States that September to restructure the company, but he failed and then resigned, leaving Harry Adler in Geneva with debts of $3,700 and assets of $1,700 in perfume stocks. On the day Feeney turned up, Adler was paying some overdue bills and clearing out his desk. He and his wife and two small children were getting ready to fly back to New York on money borrowed from relatives. It was his last day of business.

Then this "blond, blue-eyed youngster appearing no more than twenty-ish" walked into the office and introduced himself as Chuck Feeney, recalled Adler. Not knowing the dire straits the company was in, Feeney, who was in fact almost thirty years old at the time, told him that he thought that his idea was tremendous and was surely very successful, and proposed to Adler that if they inserted his liquor brochures in their next catalog, he would give them a commission on all liquor orders that resulted.

"The irony of it all!" wrote Adler later in a personal memoir. "Here was another fellow who thought that the idea could not fail and was coming to us to help him distribute his cockamamy flyers. I really had no choice but to be honest. 'Dear friend,' I said, 'Our distribution was a huge one-time gamble and is, at this time, a dismal failure.'"

Feeney was visibly shocked but not at a loss for words, said Adler. "He spoke very fast with a high-pitched voice, asking what is to become of this company, these offices, and what of the orders that were still in the pipeline?" The "engaging young fellow" then pulled out a Parker pen and started making copious notes in his back-slanted handwriting. Feeney said he would call his associate Bob Miller and would come back the next day to talk business.

Feeney was convinced that the principle was sound, and that the company could still survive and thrive with proper marketing. It was the logical extension of his own ventures into the world of duty free. The next day he proposed a deal to Adler. He and Adler would travel to the United States early in the new year, where Feeney would make an offer of up to $10,000 for the company stock. Tourists International would in the meantime hire Adler at $1,000 a month, with three months' salary in advance, to work for them. Adler could hardly believe what he was hearing.

That evening, Chuck took Adler and his wife, Ella, a survivor of the Holocaust, for what he remembered as a "rather extravagant" meal. "I impressed him by picking up the tab," recalled Feeney. He impressed Adler even more by sending him a contract from Vaduz two days before Christmas, accompanied by a check for $3,000 for three months' salary in advance, and a round-trip ticket to New York. "In a matter of four days my world had changed from abject failure to a person of worth with an exciting future ahead of me," recalled Adler.

Meanwhile, the operation in Vaduz was running into trouble. The Liechtenstein authorities decided that they had tolerated Feeney's presence long enough. In March 1961, the owner of the hotel came to him in some agitation. "You've got to go. I can't hold off the police anymore," he pleaded. Feeney decided they would have to find another business-friendly location in Europe. The nearest was Monaco, the world's second-smallest independent country, situated on the Mediterranean just east of Villefranche. Tourists International in Vaduz had by then accumulated voluminous files and company records, as well as typewriters and cabinets. They could not simply hop into a car and drive across the border. "We had to cross several frontiers, the first into Switzerland," said Feeney. "We had no authorization to be there. Officials would ask, 'What's all that shit there, what are you guys doing with all these papers?' Everybody knows how the Swiss work those things out. If you have no authorization they fine you."

They decided to do a midnight flit. Lee Sterling first drove to the U.S. Army base in Ludwigsburg, Germany, where he temporarily swapped his smart little Sunbeam Alpine for the roomier station wagon of an old friend, Lieutenant Colonel Sean O'Mahony, the commanding officer of the military hospital. In Vaduz, they loaded filing cabinets and office equipment onto the U.S. Army vehicle and covered them with laundry. Feeney put files and other papers in the back of his Renault Dauphine, throwing linen and dirty shirts over them. They left Vaduz late at night on March 16, 1961, and headed south on the N-13, driving through Switzerland and arriving at the Italian border at 3:00 AM. Sterling showed his U.S. Army lieutenant ID to the border guard and explained that he had just finished his military service. The immigration official had also just been demobilized. "What can you do for an old soldier?" he asked. They tipped him and he waved them through. They reached the French border and drove on to Monaco without further incident. Though no longer physically based in Vaduz, Feeney had no intention of giving up Liechtenstein as a tax haven. He hired a permanent Liechtenstein resident named Arno Scalet to act in future as secretary and front man for Tourists International headquarters in the principality. The nameplate on Vaduz's Altenbachstrasse stayed in place.

The Mediterranean city-state of Monaco had a tolerant attitude toward foreign businesspeople. Feeney established Tourists International's new office on Rue Suffren Reymond, a quiet street of old residential houses with red-tiled roofs, and put Lee Sterling in charge. As in Liechtenstein, they had no work permits. To avoid bringing attention to themselves, they needed a local fixer, someone who could work the system, get them out of trouble when necessary, and identify French suppliers.

They found one by accident. "One day I hear someone yelling, and I come out and there is this young, fairly big guy," said Sterling. "It turns out we were blocking his truck. Several days later the same happens. He speaks English and seems sharp so I say, 'Why don't you come and work for us?'" The truck driver, Jean Gentzbourger, a French veteran of the Algerian War, was delivering wood to building sites for 600 francs a month. Sterling offered him 800 to work for Tourists International. Gentzbourger went to his boss and said he was leaving. "I'll give you 200 francs more," his boss said. Gentzbourger replied, "Too late."

The Frenchman quickly established that the American salesmen coming in and out of the Tourists International office were all illegal. "You've got to get permission to work here or you will all be in trouble," the Frenchman told Sterling. "You are the only legal person so you will be our representative," Sterling told him. Gentzbourger became the *gérant*—the legal responsible person—for the office. Part of his job was to get the sales guys out of trouble if they came to the attention of the Monaco police. Once, a salesman arrived on his moped from Genoa covered with mud, and the police picked him up. Gentzbourger went to vouch for him. His military connections got the man released. "That was the way the business was run in those days," he recalled in the villa overlooking Cannes, where he now lives.

Feeney occasionally came and went, always walking fast, even when lugging heavy suitcases filled with brochures for the fleet. He was forever thinking up new ideas. His next venture was to open a shop in Paris at 12 Rue de la Paix with a novel approach: American tourists, many of whom were doing four countries in four days, could do one-stop shopping at the store and order such items as a cashmere sweater from Scotland, a beaded bag from Austria, Waterford crystal from Ireland, and a leather wallet from Italy and have them all shipped from the country of origin to the customer's American home as an unaccompanied gift item. There was no need for an inventory, just samples of the merchandise. The shop employed glamorous sales girls to take orders in the lobbies of five big tourist hotels around Paris. Feeney sent Gentzbourger to run the Paris shop. The French fixer said he felt like a pimp when the young women arrived every evening with purses full of cash from the orders. Feeney would drop by when in town. "He would come for a couple of days, and have lunch at La Quesh," he recalled. "We would sit at the bar. He used to order the *plat du jour* and when it arrived, it was hoofed down, and we would go. I learned to eat fast. He was always talking, talking, his mind was like Speedy Gonzales, always racing."

Their antipathy for bureaucracy sometimes caught up with them. "Chuck or Lee Sterling would arrive in the Paris shop with a new model of watch and simply change it for the old model," lamented Gentzbourger. "One day a customs official came into the shop in Paris to check the merchandise. None of the numbers on the watches fitted the invoices." The shop was fined 20,000 francs. Gentzbourger, the good *gérant*, got it reduced to 1,000.

Riding the Tiger

When Feeney and Miller were collecting orders onboard navy ships, they found themselves being asked if they were the guys who sold cars. They weren't, but they soon were. They discovered that American service personnel abroad had the right to buy cars duty free and have them shipped to their home port, and some rival salesmen had already got in on the act. Miller and Feeney picked up brochures from car showrooms and brought them on board the ships. They found that selling cars was just like selling booze. They took a deposit, paid an advance to the car dealer, and ordered the car shipped to the customer's home port.

Once they did become known as the guys who sold cars, they were overwhelmed with orders. The car-manufacturing business had picked up in Europe, and European cars were popular in America. They began hiring salesmen to tour the Mediterranean ports and military bases. They employed ex-GIs like Joe Lyons and Bob Matousek, who had served in the army in West Germany, to work the German bases, where a total of 300,000 American troops were stationed. They called this venture Cars International. The business quickly expanded. Feeney crisscrossed Western Europe to set up a network of agents selling cars, booze, and cigarettes to the U.S. military. He designed flyers and put advertisements in such military publications as the *Stars and Stripes*. As with the fleet, the salesmen's success depended on getting access to the NCO and officers' clubs and military housing at army bases. Being ex-military, they knew the ins and outs, said Matousek, a former army captain.

It was a good time to be an American on the make in Western Europe. Many older Europeans saw the Americans as liberators, and the U.S. troops as protectors against Soviet communism. American movies and consumer products were popular with the postwar generation of young Europeans. The economic miracle known as the *Wirtschaftswunder* had brought a new era of political stability to Western Germany, and France and Italy were entering a time of unprecedented prosperity. The American ex-GIs who signed on with Feeney were themselves newly liberated, finished with their military obligations and unfettered by the straitlaced conventions of 1950s America. They were free to spend their money as fast as they made it and have a good time. Chuck Feeney and his team were aggressive, self-confident, and borderline legal. They enjoyed a great sense of camaraderie. The new age of affluence in the United States meant that their American customers had disposable cash, and the money rolled in. They were in the right place at the right time.

Feeney and Miller established eight car-sales offices in West Germany. They took over a Volvo showroom in Frankfurt in the heart of the U.S. military zone and got demonstration cars from other dealers to show the customers. They rented space in an old munitions factory next to a bar. They printed lavish brochures that they mailed to servicemen who could not get to their showrooms. These listed every foreign make in vogue at the time: Sunbeam Tiger, Austin Healy, Porsche 911, Renault R-8 sedan, MG sports, Spitfire, Volvo, and Volkswagen Beetle. The Volkswagen, the tough, reliable creation of the German car designer Ferdinand Porsche, was in demand in the United States as a runaround and was the most popular buy: A soldier could save $500 on a Volkswagen 113 sedan costing $1,700 in the United States. The buyer gave Cars International 10 percent of the cost, and the company booked the order for 5 percent. "The customers were funding us, and the suppliers were also giving us credit in a funny way," said Feeney, who arranged for Geico to provide financing when the soldiers or sailors needed it.

The key to their success was, as always, that they did not have to maintain inventories. They sold liquor and cars, neither of which required a dollar of up-front money. And the business was "offshore," which meant they did not have to pay U.S. taxes. It seemed the perfect business model. A customer could pick up his automobile in France or Germany, or wait until he was back in the United States. If he drove it around for a while in Europe, it was considered a used car and subject to less road tax back home. Matousek once sold two automobiles to a two-star general who had an aversion to paying the tax. "He just drove them around the block, and then we put them on a boat and shipped them to the U.S. as cars that he had already driven in Germany."

Like car salesmen everywhere, the former GIs talked up the qualities of the automobiles with the best commission for themselves. Their main problem, however, was getting their orders filled by the European car manufacturers, as the supply of automobiles in France, Germany, and Italy could not keep up with burgeoning domestic demand. In France, car ownership tripled in the 1950s to 6 million. Cars International sometimes had to make it worthwhile for contacts in the automobile factories to "gray-market" cars, that is, deliver cars to them that were meant to go elsewhere. Bob Miller recruited Hans Schaefer, head of Export Department 6C at Daimler Benz in Stuttgart that handled the Korean quota, to provide him with gray-market cars. On paper they were shipped to Korea, but in reality they went to the United States. The scheme was discovered when a lieutenant commander turned up at the Daimler Benz factory to inspect a car he had ordered for delivery to Jacksonville, Florida. He was told, "Ah, yes, commander. It will be delivered to Seoul, Korea, in about eight weeks." The game was up. Hans Schaefer was fired but instantly reemployed, along with his German secretary, Helga Flaiz, by Cars International in Frankfurt.

At its height, Cars International bought a full-page advertisement in _Time_ magazine's overseas military edition. It boasted that "Cars International's unique Stateside Delivery Program enables GIs to choose from a wide variety of 492 American and European cars at low export prices." The sales order slip printed in the advertisement carried an "exclusive guarantee from Sales Director Charles Feeney" that any customers not satisfied after forty-five days would get their money back.

Feeney also used advanced public relations gimmicks to promote sales. He donated a $2,650 MGB sports car for a charity raffle held among the crew of 5,000 on the aircraft carrier USS _Forrestal,_ hailing it in brochures distributed to the sailors as a "woman weapon . . . if you do not have a wife, the MGB might be very useful in attracting one!" The winner of the raffle, machinist's mate Wilson Hoy of Michigan, was quoted in the next brochure as saying, "Wife? Who needs one with a beauty like this little number."

Feeney went looking further afield for business. Anywhere there was a military base, there were potential customers. He took off on trips around the world, looking for opportunities to set up sales offices, touching down in

Saigon, where the American military presence was being built up, and flying via Havana to Guantanamo, the U.S. base in southern Cuba. Perhaps inevitably, the CIA saw Cars International as a good cover for its spy operations. Many former GIs were, like Chuck, approached to do intelligence work; one ex-Marine who worked for the company in Europe became a CIA operative in South America, according to former agent Philip Agee in his book *Inside the Company: CIA Diary*.

Meanwhile, another Cornellian came into the car business and would become instrumental in expanding it across the world. Jeffrey Cornish Mahlstedt, a graduate of the Cornell Hotel School from Old Greenwich, Connecticut, and a former customer of Chuck Feeney's sandwich business, was serving in the Pacific as a lieutenant JG on the U.S. Seventh Fleet when he got a letter from Feeney saying, "You need to come to Europe after you leave the navy. It's fun, and it is sunny, and there are pretty girls." But Feeney wrote soon afterward with a different proposition: Mahlstedt should stay in the Pacific and try to sell automobiles there for Cars International. "I told him how we were going to get rich and how the whole Far East was open," recalled Feeney. "I said we are going to make our first million, so Jeffrey said, 'I'm game!'"

Cars International and Tourists International were facing ever more stiff competition in Europe. Salesmen flogging everything from cars to perfume and alcohol were elbowing each other out of the way to get onto the U.S. ships. Feeney believed that there could be more lucrative opportunities in the less-crowded Pacific. He sent Mahlstedt some literature about the business.

When due for "separation" from the navy in January 1960, Mahlstedt persuaded the captain to discharge him in Yokosuka, the big U.S. naval base at the mouth of Tokyo Bay that served as headquarters of Commander Naval Forces Far East. U.S. ships were constantly coming and going, but in postwar Japan there wasn't much for the sailors to spend their money on, other than the leisure activities one found at every port in the world. Mahlstedt discovered that nobody was selling them duty-free items of any kind. There was no market for liquor because the fleet's home ports were in California, which permitted only one bottle of duty-free liquor per sailor. He set out to sell cars.

"I moved to a little Japanese inn and got a Japanese girlfriend whom I used as my interpreter," said Mahlstedt. "Each day I would go to the navy base, using my old active duty ID. And I would go on a ship and they would ask, 'What's your business?' and I would say, 'Just visiting friends,' and go down to the ward room and start talking to people." Perhaps because the sailors didn't expect salesmen, there was a lot of suspicion about Mahlstedt's pitch, and after three weeks he had not sold a single automobile. His first sale came when he took a weekend break in Tokyo and got talking with a U.S. Army captain on the train, who said he would like to buy a car and asked Mahlstedt what he would recommend. The quick-thinking salesman glanced down at a copy of *Time* magazine on his lap, saw an advertisement for Peugeot, and asked his companion, "Are you aware that Peugeot is the motorcar of the year?" Before he got off the train, the captain gave him $400 as advance payment on a Peugeot. "I think he told me how much cash he had in his pocket, and I manipulated the deposit," recalled Mahlstedt.

Mahlstedt's persistence in Yokosuka paid off, and in the following three weeks he took deposits for twenty cars. He punched out the orders sitting cross-legged on a futon in his Japanese inn and sent them to Feeney and Miller in Villefranche. He got cards made up that said he represented "Tourist Duty Free Sales Establishment, Vaduz, Liechtenstein." It was such a mouthful, he said, "No one had any idea what I was saying."

Mahlstedt believed that the real action in the Far East was not in Japan but in Hong Kong, where the U.S. Navy ships berthed on the way home, and where the sailors splurged out before returning to the United States. Early in 1960, he booked a passage to Hong Kong on a Japanese freighter. He made one last sale in Japan to a chaplain on an aircraft carrier, also Hong Kong bound, who gave him a deposit of $200, telling him that if there were any problems he could be contacted c/o American Express in Hong Kong. Mahlstedt's boat was delayed, the chaplain arrived first and couldn't find him and reported that he had been swindled. An admiral put out an all-fleet message warning sailors, "Beware of Jeff Mahlstedt, who represents himself as being from Vaduz, Liechtenstein." Mahlstedt was apprehended at immigration in Hong Kong but explained what had happened, and the chaplain did eventually get his car.

Mahlstedt set up an office in Room 1404 in a Chinese hotel on Nathan Road in Kowloon. He pinned automobile posters around the walls and registered the enterprise on June 23, 1960, as Tourist Duty Free Sales Company (Hong Kong) Limited, with directors Chuck Feeney, Robert Miller, and Jeffrey Mahlstedt. His "office" was so cramped that a customer could not get out past the bed until the ex-navy lieutenant opened the door.

Business picked up as U.S. sailors in the Pacific got wind of the deals on offer. Feeney suggested to Bob Miller that he should go to Hong Kong to help Mahlstedt expand operations in the Far East while Feeney continued developing Europe. "We divided the world, so to speak," said Miller, who arrived in Hong Kong in September 1960 to start working with the former navy lieutenant.

Two months later, dressed in dark suits and ties, Miller and Mahlstedt opened a car showroom in Rediffusion House in Wanchai. Champagne bottles popped and a long string of fire crackers was set off to dispel the bad spirits. "I know the date because we had the *South China Morning Post* open on the coffee table and it had 'JFK Elected President of the United States,' November 9th, 1960," recalled Miller. The showroom was well located. The naval launches came to a jetty in front of the building. All around were topless bars and music parlors with accommodating hostesses and just along the street was the Luk Kwok Hotel, featured in *The World of Suzie Wong*, that year's hit movie. Rediffusion House was conveniently topped with a three-pointed neon star that looked just like the Mercedes emblem, to which Mahlstedt would direct the sailors going on shore leave.

"We sold everything," said Mahlstedt. "If you wanted a Mercedes or a Sunbeam Alpine you got it. It didn't matter if we had it or not, we had it." They also began selling liquor to the navy in the Far East when the prohibition on bringing five-packs of duty-free liquor to California was lifted. Bob Edmonds, working on his own, had gone to Sacramento and successfully lobbied the California legislature for a change in the regulations, arguing that it discriminated against military personnel.

Miller, meanwhile, had learned about a duty-free opportunity in Hawaii. On the way to Hong Kong, he had stopped off in Hawaii and stayed with his old friend Peter Fithian, a 1951 graduate of the Cornell Hotel School. The blond Bostonian had set up a company called Greeters of Hawaii and employed girls to dress up in hula-hula skirts and greet incoming airline passengers with a lei and a kiss. He was once featured in the then-popular CBS show *What's My Line?*, in which contestants were interviewed by panelists who tried to guess their unusual occupation: his was kissing girls for a living. The airport terminal in Honolulu was a Quonset hut made of corrugated iron with a plywood floor. A new terminal was under construction to cope with a surge in tourism as Pan Am and American Airlines started replacing their eighty-seat Douglas DC-8 airliners with bigger Boeing 707s. Fithian introduced Miller to several of the concessionaires at the airport. "When they asked what I was doing, I told them I was in the duty-free business," said Miller. "They said, 'Oh, that's interesting, because when the new terminal is finished, there will be a tender for a duty-free concession here.'"

Over a year later, when Miller was in Japan on a business trip, he got a call from Fithian to say the deadline for bidding on the duty-free concession at Honolulu airport expired that week. If he wanted to submit a tender, he would have to get to Hawaii right away and submit financial statements and a deposit. Miller called Feeney, who was in Geneva: "Chuck, I need a balance sheet in twenty-four hours. Can you send one out please?" Feeney got the accountant in the Geneva office to work up some figures and figured out how much they should bid, then telexed them to Miller, who flew to Hawaii. The bid, in the name of Tourists International Sales Ltd., guaranteed to pay Honolulu airport $78,000 for five years, starting on May 31, 1962, for the duty-free concession. It was a huge sum for a tiny retail space in the new terminal, but Feeney and Miller were gambling on the duty-free business picking up as tourism increased. Miller hardly slept the night before the opening of the bids. There were five contenders. They assembled at a government building to witness the director of transportation write the numbers on a large blackboard. Tourists International was successful. The second-highest bidder was a company called Mercury International, which was a money changer. When they realized they had lost, their manager offered Miller $100,000 to default on the bid. "No way!" he said.

A few months later, Miller and Feeney also secured the first duty-free concession at Kai Tak International Airport in Hong Kong. A new terminal building was also being constructed there to replace the British-built Nissan huts that had served passengers since World War II, and the runways were being extended to cater to the 707s. Dick Folta, a part-time car salesman, noticed in the weekly publication of airport tenders that the Hong Kong authorities also intended to introduce a duty-free concession for alcohol and tobacco in the new terminal, so he tipped off his bosses. Feeney and Miller bid for the concession under the name Tourists International (HK) Sales. Miller dropped off the tender in a box in the Hong Kong Civil Aviation building. To get the three-year contract, they guaranteed 28 percent of their gross sales, plus a nominal sum for the concession and all service charges. There was no public opening of bids in the British colony. Miller simply received a government letter one morning informing him that they had won.

At the time, the two airport duty-free concessions were seen by the four Cornellian entrepreneurs now running the cars and liquor sales operation—Feeney, Miller, Sterling, and Mahlstedt—as sideline businesses that might or might not make money. They stocked the duty-free shops and appointed managers, but travel in the Pacific was in its infancy and the tiny stores did little business when they opened. Selling cars to the military and liquor to American tourists was where the big money was to be made. They were, however, prepared to take their chances with whatever opportunities arose. Though operating in an opportunistic manner, without a written plan or strategy, they were getting bigger and bigger all the time. "It was like riding a tiger," said Miller. "It took you wherever it was going."

As it happened, Chuck Feeney was exploring another potentially lucrative new opening in North America. He had returned to the United States in early 1961 with Harry Adler to buy out Duty Free Shoppers, the bankrupt company that had failed so badly in Switzerland. He found that the people who owned the shares had already written off their investments as a tax loss.

The idea behind the company was that duty-free goods could be sold to American tourists anywhere beyond U.S. borders. Feeney and Adler flew to Mexico City to test the market there. After a payment of $5,000 to a fixer, they opened a tiny shop in Londres Street in the heart of the cosmopolitan Zona Rosa district and stacked the shelves with samples of watches, scarves, cashmere sweaters, cuckoo clocks, and liquor bottles that they bought from neighboring shops. Except for the samples, they carried no stock. "An American tourist would come into the shop and buy from the catalog or whatever he could see in the shop," said Adler. "We would say, 'We will send it to you.' When the tourist went back to the U.S. he would declare that while abroad he purchased, say, a Pringle cashmere sweater, which would come as unaccompanied baggage. The order would go to Geneva and would be shipped from a warehouse in Amsterdam. The postman would come to the customer's door with the package. He would say, 'You have got to pay duty.' The customer would say he declared it as unaccompanied baggage when returning from Mexico and give him the receipt. The mailman would send off the receipt. It worked fairly well."

Feeney's next move was to explore the possibility of duty-free business on the Canadian border, which promised to be a much bigger market. If American tourists in France or Germany could order liquor to be sent from bonded warehouses in Europe, they could also do the same from Canada. Feeney checked and found that no one had exploited this opportunity—apart from a Canadian ship supplier in Haiti, Elias "Papa" Noustas, who had started a mail-order liquor business in Haiti in 1960. Feeney went to see him in Port au Prince to talk about how it worked. He then contacted Jeff Mahlstedt in Hong Kong and asked him to come to New York to help launch the mail-order business in Canada for Tourists International. His Cornell friend was happy to leave the Far East, as he hadn't been getting along with Miller, and he came to New York.

When it came to business, Feeney did things as economically as possible, and he and Mahlstedt would meet in a coffee shop each morning to work out their strategy. "We would scribble notes, and call people from the pay phone until they threw us out," recalled Mahlstedt. "We would go from coffee shop to coffee shop. We would sit in the coffee shops pasting up pieces of paper to take to the printer. The total up-front cost was printing the brochure. And we didn't pay our printer immediately, either. We then rented an office on the top floor of a run-down building at Fifth Avenue and Forty-second Street. My hotel room in Hong Kong was bigger! When you went in, you had to slide around the desk. Chuck's stance was, "Look, it's a great address—Fifth Avenue. How can you beat it?"

Always coming up with new ideas, Feeney devised an order form with a perforation for a tear-off portion. Mahlstedt believes this was the first time such a system was used for direct mail. He also came up with the idea of attaching blank checks payable to Tourists International for customers to use. The order form told travelers "whether you are going to Canada, Mexico, the Caribbean, Europe, the Far East or Pago Pago, you are entitled to have your duty free five-bottle pack sent to your home . . . as well as cashmeres, cameras, watches, china, crystal, silver, pearls, leather goods, jade, skiwear and many more items all at duty free prices." They should simply declare the purchases at customs as "goods being shipped to you," ask for Form 3351, fill it out, and airmail it to Tourists International, Duty Free Sales Division, 94 Rue du Rhone, Geneva, Switzerland—the office Feeney had acquired when he bought out Adler's bankrupt company. "We do the rest . . . shortly after you have returned home, we will acknowledge your order, and inform you of the approximate date your liquor will be delivered to your home."

It was a complicated procedure with a six-week wait for delivery, but the savings for the customer could be as high as 50 percent. The most important element of the operation was that the booze did not have to originate in the country that the tourist was visiting. An American in Canada who ordered five bottles of Johnny Walker would get his package from the bonded warehouse in Amsterdam after sending his customs form to Geneva.

Feeney organized electronic data processing to compile alphabetical lists showing the name and address of each consignee, the contents of each package, and a consignee reference number. Shipments averaging 2,000 packets, each labeled to show the name and address of the consignees, were forwarded from Amsterdam to the port of New York in steel containers. After clearance by customs, they were collected by the Railway Express Agency for delivery to the tourists' homes. Tourists International never owned the liquor, so there was no need for warehouses or capital investment in stock or inventories.

Mahlstedt went to Canada and set up a duty-free outlet at the Park Hotel in Niagara Falls. Within a year he had established six shops across the border, where American travelers could order five-bottle packs of duty-free booze. He distributed brochures at gas stations. He appointed area agents to go to hotels and motels frequented by American visitors and give out leaflets with order forms. The forms were numbered so that agents and hotel clerks were entitled to a commission when the orders came in. As the business grew, Feeney also got Lee Sterling to come over from Europe to help out. They opened display shops to promote a variety of other merchandise, such as hand-knit Norwegian sweaters that would arrive in the mail months later. But the big money was in liquor sales, which made what Mahlstedt called "a gigantic amount" of profit in its early days. The first summer, they were practically the only duty-free people in Canada selling liquor by mail order. Soon they were shipping half a million bottles of spirits a year into the United States. The Ontario authorities, who had a liquor monopoly in the state, saw their sales go down. Royal Canadian Mounted Police followed Mahlstedt as he went around distributing brochures, but found he was doing nothing illegal.

Some of the brochures were "politically incorrect" by today's standards. They had a drawing of a smiling family—mother, father, and child of about ten—with five bottles of liquor stacked in front of each, and the message, "Each family member can order one gallon." One was illustrated with a sketch of the Eiffel Tower in Paris with the claim that if all the liquor bottles ordered through Tourists International in a year were placed one on top of another, they would reach a height 115 times higher than the tower.

Then the competition arrived. "We didn't realize when we started up this five-bottle-pack business that we didn't have any exclusivity on it, and in no time at all there were fifteen other companies trying to do the same as we were doing," said Feeney. Hotels and motels near the Canadian border were inundated with flyers and order forms from other operators. There was also growing resistance to their business in the United States.

"In Buffalo the retail liquor people said they were just being clobbered by us," said Mahlstedt. "It was very typical that once people knew about us, they would drive across one bridge, order their booze, and drive back over another bridge saying they had been gone forty-eight hours. There was no age limit. They would put ten little kids in the car and declare all their stuff."

Inundated by complaints from American retailers, the attorneys general in U.S. states looked for legal ways to stop the booze-ordering frenzy. One day, a Liquor Authority official came into their New York office and confronted Harry Adler. "Mr. Adler, you are selling liquor to people in the State of New York without a license," he asserted. "We are not, only to tourists," retorted Adler. The New York State Liquor Authority took Tourists International to court and lost.

Soon afterward, Adler left to run a furniture business in Phoenix. "I had fun with Chuck," he reminisced. "Chuck lived out of his briefcase. Everything was connected with business. We did a lot of screwy things. I became part of what he called his 'teen-age frontier' approach to business, because he surrounded himself with smart college youngsters, mostly single and aggressive 'conquerors of the world.' I was the oldest of his 'cowboys,' always the damper, saying to him, 'Are you out of your mind?' But it was a very exciting chapter in my life."

In those days, Chuck and Danielle Feeney divided their time between New York and Paris, where they had an apartment in Montmartre. There was business to attend to all over Europe. Feeney was traveling around so much that he had no permanent address. "I didn't have a domicile at that stage; it would have been superfluous," he recalled. But the need for a family home was becoming urgent. Their first daughter, Juliette, was born in January 1962, and their second daughter, Caroleen, in December the same year, both in Paris.

On his visits home to New Jersey, Feeney did not flaunt his success—it was not in his nature and would not have gone down well with his old school pals in Elizabeth, with whom he kept in touch. But he did decide to give his parents an expensive treat. In November 1963, he persuaded his mother and father to go on a cruise. He had secretly arranged to refurbish their house on Palisade Road while they were gone. He and Arlene's husband, Jim Fitzpatrick, cleared out the house before the workmen moved in. "We went down into the cellar and threw a lot of stuff away," recalled Fitzpatrick. "Mr. Feeney would never throw stuff away. He would save newspapers and they were stacked to the ceiling. It was kind of a fire hazard. And the attic was the same way. So Chuck and I rented a truck, and we got rid of it all. Mrs. Feeney, when she got back from the cruise, was just delighted. The house was sparkling, new drapes and furniture and all that stuff. She said, 'If I had known it was going to look like this I would have brought the captain home with us!' Mr. Feeney went right down to the cellar. He wanted to kill somebody! I got out of that house in a hurry."

CHAPTER

The Perfect Storm

By mid-1964, Tourists International was operating in twenty-seven countries and had 200 employees. In New York, they had moved their headquarters into a bigger office on Lexington Avenue. But the four Cornellians running this sprawling multinational enterprise, which included Cars International and the two airport duty-free shops, had never once been together in one room. In September that year, Feeney called them to New York for their first annual directors' meeting. The company consisted of semi-independent citadels, registered under different company names in different countries, with Feeney at the center providing the drive, vision, and ideas. They needed a proper management structure.

Taking the chair, Chuck Feeney told his three partners, Bob Miller, Jeff Mahlstedt, and Lee Sterling, that he was worried about how unwieldy Tourists International had become. The prime objective, he told them, was to establish a base for the orderly growth and overall expansion of the company. The four Americans had achieved astonishing success in just five years, but they had no plan for growth, no organizational chart, no company history, no corporate objective, not even a list of company employees. "It must grow into a more efficient and vital organization," he said. To streamline operations, he assigned them each the role of managing director: Miller for the Far East, Mahlstedt for North America, and Sterling for Europe. Feeney's responsibility would be to coordinate the reports of the other three and determine policy.

As cofounders, Feeney and Miller also decided what would be a fair division of the shareholding of the business. They agreed that they would take 38.75 percent each; Jeffrey Mahlstedt would have 12.5 percent, and Lee Sterling 10 percent. Lee wasn't happy about that, as he felt he should have gotten equal treatment with Mahlstedt. It was a handshake agreement. Nothing was put in writing.

Everybody thought the company was making big profits. They were selling up to 4,000 cars a month. Cash flowed through the system. But without a balance sheet, there was no way of knowing exactly how well they were doing. They appointed Desmond Byrne, a heavyset and rather bombastic English accountant hired by Bob Miller in Hong Kong, as company treasurer and directed him to bring the accounting procedures under centralized control and report directly to Feeney.

Around that time, Feeney ran into one of his buddies from New Jersey and said something about having twenty-seven companies around the world. The friend remarked: "But are you making any money?" It was a pertinent question. When the four directors met together again, at the next board meeting in January 1965, this time at their office at 76 Boulevard Helvetique in Geneva, Desmond Byrne reported on what he had found in his tour of the branches. The company was booming but was chronically short of cash. "We ain't got no money, boys," Byrne said bluntly. "Where's the money?"

There were severe problems in the auto sales division, disclosed Byrne. There were long delays before cash was found to pay for cars when delivery time came. They were taking deposits from service personnel and using the money to pay for expenses and car deliveries.

The directors were stunned. They thought they had an excess of funds and that it was just moving around the company network. They decided to slash costs and figure out what to do. Feeney suggested that they cut their salaries as a start. They were drawing $2,000 a month each, the tax-free limit for Americans living abroad. They agreed to reduce their pay to $1,200 a month.

"We had no idea what we were doing financially," recalled Mahlstedt. "If an office was opened somewhere, whoever had money sent them money. It was crazy. There was no accounting. It was not that we weren't keeping a record. We sent money to Hong Kong, or Hong Kong sent money to Canada, but there was no tying together." With the business expanding so rapidly, they hadn't paid enough attention to bookkeeping. "We hadn't spent any time on corporate structuring or anything like that, we were just simply busy selling cars, duty-free liquor, making the cash, putting the cash in the bank, cash in, and cash out," recalled Miller.

The Cornell graduates had learned well how to operate hotels and restaurants in the Hotel School, but they were now having to master the principles of managing a global business network on the run. They passed around among themselves Alfred P. Sloan's 1963 bestseller, *My Years with General Motors*, in which Sloan attributed his success in running GM to decentralized management and financial controls. Tourists International had the former but not the latter. "Financial controls weren't necessary," quipped Feeney, looking back. "We didn't have any money!"

One of their problems was that the car business was now coming up against serious competition from the U.S. military. Before 1960, the Army Exchange Service stores overseas, known as PXs, did not sell automobiles and luxury goods made in the United States. Now the PXs had begun selling American cars—duty free—to military personnel in Europe, for delivery back home. They gave showroom space to the three American car manufacturers: General Motors, Ford, and Chrysler. "And of course they had very attractive deals," said Feeney. "You arrived back from your overseas tour, went to your local Ford dealer, and picked up your car, which you had ordered in Europe. They sort of closed us out of that."

In Hong Kong, car sales were also coming up against other competition. Feeney and Miller's salesmen had the Pacific to themselves until a ship from the Seventh Fleet was transferred from the Pacific to the Mediterranean and docked at Naples in Italy, and the first rival car salesman to come on board found that the officers had already bought cars in Hong Kong. With that, the secret was blown.

Money had been pumped into the arteries of Cars International from Feeney's mail-order liquor business on the Canadian border, but as it had been assailed by copycat competitors, it too was in decline. It went from $20 million per year in 1963 to $5 million per year in 1964.

Through a chance encounter on a New York street a year earlier, the partners had learned that they were in deep trouble of a different kind—that could land them in court. Lee Sterling bumped into a rookie lawyer, Harvey Dale, an old school friend from Great Neck, New York, and a fellow Cornellian, and told him about the car business in which he was involved. Dale had just started work with the law firm Curtis, Mallet-Prevost, Colt & Mosle in New York. The rookie lawyer knew enough about international law to realize that the entrepreneurs had potentially serious tax problems. "You guys better get yourselves sorted out, because the laws are changing," he said.

When Lee Sterling reported back what he had heard, Feeney and Bob Miller went to the Curtis Mallet office at 101 Park Avenue to find out more. The lawyers shook their heads in amazement when Feeney outlined how they financed their operations. They explained that the United States had that year tightened tax regulations for U.S. citizens living and doing business abroad and that the partners in the car and liquor business faced enormous tax and liability issues.

Harvey Dale sat in on the meeting. The young lawyer knew Feeney slightly from Cornell, where he had studied philosophy before going on to graduate cum laude from Harvard Law School. Feeney and Miller asked him to do a tour of their global operations to see how the company could be restructured to avoid crippling tax liabilities. It was the start of a relationship that would eventually make Harvey Dale the most influential person in Chuck Feeney's life.

The tax problem also brought Chuck Feeney into contact with another lawyer, a colorful and voluble Italian American, who too would play a large role in Feeney's business affairs. Anthony M. Pilaro, fresh out of the University of Virginia Law School, had just joined the law firm and had been brought into the meeting to take notes. Despite his diminutive size, Tony Pilaro had been captain of his high school baseball, football, and basketball teams. Feeney was impressed by the smart, cocksure, junior associate, and later, in December 1964, when he heard that Pilaro was planning to take a job with a law firm in the Bahamas, he persuaded him to join Tourists International instead. Sensing that Feeney was a gifted entrepreneur and destined to be enormously successful, Pilaro agreed. He didn't quite know what was expected of him, but he guessed he would be a tax consultant and deal maker.

Harvey Dale soon established that what the four Cornellians were facing was more serious than bankruptcy. "The way they were operating carried legal risks that could have put them in jail," he recalled. "It was very serious because what they were doing, not intentionally, was they were taking trust funds that were there for Jones, and spending the deposit to make delivery to Smith—that is a Ponzi scheme, and that's a fraud. If things had gone in the worst possible light there could have been criminal liability for that. It involved serious risk, financial and criminal for the owners."

The financial crisis brought another figure into the company who would play a pivotal role in years to come. A senior partner at Price Waterhouse who was going through their books advised them to get a good accountant and gave them the name of Alan Parker. Born in England and raised in Rhodesia, Alan Moore Parker was a talented forensic accountant with a high-domed forehead and large spectacles, then living in Geneva. Feeney asked him to come to London for an interview. Parker remembered the occasion chiefly for the speed at which Feeney walked along the street in London. "I was always three steps behind him," he said. "No matter how fast I walked I could never catch up with Chuck." Feeney's fast walking was by this stage legendary. Bonnie Suchet, his London office manager, said, "Sometimes he would talk to you while he was walking away, and you had to run after him down the stairs."

Parker was hired and quickly established that "people were spending money like crazy. In Geneva everybody had gone out to lunch on the company. Bob Miller would pick up the bill, or Jeff Mahlstedt. I stopped it pretty quickly. I said, 'You just can't go on like this.'"

Worse was to come. What Feeney had started on the Canadian border had become too big, and under pressure from members of Congress whose states were hurting, the White House had stepped in to stop the mail-order liquor sales. On February 25, 1965, President Lyndon Johnson announced legislation to cut the five-bottle duty-free allowance to one bottle and to restrict the privilege to adults of at least twenty-one years old. No longer could a traveler claim an allowance of five bottles for everyone in his car, including the kids. Johnson justified his move by arguing that in the light of a balance of payments problem, the spending by Americans who were going abroad in record numbers "is not presently warranted."

His bill had to be passed by both houses of Congress before it became law. Feeney flew to Washington to lobby House and Senate members against the measure. He took Tony Pilaro with him. They were young enough—Feeney was thirty-three, Pilaro twenty-nine—to believe they could take on Washington and win by force of argument. Said Pilaro, "We just had balls." They set up camp in the Hilton Hotel and hired a well-connected law firm in the U.S. capital, Arnold, Fortas & Porter, to lobby for them. Abe Fortas was a friend and confidant of the president, and Paul Porter was one of the most influential lawyers in town. Porter told them, "If you can show me an argument that does not embarrass the president, we will take this on."

Knowing that a firm with registered headquarters in Vaduz, Liechtenstein, would evoke little sympathy with members of Congress, Feeney and Pilaro presented themselves as president and secretary of the "American Tourist and Trade Association," a body they simply created for the occasion with the motto "Tourism in Trade." They got several competitors in the five-bottle business in the United States to sign up. It was now an all-American effort.

Paul Porter arranged a ten-minute audience for Feeney with Republican senator Everett Dirksen of Illinois, the strongly anti-Communist Senate minority leader, most often remembered for the quip: "A billion here, a billion there, and pretty soon, you're talking about real money." The gruff senator with thick white hair and heavy jowls was initially skeptical. "He sat Chuck and me down and served us brandy from grapes in Indiana, so we sort of got the hint that he didn't give a damn about all this French brandy acquired abroad," recalled Pilaro. Feeney talked as fast as he could, pleading that "this bill would be a terrible injustice, and would take away the booze from all these military guys who were sticking their ass out for everybody." Dirksen didn't take a note and didn't ask any questions, recalled Feeney, "but he was interested in fairness to the military guys and walked out on the floor and made the most impassioned speech you can imagine."

Feeney placed his hopes on testifying before the House Ways and Means Committee as president of the American Tourist and Trade Association and as director of Tourists International, Inc. He spent several days in the Hilton drafting his statement against the passing of the legislation, listed as House Bill HR 7368.

When he arrived on Capitol Hill for the hearings, held on May 3 and 4, 1965, he found himself up against the big guns of the administration. Treasury Secretary Henry Fowler appeared first to tell the committee that with a national budget deficit of $3.1 billion, "this is no time to encourage foreign travel." The bill would have a beneficial effect on the balance of payments position and on Customs administration, declared Fowler. It was necessary to eliminate the "articles to follow" privilege that had deeply troubled a number of states that had lost state liquor taxes, and which he claimed was widely abused.

Porter countered on behalf of the American Tourist and Trade Association that the booze brought in as "articles to follow" accounted for only 450,000 gallons out of a total U.S. consumption of 275 million gallons of liquor. He added to laughter—he was known as a tippler—"I don't know whether I've been getting my share or not."

Feeney was called on the second day by the presiding chairman, Democrat John E. Watts of Kentucky, home of the American bourbon industry. He acknowledged in sworn testimony that the idea of a home-delivery service had been his but was now used by about fifteen companies. Its elimination "will brutally terminate an entire industry," Feeney pleaded. Moreover, the bill would not achieve its objectives. It would have a negligible impact on the outflow of dollars, and it would throw out of work hundreds of people in the United States.

Feeney plaintively described the extra hardship the measure would impose on travelers at Kennedy International Airport as they struggled through the equivalent of a "varsity football scrimmage" to declare their packages of liquor, and he appealed to the patriotism of the House members not to discriminate against returning military personnel such as the "young flyer, who has spent the past months stemming Communist aggression."

None of it swayed the committee. The Democratic majority voted to approve President Johnson's bill, and it sailed through the Senate. But the appeal to Senator Dirksen had some effect. Dirksen and Senator Jake Javits on the Senate Finance Committee combined to put back the effective date of the measure from June 1 to October 1, 1965. Feeney and Pilaro had gained four months.

Feeney never had a hope of winning the argument, according to a lawyer from their lobbying firm who told them later that "when this thing came down to push and shove, President Johnson literally called the leadership of Congress into his office and said, 'This is the way it is going to be. We are changing the duty-free allowance. There is no discussion on it.'" The attorney said he had never in all of his years in Washington seen such arm-twisting as Johnson pulled that day. At the time, bourbon popularity had slid dramatically, though not only because of them, and bourbon makers were accusing the duty-free businesses of "selling nothing but Scotch and French brandy." A newspaper columnist later wrote that American liquor interests were behind Johnson's legislation, helped by a legendary Washington lobbyist, Tommy "The Cork" Corcoran, who frequently enjoyed a glass of bourbon with Johnson. Meeting Corcoran years later at a business conference in Saipan, Pilaro asked the lobbyist about the allegation, but The Cork refused to be drawn on the matter.

Thus it was that in midsummer 1965, eight years after founding their company and seeing it expand into one of the world's first global retailers, Chuck Feeney and Bob Miller faced the perfect storm. The company was buffeted by a series of setbacks: President Johnson's smashing of the five-pack business, the cutthroat rivalry in the Mediterranean and on the Canadian border, competition in auto sales from the PX stores, the end of the car-sales monopoly in Asia—all combined with bad bookkeeping and extensive overspending to provide a classic example of how an innovative business with a visionary leadership can be sunk.

A few days after his defeat on Capitol Hill, Feeney began a salvage operation. He closed the office in Geneva and concentrated everything in New York. One of those let go was Alan Parker, just four months after being hired. Lee Sterling sold the thirty-six Swiss work permits they had acquired to Bernard "Bernie" Cornfeld, the international financier who was using Switzerland as a headquarters to sell investments in U.S. mutual funds through a company that later collapsed and ruined a number of American and European banks.

As Parker looked around for something else to do, Jeff Mahlstedt called him from New York and offered him his job back. Mahlstedt had been impressed with how Parker had been making sense of the figures in Europe. He asked him to come to the United States urgently and help sort out the company finances. The accountant was just about to get married, but he agreed. After their wedding on June 12, he and his Danish wife, Jette, took a plane to New York. It was a bit of an adventure, he felt at the time. He had never been to the United States before.

Bob Miller had also just gotten married, in May, to an Ecuadorian beauty, Maria Clara "Chantal" Pesantes. He was on his honeymoon in the Cameron Highlands in Malaysia when Feeney tracked him down with the message, "We've got huge problems. You've got to come to New York immediately." Miller cut short his honeymoon, and he and Chantal also made their way to the United States.

In New York, Parker found a situation out of control. There was a "fantastic" cash flow but a chronic shortage of funds to pay the suppliers when delivery time came. They were faced with a conundrum. They had to close down the car operation but couldn't do it right away because it was generating the cash.

Self-confident and unruffled, Alan Parker went through the books with a small team of auditors. Three days after arriving in New York, he was finally able to announce how bad it was. There was a deficit of $1.6 million, "which is peanuts today but in those days was a massive amount of money." They were on the verge of going bankrupt, perhaps already were.

On that bleak midsummer day in 1965, everybody in the organization with a professional qualification took fright and walked out. Desmond Byrne, Tony Pilaro, and a Canadian accountant named Bob Lewis came as a group to see the owners in the Tourists International office on Lexington Avenue and announced they couldn't risk their professional reputations by staying, recalled Jeff Mahlstedt. They feared getting caught up in a financial scandal. Desmond Byrne was blunt: "You guys are going bust. The company won't last for more than another two or three months at most. I'm out of here. I'm a chartered accountant and if this company goes bankrupt and I'm still here, it will ruin my name." Miller asked him what the chances of surviving were. "A million to one," said Desmond as he exited.

Tony Pilaro was next. "He said in a panic that he had to leave also," said Miller. "So Tony left. And Desmond left. They were like rats jumping off a sinking ship." It always stuck in his mind about Pilaro, he said, that "when the going gets tough, Tony freaks."

Mahlstedt also left. He wasn't too bothered by the debt, he said, but he had been working seventeen hours a day, seven days a week, for five years, and this was too much. "My butt was dragging. I was absolutely zapped," he said, and Tony advised him to "get out of it as fast as you can." Pilaro's warning "unfortunately influenced my decision." Mahlstedt told Chuck and Bob he hoped they would hold on to Alan Parker and give him his 12.5 percent shareholding—not that it was worth anything at that point—and he then drove off toward the Canadian border in a $6,000 Cadillac they gave him as settlement. He opened the Speakeasy Restaurant in Niagara Falls on the site of a real speakeasy that had been there in Prohibition times—when it was people like President John F. Kennedy's father, Joe Kennedy, who were responsible for the flow of liquor from Canada to the United States.

Dick Bradley, a Cornell Hotel School graduate and friend of Feeney who was helping to run Cars International, also left shortly afterward to cofound

Victoria Station, a restaurant chain that grew to 100 outlets in the United States, Canada, and Japan.

"These were really tough times," said Miller. "I had a young bride of two months. The company looked like it was going bust, and our key people were running for the exits." He asked an outside accountant, Lester Wulff, from the auditing firm of Larsen and Wulff, to go through the books independently and find out if they were dead in the water. Wulff studied the cash flow of the entire operation and figured out how much money was in bank accounts, how many cars had to be delivered, how many employees had to be laid off, when bills were due. After several hours going through the numbers, Wulff said, "You know, I think you and Chuck can make it. But you have too many expenses and you have to cut them quickly." Miller jumped up, gave the startled accountant a hug and a kiss, and declared, "Mr. Wulff, I love you!"

Miller called Alan Parker back to the office and asked him not to leave. "I have got to have a chief accountant here, to figure out what to do," he told him. Parker was in an awkward position. He had been in the United States for just a few days. He had no right to work there, and the business looked dodgy, but he did not have enough money to go back to Europe. He said he would stay and work with them for five years if he got a promise of a share in the company. "The company looks to be going bankrupt so any equity I give you now would be negative," Miller said. But he talked to Chuck "and we agreed and made equity available for him." This decision was to make Parker one of the richest men in the world.

Feeney and Miller were almost back where they started. They went out for a tuna fish sandwich at a New York deli. Miller recalled telling Feeney, "Well, Chuck, it's just you and I now. Looks like the shit's hit the fan. We've got to get out of this thing. It's back to you and I to figure out how to do it." There was still a chance of getting out of the mess, said Feeney. They couldn't close down the car operation right away because it was generating the cash flow, but they could perhaps boost the cash flow from the duty-free shops in Hong Kong and Hawaii to clear off the debts.

Feeney had moments of despair. "Of course. It goes with the territory. But there wasn't much we could do. It was something we had started, and we thought we were going to make a million dollars out of it. We had no choice but to salvage the company or go over the cliff." Harvey Dale was struck by their determination to straighten things out. "Both Bob and

Chuck felt the honorable thing to do would be to try to pick up the cash flow and redeem themselves and get out of trouble," he recalled.

Danielle Feeney saw a change in her husband during the crisis. To her, Chuck had always seemed driven by the desire to succeed. She admired him tremendously—how he had gone to Cornell, learned French, and finally become a success and a citizen of the world. When they got married he never talked about money, only making a go of his business ventures. A fortune was not his real goal, she perceived; his work was his challenge. Now she saw how his hopes had been shattered and his ego wounded. At home he could still be fun, charming and kind, but at times he was unsettled and angry, working tirelessly with people coming and going at the house to cope with the crisis. The family was growing—a third daughter, Leslie, was born in Paris in June 1964—and with that came more financial responsibilities. But Danielle never doubted that Chuck would find a way out of the situation.

To reduce costs, Feeney and Miller moved the Tourists International offices from Lexington Avenue to a less-expensive building in Fort Lee, New Jersey, just across the George Washington Bridge from Manhattan. There, Parker began squeezing everybody for nickels. Harvey Dale came by and saw a discarded briefcase on the floor. "It was old, made of cardboard. It was empty. I needed an attaché case as I wasn't making much money. I asked Alan whether I could take it, and he looked at me and said, 'Sure. That will be $5.' And I paid for it." The entertainment budget was slashed to zero. If there was a business lunch, the other party paid. The new regime impacted seriously on Bob Miller's personal cash flow. At a lunch with bankers where everyone had agreed to pay their share, Miller collected cash from each person around the table and paid with a credit card. Parker imposed financial control by the simple method of keeping the company checkbook locked in a drawer. Bob Miller would plead, "Alan, we've got to pay this bill," and the unsmiling accountant would say: "Tell them we will release the check in ten days."

The next to leave was Lee Sterling. In early 1965, Feeney had asked him to go to Hawaii to manage the duty-free store and try to boost sales. At the time, they were paying Peter Fithian to supervise it. But Sterling was newly married, and his wife didn't like life in Honolulu. Like Mahlstedt, he found Miller difficult. The last straw, he recalled, was a letter Miller sent that demanded "in an imperious tone" that he transfer $65,000 to him from

Hawaii for Cars International. "Bob and I were never going to get along," he reckoned. Sterling's father died, and he wanted to take time out to sell his father's business in New York. He told Feeney he would have to find someone else, and left, later in life becoming a successful real estate lawyer in Colorado.

The inability of Bob Miller to get along with Lee Sterling and Jeff Mahlstedt, both friends of Chuck Feeney, cast a shadow over Feeney's relationship with his original partner. Although they had good times when starting up and shared the same goals as Young Turks together, Feeney never developed a close friendship with Miller, and a coolness set in that did not bode well for their relationship in the years ahead. But the immediate need was to manage the rescue mission. To accomplish this, they divided the world between them. Feeney would go to Honolulu and try to improve the duty-free business. Miller would work out of New York to cut expenses around the world as fast as he could.

As the dust settled, the shareholding was redistributed. The departure of Mahlstedt and Sterling left 22.5 percent of the equity available. They agreed to give Alan Parker 20 percent. Parker would have liked one-third of the shareholding, but when Bob mentioned this, Chuck retorted, "No way! Give him some of your share if you like." Again nothing was put in writing. This left 2.5 percent. They offered it to Tony Pilaro to do pro bono work for them, even if he was making his career elsewhere. Chuck Feeney didn't like to lose such a bright legal brain. They had fought the Johnson administration together in Washington, and Feeney knew how sharp and dedicated Pilaro could be. The lawyer was feeling guilty and upset about quitting, and he accepted.

Jean Gentzbourger was another victim of the cash crisis. Before going to Hawaii, Feeney instructed him to liquidate the French company they had set up to run the Paris shop. When back in France, Feeney went himself to see what could be salvaged and told Parker in a memo that he had found an electric adding machine and a Grundig tape recorder that could be put to good use elsewhere. More than ever, Feeney was aware of the need to avoid waste of any kind.

On the advice of Harvey Dale, Feeney and Miller transferred their ownership of the company to their foreign-born wives so that it was no longer subject to U.S. tax laws. The major shareholders became Danielle Juliette Feeney, listed in company filings as a "directress," of Neuilly-sur-Seine in

France, and Maria Chantal Miller, described simply as a "married woman," of Guayaguil, Ecuador.

With the collapse of the car and five-pack business, Feeney and Miller dropped the names Tourists International and Cars International. Now that they were reduced, more or less, to retail ventures at Hong Kong and Honolulu airports, they adopted the name that Feeney had bought from the defunct New York company. In the future they would be known as Duty Free Shoppers, or DFS.

CHAPTER 7

The Sandwich Islands

The duty-free shop at Honolulu International Airport, when Chuck Feeney arrived to run it in late 1965, was little more than a market stall. Situated in the Overseas Waiting Lobby, its floor area was just over 100 square feet. It had three four-foot counters held together with Scotch tape.

The concept of a store selling duty-free merchandise in an airport was relatively new at the time, though the first known duty-free agreement in the world dated as far back as 700 AD, when King Ethelred of Mercia granted the bishop of London exemption from customary duties on imports. The idea was adopted by European armies, which supplied duty-free liquor and tobacco to soldiers, and embassies traditionally enjoyed duty-free supplies in their host countries.* Most countries eventually established duty-free zones at seaports where imported goods were stored in bonded warehouses and used only to supply ships. They were not taxed because they never entered the domestic economy.

The first duty-free stores anywhere were gift shops on pre–World War II ocean liners, and passengers patronizing the bars could enjoy drinks at duty-free prices. After the war, the privilege was extended to international aircraft passengers, but airports in the 1940s and 1950s were slow to respond, as air terminals tended to be primitive structures with little space for

---

*Julian Fox, *The Golden Book: 50 Years of Duty Free* (Tax Free World Association and Raven Fox Cohen, 1997).

commercial activity. The first airport duty-free shop was established in 1947 at Shannon airport in the west of Ireland, where transatlantic airliners stopped to refuel. The brainchild of the airport's catering boss, Brendan O'Regan, it started as a six-foot wooden counter backed by shelves of Irish whiskey and cartons of Carroll's Irish-made cigarettes and staffed by three men in double-breasted suits. The concept was so novel that suspicious Irish customs officials accompanied every carton of liquor from the bonded store to the shop, and stocktaking by hand was required three times a day. Bottles could not be opened at the airport: if a bottle was dropped, it was counted as opened and a customs officer was called to inspect the broken glass and levy an excise charge on the spot. In the 1950s, the shop expanded and began selling perfumes, watches, and cashmere to mostly American transit passengers. These were supplied directly by the manufacturers in London and Paris, an important precedent that Shannon established for other airport duty-free shops to follow.

Feeney found that Hawaii was in the early stages of a tourism boom. American tourists were starting to arrive in significant numbers, following the granting of U.S. statehood to Hawaii in 1959 and the introduction on the Pacific routes of Boeing 707s, which could ferry passengers from California in only three hours.

With balmy weather, swaying palm trees, and azure ocean waters, the Hawaiian Islands were close to the American idea of paradise. Hawaii had been popularized for Americans by the 1958 Oscar-winning movie *South Pacific,* and a nightlife culture had developed in Waikiki, Honolulu's beach resort, where mainlanders came to hear the crooner Don Ho and other popular Hawaiian entertainers. It was here in 1959 that Feeney's Cornell buddy, Chuck Rolles, had opened the first American restaurant with a salad bar, the forerunner of a chain of fifty Chuck's Steak House restaurants across the United States. New hotel developments in the mid-1960s were transforming Waikiki into an oceanside Manhattan. The sedate old Waikiki Beach hotels, the Royal Hawaiian and the Moana, once sufficient to cater to the rich tourists and Hollywood stars who patronized Hawaii, were being overshadowed by package-holiday hotels. There was so much construction going on, people said that Hawaii's national bird was the crane.

Most of the tourists milling around the DFS store in the Overseas Waiting Lobby were Americans traveling to and from the mainland, and they were not therefore permitted to buy duty-free goods as they were going from one U.S. state to another. Under international law, only travelers going to foreign destinations could buy duty-free goods. Feeney often had to turn away Americans from the store who thought Hawaii was a foreign country. The store got busy, however, between noon and 2:00 PM, when a small number of flights landed to refuel en route to Asia. An increasing number of the passengers who wandered over to inspect the shop's display were Japanese. They were still a rare sight abroad in the mid-1960s. In order to revive its war-shattered economy, the Tokyo government for many years banned ordinary Japanese citizens from traveling outside Japan for pleasure. It issued passports to business travelers for one journey only and imposed a severe limit on the amount of foreign exchange that could be taken out of the country. All that began to change when the ban on leisure travel was eased to coincide with the 1964 Tokyo Olympics. By then, Japan was well on the way to transforming itself into an economic powerhouse. Chuck Feeney, who had served in Japan and had attended the Tokyo Olympic Games, sensed that the country of 100 million people was ready to burst out of its postwar isolation. In 1964, some 20,000 Japanese were allowed to go abroad on pleasure trips. This was no more than fifty-five people a day, but most headed for Honolulu. The resentment over Pearl Harbor had faded with time. Hawaii was attractive to Japanese tourists not just because of the subtropical climate and sandy beaches, but because it was easily reached, many local people had Japanese ancestry, and it was America, the world center of consumerism.

The main goal of the first Japanese tourists was to spend their pent-up savings on foreign luxury items that were not available or were prohibitively expensive at home. They wanted quality liquors, perfumes, watches, pens, jewelry, and leather goods. "The ones who came out in the very beginning were these hicks, these *noukas*," said Feeney. "They would walk into the store, open their belt, drop their pants, reach into their crotch and pull out a pile of yen. This was cash they had in the house."

From his military service in Japan, Feeney was aware of the complex Japanese gift-giving culture, which employed thirty-five words to describe the act of giving. *Senbetsu* was the custom of giving money to departing travelers, and *omiyage* the reciprocal buying of presents for bosses, colleagues, family, and friends. Whenever a Japanese citizen went abroad, bosses, clients, and a range of friends would provide cash for the journey, creating an obligation for the traveler to bring back a present. Also at *oseibo*, year's end, and *ochugen*, midsummer, employees received envelopes stuffed with money. Standing behind the counter in Honolulu airport, Feeney learned more about how it worked. He would see a Japanese business type buying fifteen lipsticks for his staff, a leather purse for a junior worker, a watch for a big boss, and a bottle of whisky for a supervisor or family friend.

As more and more Japanese crowded around the counter of the little store, Feeney signed up for early morning classes five days a week with a Japanese teacher, Tachi Kawa, to brush up on the Japanese he had studied in military service. He memorized phrases and was soon able to handle customers in their own language. He insisted that anyone working behind the counter speak Japanese to the customers. Some of the salesgirls were natives of Japan who had married American ex-servicemen. They marshaled themselves behind the tiny counter when the Japanese planes were due. "I used to stand in the middle of the girls and line them up like last night's game when they were ready to take a free kick," said Feeney. They were squeezed so tight he would joke, "Don't put on any weight."

Feeney organized a system of red-dot specials so the sales assistants got commissions for pushing merchandise with the best markup. "If you have a sloppy display you have a sloppy customer," he told the staff. "And selling to customers is like catching flies. If you snap, then the fly is dead." He trained the girls "but some of them trained us," said Feeney. "We had one girl who, after selling six $50 pens, would say, 'Is that all the friends you've got? If I were you I would buy six more, and better, pens at $65 each.'" One hard-as-nails Japanese assistant was so good at selling that the Japanese customers often went out not knowing what they had bought. A customer came back once to complain that the cigars he had bought were difficult to smoke because they had holes in them: Rather than admit they had been eaten by worms, she convinced him that the perforations signified high quality.

The Japanese were genuinely astonished at the duty-free prices. Because of a policy of protectionism, Japan levied a 220-percent tax on imported premium cognac and whisky. In Tokyo a bottle of whisky that retailed at $25 cost only $6 in the duty-free shop. A $50 bottle of cognac in Tokyo cost a mere $10 duty free.

Within a year, the trickle of Japanese tourists turned into a stream, then a river. "Business is booming along here," Feeney wrote to Jean Gentzbourger in Paris on March 23, 1966. In less than a year, the crisis that almost bankrupted them was beginning to ease. The profits from duty-free sales enabled Miller to pay off the debts in the car business. More important, Feeney was succeeding again in business. There were parties at the house he rented for his family at Aina Haina Beach, a twenty-minute drive from Honolulu. He was thrilled with his three daughters, Juliette, Caroleen, and Leslie. "Kids are good—make some!" he wrote in another letter to Gentzbourger, in which he joked that Danielle was getting so dark "we may have racial problems if she doesn't stay out of the sun a bit."

Things looked so promising that Feeney and his co-owners felt confident enough to bid $1 million to renew the exclusive duty-free concession in 1967 for another three years. It made headlines in the Honolulu newspapers. It seemed an outrageous amount to undertake to pay for a tiny airport concession. But the owners knew what they were doing. Japan's postwar recovery was so successful that by 1968, it was the second-largest free-market economy in the world. The exodus of free-spending Japanese tourists was only getting under way.

In January 1968, Feeney and his young family went back to Europe and set up home again in Paris. Alan Parker went to Hawaii to run the operation as general manager, with Joe Lyons, the top car honcho in Europe, as sales manager. Like Feeney before him, Parker was astonished at what he found. "The original shop in Hawaii when I arrived was no wider than a desk," said Parker. "I can remember the pressure building—it grew so quickly, there were times the counter was being forced over on the salesgirls. The crush was incredible to buy items that were either not available in Japan or cost ten times the price. The first Japanese tour groups were company-sponsored trips, and that's really what took off the business. We were in the right place at the right time, and we were very lucky. The smart thing . . . was we realized that Japan had to explode from the point of overseas tourism." They expanded the airport store to 400 square feet and stocked it, according to a contemporary article in the Honolulu Star-Bulletin, "with alligator handbags, watches, jewelry, leather goods, pen and pencil sets and diamonds in addition to liquor, cigarettes and perfume."

Feeney commuted to Honolulu to work out with Parker and Lyons more ways of capitalizing on the Japanese tourism wave. In 1969, they established an 8,000-square-foot downtown duty-free store. There was nothing in the terms of the concession to prevent them from expanding out of the airport. They located their new store in the Waikiki Business Plaza atop Japan

Airlines' headquarters. Vacationers could stroll in, pick what they wanted, and have their purchases delivered to their planes. The tourists by then had even more money to spend. In 1968, the Japanese government had raised the foreign exchange allowance per person to $500 and further relaxed travel restrictions. By 1969, four out of every five Japanese travelers were tourists, with shopping rather than recreation their main priority.

The owners became skillful at enticing the Japanese into their downtown duty-free store, which eventually became as big as an aircraft hanger. They paid travel agents to bring tourists there even before they checked into their hotels. They ensured that the local guides, the bus drivers, and the taxi drivers were well looked after by providing a waiting room with refreshments and a television, so they were not in a hurry to get away after delivering their charges to the mercy of the salesgirls. As customer relations manager, Maurice Karamatsu, a Japanese speaker from Hawaii, greeted tour guides at the airport and befriended the drivers who brought the groups to the downtown store. He had gifts for everyone. When escorting Japanese into the store, Karamatsu always said, "Now you will be going into little Tokyo—except much cheaper!" The customers were given a card so that they could claim special gifts on second or third visits. In Honolulu, they averaged more than two shopping visits per Japanese.

Word got back to Feeney's Cornell friends about his success in Hawaii, which was known also as the Sandwich Islands. The name was given to Hawaii in 1778 by Captain James Cook of the British navy, in honor of his patron, the Earl of Sandwich. They sent him a mock newspaper. The headline read: "The Sandwich Man Makes It Big in The Sandwich Islands."

One day in 1965, when things were still financially precarious for Feeney and Miller, a tall, dignified Frenchman came through the Overseas Waiting Lobby in Honolulu airport and strolled over to the DFS shop. Michel Camus, president of the Camus cognac company, was on his way to Asia to promote his brandy, then little known around the world. "Why is there no Camus on display?" he asked. On hearing the reason—the difficulty of getting credit because of their cash-flow problems—he invited Chuck Feeney to come and see him in Paris.

Michel Camus and Chuck Feeney had done business before. Some years earlier, when selling booze to the U.S. Navy in the Mediterranean, Feeney had asked Jean Gentzbourger to find an inexpensive brandy to include in their portfolio. The Frenchman had gone to the International Food and

Wine Fair in Paris and found a stand marked "Camus" manned by a gentle-man who reminded him of Charles de Gaulle. Michel Camus invited Gentzbourger to visit his cellars near the town of Cognac in western France, and he sold him fifty cases of cognac at a bargain price. Feeney and Miller became clients. The president of the French company even created a "Camus Celebration" bottle for Feeney in 1963.

When Michel Camus turned up in Hawaii in 1965, Duty Free Shoppers was having trouble getting credit from most suppliers. "If you were a boom-ing success they would give you credit, but if you were just starting out, they wouldn't," said Feeney. The duty-free business was seen by most luxury goods manufacturers as a rather shady operation, run by hustlers in small, cramped shops. The elite sellers felt their brands would be diminished by as-sociation with a "discount" store. "Duty free in those days was like tax dodgers," explained Jean Gentzbourger, who had joined Camus as export sales manager. "People didn't understand it, they said there must be some-thing wrong with it."

Distributors also hated duty free because the store owners always tried to go directly to the makers and get factory prices, thus cutting them out—which was another disincentive to extending credit. Suppliers of liquor were exceptionally hard-nosed with DFS. Normally they would extend retailers sixty-day credit for spirits. They gave Duty Free Shoppers only fifteen- to thirty-day credit and sometimes asked for payment in advance. When he needed 1,000 cases of liquor at $20 a case, Feeney might have to find $20,000 cash, and that was before any of it was sold.

The established cognac makers, Hennessy and Martel, were "very snob-bish with us" because DFS was so small, recalled Bob Miller, and Chanel would only allow its perfume to be sold in the grandest shops. Alan Parker was once brusquely turned away from the office of Patek Philippe, the pres-tigious Geneva watchmaker, as "we weren't a place that could sell watches of their quality." Feeney recalled that the watch companies were "very tough operators," and the major watchmakers wouldn't deal with them—though when he found out that the head of Rolex had an Irish wife, he got chatting to him after a business function, made the ethnic connection, and got per-mission to sell Rolex.

This credit dilemma prompted Feeney to fly to Paris for a meeting with Michel Camus. He told him about their struggle to get merchandise on ac-count and their efforts to wind down the car business, but he talked up the prospects of retail success for DFS in Honolulu and Hong Kong. He said he needed to buy directly from the cognac maker, and he needed generous credit. In return, DFS would promote Camus and give it a much-needed distribution network in the Pacific and the Far East, where the Japanese were beginning to travel around and spend in large numbers.

Michel Camus had little to lose. The Camus family had once thrived exporting brandy to Saint Petersburg, where it was the official cognac at the court of the last tsar of Russia. That ended with the revolution, and Camus switched to bartering cognac for vodka from the Soviet Union, but it was not a lucrative business. By the mid-1960s, he had sizable stocks of cognac but was almost bankrupt, and Camus was ranked a lowly twentieth in world cognac sales.

The sophisticated and charming Cognaçais took a great liking to the blue-eyed former GI from New Jersey. Both were underdogs, Michel Camus in the world of cognac wholesalers and Feeney in the liquor retail trade. Camus offered Feeney direct sales and credit of 120 days, a concession unheard of in the "juice" trade. They could now acquire Camus at $2 a bottle compared with $6 for Courvoisier, and sell both for $9.95 a bottle.

The Camus connection was, however, to become much more important to the DFS owners as they struggled to clear their debts. With no reserves, DFS needed a major line of bank credit to capitalize the company and generate more cash to close down Cars International. Tony Pilaro tried to arrange credit through the Swiss banking system but was rebuffed when he approached Lombard Odier Bank on Rue de la Corraterie in Geneva and asked for a million dollars. "The guy looked at me as if I was crazy." Pilaro eventually found a banker willing to take a risk with them. Allan C. Butler, who owned Butler's Bank in Nassau in the Bahamas—where Pilaro had spent some time working—agreed to extend a credit line of $500,000 under a scheme worked out by Pilaro and Parker. DFS would set up an agency in the Bahamas to become exclusive worldwide distributors for Camus cognac. The agency would purchase large stocks from Michel Camus, which would be sold on to DFS and *other* duty-free companies in Asia, creating tax-free cash profits for the DFS owners in the Bahamas. Camus would get its distribution network; Feeney, Miller, Parker, and Pilaro could get cash to help extricate themselves from the car business; and the money flowing through Nassau would guarantee Allan Butler security for his bridging loan. In September 1965, they registered the distribution agency in

Nassau as Airport Chandlers Ltd., with the four shareholders as owners in proportion to their DFS equity.

It worked as intended. "Airport Chandlers placed the orders from Duty Free Shoppers to Camus, Camus billed Airport Chandlers, and Airport Chandlers billed DFS, and DFS paid Airport Chandlers, and Airport Chandlers paid Camus and sucked in the profits," explained Gentzbourger. The Nassau agency was soon handling 90 percent of all Camus production.

For the scheme to work, DFS had to wean Japanese tourists off their traditional liquor-buying habits and persuade them that Camus cognac was top of the line. Motivated by bonuses worked out by Feeney, the sales staff in Hawaii started cajoling tourists to switch to Camus. "The Japanese guys would come and ask for two bottles of Johnny *Kuro* [black], which is what they called Johnny Walker Black Label," said Bob Matousek, the always cheerful former car salesman whom Feeney had brought to Honolulu to run the airport shop when the downtown store was opened in Waikiki. "At the time they were allowed two bottles into the country, and Johnny Walker was a big gift to bring back to Japan. The girls would say, 'Oh no, no, aren't you aware of the new cognac, this is the latest thing,' and they would switch it to Camus. It reminded me of the car sales, switching the guy out of a Triumph to a Volvo because we made more money. But that was the name of the game, and it was very successful, it was phenomenal."

By March 1966, Feeney was selling 1,600 bottles of Camus a month at the tiny Honolulu airport shop, and he wrote to Gentzbourger to tell him how the salesgirls "really pound the customers" to sell Camus and get their bonuses. He also noted that sales of Camus were nil in Hong Kong, and said he was going to go there for a few weeks "to stir things up a bit."

The DFS sales people had fun pushing Camus everywhere they went. When in Japan on business trips, they made a point of asking for Camus cognac in nightclubs and would feign horror and surprise if none was available.

Feeney noticed, however, that when it came to brandy, the Japanese tourists liked to buy Courvoisier Napoléon in preference to any other brand. The Courvoisier label carried the trademark silhouette of the French emperor and boasted that it was the "Brandy of Napoléon," a claim based on the fact that Napoléon Bonaparte had ordered several barrels of Courvoisier to be sent with him when he was exiled to St. Helena. In Asia, the name Napoléon signified legitimacy and virility. Courvoisier dominated the world markets and was the only brand imported into Japan under license. It seemed to have the Napoléon market cornered. But there was a flaw in Courvoisier's marketing. The Japanese identified the brand with the word "Napoléon" rather than the name of the maker. No one had a patent on the word "Napoléon." Feeney suggested to Michel Camus that he promote a Camus Napoléon cognac. Camus was reluctant to go head-to-head with Courvoisier, fearing that his Napoléon would be seen as a blatant imitation and would flop. Feeney suggested a progressive redesign of the label, adding the word "Napoléon" in small letters and over a period of time making the word Camus smaller and the word "Napoléon" bigger. Few noticed what they were doing. When buying brandy, the Japanese looking for the word "Napoléon" soon did not distinguish between Courvoisier and Camus.

The marketing of Camus became something of an obsession with Feeney. He once wrote to Michel Camus asking that a promotional photograph of two Camus bottles standing beside a book showing a cover of Napoléon be professionally redone, with better serigraphy and labeling, and with the cognac snifter in front of the bottle moved "to give a better visual effect." For good measure, he attached his own sketch of how he thought the final advertisement should look. He detailed a list of other changes, such as "Move book slightly to left; move CAM NAP [Camus Napoléon] equal distance [as book] to left; move NAP EXTRA [Napoléon Extra] slightly to left to show full wording."

As Japanese business travelers often had to give presents to the same bosses, Camus poured lots of old brandy into different bottles to widen the choice, such as Baccarat crystal decanters, Limoges porcelain books, and busts of Napoléon in various colors, which made excellent gifts for Japanese business clients. One of their most successful was Camus Josephine Pour Femme, a lighter cognac in a slim bottle with a label showing a willowy lady in the style of Art Nouveau artist Alphonse Mucha. It was a big hit with the Japanese "office ladies."

DFS also got involved in the "creation" of an armagnac—a brandy made in the Armagnac region of the Pyrenees, which, unlike cognac, is distilled only once—and made it into a recognized global brand. At Gentzbourger's suggestion, Michel Camus bought an old unused label called Chabot that originated with the Chabot family in the village of Labastide d'Armagnac near the Spanish border, and established a production unit. Gentzbourger designed the first bottle of Napoléon Chabot, and called it Prince de

Chabot—a name they dropped after a person claiming the title called one day and asked for a percentage of the sales for use of his name.

Michel Camus was not the only French product maker to put his trust in DFS. Gilles Fuchs, son-in-law of Robert Ricci, who with his mother, Nina Ricci, founded the famous French perfume house, called to see Alan Parker when DFS was still struggling. "This guy wanted to sell me a thousand bottles of quarter-ounce Nina Ricci for $3 a bottle," recalled Parker. "I said to him, 'Tell you what we'll do. We'll buy 3,000 bottles at $1 each.' And he went for it. We kept on buying it at a very low price, and it created a very good margin for us so we pushed the hell out of it, and it created an enormous market for them over the years in Japan. He was smart enough to realize that if he got us hooked on his perfume, those millions of bottles would flow in, and he doesn't have to spend money on marketing in Japan, which he couldn't do anyway as he couldn't get into Japan. We could buy Nina Ricci at maybe a third of the price and make twice as much money."

The salesgirls got a special commission for pushing Nina Ricci on the unsuspecting Japanese shoppers. "They were very smooth and adept at this also," said Matousek. "They would try it on the person's hand and say, 'This is a new perfume; this is the top fashion now.'" As the company got bigger, Japanese tourists were confronted with displays of Camus and Nina Ricci at the entrance, and over time came to accept them as the gold standard of Western luxury goods.

Within two years of the Camus deal and setting up Airport Chandlers, the DFS car debts were paid off, and Airport Chandlers was making money. The four shareholders were able to meet their obligations to the admirals and generals who had ordered cars, and to deliver everything on time, even ahead of time. Airport Chandlers paid out dividends even before DFS. It was the "cash cow" at the time, recalled Parker. The first dividend was $31,250, divided proportionately among the four owners, in 1967. Chuck Feeney and Bob Miller each received $12,110; Alan Parker, $6,250; and Tony Pilaro, $780.

The DFS owners had long memories. It would take years for better-known cognacs, whose makers had snubbed them in tough times, to find a place on the shelves of their stores. By the mid-1980s, Camus was retailing almost half a million cases of cognac, mostly through DFS, and had become the number one cognac in Japan and the number five cognac in the world. Chabot went from zero to the number one exported armagnac in France.

At its peak in the 1980s, the arrangement would provide the four share-holders with total cash dividends averaging $50 million a year. And no one ever knew about it outside the company. It was a retail coup on a global scale. "We had the worldwide rights, we set the price, and we sold to our-selves," said Feeney.

Chuck Feeney never forgot Michel Camus's act of trust in him. "It was the start of a wonderful relationship and one of the great strokes of fortune we had," he said. Michel Camus became something of a father figure and mentor to Feeney. The Feeney and Miller families became regular visitors to the Camus chateau just outside the village of Cognac in the west of France. Michel Camus loved to tell his visitors: "Making a great cognac is easy. All you need is a great-grandfather, a grandfather, and a father who have dedi-cated their lives to it."

Hong Kong Crocodiles

While Feeney was raking it in at Honolulu airport and Miller was closing down Cars International, they entrusted the management of the Hong Kong duty-free shop at the new Kai Tak terminal building to John Monteiro, a savvy local accountant of Portuguese descent. Monteiro had been a manager with the China Light Company and was about to emigrate to a job in the United States when the two founders persuaded him to join DFS. They needed somebody with his street smarts. They promised they would transfer him to the United States sometime in the future. They wrote it into his contract.

The British colony in the late 1960s with its population of 4 million was the world capital of laissez faire capitalism. Everything and anything could be bought and sold. The harbor had no seagulls, it was said, as nothing edible was ever thrown away. Authority was invested in the British governor, but real power resided in the boardrooms of the Hong Kong and Shanghai Bank and in the big "hongs," or trading companies, like Jardine Matheson, Butterfield & Swire, and South Sea Textiles.

Hong Kong was just three hours' flight time from Tokyo. It had Western stores, double-deck buses, and English street signs. To Japanese tourists looking for a foreign experience and bargain prices, it was the number one destination in all of Asia. It was almost like going to England. And everything was duty free, except liquor and tobacco. The only people who could sell liquor and tobacco without charging duty were DFS.

As in Hawaii, the airport duty-free shop was like a huckster operation, with just two fifteen-foot counters. It had been badly run in its first few years when the owners were not paying attention. A manager once gave the staff Christmas Day off and went to play golf, forgetting that dozens of Japanese tourists were due to pick up duty-free liquor that day, and a mob of angry Japanese had gathered at the shuttered store.

Just as in Hawaii, the airport shop found itself overwhelmed by Japanese tourists after 1964. The salesgirls couldn't take orders fast enough for duty-free booze and cigarettes. Monteiro employed a team of Japanese-speaking people to ride on the tour buses and take orders for collection at the airport. As Japan eased restrictions further on foreign travel, the business began to double every month. It came to a point where "it was wild, we just couldn't handle it," said Monteiro. The sales generated by DFS were in time estimated to be fifty times higher per square foot than in Harrods, the London department store.

But as quickly as it made money, the owners were siphoning the profits off to wind up the car business. This meant that Monteiro had to delay payments for supplies and use his wits to keep afloat. The agent for a top-selling whisky lost patience once and said, "We won't deliver till you give us a check." Monteiro sent a check on which the numbers and figures did not match so it would not be honored by the bank. When the agent called to ask, "What the hell is this?" Monteiro said, "Oops, sorry, bring it back, and I will write another check." This bought him another two weeks. "It was fun and games," he said.

Monteiro came up with the idea of building a bigger shop downtown to cope with the growing demand and to expand the range of merchandise. The Kai Tak terminal shop was handling only 20 percent of the tourists' needs. The Japanese wanted to buy cameras, perfumes, cosmetics, expensive pens, and other luxury items. There was nothing in their contract to confine DFS to the airport or to restrict it to selling only liquor and tobacco. The company could open a store downtown for "one-stop" shopping and make it attractive to the tourists by offering to deliver all their purchases at the airport.

The four owners consulted and agonized over the proposal. They would need funds to rent premium space in downtown Hong Kong for a new store, then design it, refurbish it, and increase the staff fourfold. If they made a mistake in their calculations, it could sink the company again. Hong Kong was a more cutthroat place than Honolulu. And a downtown store would not prosper if the Chinese travel agents refused to deliver the Japanese tourists. Many of the travel agents had their own overpriced general merchandise shops or friends with stores who gave them huge kickbacks for delivering tour groups. It was a racket that everyone except the tourists knew about.

Monteiro went to see the top twenty travel agents in Hong Kong who controlled almost all the business, and put a proposal to them. If the agents would give up their own retail operations and bring all the Japanese tourists to the DFS downtown store, he would give them good commission on the items their tour groups bought, such as handbags, fountain pens, and watches. "Why do you want to run a store," asked Monteiro, "when I'll run it for you, with a better selection, better price, and I will give you the commission?"

"With the exception of one or two agents, they said they thought it a great idea and they would go along with it. So I brought that back to Chuck and Bob and they said, 'Let's do it.'"

DFS located the downtown store on the first floor of Hotung House on Hankow Road in Kowloon, behind the Peninsula Hotel, the "grand dame" of Far East hotels. They hired two managers and a staff of salesgirls. The feng shui—the placement and arrangement of things to ensure harmony with the environment—was judged to be excellent. They had a formal opening and a party.

However, the travel agents who had seemed so willing to cooperate were not going to give up their own businesses so easily. They threatened the providers of luxury goods and souvenirs in Hong Kong that they would drop them if they supplied wholesale items to DFS. "The travel agents 'locked' those guys up," said Monteiro, recalling the early days over tea in the Portuguese Club Lusitano in Hong Kong. "ST Dupont lighters were an absolute item every Japanese bought in those days, and ST Dupont would not supply us. Rolex would not supply us. Chanel would not supply us."

Monteiro called Feeney. He told him, "I have all these travel agents to deal with. I have to build the store. I have to hire the staff. I have got hardly any management working for me because we can't afford it, and I have got to see all these suppliers to get supplies. I just can't do it by myself. You've got to help."

At this point, Miller had taken a leave of absence from active involvement in the company. He had been working the business with Feeney for ten years. He had gone around the world to terminate the offices of Tourists International and Cars International, which hadn't been pleasant work. He now wanted to do other things by investing the dividends. He and his wife, Chantal, with their infant daughter, Pia, took up residence in London.

Feeney realized that he would have to move to Hong Kong himself. In September 1967, he flew into Kai Tak airport, in those days a memorable experience. Approaching at low altitude, passengers could see the flickering blue lights of television sets in the six-story apartment blocks of Kowloon. No other airport in the world required pilots to make such a tight, curved approach across the heart of a city.

Feeney and Monteiro split the suppliers into two groups and did the rounds. They offered to buy at "dead margin" simply to get stock. Still the business didn't come. The agents who had originally tried to get the distributors to boycott DFS had also lied about bringing tour groups to the store. They were up to their knees in crocodiles. "It was the worst nightmare of my life," said Monteiro. "It was hell. I went back to the twenty agents to see what the hell was going on. I said, 'OK, you bastards, you screwed me. This is what I propose, you either come to my store and support me or I won't sell duty-free liquor to your customers.'"

Monteiro told the travel agents he would continue filling their booze orders for one week, and then he would cut them off unless they also brought the Japanese to the shop. They capitulated. They started bringing tour groups to the downtown shop. Within a week, the DFS store was so busy, they could not find enough salesgirls to hire.

"The travel agents would work with anybody who gave them a kickback, and they realized after a while we were the best game in town," said Feeney. "They made more commission from us. To this day still do. They might make $1 a head for bringing people to a restaurant for lunch, but when it came to us they made serious money." Some of the travel agents found that when they did bring people to the DFS stores, the commissions they got were so big that they closed their own stores down.

One of the most audacious gambles in the history of Hong Kong retailing had paid off. Duty Free Shoppers could now sell high-end luxury goods of every description to tourists who might imagine they were in a store where everything, not just booze and tobacco, was duty free. "We were using the carrot of the liquor and tobacco to bring them in to buy watches," said Feeney.

The pressure on the salesgirls was unrelenting. They worked fifteen hours a day, seven days a week. Their husbands began complaining. They called up the store saying, "Hell, I don't see my wife any more, the kids don't see their mothers any more, you know, when will it stop?" Finally, the angry husbands got together and confronted management in the downtown shop. Feeney and Monteiro faced them together as they screamed abuse. "Please be patient," pleaded Chuck. A few of the women left, but most stayed. The pressure eased as the staff was doubled, then doubled again.

There was no letup for Monteiro. On New Year's Eve, he and a manager did stocktaking in tuxedos while their fiancées waited for them to finish. At 2:00 AM they were still working, and the women had gone home.

The demand was so heavy that the downtown store had to be expanded, which meant asking the landlord to persuade other tenants of Hotung House to leave. Some of them saw how much business their neighbor was doing and decided they wanted to stay put. A Hong Kong manager suggested the "Chinese cricket attack" to get them to leave, covering a cricket with human excrement and letting it loose in a rival store. "We told him that it was very creative but that we wouldn't do it," said Monteiro with a laugh.

Feeney and Monteiro did a study of the Japanese visitors' shopping habits. They discovered that tourists spent 30 percent more money on the third day of a four-day visit than on the first day. By the third day the Japanese had figured out prices and were anxious to complete their shopping. Monteiro went to the agents again to get them to bring the Japanese shoppers back a second time. "Some agents would, a lot of agents resisted it. They would give me this bullshit, 'I have already taken them to six stores, and they have already been to your store. So what excuse have I got to bring them back to the same store?' I said, 'OK, I will build another one, so that you visit this one and then you go to that one.'"

Which is what DFS did. The company opened a second downtown store—called the "repeater" store—at the junction of Nathan Road and Granville Road in Kowloon's "Golden Mile." Monteiro promised the agents they would get commission on anything bought by tourists on a visit to the second shop, even if they wandered in of their own accord. He would know who the agent was by the shopping cards the tourists got in the Hotung House store for delivery of their purchases to the airport.

Some agents were again skeptical. Monteiro took them to dinner and showed them calculations of how much money they would make from the scheme. "Their jaws would drop. They would say, 'You're bullshitting me.' I said, 'It's true! Try it next month!'"

Liquor and tobacco was the come-on, but general merchandise was turning out to be the biggest part of Duty Free Shoppers' business from the status-conscious Japanese travelers. However, the claim that the store was "duty free" created some problems with competitors. There was considerable resentment among other Hong Kong businesses that tourists might gain the impression they were getting better prices than in regular shops for everything. The company started using only the initials DFS to avoid trouble.

The venerable companies in Hong Kong and Hawaii missed out on the duty-free business. "At the beginning, the Jardine Mathesons, the Hongs, the equivalent of the big five in Hawaii, were asleep," said Alan Parker. "It was amazing that they missed it."

After the car debts were paid off and the duty-free shops began to make substantial profits, the owners agreed to take 90 percent of the dividends in cash, a practice that would continue for a quarter of a century. "We didn't want the cash to build up in the company," said Feeney, "so from the time that DFS worked, we did nothing but distribute the money out in dividends." "Usually every three months there was a cash pot," said Miller. Three years after facing bankruptcy and disgrace, Feeney and Miller were well on their way to achieving their goal of making a million. And the duty-free shops had become spigots producing a cascade of money that just got bigger and bigger.

On March 18, 1968, about six months after Feeney flew in to help Monteiro, Danielle arrived in Hong Kong to join her husband. They now had four daughters. The youngest, Diane, was just ten days old. Feeney had found for them a beautiful twentieth-floor apartment in Cape Mansions on Mount Davis Road high above the sea. At the age of thirty-seven, Chuck Feeney was now, by the standards of the day, a wealthy man. The fact that they had become rich did not impact on Danielle's consciousness until she and Chuck settled in the British colony. It was not so much that the reality of having a lot of money dawned on Danielle suddenly, but mostly the realization of it through the eyes of others. People looked at them and treated them in a different way.

The Feeneys began sharing a life with wealthy and extravagant people. They bought a Jaguar and a small boat. They employed a driver named George and several other domestic workers. They joined clubs and gave parties. Feeney in those days had two tuxedos. They patronized the Ladies' Recreation Club at Midlevels, one of the most exclusive and prestigious clubs in the colony, where the kids would splash around in the pool on Sundays while the parents played tennis. Danielle found it easy to live in luxury in Hong Kong. Domestic help, construction, and food was cheap. She bought jewelry and antiques and made the apartment a showcase of décor and beautiful objects.

Danielle was not from a wealthy background. Her family had moved from Algeria to Paris and endured a catastrophic financial situation before her father was able to establish himself as a prominent psychiatrist. She had lived through World War II in difficult circumstances, then endured many moves from country to country because of Chuck's business, and now in Hong Kong she felt that money was there to be enjoyed. She liked the colonial life, though she was quite aware of its futile aspects.

Chuck Feeney, fit and tanned with neat haircut and short sideburns, exuded the confidence and dynamism that typified the postwar generation of U.S. entrepreneurs. He was the decent American, generous, hardworking, and family oriented. Feeney enjoyed his work, he was pleased with his business accomplishments, and he seemed, at first anyway, to be taking some enjoyment from the comfortable life he led. The DFS people loved him. He gave loyalty, and he expected loyalty. He knew the names of every sales assistant and took an interest in their families. He got a reputation for helping staff with problems. When John Monteiro's eight-year-old son Michael was badly burned after throwing a lit match into a motorcycle gas tank, Feeney had the boy transferred to a first-class hospital in New York for multiple operations and paid all the bills.

In Hong Kong, Feeney displayed a concern for the well-being of less fortunate kids that was to characterize his whole life. His eagerness to look after children in the camp on the Villefranche beach had not been simply a commercial exercise. He obsessed about getting the best treatment for a girl named Susanna, who lived in an apartment below theirs in Hong Kong and suffered from deafness. He worried about the children he saw in a minibus en route to the American School whose driver allowed them to stick their heads out of the sun roof. "If she jams on the brakes or has an accident, they will get such injuries!" he would say. He called at the woman's apartment to express his concern, and when she told him, "Go to hell," he went to each parent and eventually got the practice stopped.

The duty-free business got so big in Hong Kong, and the potential for expansion around the Pacific was so great, that in 1969 Feeney persuaded Bob Miller he should come back into the firm. "Frankly I wasn't capable of looking after everything in Hong Kong," recalled Feeney. "I said, 'Bob, everybody should get back in. There is potential to do so much more.'" He was eyeing the possibility of expanding, of opening up the first duty-free stores in Alaska and the Pacific Islands. "'OK, I will go back,' said Miller." He and his young family returned from London to the British colony in a move that would prove permanent. With Alan Parker running Hawaii and Miller taking care of Hong Kong, Feeney could now operate out of Hong Kong to look for new opportunities.

The Feeneys and the Millers were both part of the social set in British Hong Kong, but they rarely socialized together. Danielle liked Bob and got on well with the Millers, but Chuck recalled only one occasion when the Millers visited their home and only once when he went to the Miller residence. The coolness between the two founding members was exacerbated by their different social aspirations. Bob and Chantal Miller believed in spending on the best things and aspired to elegance and the highest social status. Chantal once pledged to Danielle, "My daughters will marry princes." (Two of them did.)

As time went by, Feeney, however, was starting to rethink his attitude about that kind of life, so far removed from the life he had lived—and which his family and friends continued to live in Elizabeth, New Jersey—and the values of thrift imbued in him from childhood. It only became clear to Danielle afterward how strongly her American husband felt that he did not belong to the world of black-tie dinners and leisure yachts, and how much he was coming to hate ostentation and to despise the life of wealthy socialites in Hong Kong.

The differences between the two DFS founders expressed themselves in disagreements over the company's charitable giving. When they got into the black, Feeney suggested giving 5 percent of pre-tax profit to good causes. Donating such a proportion of profits ran against the corporate ethos of the time—in 1970, Milton Friedman made his famous comment in the *New York Times Magazine* that "the only social responsibility of business is to increase its profits"—and only about ten Hong Kong companies gave anything significant to charity. Miller thought it was excessive, but he went along. Chuck got the company to set up a charitable trust administered by

Monteiro, who recruited several notables to serve on the advisory board, including senior government official (and later chief secretary) Anson Chan, former governor Sir David Akers-Jones, and former chief secretary Sir Denis Brady. The company's trust, which made donations to the homeless, the blind, and the aged, also helped give DFS respectability.

The personal relationship between Chuck and Bob became further strained over who was doing the most to develop the business. To insiders, it was Feeney who was doing all the work. On the other hand, it was Miller who had secured the two key DFS concessions in Hawaii and Hong Kong at the very beginning. "Bob wanted to have fun, and Chuck wanted to make the business successful," said a DFS manager, who recalled Feeney saying that he would never do another business deal with Miller. "That doesn't mean Bob wasn't an astute and smart businessman; it's just that Chuck was doing a lot more hours." Bob Matousek recalled Miller as "a classy guy and a raconteur" and someone who enjoyed the good things in life to the full. Alan Parker believed that Feeney, as the company's leader and the one who came up with almost all the creative ideas, felt he should have the controlling say in DFS.

Perhaps unsurprisingly, Feeney started to take some business initiatives on his own. He saw an opportunity to set up a venture on the side to sell Camus cognac and armagnac to *domestic* markets in Asia, and also to act as the agent for Chanel perfume in the region. Without telling his duty-free partners, he registered a separate company in the Bahamas on April 1, 1970. He persuaded Jean Gentzbourger to join him full time on the basis of a profit-sharing arrangement. To convince the Frenchman it was a good deal, he sketched a potential month's activity on a page of a grid-lined workbook showing Gentzbourger getting 50 percent of the profits, minus operating expenses, while Feeney got the other 50 percent. They both signed it and shook hands. They would trade under the name Airport Chandlers Incorporated to distinguish themselves from Airport Chandlers Ltd., which was owned by the four DFS shareholders. Gentzbourger and his dentist wife, Irene, moved from France to Hong Kong two months later to start trading.

Feeney later justified setting up his separate Camus distribution operation on the grounds that he simply saw the opportunity where no one else did. Camus "was fated to be a kind of second-class brand unless the brand was selling all over Asia and not only in DFS," he said. It was in fact a logical step that would ultimately benefit his partners. The higher the profile Camus got throughout Asia, the more Camus would be sold by DFS.

Tony Pilaro said he found out about Feeney's operation a year later when he met Gentzbourger in Tokyo and asked him, "What the hell are you doing here?" He and the other DFS shareholders were affronted to discover that Feeney had struck out on his own. As far as Alan Parker was concerned, Feeney's relationship with Camus came out of the relationship DFS had with the cognac maker, and if it belonged to anybody, it belonged to them all. "Chuck couldn't see it that way," he said. "He just has a block. He probably doesn't see it to this day."

They confronted Feeney, recalled Pilaro, and he simply agreed to fold his duty-paid Camus distribution into Airport Chandlers Ltd. "He just let it go," recalled Miller. "I think he let it smolder inside him, as he does." They bought Jean Gentzbourger out—to his huge delight—for $375,000. The integrated company was eventually renamed Camus Overseas Ltd. (COL) and went on to become the world's largest distributor of Camus cognac, providing handsome dividends for its four owners.

Surrounding Japan

In 1969, John Monteiro prepared to leave Hong Kong and move to Honolulu. He reminded Chuck Feeney of the clause in his contract that they would get him a visa to transfer to Hawaii. It proved difficult. DFS had to employ lawyers in Honolulu to show U.S. immigration authorities that they absolutely needed someone skilled in management who could speak Portuguese, Cantonese, English, and a bit of Japanese, and that only John Monteiro met those requirements.

"I finally got permission to go to the U.S., so I packed all my stuff, put it on a ship, and bought my ticket," said Monteiro. "And Chuck Feeney calls me up to meet him, and says, 'I hope you don't mind but the company really needs you in Alaska, not in Hawaii.'"

Monteiro and his wife, Carol, had always lived in the steamy climate of Hong Kong. Now they found themselves at Feeney's behest in the city of Anchorage, where the winters were frigid, with an average sixty inches of snow. With a population of just over 100,000, Anchorage in those days had the atmosphere of a frontier town and was plagued by crime. It was still recovering from a devastating earthquake in 1964. It was the last place on earth Monteiro wanted to be. They had a one-year-old boy. Carol was pregnant. She was used to two maids in the apartment in Hong Kong, and now she was in Alaska with snow everywhere and unable to drive, and her husband working from morning to night. Stick it out for a year, Feeney had said, then they could go to Hawaii.

Feeney needed someone of Monteiro's drive and experience in Alaska because in 1969, he had gone to the state authorities and persuaded them to grant DFS a duty-free concession at Anchorage airport. The cash-rich Japanese tourists were not only flocking to Hawaii and Hong Kong, they were now heading to destinations in Europe and the mainland United States. The era of the Boeing 747 jumbo jets had arrived, making the world more of a global village. Anchorage was a refueling stopover for planes that were obliged to fly to and from East Asia across the North Pole, as they were not permitted to enter Soviet air space. The passengers had to disembark during refueling and hang around the primitive terminal building.

"Who would have thought of going to Alaska, a fueling stop, to open a duty free there?" said Bob Matousek. "Chuck did. He was prepared to take the risk. He had an uncanny quality, a perception, an ability to see business opportunities that no one else could. The 747s exploded the business, opened the floodgates."

The Alaska store, dominated by a stuffed polar bear, was an instant success. When the half-dozen morning flights arrived from Japan en route to London or Paris, the passengers would stream into the terminal, shriek at the low prices in duty free, and plunge into a frenzy of shopping. There was mayhem again in the afternoon as planes arrived bound for Europe or Asia and travelers snapped up liquor, watches, perfumes, and furs. They could leave their purchases there and collect them on the way back, when they could also stock up on Alaskan king crab and salmon.

Feeney stopped over in Anchorage once on a trip with Jean Gentzbourger. Carol Monteiro had given birth to a son. They were Catholics, and they asked Feeney to become his godfather because, they joked, he was the only Catholic around at the time. Monteiro took Feeney and Gentzbourger on a tour of the city sights, which included a raunchy bar where scantily dressed women took the drink orders. Gentzbourger went to the fattest hooker in the bar, a 250-pound toothless woman, gave her $20 and told her Feeney really admired her but was very shy. She said she knew how to handle such guys and went and sat on Chuck's knee. She was so big he couldn't move. "No, no," protested Feeney as she said, "Don't worry. I know you are a shy man." His friends fell about laughing.

The success of Anchorage also led to what Feeney called "a complete debacle," the decision to set up a duty-free shop for Japanese tourists in Paris. It was our "biggest fiasco," said Bob Matousek, who had become a close friend of Feeney and who went to manage the DFS shop when it opened on the Avenue de l'Opéra in 1970. The idea was that when Japanese tour groups transited through Anchorage or Hong Kong on their way to Paris, the store managers there would get information about the flight and telex the details to Paris. DFS in Paris would arrange for the group to be driven to the store, where the tourists could buy cheap liquor and tobacco, and Parisian merchandise such as perfume, ties, scarves, and leather goods on which the tax could be claimed back at the airport.

The Americans, however, were no match for the Parisian "crocodiles." Rival stores and agents turned DFS tactics against them. "Paris is a city of a million stores, and the Japanese travel agents were growing more and more sophisticated as they grew older, and so they were getting paid off in cash," said Feeney. "The biggest mistake was simply not realizing that the tour escorts would finesse us. We reached the conclusion that this was madness. So we eventually closed the store."

The success of other DFS stores, however, particularly in Hawaii, was becoming the talk of the travel trade. The duty-free concession there was clearly a gold mine. Only the owners knew how much cash they were generating, but other retail outfits were taking notice. DFS had renewed the Hawaii concession in 1967 for three years without serious opposition. They feared that when it came up for renewal in 1970—this time for a ten-year period—they might lose it to a higher bidder. All the goodwill and effort would go to benefit someone else.

In July 1970 Feeney, Miller, Parker, and Pilaro flew to Honolulu to decide what they should bid to renew the Hawaii concession. They picked up rumors that a Japanese company called Empire Boeki was going to put in a serious bid against them. Alarmingly, the Japanese were being advised by Desmond Byrne, DFS's former chief accountant, who had moved to Hawaii after jumping ship during the 1965 financial crisis. Byrne knew the numbers. He knew how DFS operated and its potential.

Secrecy was all-important. Bidders were required to put up a large bond that had to be a certain percentage of the bid. The partners knew that if they went to a bank and bought a single certified check for the bond, somebody in the bank could figure out their total offer. To disguise what they were doing, they went to different banks and bought five or six certified cashier's checks. The four men gathered to do their calculations at the house Feeney rented at Aina Haina Beach. The bid was the minimum they would give the

Hawaiian government for each year of the ten-year concession. As the numbers man, Alan Parker supplied the raw data. Feeney was the most bullish about projections for sales. They settled on an offer of $69 million—just short of $7 million a year.

They gathered for the formal opening of the sealed envelopes at noon on Tuesday, September 1, 1970, in a drab Department of Transportation office with a fan turning at the ceiling and chairs facing a blackboard. Feeney and Parker took their seats, along with Bob Matousek and finance director Mike Windsor, an Englishman the company had hired in Hong Kong. Some airport staff came in to watch the proceedings. Kay Lund of the *Star-Bulletin* took a seat. Alan Parker looked nervous, recalled Windsor, though Feeney seemed pretty calm.

There were four bids, but only two were serious, those from DFS Ltd. and Empire Boeki. An official wrote up on a blackboard, year by year, the annual guaranteed rent each company was bidding. It was very close. Empire Boeki bid $65 million, just $4 million behind DFS. Kay Lund noted that although it had been anticipated that the winning bid would be big, airport officials gasped when the top figures were revealed. The phenomenal sums, she wrote, illustrated how lucrative the duty-free business had become, not just for DFS but for the State of Hawaii.

That successful bid "changed the owners' lives forever," reflected Mike Windsor years later. If DFS had lost the bid, he said, it would have been a huge setback from which they might not have recovered. By retaining it, they could ride the wave of Japanese expansion.

In the next three years, the total number of Japanese overseas travelers— "OJs" as they called them—doubled, reaching 2.3 million. The number of salesgirls in the Waikiki store rose from six in 1962 to 160 in 1972, still standing shoulder-to-shoulder taking orders. The Japanese had the highest savings rate in the world, and they arrived with dollars and yen stuffed into their money belts. DFS took both currencies. One-third of the purchases were in yen, and DFS became one of the major foreign receivers of yen currency. The executives would sometimes take suitcases full of yen notes to Tokyo to exchange for U.S. dollars through banking channels. In Hong Kong, they accumulated so much yen they had to use metal trunks. "We were convinced the currency would have to revalue," recalled Alan Parker. "We rented an enormous safety deposit box in the Hong Kong and Shanghai Bank and for months would just accumulate this yen. Then our financial guy in Hong Kong, Colin Wright, would buy one of these old trunks, and we would fill it with 10,000-yen notes and he would fly to Tokyo and pay it in, and we'd change it into dollars." The yen strengthened from 360 to 280 to the dollar in the early 1970s, giving DFS a huge profit on their accumulated Japanese banknotes.

They arbitraged the yen in other ways. DFS set up a company in Honolulu called Kinkai Properties Ltd. to buy the real estate for the downtown shop. "Kinkai owned and leased the building to DFS and the lease was in yen," said Tony Pilaro. "So we went to Sanwa Bank and borrowed yen at 1 percent interest for the mortgage, we took $55 million, put the $55 million on deposit, invested in treasury bills at 7 percent. Zero risk. Six percent. It was a Christmas tree!"

Feeney went to Tokyo in 1970 and hired a "very smart" Japanese woman, Noriko Sagawa, to manage a DFS office from which they could watch trends in tourism and engage in "wholesale" trade with Japanese tour organizers. He rented space in Tokyo's Imperial Hotel, and later established an office and showroom in a building where half of Japan's prospective travelers picked up their passports. He got friendly with the major Japanese travel agents, who organized tours a year in advance, and found out where their clients would go the following year. He studied Japan Airlines' projections for passengers and routes. He retained the Nomura Research Institute of Japan to prepare a regularly updated "econometric model" to predict Japanese travel plans. The research had to be accurate, as by this stage DFS was ordering its stock six months in advance.

DFS also started providing an after-sales service at Narita airport in Tokyo and Osaka airport for customers returning from abroad who found missing or broken articles in their duty-free packages. Feeney wanted Japanese customers to see DFS as a natural and positive part of their holiday abroad, a company that would look after them and see to it that they got their purchases in good order. All merchandise was guaranteed genuine—important in a part of the world where fake consumer goods flooded street markets—and all defective or broken articles were replaced. The claims offices also reassured the Japanese customers that if their purchases were not delivered to their returning flight—as sometimes happened—they would eventually get them. The offices were stocked with an array of duty-free samples, and tourists could pick up the four-page brochure, *Passport to Shopping*, which detailed the merchandise available at the DFS stores at their destination. Later, they could apply for a DFS credit card. DFS looked after its friends and staged a $200,000 golf tournament in Japan each year. The company successfully lobbied in Tokyo to block legislation that would have allowed Japan to sell duty-free goods to tourists arriving home.

"We set up a whole staff of people in Japan that would liaise with all the travel agencies so they knew when the tour groups were coming and what flight they were arriving on," said Bob Matousek. "Customer relations staff would meet the tour conductors off the flights and they would come en masse to the downtown store with the tour conductor, and the travel agency would get a commission." DFS gave the tour operators and travel agents $1 for every traveler they brought to a DFS store and a 5-percent commission on all sales made to their groups.

Feeney drew an imaginary compass around Japan, looking for other destinations where the Japanese tourists might go. He visited the Philippines but Imelda Marcos, first lady and governor of Metro Manila, made too many demands. "Imelda Marcos was trying to line up a partnership in which we did everything, put the money up, ran the shops, took all the risk, while she was supposed to get kickbacks," said Feeney. "When the word 'corruption' came up, we ran." Paying commissions to travel agents was one thing—but getting ensnared with corrupt politicians was another.

Feeney set his sights instead on Guam, the Pacific island where America's day begins, as a possible future destination for the Japanese. He took the four-hour flight from Tokyo to have a look around. Guam, the southernmost island of the Mariana Archipelago, was American territory, ceded to the United States after the Spanish-American War in 1898. It had been seized by the Japanese in 1941 and recaptured by American forces three years later. About three times the size of Washington, D.C.—with one-third of the surface taken up by U.S. military installations—Guam had an indigenous population of only 65,000. The currency was the U.S. dollar, and stores stocked American goods.

The Japanese hadn't started coming yet, but it was evident they would, concluded Feeney. With its American culture, pleasantly warm climate, and coral reefs, Guam had the potential to become Japan's Miami Beach. "I realized this was a place we wanted to be. It was a natural destination. It was like Hong Kong: The only taxes were on liquor and tobacco. So we could open up a store and sell products other than liquor and tobacco. It was a no-brainer."

"Tony, we could own this place," Pilaro recalled Feeney telling him on a flight to Guam in 1971. "He hands me this mythical flag—on the plane as we are flying in—and says, 'I want you to take over.' I went in and bought the living shit out of everything, bought the airport concession, bought the hotel shops, I moved very fast."

Guam had no civilian passenger terminal at the airport, then known as Naval Air Station Brewer Field, other than a wooden shack. An elderly American, Kenneth T. Jones Jr., who in the wake of the U.S. victory in 1944 had established a retail company on Guam called Jones & Guerrero, had the retail concession at the airport, but Feeney saw that he had no idea how to run it. DFS established a shop in the Dai-Ichi Hotel, Guam's first international hotel, situated on Tumon Bay and overlooking sandy beaches and a lagoon of jade green and cobalt blue. With its Nina Ricci fragrances, and displays of Camus cognac, "we brought a little bit of Paris to Guam," said Pilaro. In 1972, they opened a second store downtown, and at the end of that year got the duty-free concession for the airport. They opened four more stores in a row of first-class hotels that were built on Tumon Bay. Chuck brought in one of his best car salesmen, Bob Bruso, a former supply officer in the U.S. Navy, to manage Guam as the Japanese tourists, just as Feeney predicted, started coming in large numbers.

Guam was such a success for DFS that Feeney decided to have a look at Saipan, an island one-fifth the size of Guam lying in the Northern Mariana Islands, 200 miles closer to Japan. Saipan did not even have an airport. Island-hopper planes taxied up a dirt runway to a Quonset hut. Before the war, it was administered by Japan, but U.S. Marines expelled Japanese forces in June 1944 after one of the most fiercely contested battles of World War II. Of the 32,000 Japanese soldiers on the island, 29,500 were killed in the fighting. In one of the most tragic episodes of the war in the Pacific, hundreds of Japanese soldiers and residents along with their families threw themselves to their death over the 800-foot high Laderan Banadero cliffs at the island's most northern point, rather than surrender to the Americans. Under a postwar United Nations agreement, Saipan was recognized as a trust territory administered by the United States. When he arrived in 1974 on a small propeller-driven aircraft, Feeney found the island still bore the scars of the fighting. But it had better beaches than Guam and a spectacular coral reef along its western shores. It was also becoming a place of pilgrimage for Japanese remembering their war dead.

"Saipan had no tourism and didn't even have a hotel," recalled Alan Parker. "Chuck came up with the idea that this has to be a good place for tourism, but all that existed from the war was this runway, old and long and overgrown. We went to the government authority and said, 'We will finance the building of an airport, the redoing of the runway in return for a twenty-year concession on the duty free in Saipan.'" "Then we did the best tax deal in the world," said Pilaro. "We made Saipan the biggest tax haven in the United States, waving the flag. We had legislation enacted that exempted Saipan-sourced income from being taxed. We built the whole thing. It was a gold mine. No tax."

DFS paid $5 million toward construction of the terminal, and when the civilian airport opened in 1976, DFS operated everything—the duty-free stores, the gift shops, the cafés, and eventually four hotel shops and a downtown store. Among themselves, DFS people called the airport runway the Pilaro Runway because of his role in building it. Soon, 100,000 visitors a year were coming to the island, almost all of them from Japan. The big hotel chains came to Saipan and the number of Japanese tourists increased again. "It was a wonderful jewel of a business. There wasn't anything to do but go to the beach and our shops," said Pilaro.

It was for quite a long time cheaper to fly from Tokyo to Guam or Saipan, play golf for the weekend, purchase $200 or $300 worth of goods, and fly back, than to pay for one round of golf in Japan.

In this era of rapid expansion, DFS was also able to secure the first duty-free concessions at Toronto airport in Canada and at San Francisco and Oakland airports in California, and open downtown shops in San Francisco and Los Angeles for overseas travelers. It became a roaring capitalistic venture at a time when Wall Street was in retreat. From 1968 to 1974, the average stock on Wall Street fell 70 percent. In the same period, DFS cash dividends were rising by several hundred percent a year. By 1977, the annual dividend was $34 million. Feeney and Miller each took $12 million, Parker almost $6 million, and Tony Pilaro almost $1 million. It was all in cash. They were becoming seriously rich.

PART TWO
GOING
UNDERGROUND

How Much Is Rich?

After four years operating out of Hong Kong, Feeney had sufficient financial reserves to start more new business ventures outside of DFS. He told his partners that he was stepping down from day-to-day management of the company. At a board meeting in 1971, he suggested that Tony Pilaro should take over as chief executive. Feeney would still be involved as an owner in seeking new locations, developing overall strategy, and jointly deciding on bids to renew concessions.

Feeney had had enough of the artificial expatriate life in Hong Kong. He and Danielle returned to France, mainly so that their children could attend French schools. They now had five, the fifth, Patrick, born in November 1971. They first went to Paris but moved to the French Riviera, where Feeney bought a magnificent villa in Saint-Jean-Cap-Ferrat, a favorite holiday destination for wealthy Europeans on the Mediterranean coast. It overlooked the beach at Villefranche where Chuck and Danielle had met fifteen years before. The couple moved there in May 1972. The house was in poor shape and the garden was overgrown. But the family loved it. Feeney insisted on keeping the old rattan chairs and velvet-covered furniture. Danielle found him reluctant to invest in décor. It was as if he were torn between the enjoyment of what wealth could bring and his discomfort with the elegant lifestyle. Buying the house was an investment for the cash he was accumulating, but Feeney was showing increasing signs of discomfort with the trappings of wealth, and with the sense of entitlement to the expensive things that went with it.

He was even beginning to have doubts about his right to have so much money. When asked many years later if he was rich at this point in his life, he replied: "How much is rich? Beyond all expectations. Beyond all deserving, so to speak. I just reached the conclusion with myself that money, buying boats and all the trimmings, didn't appeal to me." He consciously cultivated a frugal lifestyle, wearing a cheap Timex watch and buying a second-hand Volvo. He insisted that he and his family fly economy class, even on long transoceanic flights, as it was better value for money. He reluctantly attended a few black-tie dinners in Paris and Monte Carlo but when a picture of him and Danielle appeared in *Paris Match*, he was furious. He stopped attending such events and broke off all connection with the wealthy social group the couple had started to become part of in the south of France.

Feeney showed his dislike for ostentation by how he dressed. Thomas Harville, a former member of the management consultants Cresap, McCormick and Paget in Manhattan who was hired by DFS to help evaluate Japanese tourism trends, recalled going to Honolulu to meet top DFS executives. "In walked this man dressed in a faded aloha shirt, white dungarees, and shoes with no socks. Of course, this was Chuck Feeney."

He had another reason for keeping a low profile as a successful businessman. The kidnapping of children for ransom was rife in Italy in the 1970s, at a time when the Feeneys were living in France just thirty miles from the Italian frontier. Between 1970 and 1982, criminal and political gangs in Italy carried out 512 kidnappings. He feared that one of his children could end up like Christina Mazzotti, an eighteen-year-old Italian girl who was killed by abductors despite payment of a $2-million ransom in 1975. He would not let his daughters visit Italy, and they didn't until they were adults. The kidnap gangs sometimes crossed the border: In 1977, a five-year-old Italian girl was seized on her way to school in Geneva and released after a $2-million ransom was paid.

Feeney's concern for the safety of his children was heightened when his daughter Caroleen befriended Isabella Rizzoli, the daughter of Angelo Rizzoli, the Italian moviemaker and publisher of the Milan newspaper *Corriere della Sera*, whose home was a five-minute drive away. They both attended the same school, and Caroleen started bringing Isabella to their home. When Caroleen visited Isabella's house, she saw guards with Uzi submachine guns patrolling the grounds. Once, when the two girls went to an amusement park together, Isabella's father provided armor-plated cars and six armed bodyguards. "Her father was a very high-profile target and I was always nervous," said Feeney. "They used to flaunt their money and drive up to school in a huge car." He refused to let Caroleen accompany her friend to Italy "because they would have got two for one." Isabella Rizzoli loved the Feeney family so much that when the Feeneys moved to the United States some years later, she begged her parents to be allowed to go with them. They sent her instead to a school for the rich in Switzerland. There she got hooked on drugs, and in 1987, a month after her twenty-third birthday, she committed suicide. "This beautiful girl, Caroleen's friend, got drugged up and threw herself off a building in Monaco and killed herself," said Feeney. Her short life illustrated dramatically that money did not guarantee happiness.

Feeney made a practice of welcoming at the house lost and unhappy people like Isabella, especially children from broken homes. He gave teenagers jobs or sent them to college and became their mentor. It was something his own kids had to learn to cope with. In his teenage years in New Jersey, Feeney was noted for bringing friends home to be looked after. A boy from a single-parent family came for one night and stayed the summer, recalled his sister Arlene.

People close to Feeney saw a change in his personality during this period of his life and noted how, as he approached middle age, he worried more about the state of the world. The early days of business had been a time of optimism for Americans and Feeney had discovered a new, vibrant world where everything seemed possible. Following the Great Depression and World War II, the world was enjoying an unprecedented period of stability and prosperity. Then came the assassination of President John F. Kennedy in 1963, the war in Vietnam, and anti-American protests around the world. "He and so many of his friends were able to pull themselves up by their bootstraps," reflected his son, Patrick. "I think with that momentum he was expecting the world to be a better place. As he grew older that hasn't happened. His disappointment comes from having so much hope when he was younger."

Paradoxically, while Feeney became more frugal, he was pushing himself ever harder to build up the global duty-free business that was making him even richer. To Danielle, he seemed more driven, more involved in his professional interests. He read business books and biographies of successful businessmen. He was constantly traveling, to London, New York, Hawaii,

Hong Kong, Tokyo, Guam, Saipan. Associates such as Tom Harville remembered Feeney in those days as "a driven man, constantly searching for new opportunities, constantly traveling and constantly studying, rarely traveling with luggage, preferring to leave a change of clothes at each of his many travel ports."

But for his children these were the happiest times. They loved their school on the French Riviera. They remembered that when they went to "snow school" up in the mountains, their father would drive for three hours with projector and screen in the car to show their class the latest movies, for instance, *The Sound of Music* and *Born Free*. Feeney brought his elderly father out to Saint-Jean-Cap-Ferrat and organized trips to New Jersey for the family. There were frequent guests, and always, a sense of fun.

Feeney established a personal business office in Monaco, a short drive along the Côte d'Azur, where he could do his dictation and manage his growing business interests. He recruited a tax specialist, Jack Moore, and employed Helga Flaiz, who had been with DFS since the Cars International days, as his secretary.

Feeney was drawn back to an executive role in DFS by a management crisis in 1975. Tony Pilaro, having assumed the role of chairman, had brought in professional management, hiring Ed Attebury, an abrasive American retailer from Hawaii's Liberty House, as the first outside executive, to help grow the business. Attebury brought in his own people and stripped the division presidents, Joe Lyons in Hawaii, Dick Wade in Guam, and John Monteiro in Hong Kong, of much of their autonomy. He centralized warehousing at Geneva and called it Central Buying Office Switzerland (CBOS). It was a nightmare, recalled Monteiro. "The result was that Hawaiian shirts were ending up in Hong Kong, and Hong Kong specialty gifts were going to Waikiki." Worse, he abused people who had sweated to build the company. "He would belittle us and berate us," said Monteiro. "Every time I was called to his office, it was a screaming session." With the regional presidents all threatening to quit, Feeney came to the conclusion that Attebury had to go. Bob Miller and Alan Parker agreed. Feeney told Pilaro, "Fire him!" There was always friction between the corporate head office and where the cash register rang, reflected Pilaro, but Attebury failed to understand the nature of the business and had to go.

Feeney took the chair at a DFS board meeting in the CBOS office in Geneva, at which he resumed control of the company as chief executive officer. Monteiro remembered that Feeney pulled no punches. With Attebury and his team gone, the owners hired an experienced retailer from Boston, Bob Futoran, to manage the company professionally, and Feeney stayed on for some months to make sure the new man understood the culture of DFS. Under Futoran's management, CBOS was wound down, the regional presidents became barons again, and DFS continued to expand.

As the flow of cash into the owners' pockets increased, some DFS executives thought they were being too greedy. Thomas Harville, who had been promoted to DFS vice president for planning and administration, quit in disgust in June 1977. He sent the owners a letter that made clear his problems with the ethics of what they were doing. He left, he explained diplomatically many years later, because of his "philosophical distaste for devoting the prime years of my business career to the sole benefit of four shareholders who seemed to be accumulating a quantum amount of wealth beyond their needs."

With the company under Futoran's management, Feeney stepped down again from active involvement and distanced himself further from his co-owners. Without a majority shareholding, he could never guarantee that he would get his way on policy matters, and friends thought that this troubled him. In late 1977, he stopped attending board meetings, nominating George Parker, a friend and a U.S. Navy comrade of Jeff Mahlstedt, to represent him instead on the DFS board. In future he would only see his partners when necessary, such as when they gathered to decide on the renewable concession bids on which the company's survival depended. On November 24, 1977, he wrote to Jean-Paul Camus, who had taken over the cognac business from his father, Michel Camus, that he was stepping back "to devote more time to my fast-growing family."

Feeney was clearly frustrated that he did not control the destiny of the company he had co-founded and built up. "I frankly wanted out, for one because I said if I am going to do things, I am not going to do them as I did them before where I do all the work, and people pick up their share of the action," he said. He regarded Tony as "a hardworking guy" who did his share, and Alan as "a good accountant." But the old problems with Bob festered.

"In the early days they had a good partnership," recalled Farid Khan, a Hong Kong–born Pakistani who bought opals in Mexico and Australia for DFS, often at great personal risk from thieves, and who had become a family friend of the Feeneys. "They got a printing machine to print money.

Chuck was the spearhead, the mastermind, and Bob the tough driver. But Feeney became angry when the other owners tried to control him more. He was the founding member, and these little guys were ganging up on him. Chuck alone could not sign approval of the contracts. He drifted away. He could not take defeat any more."

Tony Pilaro recalled a comment made by Feeney: "Tony, you are foolish; you put 100 percent of yourself into the company and take only two and a half percent out. I'm not going to put in 100 percent and only take 38.75 percent."

Feeney had meanwhile been looking around the Pacific for his own investment opportunities. He flew to Tahiti, the French-speaking island in the southern Pacific Ocean that promotes itself as the Island of Love, and invested in a $12-million commercial complex called the Vaima Center, with shops, apartments, and offices on the waterfront in the capital, Papeete. The Vaima Center got the concession to operate a duty-free store specializing in French perfumes. When they heard about this, Feeney's DFS co-owners became upset, as they felt he was interfering in the core business of DFS, but it was so small an operation they did not kick up a fuss. It was hardly a top tourist destination for the Japanese, who faced a ten-hour flight from Tokyo to reach the Polynesian Islands. "This was peanut stuff, it didn't become an issue," recalled Feeney. Miller agreed it was "sort of irritating, but not harmful." Nevertheless, the issue led to the signing by all four owners of a noncompete clause that prohibited an individual owner from bidding on a duty-free concession in any airport in the world that was a hub for Japanese tourists. That right they agreed belonged to DFS.

Chuck Feeney's next significant investment, which would cause much more dissension, came about by chance. In December 1976 in Hawaii, he met an elderly retailer named Dick Wheeler, who with his wife, Sylvia, owned Andrade, a sleepy old Portuguese company that had thirty-four general retailing and resort shops in the Hawaiian Islands. Wheeler, who was dying, told Feeney he wanted to sell Andrade but would prefer that it were run by a single proprietor and not a corporate group. Feeney agreed to buy the company from him for $2 million. He took over Andrade's outlets. They didn't sell duty-free items, but the customers included some of the Japanese tourists that DFS specialized in corralling into the duty-free store.

Feeney moved his family to Hawaii for a year while he took over the Andrade retail chain. He founded a company there to run the stores and develop and operate other ventures in the Pacific Basin. He called it General

Atlantic Pacific (later InterPacific) and recruited Mike Windsor to run it from Honolulu. One of Windsor's earliest memories is of entering the duty-free shop in Tahiti and finding Feeney alone behind the counter conducting a sale with a Japanese tourist—in Japanese. Windsor found Feeney very focused and serious about business. "He brings a focus on business that I hadn't experienced before. If something doesn't work, he has four or so different thoughts. He has a multifaceted way of looking at business. He is detail oriented in his approach. Chuck would fly in to Honolulu in late afternoon, and before he went to bed, he would visit the main store. He would talk to the salespeople and check on display and pricing. The following morning, he would have a list of things to discuss. A lot of managers like to talk down and don't really listen. Chuck listened to the salespeople."

The next year, when back in France, Feeney engaged George Parker to group all of his investments together in a holding company. Parker identified Bermuda as an ideal location, as the U.K. territory did not tax company profits or individuals. They decided on the name General Atlantic Group Limited, or GAGL, which they pronounced "gaggle." GAGL was registered in 1978 in Bermuda as a private holding company for Feeney's 38.75 percent of DFS, plus his burgeoning investments in real estate, retail stores, and other businesses. As Feeney was a U.S. citizen and subject to the attentions of the Internal Revenue Service, everything was registered in the name of Danielle Juliette Feeney, French citizen. Chuck Feeney assumed the role of chairman and chief executive, with George Parker, Mike Windsor, Jack Moore, and Jean Karoubi as directors. Karoubi, a cousin of Danielle, was a former president of Duty Free Shoppers in Paris and would later head the Feeney family office.

The vagueness of the title suited Chuck, with his penchant for keeping a low profile. Many companies used generic words like "General" and "Atlantic," but nobody had both. The name sounded familiar to the public, but it gave nothing away. When they held a staff conference in a Bermuda hotel, a man in the lobby, spotting a notice saying, "Meeting of General Atlantic," asked Feeney, "Aren't they the people who own General Electric?" "Yeah, they're the ones," Feeney assured him with a straight face.

GAGL grew fast. Within a couple of years, Feeney's private company had established or invested in over twenty enterprises across the world in a bewildering array of locations: New York, Delaware, Texas, Illinois, Bermuda, Hawaii, the British Virgin Islands, the Netherlands Antilles, and Guam.

Investments ranged from Royal Hawaiian Perfumes Inc. and Pacific Resorts Ltd. to G.A. Land Development of Texas, Inc. and Société Civile General Atlantic of Paris. They varied in size from the Andrade retail chain in Hawaii to Ian McClean Antiques Inc. in New York. Feeney invested in a six-store retail company in San Antonio, Texas, called Solo Serve that was successful for a time selling seconds merchandise, and in Carl's, a small chain of department stores in upstate New York. He got a multi-million-dollar contract to renovate and manage the Richmont Hotel in Chicago, and he had an interest for a time in a chain of motels in France called Mini-Mote.

Some early opportunistic ventures flopped. The mall with its duty-free store in Tahiti never really worked economically. The China Import Store in the Royal Hawaiian Shopping Center in Waikiki, modeled on the big Friendship Store for tourists in Beijing that Feeney saw on a visit to China in 1979, never caught on, despite the promotional antics of his teenage daughter Caroleen. During her college vacation, she put on a panda suit and handed out leaflets to entice customers to enter. She became such an attraction that Japanese vacationers began asking the tourist office when her performance began, and she was required to stop as she was causing "congregating in a public place." Feeney closed the store after three years, with losses of $4 million.

His multi-million-dollar investment in an 800-room luxury hotel in Guam in 1978 proved much more profitable. It was run in such a way that Japanese tourists checked out for a late-night flight as incoming groups checked in for the same bed night.

Meanwhile, the cash dividends from DFS kept getting bigger. In 1978, Feeney banked $18 million in cash. By the first year of the new decade, his share of the DFS dividend had risen to $23 million. Rarely in corporate history did owners receive such an abundance of dollars, in cash, on a regular and ever-growing basis.

As his own businesses generated a separate cash flow, Feeney set up a subsidiary capital investment company in New York in 1980, naming it General Atlantic Inc. It was headed first by former McKinsey & Company partner Ed Cohen, and then by former U.S. Navy officer Steve Denning. It invested in new ventures such as real estate, software, and oil and gas interests around the world. Wall Street was recovering from a long spell in the doldrums, and there was money to be made on speculative investments and acquisitions. Its first investment of $4 million in a company called Transportation Management Systems was a disaster, but it was to prove an exception. A $5-million investment in Universal Health Services tripled in value in three years.

Feeney continued to acquire property. Despite his unease with wealth, his lifestyle was characterized by fine family houses. In Saint-Jean-Cap-Ferrat, he bought two neighboring properties on the same road as the family home, at the behest of their elderly cash-strapped owners, who continued to live in the houses. The Feeneys kept their residence in Hong Kong until 1980. They acquired a house in the fashionable Paris suburb of Neuilly-sur-Seine, a villa in a beachside suburb of Honolulu, and a rented apartment in Manhattan. Feeney often made real estate purchases on the spur of the moment. He saw a townhouse on Fifty-fifth Street in Manhattan for sale while in a taxi stuck in traffic and bought it for offices.

On a family car journey to New York after the Olympic Games in Montreal in August 1976, he bought a mansion in just such an opportunistic fashion that would become the family holiday home for many years. Feeney had made a detour to Salisbury in northwest Connecticut to visit a Cornell classmate, John Harney, of the company Master Tea Blender. They stayed at the nineteenth-century White Hart Inn, and in the evening enjoyed cookouts in the Harneys' yard. The children loved it so much they kept pleading for one more day. At the end of two weeks, Chuck drove them to nearby Lakeville, a village on Lake Wononskopomuc, and stopped at a big white lakeside house at 9 Elm Street where a town mayor used to live. "I'm just going in to do some business," he said, leaving them in the car. He came back to say: "So what do you think of your new house?"

Lakeville became the Feeneys' summer home, where the children could bring their friends during school vacations, and where Chuck and Danielle could entertain. They often had two dozen kids in bunk beds in the front room. When Cornell friends like Chuck Rolles came to stay, the Sandwich Man would make the sandwiches. Feeney would go walking and running every day and read books and four or five newspapers spread out on a long picnic table on the back porch. It became part of the summer vacation ritual at Lakeville that he would take the kids aside for serious talks about goals and budgets, about being thrifty and sharing everything with other people. When Caroleen got a part in a play at college, he suggested that she share the role with her understudy and give the second understudy a chance—she had to tell him that the theater didn't work like that.

Both Danielle and Chuck were aware of the dangers of too much money in bringing up the children: Danielle knew she tended to spoil them more, but she saw that Chuck gave them a strong backbone of selflessness and self-reliance, and taught them to value knowledge. Like his father before him, he insisted on taking them to public libraries.

Wherever he was, Feeney liked to jog. His mother, Madaline, who had been overweight, died in 1964, aged only sixty-two, and he lectured his family on keeping slim and fit. As with everything else, he pushed himself to excel, and in 1979 he resolved to complete the Boston Marathon, one of the world's most prestigious running events. To enter, competitors had to complete a standard marathon elsewhere. Chuck and Danielle flew to Hawaii so Feeney could enter the Honolulu Marathon. He was in great shape but found the hilly twenty-six-mile course and high temperatures too much for him. Near the finish, he began to run erratically from one side to the other, bumping into other runners who shouldered him back out of their way, until he finally collapsed at the side of the road, not far from his house. Danielle and Jean Gentzbourger, who was staying with the Feeneys, saw what was happening and ran to help. Feeney was in a state of shock and quite rigid. He was rushed to the hospital by ambulance with an intravenous drip in his arm. The cardiologist told Danielle that Chuck had been very close to a fatal heart attack, due to lack of fluids and food in his body.

Feeney's pride was evidently hurt, as he didn't like talking about it afterward. He was just dehydrated, he recalled, though he admitted, "I'm a bad loser." But this intimation of mortality may subconsciously have given him pause to reflect on his life and to figure out what he really should be doing with the vast wealth he was accumulating.

CHAPTER

Boremuda

s he became more wealthy, Feeney began giving some of his money away in a piecemeal fashion. He was generous to colleagues and often paid for hospital treatment for staff or their kids. The earliest significant act of giving that he remembers was a donation of $10,000 that he sent in the 1960s to his friend and former professor, Robert A. (Bob) Beck, who was dean of the Hotel School from 1961 to 1981. The Hotel School had asked for $1,000, but "I wanted to make a gift that was meaningful, and I reckoned $10,000 was meaningful," he said. He recalled with a laugh how Beck, who had lost a leg in Normandy, told him that he was so excited at getting such an amount that he held up the check to get a good look at it and a gust of wind came along "and the next thing he was running across a field to catch up with it."

The first instance of active philanthropy was the provision of a sports center for the Blanche de Castille Catholic school in Nice, which his children attended. He paid to have a sports complex carved into the slope of the hill, with indoor facilities and outdoor tennis courts that could also be used for basketball and handball. Thereafter he contributed to various charities, but he was not satisfied with being just a donor. He told a persistent correspondent from *Pacific Business News* who caught up with him in Honolulu in June 1980 that his idea of helping charities was not simply handing money over but personally seeing that it was effectively used to help as many people as possible.

"I am not really into money," he told the reporter. "Some people get their kicks that way. That's not my style." He was "intensely competitive," but his motivation was derived from the creative challenge of applying a better approach to something that already existed. His definition of success, he said, was not having all the money one desired, but being able to raise a happy, healthy family. "There has to be a balance in life. A balance of business, family, and the opportunity to learn and teach."

He had already begun to tease out these themes in conversation with Harvey Dale. Feeney and the lawyer had become friends since Dale first advised Tourists International on restructuring company finances in the early 1960s. The New York attorney had established himself as the Feeney family consigliere, advising Chuck and Danielle, mostly on tax issues. An accomplished pianist with a passion for Mozart and a gift for mastering complex tax issues, Dale had become a partner in a number of New York law firms and was made professor of law at New York University in 1979. He was intense, focused, and legalistic, but had no operational background, a perfect foil for Feeney, who was restless and business oriented. They balanced each other, observed Mike Windsor, like yin and yang. Dale considered Feeney a brilliant retailer, while Feeney was in awe of Dale's intellectual powers. "If you were to ask me who is smarter, Harvey or myself, that's a dumb question," he said, "It's Harvey. He is a brilliant lawyer with a mind like a machine."

Over a number of lunches and dinners in the late 1970s, as Feeney's estimated wealth approached a quarter of a billion dollars, he and Dale began talking about serious philanthropy. Fond of telling business associates that they should think big, Feeney applied the same advice to himself as he struggled with the concept of serious giving. It wasn't long before Dale realized that what was gestating in Feeney's mind was something radical, that while Feeney relished his continuing success in business, he wanted not just to be a generous donor but to shed the burden of wealth and assume responsibility for its charitable use.

As their conversations progressed, Dale introduced Feeney to the literature of giving. He quoted to him the advice the Reverend Frederick Gates gave to his employer, John D. Rockefeller, the world's first billionaire: "Mr. Rockefeller, your fortune is rolling up like an avalanche! You must distribute it faster than it grows! If you do not, it will crush you and your children and your children's children!" They discussed the writings of Andrew Carnegie, the son of a Scottish immigrant to the United States, who accumulated a massive fortune providing iron and steel for American railways in the late nineteenth century, and who gave away much of it during his lifetime to fund the establishment of libraries, schools, and universities.

Feeney reread several times Carnegie's famous essay, "Wealth," first published in the *North American Review* in 1889. The philanthropist argued that there were three ways to dispose of surplus wealth: It could be left to the family, bequeathed to the government, or given away while alive, preferably to those who could use it well. The first was motivated by vanity and a misguided affection for the children, who were so burdened that it amounted to a curse; the second required the owner to die before the wealth was used and his wishes could then be thwarted; and the third ensured that surplus wealth was put to good use and not dispersed over hundreds of years in trifling amounts. The best way to use wealth, concluded Carnegie, was to provide "the ladders upon which the aspiring can rise"— such as universities and libraries. Carnegie also cautioned that a man of wealth should set an example "of modest, unostentatious living, shunning display or extravagance."

What Carnegie advocated was to have a profound effect on the New Jersey entrepreneur. "I do remember somebody gave me a copy of a speech that Carnegie had given at Cornell, and for some reason I researched that speech and read two books on Carnegie," recalled Feeney. Harvey Dale, who is Jewish, also introduced Feeney to the writings of Maimonides, the twelfth-century Jewish philosopher who taught that the highest of eight levels of *tzedakah,* or giving, was to help a fellow Jew to become self-sufficient through training and education, and that the second-highest level was giving in such a way that the donor did not know the donee, nor did the beneficiary know where the money came from. They discussed the fact that among all religions, the highest form of giving had always been that which was not motivated by ego, or by the prospect of political or social leverage, which relieved the beneficiary of any feeling of shame or indebtedness or the expense of a public ceremony to honor the donor. Jesus Christ advised givers in the Sermon on the Mount: "When you give alms, sound no trumpet before you, as the hypocrites do in the synagogues and in the streets, that they may be praised by men." The Qur'an stated, "If you declare your charities, they are still good. But if you keep them anonymous and give them to the poor, it is better for you and remits more of your sins."

Dale guessed that Chuck wasn't initially motivated by anything that had to do with Carnegie or Maimonides, or indeed with any religious teaching. He felt it was inevitable, given Chuck's natural goodness and the culture he brought with him from his boyhood in New Jersey, that he would consider using his fortune to help others. "He just became more and more interested in giving back and not owning," he recalled.

Feeney also decided that whatever he did it would be done anonymously. There were two principal reasons for this, he reflected. He did not want to "blow my own horn"—just as his mother never let the neighbor with Lou Gehrig's disease know she was going out of her way to give him a lift—and he did not want to discourage other contributors from giving to the same deserving cause, which he thought would be the inevitable outcome of publicity. He had also been inundated with requests after giving sizable donations to Cornell, and he did not want that to continue.

Giving away large amounts required the setting up of a specific foundation in a carefully chosen location, especially if Feeney decided he wanted to transfer to such a foundation any of his business assets as he seemed to be indicating, and if he wanted his giving to be international in its scope. Harvey Dale set out to do a worldwide survey of jurisdictions that would accommodate Chuck's requirements. The United States was ruled out as a base. Anonymity would be almost impossible, and the U.S. government was at that time moving to bar foundations from holding a concentration of business assets, as federal authorities had found evidence that many wealthy Americans were using philanthropies simply to perpetuate control of their corporate interests.

Dale considered the Channel Islands and the Bahamas and finally settled on Bermuda. The twenty-one square miles of self-governing British territory in the middle of the Atlantic imposed no direct taxes on personal or corporate income, did not levy taxes on charities or foundations, and did not require public disclosure of foundations. Bermuda also allowed a philanthropy to fund good causes worldwide. It had a highly developed economy and financial structure, and Feeney's company, General Atlantic Group Ltd., was already registered in Bermuda, in a little office opposite a bakery delicatessen on Washington Mall in the capital, Hamilton.

But to set up a foundation in Bermuda, a person had to be a resident for a year. And that meant not just Chuck but Danielle, as everything was in her name. In March 1978, Feeney bought a large villa in Bermuda with the help of a local banker, Cummings Zuill, a member of an old Bermuda family whom he had met when Zuill was working in Hong Kong for the Bank of Bermuda. The Feeney family moved there in the summer of 1978. "Chuck will say that was my punishment visited on him," said Harvey Dale. "Danielle will certainly say that!"

Called Woodlands, the Bermuda villa had lush gardens, a pool, and a tennis court. It was located on a country road lined with yellow and white oleander hedges, brightly colored hibiscus, and manicured lawns near the coastal town of Paget. There were pink beaches nearby and inlets lined with palm trees. Golf clubs and yachting marinas were within easy reach. All around stood fine old colonial houses with coral stone walls and cedar beams. Right next door was an eighteenth-century colonial building housing the five-star Fourways Inn, where the piano player wore a tuxedo, and the waiters sported shirt, tie, and shorts with knee-length socks. The capital of Hamilton was only a short distance away.

Danielle hated it. It was 640 miles from the United States and 3,500 miles from Paris. She didn't know anybody, it rained a lot, and she failed her Bermuda driving test and had to rely on the gardener to go into town. The house was run down inside. She found little cultural life to her liking in the semitropical Atlantic island. "Bermuda was small town, middle class with English expats, the ladies lunched, played tennis and had tea," recalled their daughter Leslie. Her vibrant French mother "stuck out like a sore thumb."

Chuck was often away on business. He didn't like Bermuda that much, either. He had no interest in the golf, sailing, or deep-sea fishing that consumed the free time of other foreign businesspeople who took up residence in the British territory. When he was there, however, he did what he always loved doing, helping organize kids and giving others the benefit of his expertise. There was a school next to where they lived, and he helped coach the basketball team. He also became a member of the Bermuda tourism advisory board. Their youngest children, eleven-year-old Diane and eight-year-old Patrick, were enrolled in Bermuda schools. The teenagers, Juliette, Leslie, and Caroleen, moved into the Manhattan apartment on Fifth Avenue along with a Chinese amah Chuck brought over from Hawaii, and were enrolled in American schools.

The Feeney kids, too, were less than enamored of "Boremuda," but they had some fun times there, especially during school vacation, when Feeney would entertain the friends they brought from abroad in the sprawling house, up to two dozen at a time, with the girls sleeping upstairs and the boys in downstairs rooms that were turned into dormitories. He could be a demanding parent. He required the children to work on vacation—Patrick sold ice cream—and to adhere to strict budget rules. He gave his daughters in New York responsibility for paying their expenses out of budgets he allocated so they would learn the value of money. He took this to some lengths. When his daughters and a teenage friend ran up a large phone bill calling boyfriends in Europe from the Manhattan apartment, he came to town, disconnected the telephone, and put a map of New York City on the wall of the living room, on which he circled neighboring pay phones. He hung from it dimes stuck on scotch tape. If friends called on the second phone, which was in the spare bedroom he used, and he happened to be there, he would tell them to call the public phone on Sixty-first and Fifth in five minutes. When guests came to the apartment after celebrating his fiftieth birthday in a restaurant, his daughters begged him to take the dimes off the wall, but he wouldn't. The adult guests saw the funny side. One said, "I'm going to do this for *my* kid!"

Shortly after arriving in Bermuda, Chuck and Danielle created their first, named, charitable venture. They called it the Davney Fund. The word Davney was an amalgam of his mother's maiden name, Davis, and his father's name, Feeney. It was not registered as a foundation, as it was just a way of "test-driving" a system for making anonymous payments to individuals and educational and charitable organizations, prior to setting up a real foundation. Having gotten ahead in the world through a GI scholarship, Feeney used the fund mainly to give a leg up to other talented, aspiring kids of modest means, especially the children of his employees. "Davney was my first real attempt at putting something back," said Feeney, who channeled $1 million into the fund in its first year.

Chuck recruited his sister Ursula in New Jersey to administer the Davney Fund. She flew to Bermuda to create a bank account. "I can remember Cummings Zuill going to the bank to set up the account, and he was in shorts and I thought, 'What kind of a banker is this, dressed like that?'" Among the first beneficiaries were the four children of a fireman who looked out for Feeney in military service, and who had died of a heart attack. "I want to make sure all those children are educated," Chuck told his sister. Ursula also ran a two-week camp in Hawaii for about two dozen deaf and blind kids with money from the Davney bank account. She learned a lesson in giving: The beneficiary has to deserve the help. The fund provided grants of $2,000 each for some twenty children of DFS employees in Hawaii. "The kids went to a particular college where they got their degree by just signing in and out," recalled Ursula. "I decided, witch that I am, that maybe they ought to send me their grades. You'd be amazed how quickly a couple disappeared. The candidates weren't getting a free ride to college. They had to get their grades up to snuff."

The dialogue between Chuck and Harvey, meanwhile, had evolved to the point where it became clear that he was intending to put everything into a foundation—the DFS shareholding, the businesses, and all his investments. He would make sure Danielle and the children were taken care of, and the houses would remain in the family, but that was all.

It was a progression of his thinking, a "slope line," recalled Harvey Dale, who thought Feeney reached the decision sometime between 1980 and 1982. "Chuck's time clock is different from that of anybody I know. He quite often takes important decisions and sort of lets them marinate. Time passes until he gets to some place internally where he has comfort with a direction." Feeney himself cannot remember a "going-over-the-cliff" moment. Nor did he philosophize much about his decision after he reached it. "I came to the conclusion I didn't need a lot of money because I didn't intend to live a lifestyle that required it," he said simply.

While he was mulling this over, Feeney made his first major individual gift. In 1981, he was contacted by Ernie Stern, the fund-raiser for the twenty-fifth anniversary of the Cornell Class of '56. At that time it was the custom for alumni from Cornell to get together to give a total gift of $250,000 to the university on the twenty-fifth anniversary of their graduation. Stern was persuaded to aim for $1 million by one of the wealthier alumni, John Lindseth, whose father, Elmer, was president of the Cleveland Electric Illuminating Company. The university development office warned him that he was setting goals that were unrealistic. Stern tracked Feeney down to help. "I remembered him vaguely as the sandwich guy. I think his main thesis was—not too heavy on the salami or the bologna, more bread!" Feeney responded by writing a check for $700,000. "We ended up raising $2 million," said Stern.

Feeney thought the exercise made his class look good, but he felt that it didn't resolve any specific need of the university. His urge to give came with a strong belief, drawn from the example of his parents and based on his own entrepreneurial bent, that he should bring into play the talents that had enabled him to amass that money to make sure it was put to good use, which meant more than just writing checks.

Setting up a registered charity with the specific provisions Feeney wanted proved complex. The foundation had, for example, to get around Bermuda's very narrow interpretation of charitable activities—which did not permit giving to sports, something that with his love of sport Feeney might want to do. Establishing a unique charity that could give anonymously, possess businesses, and operate worldwide required in the end a special act of the Bermuda parliament. In 1981, Harvey Dale engaged an English-born lawyer, Frank Mutch, from the island's biggest law firm, Conyers Dill & Pearman, to help draft the necessary legislation. A year later, they presented their draft bill to the Private Bills Committee in the Bermuda Assembly. It provided for setting up a charitable foundation to be called the Atlantic Foundation. To reassure the parliamentarians they were genuine, the bill empowered the Bermuda Charity Commissioners to oversee the Atlantic Foundation's operations. The committee approved the Atlantic Foundation Company Act, 1982, and it was nodded through the red-carpeted House of Assembly.

The foundation documents were lodged with the company registrar at 30 Parliament Street in Hamilton, and the Atlantic Foundation was officially set up on March 1, 1982, with an initial lodgment of $5 million and the declared aim of helping projects across the world to relieve poverty and suffering, to advance education, and to help causes such as health, children and youth, old age, and international justice. It did not limit its activities with respect to projects and directions. Its directors were listed as Chuck and Danielle Feeney, and Harvey Dale. Feeney recruited Ray Handlan, a former director of development for Cornell, to act as president and a board of advisers was recruited: three Cornellians—Chuck Rolles, Bob Beck, and Fred Eydt—and Jack Nordeman, a friend of George Parker.

Feeney gave all the people involved in the foundation a copy of Carnegie's essay on wealth to read. Although brilliant when talking about business, Feeney was never good at articulating his philosophy of life. It embarrassed him. He used quips as a defense mechanism against introspection. Acquaintances remarked that they never heard him engage in introspection and that he used his sense of humor to keep his inner self at a distance. Instead of explaining what was going on in his mind, he would give friends and family members articles or cuttings from magazines and newspapers. They had to infer the message. Giving out copies of "Wealth" was a clever way of enlightening them on the essence of his giving. He also kept a copy of Carnegie's essay on his desk.

Andrew Carnegie was not a precise role model for Chuck Feeney. The Scottish philanthropist made his fortune through harsh and ruthless business methods, and he loved having his name on libraries and schools, neither of which applied to Feeney. But his basic message was clear—give while alive. Those to whom Feeney handed a copy of "Wealth" were left in no doubt that he was intent on giving away most if not all of the fortune he had accumulated in the duty-free business, and that he meant to turn his back on the conspicuous consumption that in the 1980s was coming to characterize what would be known as the "Decade of Greed."

All Feeney's instincts, instilled in him by the example of his parents, by the sharing culture of his blue-collar upbringing in New Jersey, by his desire not to distance himself from his boyhood neighbors and friends, and by his own innate kindness and concern for others, undoubtedly shaped his decision. In New Jersey's Elmora neighborhood, you helped people and you didn't flaunt riches that came with success or boast about your good works.

Although the mechanism had been put in place, Dale was unwilling to let Feeney commit substantial assets to the foundation until he saw that it was working in the way they intended. He counseled Feeney to run it for a couple of years as a "pass-through entity" with money going in and being donated out. Also, there had not been complete discussion or agreement between Chuck and Danielle about the amount that would be set aside for her and the kids. "But Chuck was clear then that this was the only exception. Everything else was going to go in."

There was an added consideration: as everything was in the name of Danielle Feeney, a French citizen, it would under French law all pass to the children, also French citizens, if anything should happen to Danielle. "They were potent tax problems in that Danielle was a French citizen and had residence in France and the children had French nationality," explained Frank Mutch. "Chuck was an American citizen, taxable worldwide. If Danielle had died when she was owner there are rules under French law which would have dictated the inheritance of those shares to the children. You can't get round them unless you sell them. The question would be where do you put the ownership. The tradition would be to put it into a Bermuda trust, but the trust would have to have beneficiaries. And there you fall right back into the French rules. The idea of the foundation or a charity got around that French problem and also relieved Chuck of any liabilities in the United States. It wasn't an unusual structure in that sense. The unique feature was the extent of the amount of assets that Chuck was putting into it. To put the whole share of the business in was unique. I've seen a number of European foundations where at least 30 percent of an international business was put in the foundation. The unusual factor was that it was substantially all of Feeney's wealth."

Feeney and Dale had "serious conversations" about the enormity of what he was set to do. "One of the things we both understood was that whatever the value of the assets was, except for the amount that was set aside for Danielle and the kids, all of that was going in, and this was a very unusual decision, probably unique in the history of the world. I said, 'You ought to be sure about this because if you change your mind in three weeks it's too bad. The assets are gone, and you can't get them back, and you can't use them,' and I was very stern with him about that. That made no impact on him because he knew that he understood that, and that was exactly and precisely what he wanted."

Four Guys in a Room

While Chuck Feeney was secretly setting up the philanthropy in Bermuda, some of his friends were conspiring with equal stealth to make sure he would be in New York on April 26, 1981. Jeff Mahlstedt and Ara Daglian, a Cornell alumnus and sometime sandwich maker for Feeney, were organizing a roast in the Metropolitan Club on Sixtieth Street and Fifth Avenue to celebrate Feeney's fiftieth birthday, which fell on April 23. They told Feeney the event was to be a surprise party for Bob Beck, given by the Cornell Society of Hoteliers, and it was his responsibility to get Beck to attend. As Feeney settled down at a table with Bob Beck, a curtain was drawn back to reveal a roomful of revelers, including Chuck Rolles and Lee Sterling. A fraternity brother, Tony Cashen, who acted as MC for the roast, gave a performance of the Sandwich Man in action, wearing an army field jacket like the one Feeney used to pocket coins when delivering sandwiches at Cornell. Mahlstedt recalled for the assembly that in 1960 Feeney had a Mercedes in Geneva that he took out for the only time one Saturday and was hit by a car driven by a Japanese tourist—"and he's been getting repaid by the Japanese ever since."

None of Chuck Feeney's partners in the duty-free business were at his fiftieth birthday party in New York. All four owners had by then accumulated so much money that they were busy developing their own investment companies and family trusts in different parts of the world. The more successful they were, the weaker the bonds of friendship became. Things had changed since the 1970s when, as Tom Harville remembered, the company was still "young, energetic, entrepreneurial, and fun, and we could argue and debate each other during the day and go out to dinner that night with our families and never mention work." Alan Parker and Tony Pilaro maintained cordial relations with the two founders, but the bond between Feeney and Miller that they formed chasing the U.S. fleet in the Mediterranean was now practically nonexistent. The different courses their lives had taken emphasized the gulf between them. The former St. Mary's boy from Elizabeth, New Jersey, was domiciled in Bermuda trying to figure out how to get rid of his surplus wealth, while the salesman's son from Quincy, Massachusetts, was scaling the dizzy social heights of Hong Kong. Alan Parker, the son of a low-salaried Rhodesian civil servant, had settled in Switzerland and was quietly making investments that would multiply his riches, and Tony Pilaro, with just 2.5 percent of the equity, was well on the way to joining the *Forbes* 400 list of the world's richest Americans.

The only thing that united them was the process of extracting money from their duty-free empire, and for that they still occasionally had to get together, just four guys in a room making a business decision. When the time came to renew the duty-free concessions, they had to get the bids right. This was the key to Duty Free Shoppers' continued success. The owners relied a lot on accounts and predictions from their financial staff, and they studied forecasts of Japanese travel, spending patterns, and yen-to-dollar rates. But they would entrust no one but themselves with the final throw of the dice. They made the judgment on how much the business was going to grow, and how much they wanted to split with a government. The need to renew concessions was both the strength and weakness of the business model. The sheer size and power of DFS, and its command of the duty-free system, was now sufficient to intimidate potential competitors. But the fear of being outbid pervaded the room when they met to do their final calculation.

"It was one of the greatest success stories in private enterprise and when it came down to it, it was four guys in a room, picking a number," said Tony Pilaro. "The last person in the room who came up with a number prevailed, because no one would have the courage to say no. There's no second prize in bidding for airports." They had learned to be bullish and had lots of cash reserves, which enabled them to succeed as often as they did. "We had big balls and big bucks," said Pilaro.

"It was four guys in a room, without any doubt," agreed Alan Parker. "We always did the bid, the four of us, with almost no involvement of anyone else. We would get together at least a week before a bid and start grinding through it. Chuck probably got his way more than anybody else, because Bob would fold. Chuck would sit down and say, '210,000 passengers times $302 with inflation, growth of passengers this, growth of spending this,' and I would do those maths. Bob is probably as bright as Chuck but never really applied himself in my view. He never spent the time—what Chuck always called 'mulling.' Chuck used the term a lot, whatever it means. He would go off for the night and get back the next morning, and Bob would have spent five minutes on it and have had a few beers."

When the four guys in the room finally decided on the number, they would put the tender in an envelope and seal it. Chuck would always produce a little shillelagh and rub the envelope. "I used to bless the bids," he said with a chuckle.

In 1980, the four owners came together in Honolulu to decide on one of the most profitable concessions, that for Guam in the Pacific Ocean. Guam had become a top Japanese tourist resort. Every month, scores of planeloads of Japanese consumers arrived in what they almost regarded as a duty-free extension of Japan. DFS had become in effect a Japanese retailer, selling to Japanese in what amounted to an overseas "suburb" of Tokyo. It conducted its monopoly retail business in such "suburbs," unencumbered with the multitude of impediments facing foreign companies doing business in Japan.

DFS had become so dominant in the Pacific that there were few competitors in the duty-free business big enough or bold enough to take them on in their strongholds. But there was one they feared. Host International had built up a chain of catering and shopping concessions at twenty-five U.S. airports and had eight duty-free shops at JFK airport in New York. It had beaten off DFS in Los Angeles and was now gearing up for an epic battle with DFS in their Pacific strongholds.

As the winner in Guam had a say in determining the length of the duty-free concession, Feeney took the view that a short-term concession was more desirable, as it would deter a competitor who would have to build a shop for twenty years without a guarantee of lasting that long. Pilaro disagreed. "Chuck thought if we have a two-to-three year bid, nobody else will come in because we have this huge downtown shop. But we also had the capacity to bid a lot because we had the money." He wrote a memo headed

"Big balls, big bucks," arguing that with a longer concession they would not have to risk losing it each time it came up for renewal. They finally agreed on a bid of $105 million for ten years, $2.75 million of which would be spent on construction of new airport facilities, and Feeney "blessed" it with his shillelagh. Pilaro set off from Honolulu on an island-hopper plane to Johnston Atoll, Truk, and eventually Guam, to lodge the sealed bid. In Guam, however, he picked up a tip from a consultant that Host International was preparing to outbid DFS for the concession. "I got on the phone and said, 'Chuck I want to increase it by $10 million from $105 to $115,'" said Pilaro. "He didn't want to do it. I got hold of Alan. He said yes. Bob said yes. The rules of the game were that the majority controls, so we did it. We bid $115 million."

The challenge from Host did not materialize. "They were there; they just said, we are not going to bid," said Pilaro. "On the day the bids were opened, Host International chickened out and put in an empty envelope. So theoretically, Tony Pilaro pissed away $10 million." But they got the concession for fifteen years, not ten, he said, "and we made a gazillion dollars." Pilaro helped organize a finance package with a Dallas, Texas, investment bank so Governor Carlos G. Commacho could start building a new airport, right in the heart of Guam's business district. The state-of-the-art terminal was completed in 1982 with $43 million in revenue bonds. It was called a white elephant by island leaders because they thought it would never reach capacity. But in that year alone, over 300,000 visitors used the airport, of whom four out of five were Japanese. Five years after that, it was bursting at the seams as the annual number of Japanese vacationers soared toward 1 million and a second terminal had to be constructed. DFS had to invest in dozens of new cash registers.

The four DFS owners came together again later in the year in Honolulu to renew the Hawaii bid. There was no sign that anyone from Host International was in town. But the consequences of losing the concession there were so serious that they flew in months in advance to prepare. Hawaii was the mother ship, the beating, pulsing heart of their business and by then the biggest retailer in the state.

The Hawaiian concession was to be bid for another seven and a half years, but this time there was a complication. The Hawaiian Department of Transportation split it into two concessions to avoid possible federal antitrust violations. The department invited bids for the total minimum guaranteed rent for airport shop space, with the highest bidder getting the best airport locations for selling duty-free merchandise, that is, right beside Japan Airlines' gates (concession A) and the loser getting secondary positions at the domestic gates, where business would be much slower (concession B). However, both top bidders—winner and second—could operate a duty-free store downtown.

Joe Lyons, head of the Hawaii DFS operation, created a small separate office in Honolulu to prepare sales and projections to help the owners calculate their bid. He brought in Phil Fong, a Hong Kong–born accountant from Price Waterhouse to work the numbers. Fong remembered Feeney arranging morning meetings in the lobby of the posh Waikiki Parc Hotel because there was complimentary coffee.

"I spent a lot of time just listening to Chuck and Alan and built a financial model of the bid," said Fong. "This was before computers. We used to do everything on calculators. I went to IBM and learned an advanced financial modeling software program called Plan Code, a very simplistic version of the state-of-the-art Microsoft system called Excel that is used today. I had a data terminal in my office. I would key data in that would be transmitted to our computer room several miles away, and we would have the data scrambled at both ends because we were concerned that someone could tap into that line and figure out what we were doing." Such was their fear of spying by competitors that all papers and notebooks used to make calculations were regularly shredded, and Joe Lyons took the shredded material away in the trunk of his car.

Then Miller, Parker, and Pilaro picked up an astonishing piece of information. Their competition might be Chuck Feeney. They heard he was thinking of bidding himself to be the second operator at the airport. "Chuck clearly had a plan to have an A shop which was owned by Chuck Feeney or Chuck Feeney interests, and a B shop which was owned by DFS," said Alan Parker. "How you can't see that as a conflict is beyond my comprehension." The prospect of Feeney bidding offended them, said Pilaro. But it didn't happen. Feeney's explanation was that "we talked about it cautiously because we couldn't collude, that would be against the regulations, but it was a guarantee for someone to get the concession. But we decided against it."

Fong's analysis showed that only 20 percent of the duty-free business was done at the airport and 80 percent downtown in Waikiki. If they lost the best airport position, they still had downtown, and "any competitor would have to build a new store in Waikiki very quickly, build up all the suppliers, get marketing in place, and get the customers accustomed to it."

The four owners finally settled on a bid of $165 million. This meant lodging a deposit of over $6 million—which was 2 percent of their total bid for each concession, plus a fee of $2,500—with the transportation authority. As before, they went to different banks to accumulate cashier's checks, rather than risk a leak from any one bank. On September 16, 1980, they made their way to the Department of Transportation office in Honolulu for the opening of the bids by Transportation Director Ryokichi Higashionna. There were the usual onlookers and financial journalists and a few strange faces. The officials chalked up on a blackboard the yearly guaranteed rent submitted by each bidder. The DFS owners discovered they had been ambushed. Host International bid $246 million, topping DFS's bid by $81 million.

"They were very crafty," said Feeney. "They were really irritated they had lost before, and they decided to go very quietly, and this time around there was no notice, and we didn't detect that there was anyone out there bidding." Host made their pitch through a subsidiary called DFI Financial. The DFS radar hadn't picked them up, or the fact that their own former accountant, Desmond Byrne, was advising them as a consultant.

As the numbers went up on the blackboard, the four DFS shareholders looked on shocked, not just because they had been beaten for the prime airport space but because they knew the Host figures were too high. "We sat there, stunned, listening to their yearly come-out, and I knew that that bid would put them into bankruptcy," said Pilaro. "It was a major mistake on the part of Host. I was looking at Chuck, and he was shocked. We were all shocked by their bid. They couldn't do it."

The head of Host's duty-free operations, Ira Schechter, moved immediately to open a duty-free shop in the prime air terminal location, from which DFS was now ejected, and to construct a rival downtown store on the mezzanine level of the Waikiki Trade Center on Kuhio Avenue, a couple of blocks from the DFS shopping mall. Host's downtown store opened on January 1, 1981, and was hailed as one of the most lavish duty-free outlets in the world. This was a real fight.

Feeney called on his old friend Maurice Karamatsu, who for years had "looked after" the ten principal travel agents serving Hawaii to make sure they didn't desert DFS. "I told him, 'We have a second competitor here. We want to hold on to as much of the business as we can, 80 or 90 percent.'" Karamatsu replied, "I have been working with these people for a long time, and it would be bad for them in Japanese culture to walk, and start supporting someone new, especially as we have been giving them checks for all this time." He went to the travel agents and said, "You have got to live with the people who put you in business." Host International found out what DFS was paying in commissions and offered 20 percent more, but the agents stayed loyal and continued to bring the Japanese tour groups to the DFS stores directly from the airport.

"DFS had the advantage of brand recognition," said Phil Fong. "Chuck knew that the Japanese-speaking sales associates were very loyal and hard-working and hard to come by. There was a scarcity of such bilingual staff. We also had special arrangements with the tour guides, the local guides, the bus drivers, and the taxi drivers. We gave them lunch, and we had a comfortable TV lounge to encourage them to stay longer so their customers could shop. They knew they could relax, and that we had more to sell, and they would get more commission."

DFS employees also felt a loyalty to Feeney himself, which counted for a lot when the rival store began desperately looking for experienced Japanese-speaking assistants. Having a kind and considerate owner meant more than a salary increase. "He took a personal interest in everyone," said Fong. "He called employees by their first name. He said, 'Call me Chuck.' He stopped by my office along with his children one Christmas to say Merry Christmas. That is more to me than any pay rise or bonus."

It was all over in nine months. Host International needed one-third of the Japanese market to break even. It didn't get one-sixth. It closed the store in September with losses of $25 million. They could not entice the Japanese tour operators to shepherd their flocks through their doors, even by dropping prices. "In Hawaii they used to call us *yoku bari*, which means 'the greedy ones,' because we were always trying to close down any type of opportunity that came up," recalled Feeney with a laugh.

In November 1981, the action moved to New York. At Pilaro's urging, DFS made a bid for their hard-hit rival and Host agreed to sell at $24.25 a share, but on the Friday afternoon they were to close the deal, the Marriott Hotel chain topped the offer with $29.00 a share. Feeney was nervous about getting into a bidding war, but on Monday DFS upped the ante again to $29.25 a share. Marriott topped that with an offer of $31.00 a share. The issue was resolved when Bill Marriott called DFS, and they agreed to divide up the company. DFS acquired Host's duty-free concessions at Los Angeles, Boston, and JFK airports at $29.25 a share—a total of $31.6 million. Marriott got the hotels for $31.00 a share. They had been lucky again: Los Angeles turned out to be, in Pilaro's words, "a gold mine."

The outcome of the whole thing, said Phil Fong, was that "it took DFS to a new level, strengthened our position on the Pacific Rim, gave us a stronger position on the West Coast and made us a legitimate operator on the mainland U.S."

It wasn't long before a new front opened, this time in Anchorage, Alaska. In 1983, the four DFS owners bid $71 million to renew this lucrative concession for five years. Feeney was decisive in fixing the final amount. They were topped by a bid of $76.6 million, entered by an outfit calling itself International Duty Free Ltd., of Anchorage. Only someone with inside knowledge could have finessed them. It turned out to be Richard Wade, who had been Pacific regional president of DFS until two years before and had left with a generous settlement.

The owners were outraged. They decided they would not take this lying down. "Chuck didn't like to lose a bid," recalled Adrian Bellamy, who took over as chief executive of DFS that year. "We moved in with lawyers all over the place to try and find some gap in Wade's bid. Chuck was very much involved in marshaling everybody, and he was particularly good about keeping our chin up." A handwritten note by Feeney, "It ain't over till it's over," was pinned up on the wall of the Anchorage office. DFS filed a $20-million damage suit against Wade for allegedly violating a termination agreement not to compete against his old company.

In the end, Wade was unable to come up with a required $17.2 million letter of credit, his bid was declared invalid, and DFS got the concession back by default. It was an important victory. The Anchorage store was ringing up about $100 in purchases from every international passenger, about ten times higher than the global average, in two bursts of frenzied shopping in the morning and the afternoon, when a dozen long-haul flights arrived on the way to or from Europe and Japan.

CHAPTER 13

Rich Man, Poor Man

With the future of DFS secured for several years after the renewal of the Hawaii and Alaska concessions, Chuck Feeney reached an agreement with Danielle that when the day came to sign everything away, $40 million and the houses would be held back for her and the children, and the money paid out over a few years. It was the figure thought necessary to take care of "the houses and the kids and education and clothes and boats and artworks, jewelry," recalled Harvey Dale.

The Atlantic Foundation had worked well in the two years since its creation in 1982. The Feeneys channeled $15 million through the foundation in that time, of which $14 million went to Cornell. Cornell had given him everything, his Ivy League education, his launchpad to the world, his network of loyal friends. It would always have first call on his generosity. Feeney was overwhelmingly grateful to the Ivy League university for giving him the self-confidence to prosper in business. "I got a lot out of Cornell, more than a simple diploma," he once explained to students on a visit back to the Hotel School. "It prepared me. When you come out of Cornell you have got good baggage. When you say 'Cornell University,' everybody knows it's a damn good university, and the Hotel School is the best in the world." Danielle was supportive, and was happy to receive thank-you letters addressed to Chuck and Danielle. They gave $2 million for a challenge grant to build a performing arts center at Cornell, for which Bob Miller put up a matching grant of $2 million. Their gifts also provided for scholarships for students from modest backgrounds to study at the Hotel School.

By November 1984, they were ready to transfer everything into the foundation. But a wealth transfer of great magnitude in the territory of Bermuda would require the payment of stamp duty that their lawyer Frank Mutch reckoned could be in the region of $40 million. They decided to do the transaction in the Bahamas. There would be no stamp duty, if it was not a gift to the foundation but a *purchase* by the foundation, and if this occurred outside Bermuda. As everything was in Danielle's name, it was arranged that the foundation would issue promissory notes to purchase the assets from her, namely, the DFS shareholding and the businesses, over a specific time period.

They set a date for the transaction: Friday, November 23, the day after American Thanksgiving. It required the presence of Chuck and Danielle and the two lawyers, Frank Mutch and Harvey Dale. The Feeneys and Mutch arrived that morning at Nassau International Airport on flights from New York and Bermuda. Dale was due to fly in from West Palm Beach, but a thunderstorm lingered over the airport and delayed his flight. When the passengers were finally boarded and the captain announced, "I think there's a window in the weather, and we can get out if you all are willing," he found himself almost shouting, "We're all ready to do it." He remembered the occasion as being as near to a disaster as he could imagine. "It was midafternoon, almost four, when I arrived," said Dale. "The Trust Company closes at 5:00 PM. The plane landed, I ran out of the plane, jumped into a taxi, ran up the stairs to the conference room, everybody was sitting around twiddling their fingers waiting for me. The closing had been scheduled to take two to three hours. We had one hour." "Good to see you," said Feeney as Dale entered, and they rushed through the closing.

When all the documents were signed, the Atlantic Foundation had purchased the assets from Danielle by issuing non-negotiable promissory notes, through an underlying company called Exeter, for payment to her of $40 million over a number of years. In addition, Danielle retained the nonbusiness assets, principally the Feeney homes in various parts of the world, valued at $20–$30 million.

With the stroke, or several strokes, of a pen in the law office, Chuck Feeney, at the age of fifty-three, had signed away his fortune, though as chairman of his foundation he could influence what was done with it. He was by no means a pauper, and he would also still be running the businesses as chairman of General Atlantic Group Ltd. and drawing an annual salary, even though his business empire was now wholly and irrevocably owned by his foundation. But he had gone from the cusp of billionaire status to someone with a net worth of less than $5 million. He would joke later: "How to become a millionaire? Become a billionaire first!"

Although it was one of the biggest single transfers of wealth in history, not one of the people intimately involved could put a precise figure on what it was worth, even to the nearest hundred million. The foundation would later put it conservatively at $500 million. Frank Mutch believes that the total value of Feeney's assets then could have been $600 million. Harvey Dale reckons it could have been as high as $800 million, a sum equivalent to the gross domestic product of Fiji or Barbados (that if invested at an annual return of 7 percent would be worth $3.8 billion in 2007). Paul Hannon, hired by Feeney as his general counsel two years earlier, suggested in a contemporaneous private memo that the assets were worth between $500 million and $1 billion, rivaling the capital of sizable investment banking firms such as Bear Stearns and far outstripping Morgan Stanley.

The difficulty in making a precise calculation arose from the fact that DFS was a private multinational and the value of Feeney's 38.75 percent shareholding was "in the eye of the beholder," as he put it. On the basis of an offer for the company that Tony Pilaro had made that year to buy out the other owners for $610 million (in the end he couldn't raise the cash), Feeney's equity was worth some $236 million. But if DFS had been floated on the stock market, its value could have been much higher. On top of that, General Atlantic's fast-growing holdings and investments were by this stage worth several hundred million dollars, perhaps half a billion or more.

Among themselves, Feeney and Dale referred to the foundation's assets as being divided into "church" and "state," with "church" signifying liquid assets for making grants and "state" being the businesses and the DFS shareholding. With the transfer, 90 percent of the assets were in "state"—an unheard of proportion among modern charitable foundations, which rarely control any businesses at all.

There was no celebratory drink or meal after the signing. Everyone rushed to catch their evening flights out of Nassau, Chuck and Danielle heading to New York, Harvey Dale back to West Palm Beach, Frank Mutch to Bermuda.

As far as Danielle was concerned, it was just another of her husband's business transactions, though one of great importance. She always did what her husband decided in such matters and she knew the assets weren't hers, though they had been in her name. Harvey Dale was her lawyer, too, and they were both friendly with Dale's family. She felt it was not for her to refuse, and she did not want it to become an issue in their marriage. She did not feel deprived in any way, though the $40 million was a fraction of the actual value of the assets.

But she would not look back on it in time as a happy event. As the 1980s progressed, friends noted that she and Chuck were living increasingly separate lives. Feeney was always on the road, now more than ever, as his business and philanthropic interests consumed almost all his time. Sometime afterward, she began to feel resentful and confused about the future. She felt something very bad and serious had happened in her life. She began to worry about the children being disinherited. Her relationship with Harvey Dale became very strained. She believed that the lawyer had too great an influence on her husband, and she made her feelings known to him in verbal exchanges in no uncertain terms on a number of occasions when they met.

The Feeney children were not sure what to make of their father's relationship with the New York lawyer. They wondered among themselves about the extent of Harvey Dale's influence, whether he had manipulated their father in any way, or if it was a case of Maimonides influencing Dale and Dale influencing their father. But they had little doubt that the idea of giving while living had germinated in their father's mind for a long time.

Feeney readily agreed that Harvey Dale was the most influential person in his life. "Yes, absolutely," he said. "He is impeccably honest and is also a good person as a human being. He knew my motivations. The idea never changed in my mind—use your wealth to help people, use your wealth to create institutions to help people. I think he has the same pragmatic view that I have."

"Harvey was very influential," said Frank Mutch. "He was the one behind it all, really. He espoused Chuck's ideas. The unique feature was that Chuck never made any arrangement for himself to be provided for." Feeney's legal counsel, Paul Hannon, felt that Dale not only interpreted his wishes but "to some extent he created Chuck's wishes."

Diane Feeney, the youngest daughter, recalled that sometime after 1984, Harvey Dale explained the implications of the creation of the foundation to family members. "I remember Harvey coming to see every single one of us," she said. "I was in Cornell at the time. He dragged me out of a football game, so you knew it had to be pretty major, sat me down and explained that Dad wanted to give all his money away to charity, this was in the process of being implemented, and he wanted to tell us about it."

The cleverly constructed setup in Bermuda was flawed, however, as they discovered to their acute dismay a year later. Under Bermuda law, the Articles of the Foundation, lodged with the company registrar on Parliament Street, was a public document. Anybody could inspect it and ascertain that the members were Chuck Feeney, Danielle Feeney, Harvey Dale, Frank Mutch, and Cummings Zuill. There was no evidence that anyone undesirable—for example, a financial journalist—had inspected the register, but at any time Feeney could be "outed" as a member of the board of a secret philanthropy. There was only one solution—to have the law changed.

Happily, the Bermuda attorney general was a former partner of Frank Mutch and understanding of their dilemma. The Atlantic Foundation lawyers drew up an amending act, inserting a new clause, 17A, into the Atlantic Foundation Company Act, 1982. This stated that only the attorney general, or a person named by the Charity Commissioners or by the Supreme Court, could inspect the register of Atlantic Foundation. Otherwise, it was to be kept secret from the public.

"We put up a rationale," said Mutch. "We said the members or the board didn't want to receive solicitations; we didn't want to be bothered with phone calls. We were a private foundation, but were not trying to hide anything." The amending act went through before anyone noticed what was going on. "We closed the door before reporters got the names," he said.

It was a coup against freedom of information in Bermuda. The *Royal Gazette*, Bermuda's daily newspaper, realizing what had happened, protested in an article about restricting the freedom of the press. It was too late. But for the first time, the name Atlantic Foundation came out in a newspaper report.

In 1986, Feeney established a second foundation in Bermuda called the Atlantic Trust to handle U.S. giving. This was made necessary by new U.S. federal tax legislation that prompted the four DFS owners to restructure the company into two groups: the U.S. and Guam operations and the non-U.S. and Pacific Rim operations. DFS holdings in the United States and Guam went into the Atlantic Trust and those in the non-U.S. and Pacific Rim into the Atlantic Foundation.

No one in the world of philanthropy in the United States or elsewhere was aware that a major new player had come on the scene. Dale, who assumed the role of president and chief executive of the Atlantic Foundation, required everyone involved in setting up the foundation to sign a highly lawyered confidentiality agreement, drawn up by the Manhattan law firm Cadwalader, Wickersham & Taft, to protect Feeney's privacy. Strict rules were formulated for the conduct of the foundation. No solicitations would be entertained. Gifts would be made anonymously, and those who received them would not be told where they came from. The recipients, too, would have to sign confidentiality agreements. If they found out anything about the Atlantic Foundation or Chuck Feeney and made it public, the money would stop. The Atlantic Foundation would be the biggest secret foundation of its size in the world.

From the start, Chuck Feeney was adamant that he did not want recognition for his giving. There would be no plaques or names on buildings he funded, no black-tie "thank-you" dinners, no honorary degrees. People should not know that he was behind the foundation. Beneficiaries should not even be told its name.

While this stemmed from the absence of a demanding ego, being secretive had become almost second nature to Feeney. Practically everything he undertook in his life depended on keeping confidences and maintaining a low profile. His family in New Jersey believe that it started with his intelligence work in Japan during the Korean War, which had been so sensitive he was not allowed to talk about it. In Europe, he had operated out of Liechtenstein like a character in a spy movie, always one step ahead of the immigration police. When selling booze to the fleet in Europe, he and Bob Miller had to rely on classified information on fleet movements, and their car sales in the Pacific depended on no one else knowing about it. Similarly, in the United States his monopoly on the five-bottle import scheme only flourished until competitors found out and muscled in. The whole edifice of DFS was based on secrecy. If a rival company learned how much DFS planned to bid for a major concession, it could outbid them and force them out of business. The key to getting some of the most profitable concessions was not letting airport authorities know just how much money they were making. As a private company, DFS did not have to declare its profits to anyone. Top managers in DFS had to sign strict confidentiality pledges about financial returns, and there was a written agreement among the four DFS owners that they would give only one response to press queries: "I would like to answer this question but I am bound not to." John Monteiro recalled Feeney insisting at meetings, "Don't go out and blow your horns about how big and successful we are." And of course, when living in France, he was always apprehensive that his children might be kidnapped for ransom by some gang that thought, "Here is another guy who has got a lot of money."

Feeney had been dismayed when Bob and Chantal Miller threw a lavish three-day party in Hong Kong's Repulse Bay in 1978, with a Caribbean steel band, a South American rock group, and a disc jockey flown in from Paris, during which Chantal descended among her guests in a hot-air balloon dressed as an Inca princess. It was reported in the social columns, along with the Millers' announcement that they gave the equivalent cost to charity.

"I always said, and I was preaching it, the less you speak and the less ostentatious you are, the fewer people who will be angry and jealous," said Harvey Dale. "Bob Miller did not keep to that style, but the other partners really did. From Feeney's point of view Bob was increasingly ostentatious, a shogun, a big man in Hong Kong, all of which was personally distasteful to him."

Tony Pilaro was less troubled by Bob Miller's high-society profile. "The fact that Miller drives a Rolls Royce doesn't mean people will make assumptions about the business model. Everyone, the travel agencies, the people who sold us Chanel, the airlines, they all knew we must be making a lot of money."

The perception that duty-free shopping may not always be such a great bargain for shoppers was also something they did not want publicized but which was gaining ground. In March 1985, an article in the *Far Eastern Economic Review* warned travelers to be careful about the duty-free shops in Hong Kong, "which charge at least ten percent more than the thousands of shops in this duty free city."

Ironically, after 1984, when he gave the vast bulk of his fortune away, everyone not in the know continued to think Chuck Feeney "was another guy who has got a lot of money." By keeping what he did a secret, he allowed people to assume he was still very rich. Even his DFS partners did not know that Feeney or his wife personally no longer owned 38.75 percent of the company. He still turned up as co-owner of DFS when concession bids had to be decided, and he continued to act as chairman and chief executive of General Atlantic Group Ltd., drawing a reduced salary of $200,000 a year. His philanthropic foundation owned all the business assets in GAGL, but outwardly nothing seemed to have changed.

Feeney, however, would sometimes hint at the real state of affairs. "He spent about two and a half hours explaining to me that he did not own what he owned, as it were, that he was its custodian and that he saw himself as being lucky enough to have made money but it was not his money, he was just essentially recycling it," recalled Adrian Bellamy, who succeeded Bob Futoran as DFS chief executive in 1983. "I don't know that I ever knew he had irrevocably given it away."

Paul Hannon recalled that after he was hired as general counsel for General Atlantic Group Ltd., Feeney gave him a copy of "Wealth," and Harvey Dale took him aside to explain he would be working for a charity. "Chuck has a love-hate relationship with money," Dale told him. "He likes to make it because it is his scorecard, but he doesn't like to keep it." Hannon realized that Feeney wanted him to know he was working for something more important than making him rich. The Yale-educated lawyer was surprised to discover that his annual salary would be greater than Feeney's. "That made it difficult for me. If the boss is making a lot less than you, and you ask him for a raise, he says, 'OK, but you're taking it from the starving children in Africa!'"

By the mid-1980s, General Atlantic Group was getting too big to stay under the radar of financial institutions and the media. Aside from DFS dividends, General Atlantic Group's annual income in 1984 was $30 million.

On May 23, 1985, Hannon presented Chuck with a confidential report, "The Benefits and Burdens of Secrecy," in which he warned that a great deal of information had become a matter of public record. If domestically owned, the U.S. Internal Revenue Service would have taken half the $30 million and if the IRS focused on General Atlantic and prevailed in such a determination, "the cost would be horrendous and could easily reach into hundreds of millions . . . hence strenuous efforts should be made to conceal from the IRS by all legal means the offshore corporate structure, the identity of the owners and the extent of the wealth they control."

It was difficult, Hannon warned, to deal with banks, partners, and employees when the company was presented as a "pool of capital of mysterious origin," conjuring up "images of oil sheiks, mafiosi and others who need to conceal their identity." The banks they dealt with had agreed to keep separate secret files on transactions with General Atlantic, but Hannon guessed about 200 members of the financial community knew something about the undisclosed wealth, and that someone called Feeney was behind it. Atlantic's part ownerships of a number of U.S. companies were filed in those companies' Securities and Exchange Commission (SEC) returns. Acquisitions in the United States of a certain size had to be filed with the Justice Department, and it was already a matter of public record from concession bids in Hawaii and Alaska that an entity called General Atlantic held 38.75 percent of DFS. He concluded: "I believe it virtually inevitable that within the next few years, if we continue to invest as we have, we will be the subject of a big investigation by *Forbes*, the *Wall Street Journal*, or another member of the financial press. We are just too big and interesting to be ignored."

To make his point, Hannon compiled a mock version of a story the *Wall Street Journal* might run if a dogged reporter got on their tracks, with some of the damaging assumptions that a reporter might make.

AMERICA'S UNKNOWN MULTI-MILLIONAIRE

The Feeney Fortune. Is It Millions or Billions?

Despite Obsessive Secrecy, Mafia Ties Unproved

Around noon last Tuesday, Charles F. Feeney passed through the swinging doors of Clarke's, the raffish Irish saloon on New York's Third Avenue. . . . the slight, agile Feeney made his way to his regular table, accompanied by several business associates, [and] settled the affairs of the vast General Atlantic empire over a meal of hamburgers and white wine.

Feeney and his associates consistently declined to answer questions and return telephone calls from the *Wall Street Journal*. However, an in-depth *WSJ* investigation reveals that Feeney's wealth far exceeds that of the far better known American rich. T. Boone Pickins, Ivan Boesky, Donald Trump and Doris Duke are pikers compared with the self-effacing Feeney . . .

The Feeney financial empire is characterized by obsessive secrecy. Its holdings are concealed in a web of foreign foundations, trusts, various family members, and over 50 separate corporations. However, legally compulsory filings with Government agencies, a handful of sometimes contradictory press clippings, and background interviews with bankers and former employees who uniformly decline to be quoted for attribution reveal the outlines of Feeney's extensive holdings.

A 38.75% interest in Hong Kong's Duty Free Shoppers is the keystone of the General Atlantic Group . . . reports filed with airport authorities lead *WSJ* investigators to estimate DFS sales in the $750 million–$1 billion range and profits after tax of approximately $60–$100 million per annum.

A small shareholding in DFS by New York financier A. M. Pilaro has given rise to persistent rumors . . . Pilaro was at one time a close adviser to fugitive financier Robert Vesco. . . .

In Feeney's sole example of personal extravagance, he maintains homes in New York City, Paris, Bermuda, Honolulu, San Francisco, and reputedly owns, through nominees, several large homes at Saint-Jean-Cap-Ferrat, a secluded enclave of the Super-Rich on the French Riviera.

Feeney's smaller, but specialized, holdings in retail sales operations include Andrade, the second largest chain of retail stores in Hawaii, Solo Serve, a profitable string of off-price department stores in the South West, Carl's, a group of traditional department stores in upstate New York, and N. Peal, an elegant cashmere shop in London's Burlington Arcade.

General Atlantic . . . has invested shrewdly in computer software companies, oil and gas operations, and health care concerns . . . General Atlantic also owned for some years a significant interest in Inflight Services. Typically, SEC filings show Feeney's interest in Inflight held indirectly in the name of his wife, Danielle J. Feeney, a French national, purportedly resident in Bermuda. However, neighbors report seldom sighting any Feeneys at Woodlands, the palatial, though somewhat neglected Feeney house in Bermuda.

Feeney was horrified that such a worst-case newspaper story might actually appear, and Harvey Dale was so alarmed that he wanted to destroy all copies, recalled Hannon. If anything, it reinforced Feeney's determination that everything be kept secret and security tightened.

CHAPTER 14

Don't Ask, Don't Tell

At the time he set up the Atlantic Foundation in Bermuda in 1982, Chuck Feeney created a structure for giving in the United States that would protect his anonymity. He established an office in Ithaca, New York, the hometown of Cornell University, and gave it the innocuous name of the Atlantic Foundation Service Company (later known as the Atlantic Philanthropic Service Company). It was registered as a "for-profit" company to avoid disclosure rules. Ray Handlan was put in charge to help identify beneficiaries and arrange payments.

Feeney also created an advisory body made up of several trusted friends, including Chuck Rolles, to vet grant recommendations. He transferred $25,000 of the foundation's money to each member per year to donate to a charity of their choosing. This enabled the service company to claim, as it did in a brochure, to be a consulting company that dealt with "*a number of individuals*" who wished to make grants anonymously. They said they had eight or ten donors on their books. "This was not an outright lie," said Handlan. "It was all Chuck's money, but other people were giving it away." Handlan maintained the fiction even in his confidential internal reports to the directors in Bermuda on the work of the service company, once noting, "It is a pleasure and joy to work for and with our clients, who are such caring people."

The same discretion was employed by Sterling Management, a private company in Hamilton, Bermuda, commissioned to manage Feeney's and

GAGL's bank accounts and other affairs. Sterling Management's account manager, Margaret Hern, established a full-time office for what the company described, accurately if somewhat misleadingly, as a "group of substantial private charitable foundations."

As a further measure to ensure that beneficiaries could not know who the "donors" were, grants were transferred from the foundation's bank in Bermuda to the Bessemer Trust Company in New York, a private bank that serviced high-net-worth clients, family endowments, and foundations. Bessemer made the checks out to the donees, without any indication of the source of the money.

The check arrived in the mail, accompanied by a letter that laid out the conditions to be observed by the donee.

The basic message of the letter was, "Don't ask, don't tell." It stated: "The donors do not want to receive any recognition for this gift. And our ability to seek out, assess, and assist worthwhile projects on their behalf is greatly dependent on being able to do so confidentially. Thus the issue of confidentiality is a matter of the utmost importance to the donors. We specifically request that this gift is referred to—both externally and internally—as a private donation and that it is not stated, orally or in writing, that it has been received from our principals. Please list it in this way in your annual report and in internal reports. In addition, it is recommended that the papers relating to this gift be retained in a confidential file. . . . I would ask you to confirm your acceptance by countersigning a copy of this letter and returning it to us."

"It was all very strict and there was a convoluted way of getting the donees the money so it couldn't be traced," said Cummings Zuill, who recalled that the anonymity rules created a problem for foundation staff as they couldn't tell their families what they were doing or get a job reference. "People would tell their wives they were in a pub to keep secret that they were at an Atlantic Foundation meeting," he said.

Harvey Dale, as president of the Atlantic Foundation, would often lecture the advisory board members on the need for absolute confidentiality. "My favorite definition of a secret is something that you tell other people one at a time, and I did not want that scenario, so I was busy pushing the pendulum as far as I could on this," said Dale. "Almost every time we got together I would remind them that this was confidential so they had no excuse for not knowing it and how they couldn't say it." It got to the point where even Chuck felt that Dale was laying it on too thick. On one occasion when he and Dale were conducting a meeting with board members Ray Handlan, Chuck Rolles, Fred Eydt, Jack Nordeman, and Bob Beck in the office in Ithaca, the secretary, by arrangement, called Dale out to take an urgent phone call. When he came back, he was momentarily nonplussed to see everyone had their backs to the door. On a signal, they turned toward him. Everyone was wearing a Groucho Marx disguise—false nose, mustache, and big glasses—that Handlan had handed out. Dale roared with laughter, and they all posed for a photograph.

The members of this covert group also derived some amusement from the fact that the program manager appointed by the foundation was named Angela Covert.

Dale had his own reasons for enforcing secrecy. He worried about how people would relate to him if it were known he controlled a huge foundation. It was a truism in philanthropy that once a person became a philanthropist or a foundation executive, he had eaten his last bad meal and told his last bad joke, he said. He cited the warning of an adviser to the Rockefeller family that "if you are perceived to have the ability to give away money, everybody lies to you, always."

"I was always terrified by this," he recalled. "I worried that I would become 'very handsome and a good dancer.' I think Lord Acton understood human nature better than anybody when he said that 'power tends to corrupt and absolute power corrupts absolutely.' You get seduced by being in the position of giving money away, and the arrogance and certitude that comes with that is awful. I hate it, it's really evil, but the tendency for that to happen is very big. I was much more comfortable not having my friends and colleagues thinking that I was president of a major foundation."

Looking back long after leaving Atlantic, legal counsel Paul Hannon thought the secrecy made it more difficult for the foundation to operate properly. "Harvey Dale liked to play Santa Claus, in my view," he said. "Chuck would say, 'I'm interested in aging,' for example, and so Harvey would go out and find somebody who was big in the field, and they went out and supported a guy called Bob Butler, and we gave quite a bit of money to him." Dr. Robert Butler, president and CEO of the International Longevity Center, later met Feeney when pitching for finance to an advisory board that reviewed grant proposals but had no idea he was his anonymous benefactor.

The main beneficiary of the foundation in the early days was Cornell. Ernie Stern, who secured the first big gift from Feeney in 1981, believes that

Feeney's giving to Cornell, like his own, derived from a sense of *owing*. Neither could have expected early in life to have ended up graduating from such a prestigious university. Stern was born in Nazi Germany and escaped with his parents to America in November 1938, four days before Kristallnacht, and had risen in the corporate world to become chairman and CEO of Thales Components Corporation, a global supplier of professional and defense electronics. He reckoned they both felt enormously indebted to Cornell for their success and their friends.

After that first gift, Feeney and Stern cooperated to get their class to set new levels of giving when it was required, by tradition, to make a special effort once every five years. They would meet to figure out a way to encourage the class to give more. Stern would send the word out to alumni: If anyone gives $5,000, a group of anonymous donors—that is, Feeney—would match it two to one, or even three to one. "His motivation was to prime the pump," said Stern.

Feeney primed the pump for construction of a new 150-room Statler Hotel on the Hotel School campus. There was a down-at-heel fifty-two-room hotel on the site that was losing $150,000 a year. Jack Clark, who succeeded Bob Beck as Hotel School dean in 1981, and who was let in on the secret of Feeney's giving to the university, got the idea of replacing it in 1983. Feeney came to look at the architect's drawings in Clark's office. "I like the plans," he said. "But if you are looking into the future, how big should the hotel be?" Clark replied, "To be honest, if I could I would make 150 rooms instead of 100." Feeney said, "Let's do it!" Feeney's initial funding of the $50-million project helped pull in gifts from industry leaders like Bill Marriott of Marriott Hotels, Dick Ferris of United Airlines, and John F. Mariani Jr. of Banfi Vintners. On completion, it became a "cash cow," said Clark, and today is always full and makes over $1 million a year.

Clark recalled that Feeney would turn up on campus always wearing the same light khaki raincoat until it was falling apart. Feeney joked about being the "shabby philanthropist."

One of his most innovative gifts was $7 million to set up a scheme that became known as the Cornell Tradition. It allowed bright students from modest backgrounds to earn scholarships to Cornell by combining study with work on the campus. Feeney liked it because "it was a hand up rather than hand out," said Handlan. The Cornell Tradition became self-sufficient and went on to award 600 fellowships each year. "The kids who staff the desk and do other stuff at the tennis courts here are all Cornell Tradition," said Clark on a stroll across the campus. "They sweep the floor, they keep the place going, they check you at the desk." The idea had the enthusiastic support of the president of Cornell, Frank Rhodes, who was also brought into Feeney's confidence from the beginning and would later become a close associate. It caught the attention of the *New York Times*, which hailed it as a landmark in the financing of higher education.

Ray Handlan recalled that when Feeney came to Cornell, "he did not want to sit necessarily with the president; you see him maybe downstairs at the faculty club or sitting in the lounge at the Hotel School, or whatever, talking with kids. He is a very caring person, he is a very human person, so he can sit down with young boys and talk about their future, their career, and they seem to know that he is there to help them in whatever way they might need help through financial support or guidance."

Handlan's main responsibility was to find other worthy causes across the United States. He came across a privately funded program in Boston called City Year that began in 1988 as a summer community service program for about seventy volunteer students who would paint schools, renovate home-less shelters, and clean up parks. After giving a speech, cofounder Michael Brown was approached by Handlan, who put him through a rigorous inter-view about what he hoped to achieve. A grant of several million dollars fol-lowed in 1991. City Year was able to expand and within a decade was operating in fourteen cities. It became the model for President Bill Clinton's AmeriCorps program for national youth service. The Atlantic Foundation also funded the Citizens' Scholarship Foundation of America in St. Peter, Minnesota, enabling it to expand its Dollars for Scholars program nation-wide and conduct follow-up research to ensure it was effective.

The anonymous Atlantic checks, even for Cornell, did not arrive until due diligence had been done by the "service company." "These guys really kick the tires," said Chuck Supple, president of Public Allies, which pro-vided internships for young people in nonprofit organizations. It wasn't a case of Ed McMahon knocking on his door, he said, referring to the enter-tainer who arrived unannounced with a large check for winners of American Family Publishers sweepstakes. Atlantic followed up to see how effective the gift was, while taking care not to tell people what to do with the money.

Often, Handlan relied on his instincts. "I heard Howard Gardner speak at an educational conference, rode back with him on the plane, and talked to him about what his needs were." Gardner, a Harvard professor whose empirical work on multiple intelligences in the 1980s changed the way people thought and worked in education, the arts, cognitive psychology, and medicine, recalled that he had no idea who Handlan was, but that they spoke on the plane and that he drove Handlan from the airport to his hotel. "Shortly thereafter, he was offering me support at a level that I could only have dreamed about," he said. "Our research group at Harvard Project Zero received generous funding without needless conditions. This funding was absolutely essential for our continuing work . . . because funding for nonquantitative social science and for broader, progressively oriented educational inquiries was disappearing."

Gardner honored the anonymity requirements to the letter. He referred in conversation to Ray Handlan as Rex Harrison, to program director Angela Covert as Agatha Christie, and to the foundation as AF, as in Anonymous Funder. When his children later met Joel Fleishman, who succeeded Handlan as president of the Atlantic Foundation Service Company, they asked, "Is he the AF?" Gardner said, "I just smiled."

Handlan had sufficient respectability to reassure most people that the money was from an impeccable source. Beneficiaries might fear it was "tainted" money, he said, adding with a laugh, "although in fund-raising what you worry about is 'tain't enough!" He found some potential donees hesitant at first, "but I hope because of my background and my curriculum vitae they accepted the fact that it was not drug money or gambling money." A serious consideration for beneficiaries was that if the money had been fraudulently obtained, the courts would demand that it be returned to pay the donor's creditors.

An embarrassing situation arose when Columbia University in New York turned down a proposed anonymous gift amounting to several hundred thousand dollars because of objections from a board member. Handlan could not reveal the source of the money, but the gift was accepted after Frank Rhodes was recruited to contact the president of Columbia and vouch for the secret foundation's legitimacy. "There were one or two universities that thought that the anonymous offer was a very shady proposition," recalled Rhodes. "More than once I had to speak to people and say, 'This is perfectly legitimate, but there are good reasons for the anonymity.'"

"People probed at it in different ways," said Harvey Dale. "We had a standard answer that was intended to close the door, not to open up a conversation. We said sternly, and it was written into the commitment letter, 'You can't ask that question. We act for anonymous donors. And the condition under which we can give you the money—their money, not our money—is you don't inquire, you don't talk about it.'" Only about one in twenty-five beneficiaries expressed concern, said Dale. "The rest said, 'Oh! Great! Thanks! You must be very respected!'"

In one instance, Dale resorted to a ruse to give money to a not-for-profit body in New York where a board member vetoed taking anything from an anonymous source. Dale suggested to its president that he apply for the grant to another named charitable body. The Atlantic Foundation regularly gave funds to this body to make grants on their recommendation. The Atlantic money arrived at its destination without anyone being the wiser. "We also got credit for a lot of stuff that we didn't do," said Dale. "When we became somewhat known, someone would come up and say, 'I always knew it was you!' And sometimes it wasn't."

Like Pip in Charles Dickens's *Great Expectations,* who assumed his anonymous patron was Miss Havisham, when all along it was the convict Magwitch, some recipients guessed wrongly who their benefactor was. But they were never told. Harvey Dale imposed the same conditions as Jaggers, the lawyer for Pip's real benefactor, who said, "Not only is it a profound secret, but more importantly it is a binding condition that you do not inquire."

Dale could appreciate the caution of beneficiaries, as he had been an active member when in college of the National Students' Organization, which he only learned later was secretly funded by the CIA to keep track of left-leaning future potential leaders.

As president of Cornell, Frank Rhodes found it frustrating that he could not praise Feeney more in public, "but it was Chuck's wish that it should be anonymous, secretive almost, and that he shouldn't be publicly identified as the donor." When Rhodes hosted an intimate dinner for Feeney in a private room overlooking Lake Cayuga at Cornell's Herbert F. Johnson Museum of Art, he made a little speech in which he said that though respectful of the desire for anonymity, those in the room knew where the money was coming from and they could recognize Chuck Feeney's generosity.

It seemed an innocuous gesture, but Harvey Dale was upset. "What agitated me most, there were waiters walking around, and the president of Cornell was saying, 'Here's something nobody knows, the source of all this magnificent money is Chuck Feeney, I've got a great secret and I can only share it in this room,' and so that blows it. One doesn't really challenge Frank Rhodes. But I said afterward, 'Frank, you shouldn't have done that, that was a bad idea. Don't do that again.'" Rhodes recalled that Feeney would shrug off anonymity as an evil necessity, but Harvey Dale enforced confidentiality so severely that "you had almost to sign your life away" to receive a donation from the Atlantic Foundation.

In order to improve its own understanding of the issues surrounding secret giving, the Atlantic Foundation bankrolled a conference on anonymous giving at the Indiana University Center on Philanthropy. Naturally, it gave the funding anonymously.

CHAPTER 15

The Luck of the Irish

The Feeneys left Bermuda after the creation of the Atlantic Foundation. Danielle disliked the country so much that she vowed never to set foot there again. In 1985, Chuck and Danielle moved the family home to London. Feeney wanted to use the English capital as his base for running the multinational company known as General Atlantic Group Ltd. on behalf of the philanthropy. He owned neither, but he still effectively controlled both. For the first years after he created the Atlantic Foundation, Chuck Feeney had been happy to see almost all of its giving focused on the United States, and on the university that had given him such a wonderful base for his business life. But he kept an open mind about other locations for his initiatives. He spent much of his time after the move to London reading, asking questions, and looking for fresh opportunities for both making money and giving it away.

When Feeney went to register his company in London, however, he came up against an unexpected bureaucratic complication. The use in a business title of two generic names together, such as "General" and "Atlantic" was not allowed under English company law. But there was nothing to stop him from using the initials "G.A." if he had a name to match. "I went to the telephone book," said Feeney, "and found an old trading company called Gerard Atkins and Co. and bought it, so we operated under that name and used the initials G.A." The name Gerard Atkins on the letterhead was also a convenient way of maintaining discretion and anonymity.

With funds from General Atlantic, he bought 17 Savile Row, a rambling building in the heart of London's fashionable custom-tailoring district, to serve as world headquarters for GAGL and as a residence for himself and Danielle. He told Paul Hannon, "I like funky buildings." Feeney renovated the building with the help of Broadway theater designer Fred Fox, whom he had befriended on a plane. "Chuck enjoyed the project enormously, knocking down walls and painting," said Hannon. "He himself took the top floor, so we had to keep climbing up and down the stairs. It was good for all of us, but not very efficient. The building had five floors and no lift, and he was planning to live on the top floor with his family, but Danielle vetoed that." Feeney moved his family instead to a triplex in Mayfair and enrolled Patrick, then fourteen, in the French lycée.

In London, Feeney had already acquired N. Peal, one of the world's most famous cashmere brands, with two outlets in the Burlington Arcade and a shop in the Gleneagles Hotel in Scotland, and a factory in Hawick on the Scottish border. He liked going into the cashmere shops and checking out the displays.

A chance invitation brought Chuck Feeney to Ireland. Shortly after he moved to London, a friend of Tony Pilaro's sent him a brochure that he had come across. It appealed to Irish and Irish American investors to join an eighty-member consortium with the intent of buying and upgrading Ashford Castle, a 700-year-old stately home converted into a luxury hotel on the shores of Lake Corrib in County Mayo. The brochure arrived with a tongue-in-cheek note saying, "This is something no self-respecting Italian American would get involved in, but might interest you." Once the home of the Guinness family, the hotel was a favorite with American celebrity visitors. John Wayne and Maureen O'Hara had stayed there during the shooting of John Ford's *The Quiet Man* in 1952, and President Ronald Reagan had spent a night during a presidential visit to Ireland in May 1984.

Like most Irish Americans, Feeney had a sentimental attraction to the land of his ancestors. St. Patrick's Day was always a big event in the Feeney household. He joked to his children that he was descended from a dethroned "high king of Ireland." He did some research into his family history and established that his grandmother on his father's side came from a tiny rural district called Larganacarran in County Fermanagh in Northern Ireland. He carried in his wallet a "Thornsticks" card, stating he was an Irish

American, passionately proud of Irish culture and customs but "without publicity, fanfare, or personal reward."

He first took Danielle and the children to Ireland back in 1971. They stayed at Dromoland Castle Hotel in County Clare. They remember tears trickling down his face as he listened to a harpist play melancholy Irish melodies. He considered buying film director John Huston's Georgian manor house near Craughwell in the west of Ireland as another family home, but the price was too high.

The more he reconnected with Ireland, the more Feeney became convinced that Irish Americans like himself should be doing more to help. In the 1980s, the economy of the Republic of Ireland was moribund. One in five adults was out of work. Three out of four graduates were leaving the country as soon as they qualified. A British newspaper columnist described Ireland as a Third World country but for the climate, and many Irish agreed and emigrated. In Northern Ireland the bloody conflict known as The Troubles was raging without any sign of a resolution.

The offer to buy into Ashford Castle Hotel seemed a useful entry point, if only because the other co-owners were moneyed people and might share his interest in doing something for Ireland. It was Feeney's way of familiarizing himself with a culture: Before he invested General Atlantic money, he would find a "perch" to get a feel for the place, and he understood the hotel business. The consortium bought Ashford Castle for $7 million in 1985, of which Feeney paid $70,000. He induced Paul Hannon, and Joe Lyons from DFS, also to buy a stake each. Chuck, Danielle, and the children flew to Shannon airport and crowded into a rented Volkswagen van to drive to the hotel for a short stay. Typically, Chuck found himself helping the manager of Ashford Castle to organize the hotel shop.

Most of the co-owners in the Ashford consortium seemed more interested in playing golf and salmon fishing than anything else. If he was to get involved, Feeney needed somebody with a knowledge of the country to survey the landscape for him and suggest investment ideas, and better still if there was a Cornell connection. He found such a person in Padraig Berry, a young, intense Irishman who had gone to Cornell Hotel School on a $20,000 scholarship—made possible by funds donated to a scholarship fund by Feeney—and had worked as assistant to the Hotel School dean, Bob Beck. Feeney had met him with Beck a couple of times, and they stayed in touch.

Berry was fascinated by Feeney. "I thought at first he was quite odd. It was almost as if he was embarrassed to be recognized for who he was. I met him subsequently and engaged him in conversation. He looked at me and I remember those steely blue eyes." They began meeting for lunches and dinners in London, where Berry worked as an accountant. "Chuck would bring up ideas, without following any agenda, to see how things unfolded, to see if we would do great things together." Eventually Feeney suggested to Berry that he go to Ireland and look around for investment opportunities. Berry quit his job, loaded up his Golf GTI, and in May 1987 took the ferry to Ireland with only the vaguest idea of what he was supposed to do. Feeney gave him a large advance payment. "I worked sixteen hours a day for seven days a week for years for that man for that check," said Berry, who came to regard Feeney as a father figure. Feeney came to Ireland a number of times, and they drove around looking at potential investments. "In Dublin we'd eat out every night in Gallery 22. We would have a couple of bottles of Macon Lugny. It was always a ritual."

For a while, recalled Feeney, "we were just trucking along and doing things on an ad hoc basis." He acquired the Kilternan Golf and Country Club in the misty foothills of the Dublin Mountains that had Ireland's only—synthetic—ski slope, and Heritage House, one of the finest Georgian buildings in Dublin, which he got Fred Fox to renovate as a showpiece of period décor.

Then a newspaper article caught his eye, about the formation in Dublin of a body called the Irish American Partnership, inspired by Paddy Harte, a member of the Dail, the Irish parliament. Harte believed that there was tremendous goodwill toward Ireland among successful Irish Americans but that it wasn't being fully exploited to stimulate business development. Its director general, John Healy, was a shrewd and disarming diplomat, and a former executive of the Irish Trade Board. Feeney arranged to meet him in Dublin. Healy rang a high-level official at the Trade Board to find out in advance more about Feeney. They said they had never heard of him.

Feeney and Padraig Berry called at Healy's Dublin office on September 4, 1987. Healy wasn't sure what to make of Feeney as he briefed him on what the Partnership did. "This fellow sat there, you know, with the hooded eyes, not saying very much, looking at us intently," he recalled. Finally he turned to Feeney and said, "What we need to do now is set up a counterpart organization in the U.S. That's where the action is. Could you advise me where I could find money to do that?" Feeney didn't answer. But as they walked to lunch at the Kildare Street & University Club, Feeney told him that he knew a place in America that might entertain a proposal for a grant of $250,000. He suggested that Healy send the proposal to the Atlantic Foundation Service Company in Ithaca, care of Mr. Ray Handlan. After the lunch, Healy called a friend in New York who worked as a fund-raising professional and asked, "What's a foundation service company?" The friend replied, "I haven't a clue." Healy put together his proposal and sent it off to Ithaca. A check for $250,000 duly arrived.

The Kildare Street & University Club was a favorite dining place for Irish academics, and as they made their way to a table that day, Healy introduced Feeney to Ed Walsh, head of the fifteen-year-old Limerick Institute of Higher Education, who was in Dublin to lobby for full university status. "Any time you are in the west, you might think of visiting Limerick," said Walsh politely. Feeney replied, "I'll come down and talk to you."

Three weeks later, Feeney turned up in Limerick. Walsh was wary of Irish Americans, who were often only concerned about why "the bloody British aren't out of Ireland" and arranged to give him the usual routine: tea in his office for fifteen minutes, then a tour of the campus, situated on rolling meadows by the River Shannon. But the visitor showed an extraordinary interest in his vision for the college and hinted at access to funds. Walsh said later that he knew enough not to ask for a donation, on the basis that "if you ask for money, you will get advice; if you ask for advice, you may eventually get support." Berry recalled that Feeney allowed himself to be "baited and reeled in."

Feeney got a blank stare when he asked Walsh how much funding Limerick received from its alumni. In Ireland, universities relied almost exclusively on state subvention. There was no culture of philanthropy, and no Irish educational institutions even had a foundation or a director of development.

"I could see very quickly they could absorb an awful lot of money," recalled Feeney. "The university was on a magnificent site, but buildings were in rough condition. I recognized here was a school on the uptake and a charismatic leader. You need both things to support an organization." Feeney was also attracted by the notion of helping the underdog: If Ireland was the underdog in Europe, Limerick was the underdog in the Irish academic world.

Feeney asked his host: "What's the best university in the United States?" Walsh reeled off a few names: "Stanford? Yale? Harvard?" "No, it's Cornell," said Feeney. "Would you like to come out there?" Walsh hesitated. His visitor wore off-the-peg clothes and a cheap watch and he had no idea who he really was or what he did. But an association with an Ivy League university in the United States would do no harm to his quest for full university status so he agreed.

Walsh traveled to New York in December and joined Chuck and Danielle in their Fifth Avenue apartment overlooking Central Park. Feeney disappeared and came back with some fresh bagels and cream cheese for Sunday brunch, after which they took the short flight to Ithaca, home of Cornell University in upstate New York.

"To my astonishment," recalled Walsh, "Cornell had laid on a most exceptional visit for me. Whoever heard of Limerick, never mind of the National Institute of Higher Education in Limerick! But when we got out of the plane, the top brass was there to meet us. And clearly they were there because of Chuck." It dawned on Walsh that Feeney was "no ordinary Joe Soap." There were sly references to his generosity. Feeney introduced him to Ray Handlan, who told him that Cornell had raised more than $500 million in donations from alumni that year. This was a whole new world. The day ended with a private dinner for Walsh, hosted by Cornell president Frank Rhodes. "It was a puzzling meeting altogether," recalled Rhodes, who also wondered what Feeney was up to. After the dinner, the Irish visitor invited Rhodes to visit Limerick, little expecting that any Ivy League university president would find time to come to his struggling institute.

Within weeks of Ed Walsh's return to Ireland, however, a steady stream of visitors began arriving from the United States: James Whelan, president of Ithaca College and his wife, Gillian; the Cornell dean of business, David Long; Chuck and Danielle with a group that included the dean of the Hotel School; Jack Clark and Ray Handlan; and then Chuck again with Frank Rhodes, who spent two days asking probing questions about how Limerick might develop.

One day Feeney called to say that a friend of his—a leading faculty member at New York University who specialized in the law relating to philanthropy—was in Europe and would like to visit the university. Maybe Walsh would show him around. His name was Harvey Dale.

Any friend of Feeney's was by now given the red carpet. Walsh and his wife, Stephanie, brought Dale and his then-wife Nan sailing on Lough Derg. They took them to dinner at a traditional restaurant near Bunratty.

The Dales stayed for a few days, asking questions and looking around. Without saying what his relationship with Feeney was, the New York lawyer took Ed Walsh aside to tell him that Feeney's potential to assist the university arose more from his network of contacts than from any personal wealth he might possess and that all funding would be anonymous. He also stressed that Feeney was not to be bothered by the press, that he should not be asked to pose for photographs or give interviews, and that failure to respect these conditions could jeopardize any help Feeney might bring to Limerick.

Walsh listened and nodded. He conveyed the conditions to his board. Some members expressed unease about taking money from anonymous sources. But Walsh was able to assure the directors that the conduit for the cash flow was a person highly respected in Ivy League circles in the United States.

Feeney became totally preoccupied with Limerick, recalled Padraig Berry. "The University of Limerick was coming out of my ears for six months afterward; it was all he would talk about." Often Feeney would arrive at the university and wander about unrecognized. "What was so astonishing was his wish to be ordinary," recalled Walsh.

One of the things that attracted Feeney to Limerick was the cocky attitude of the leadership and its intolerance for bureaucratic restrictions. He learned how Ed Walsh's decision in the late 1980s to raise funds for new student accommodations had been met with outrage and opposition from the Irish Higher Education Authority in Dublin. It was conventional wisdom that any rental fees from student accommodations would be insufficient to service a building loan. John O'Connor, the university's impish finance officer, circumvented the Department of Education by creating a private company that, being legally independent, could not be issued with any directive to stop construction. The first phase of the village was being completed when Feeney first showed up on campus, and eventually expanded to house 1,000 of the 6,000 students.

Limerick provided Feeney with an opportunity he was looking for, to raise the level of spending of his Atlantic Foundation to good effect. His first significant donation was for a concert hall that became a center of musical activity for the university and the city of Limerick. Atlantic put up IR£6 million, the equivalent of $10 million, and Ed Walsh successfully lobbied the Minister for Education Mary O'Rourke to match it. "In hindsight this initiative was one of enormous importance," said Walsh, whose institute was awarded university status in 1989. "Our success convinced the state bureaucracy that the concept of matching funds could indeed stimulate major private investment in the universities."

Feeney and Frank Rhodes encouraged Walsh to establish a foundation to raise money and also to provide advice on the development of the university. In American universities, distinguished business and community leaders were avidly recruited to advise the president. Irish universities not only had no foundations, their governing bodies were made up largely of political appointees, who could be egocentric, pompous, and driven by political ambition.

Walsh brought the idea to his executive committee. There was an outcry. If they were successful in raising significant money, wouldn't the state use this as a pretext to reallocate its limited resources to other universities? But Walsh persisted. Much to the astonishment, and annoyance, of Harvey Dale, he then persuaded Chuck Feeney to become the first chairman of the Limerick University Foundation.

The interaction with Cornell and with Feeney stimulated Walsh to think big. He went to the United States to recruit prominent figures for his foundation board. He persuaded Jack Welch, then chairman of General Electric in Connecticut—who had never before heard of Limerick Institute of Higher Education—to send senior executive Frank Doyle to join the directors. Walsh also targeted Wall Street financier Lewis L. Glucksman. Born to a second-generation Hungarian Jewish family in New York, Glucksman had won control of Manhattan-based Lehman in an epic 1983 boardroom battle documented in the book *Greed and Glory on Wall Street* by Ken Auletta. Having visited Ireland as a young naval officer, he fell for the country and its literature and had made County Cork his second home. He was married to Loretta Brennan Glucksman, a famous Irish American beauty and philanthropist in New York.

Walsh and Feeney set up a meeting with Lew Glucksman in his Wall Street office. "Chuck was late," said Walsh. "He explained that things were tied up on the subway. They both then recalled how when young they managed to ride the subway by getting through the turnstile without paying. Feeney quipped, 'I was so small I could walk under it!' Glucksman said: 'I was caught once. I was taken to the police station and I was put into a cell with three or four others. I said to one guy, a young chap like myself, 'I am here because I did the subway and, why are you here?' And he says, 'I killed my ma.'"

Glucksman joined the foundation board and became a major donor, eventually taking over from Feeney as chairman of the Limerick University Foundation. He and Feeney, who shared a liking for early nights, competed at foundation board dinners to see who could slip off first with good grace. The winner got a necktie.

To deflect inquiries about his anonymous source of funding, Ed Walsh let everyone think he was going off to America once a month and collecting a suitcase full of dollars from rich American businessmen. Astonishingly, this was widely believed. When Feeney was on campus, he was shielded, sometimes physically, from inquisitive eyes. People from Atlantic stood between Feeney and anyone with a camera. On one occasion guests thought they were being photographed, but the official photographer had been instructed not to put film in his camera. Faculty members who got to know who Feeney was declined to identify him at social gatherings. Legal counsel Paul Hannon recalled that when the *Limerick Leader* published a photograph showing Feeney, Harvey Dale ordered that all available copies of the newspaper be bought up and destroyed.

Feeney poked fun at his own insistence on confidentiality. Once, he turned up at Shannon airport to greet directors of his foundation flying in from the United States by holding up a notice saying: "Welcome to Anonymous Donors."

While in Limerick, Chuck was able to spend some time with a man he had admired all his professional life. Brendan O'Regan founded duty free at Shannon airport and provided the business model from which Chuck had made his fortune. He was also an idealist who promoted peace on the island through his organization, the Irish Peace Institute. In the summer of 1988, O'Regan invited Feeney to a peace conference at Dromoland Castle. There, another chance encounter opened up new horizons for Feeney. He got talking with an Estonian delegate, Kalle Tenno, who invited him to visit his tiny Baltic republic, then still part of the Soviet Union, and see the changes starting to take place.

In September 1988, Feeney traveled to Estonia, taking with him Jim Downey, the son of his school friend, Skip Downey, who had come to Europe to help him identify and develop business opportunities. They went to the university in Tartu, the intellectual center of Estonia, becoming one of the first group of Westerners to visit the city since Estonia had been annexed by the Soviet Union after World War II. Feeney promised university leaders there that he would help Estonia build links with the West. He also provided the university with its first fax machine.

Back in Ireland, Feeney bought a former adoption home in Blackrock, County Dublin, and created the Trade Management Institute for Estonians and other Soviet citizens to take business courses and learn English, and for Irish postgraduate students to study Russian, French, and Spanish. "We bought that place for £426,000 [about $720,000] and in six months we redesigned it and turned it into a school," said Padraig Berry. A suspicious Soviet embassy official came by to ask what was going on and make a report. Feeney also wanted to motivate the Irish students. "I was so frustrated with the lack of business effort by young Irish people," he said. In March 1989, the former Irish prime minister Garret FitzGerald gave the commencement address, and Feeney arranged for lectures by faculty members from Limerick University, University College Dublin, and Cornell University.

Around this time, Feeney told Ed Walsh over breakfast at Ashford Castle about Estonia's "heroic efforts" at reform within the Soviet Union. "Would you ever think of going out there, meeting with the rector of the University of Tartu to see if you could help?" he asked. "Chuck so seldom asked and so frequently gave" that he could only agree, said Walsh. He lined up a delegation led by Gus O'Driscoll, the mayor of Limerick, and set off for Estonia, where he signed an agreement with Tartu University on an exchange of students—as a result of which his eldest son, Michael, went there to study and met his future wife, Marju. "Now my children and first grandchildren speak Estonian," said Walsh, "all triggered by Chuck."

By now, Chuck Feeney's mind was thoroughly bifurcated. The opportunistic way he did business for General Atlantic Group Ltd., acquiring elements here and there, had clearly transferred to his philanthropy. Limerick showed that. If he saw a good opportunity, either to increase the non-negotiable assets of the foundation through doing business deals, or to decrease the liquid assets through acts of giving, he would take it, and leverage it into help for other institutions in an ever-expanding network.

CHAPTER 16

Leaving Money on the Table

By 1986, DFS had become the largest retailer of liquor in the world, selling $250 million worth a year. It was the biggest single retailer in Hong Kong, Hawaii, Alaska, and Guam, and also had retail operations in Singapore, Taiwan, Macau, Saipan, New Zealand, and Australia, and in the United States in Los Angeles, San Francisco, Dallas–Fort Worth, New York, and Boston. It was paying $185 million in fees for forty concessions at twelve international airports. Worldwide, the company employed over 6,500 people, 1,200 in Hawaii alone. It was an international retailing colossus so big that it was a major reason for Japan's $10-billion tourism deficit. Japanese overseas travel continued to enjoy phenomenal growth. From 1964 to 1986, passenger growth had increased on average 19 percent a year and the value of the yen had increased by 4 percent a year.

The days were long gone when DFS was snubbed by the top-brand suppliers as a fly-by-night discount operation. Now it offered premier labels for the designer-conscious Japanese tourists in huge modern stores, though it remained fiercely loyal to those who had stood by it in tough times, and anyone entering DFS shops was confronted with prominent displays of Camus cognacs and Nina Ricci perfumes. What DFS chief executive Bellamy called their "ego-intensive merchandise" included Hermès ties, Gucci shoes,

Tiffany diamonds, Bulgari watches, Dunhill lighters, Montblanc pens, Swarovski crystal, Wedgwood china, and Godiva chocolates. Japanese office ladies crowded around the cash registers to buy Fendi bags and Chanel perfume at less than half the price at home, and Tokyo business executives handed over hundreds of dollars for bottles of vintage Chivas Regal.

In his annual 1986 report for the eyes of the four owners only, Bellamy wrote that it was a spectacular year, a "special vintage." They had caught a big wave "and we rode it all the way in."

"The great department stores are a century old, but we were born with the jet," enthused Bellamy in an interview published in the *Financial Times* in June 1986, explaining how the company had created an unequaled sales machine to cash in on Japanese consumer culture. In his interview, he explained how DFS had employed shrewd marketing to get Japanese patronage. "In the early days we were purely an operating company, now we are merchants in the fashion business, retailers to the international traveler."

When the DFS owners saw the article, their reaction was "explosive," according to Tony Pilaro. Feeney was agitated. He sent his board representative George Parker "to express his discomfort to me in no uncertain way," recalled Bellamy. The partners knew that one of the reasons for DFS's success was that its international operations were a mystery to outsiders. No one quite knew how duty free worked or how big DFS was. The owners had been alarmed at an article the same year in the *World Executive Digest* that criticized DFS in Hong Kong for trading on its duty-free franchise to promote other goods as duty free—though it gave flattering portraits of the founders: It said that Feeney remained the éminence grise who brought into the operation "all the drive and kinetic energy of a cyclone," while Miller, "banker, financier, sportsman and *bon vivant* personifies all that is acceptable and respectable of DFS worldwide."

Above all, the DFS owners wanted to keep secret the amount they were taking out of the company in dividends and their unique tax arrangements. In 1986, it was a staggering $186 million, of which Feeney—or his foundation—received $39 million in cash.

That year the free flow of cash was almost intercepted by Uncle Sam. DFS operated its business activities in the United States and Guam through a Netherlands Antilles holding company, which enabled the four foreign-registered owners to avoid paying tax on the dividends. In 1986, however, the U.S. government planned to eliminate this exemption, and the owners faced paying tax on future dividends at 30 percent. Under the new regulations the company could also have to pay double U.S. tax on DFS profits.

Pilaro came up with an audacious solution that involved liquidating the Netherlands Antilles company overnight, operating it as a U.S. partnership, and distributing all of its assets to the foreign shareholders. Through a clever revaluation (known as a "step-up") of the assets, even the one U.S. tax on company profits that they had been paying was largely eliminated, at least for several years. There was a lot of paper shuffling and filings and basically nothing changed, but the scheme resulted in an estimated cash savings of $700 million over the following decade. "In short," said Pilaro, "the plan turned DFS U.S. operations into a tax-free cash flow machine."

The "Big Bang" restructuring put more distance among the four founders. They were still regarded by everyone as the owners of DFS, but they were now, in legal terms, "shareholder representatives" of the tax shelters and charitable foundations they created.

This dissonance may have contributed to missteps in the all-important bidding process. The four had stepped down from managing the business, but they kept control of the company, and this meant getting together when the time came to calculate a bid. In 1987, they got it wrong in Hong Kong, their original base. The system in Hong Kong was different from everywhere else. On a given date, bids were dropped into a tender box situated in the lift lobby of Central Government Offices on Lower Albert Road. The four owners would walk up together and drop in the bid and wait to be notified by official letter who had won. Once, they nearly lost it by default, remembering at the last minute that they needed to include two copies and not just one.

After they submitted their tender on June 4, 1987, to renew the three-year liquor and tobacco concession, they found themselves outbid by Kiu Fat Investments Corporation, a consortium of three Chinese companies backed by the People's Republic of China. It was led by former left-wing movie star Fu Chi and his actress wife, Shek Wai, famous for their role in a 1967 real-life political melodrama when they spent twenty-seven hours on a bridge between Hong Kong and China protesting at Hong Kong's attempt to deport them for Cultural Revolution activities. Kiu Fat outbid DFS by more than 25 percent.

Hong Kong was different from Hawaii, however. This need not be a disaster. Duty free still applied only to alcohol and tobacco; DFS was selling watches, pens, apparel, and everything else the tourists might want. Feeney took the view that it was unethical to try to undermine the Chinese, and that they should be honorable and take their losses while continuing to do retail business like all other Hong Kong stores. Alan Parker agreed. "We just decided we would stay in business," he said. "The whole issue of duty free in Hong Kong is false. The whole of Hong Kong is duty free except for a tiny little bit of duty on booze, alcohol, and perfume. We had developed this whole thing, Duty Free Shoppers, we used the name [but] we sold every product in the world."

John Monteiro, who had returned to run the Hong Kong operation after a number of years in Alaska and Hawaii, took the defeat personally, however. The Chinese organization poached 20 percent of his staff, including managers, salesgirls, and supervisors, and set up a downtown store with a sign saying "Official Duty Free." He resolved to fight to get the liquor and tobacco concession back. The Hong Kong travel agents—the crocodiles—told Monteiro they might have to support the new store, not least because it was backed by the Chinese government that would one day take over the British colony. But Monteiro dropped the price of his duty-paid liquor to 5 percent below that of the new duty-free store, and every time Kiu Fat dropped its price, he dropped his further. The agents remained loyal after all and kept bringing Japanese to DFS rather than the new store. DFS also did everything it could to discourage European designer houses from supplying an operation backed by Red China.

At Kai Tak airport, the Chinese consortium had the monopoly on selling duty-free items for delivery on board the planes—a major convenience for overloaded tourists—but Monteiro went to his friends in the airlines, and they agreed to belly-load the *duty-paid* liquor and tobacco from DFS stores as unaccompanied baggage to be picked up in Japan. The airport authority tried to stop him, but Anson Chan, secretary for economic services in Hong Kong, who had been a director of the DFS charity board, ruled that it was not illegal.

"It was a huge fight, and the Chinese suffered such tremendous financial loss because they had a minimum guarantee to pay the government, and they didn't have the sales," said Monteiro.

An official from the New China News Agency, which represented the People's Republic of China in Hong Kong, asked to meet Adrian Bellamy for lunch. "He was a very intelligent guy and very impressive," said Bellamy. "He put a lot of pressure on me and on DFS to stop the fight. He said,

Already camera-shy. Chuck Feeney (age thirteen), front row, second from left, at St. Genevieve's graduation, 1944.

Chuck Feeney (right) with John Costello in Korea, September 1951.

Chuck Feeney, fresh out of the Air Force, 1952.

Already well on the way to their first billion, Chuck Feeney (left) and Bob Miller pose for a mid-1970s DFS promotion. The golden partnership would end in acrimony two decades later.

Smallest of the DFS owners with 2.5 percent of the shareholding, Tony Pilaro (left) still made it to the Forbes magazine list of the 400 richest Americans. Lacking the fare to go home to Europe, Alan Parker (right) stayed on in New York as DFS accountant and is today worth several billion dollars. He lives in Switzerland.

Chuck Feeney with Patrick, Diane, and Leslie.

Lifelong friend and colleague Bob Matousek (left), then president of the European Division of DFS, relaxing with Chuck Feeney in the south of France in the summer of 1975.

Chuck Feeney with daughter Caroleen in panda suit, promoting Chinese products at the Hawaii store.

Feeney celebrating the DFS sale with Harvey Dale.

Feeney, in background, failing to avoid the camera at a meeting in Belfast in 1994 with Sinn Fein president Gerry Adams.

Directors of the Atlantic Foundation advisory board don Groucho Marx masks to mock Harvey Dale's insistence on secrecy. Feeney sits in front row, first left.

Chuck Rolles, Chuck Feeney, Ray Handlan, Fred Eydt, and Bob Gallagher relive their youth at Couran Cove.

Harvey Dale and Chuck Feeney in a typical lunchtime setting in San Francisco.

Le Nhan Phuong, Atlantic Philanthropies country manager in Vietnam, who came to regard Chuck Feeney as a father figure.

Former Australian diplomat Michael Mann, founding president of the first foreign-owned university in Vietnam, aligned with the Royal Institute of Technology in Melbourne. According to him, "Without Chuck Feeney, we would not have this university."

Feeney in Johannesburg with former ANC general secretary, Cyril Ramaphosa, with whom he exchanged cloak-and-dagger stories of their involvement in the Northern Ireland peace process.

Then-president of South Africa, Nelson Mandela, with John Healy, chief executive of Atlantic Philanthropies from 2001–2007.

Irish Prime Minister Enda Kenny with Helga and Chuck Feeney at a government dinner in Feeney's honor in Dublin, 2012.

Christopher Oechsli and Chuck Feeney plan strategy during the struggle for power at Atlantic Philanthropies.

Chuck Feeney prepares to speak in Dublin at the conferring of his joint honorary degree by all the universities in Ireland, September 2012.

'When two lions fight, they both get hurt.' It didn't deter us in any way. Johnny Monteiro was the really aggressive one. He didn't like his marbles being taken away."

By July 1988, Kiu Fat couldn't pay the staff, and its 600 disgruntled workers staged a fifty-hour sit-in. It conceded defeat. After two weeks of day-and-night negotiations with DFS, represented by Monteiro and Tony Pilaro, it ceded the concession for a management commission that allowed it to save face. DFS officially got the concession back through the bid process the following year.

The unnerving setback in Hong Kong was a factor behind the biggest miscalculation the four guys in a room ever made, the bid they lodged to renew the Hawaii concession the following year. The new bid was for a four-and-a-half-year concession, from 1986 to 1991. Hawaii had become so important that DFS moved its international corporate headquarters from Hong Kong to Honolulu in 1982, the first non-Hawaiian company to do so. Sales at the hanger-size Waikiki store in Hawaii had soared to $400 million a year, equivalent to $20,000 a square foot in revenues—compared with $800 a square foot at Bloomingdale's in New York. By this time, Japanese investors in Honolulu owned two-thirds of the major hotels, several big office blocks, plus condominiums, golf courses, restaurants, and construction companies. Thousands of Japanese with high purchasing power—tourists, business executives, couples getting married—were arriving in Honolulu on the six-hour flight from Tokyo every day. With the strong yen, Hawaii was for the Japanese like Mexico was for Americans. Everything was cheap, and DFS was like a giveaway store.

The Waikiki store was taking in so much cash every day that DFS had created its own bank known as the "Central Cashier" to which armed guards would bring the cash every evening in armored vehicles for processing at special currency counters. The store had 300 cash registers, which meant 300 deposits every day for the Central Cashier, which had bulletproof doors and security cameras. The yen were counted separately in a special strong room. The amount of American and Japanese currency taken in every day was so great that a special department of currency traders was set up inside DFS to trade it on the overnight money markets.

Chuck Feeney, Bob Miller, Alan Parker, and Tony Pilaro flew into town to calculate their bid. They imagined they spotted rivals at a question-and-answer session with Hawaii state officials. They became neurotic, recalled Parker. "You would see people wander around outside the store, and you would imagine that every person who walked past the store was somebody who was going to bid." To put up the required 2-percent bid deposit, they started accumulating cash and buying cashier's checks from different banks. They picked up intelligence about a rival Korean company preparing to make a bid.

The day came when the four guys gathered a last time to determine how much they should put on the table. They kept nudging it upward as they studied the projections. "It was led by Chuck," said Alan Parker. "The simple bottom line was that we would have ended up bidding the highest anybody in the room wanted to bid because nobody wanted to be the guy who lost the bid."

"The dynamics of the bidding were always—where was Chuck?" said Adrian Bellamy. "His influence over the other three was very powerful. He was always a few steps ahead of everybody with his gut instinct about what to do. Chuck generally persuaded Bob on it. Alan's point of view almost always was that he couldn't be the guy who puts his number on the table, but he could always control it by waiting for one of the big guys to decide and then side with whichever won. He was in the catbird seat."

They finally settled on $1.151 billion, the highest price ever bid for a duty-free concession anywhere in the world, before or since. It was an unimaginable amount of money. It was in some ways just a number, the end figure in their calculations, but if stacked in actual dollar bills it would have been seventy-two miles high.

They were offering to pay the State of Hawaii some $2 million every three days, for the next five years, just for the right to run a couple of stores. It was more than six times what they had paid the previous year, $185 million, for *all* their concessions around the world. According to Pilaro, "Alan vigorously opposed the bid." But he wasn't in the majority.

They trooped along to the transportation office for the now-familiar ritual of the opening of the sealed bids and the chalking up of the figures on the blackboard. It emerged that there was indeed a rival. It was Hotel Lotte of South Korea, which owned a shopping complex and duty-free store in Seoul. But the bid was a mere $372 million. The DFS owners sat there, aghast. They had bid $779 million more. "We left a shitload of money on the table, three-quarters of a billion dollars," said Pilaro. "What happened? I wish I knew. We were rather foolish. We were all responsible. Maybe we were all making too much money. The last person who came up with a number prevailed." There was one upside, apart from winning the concession, he said. "In the most generous analysis, never again was anybody going to come and bid against us." Five years later, there was no counterbid when DFS secured Hawaii for a further four years for $401 million.

Looking back years later, Feeney defended the bid. "The worst thing to do was lose," he said. The truth was, they could pay this amount and still make huge profits.

In the aftermath of the Hawaii setback, Adrian Bellamy retained consultants from McKinsey & Company to do a study on how bids should be calculated. He arranged for McKinsey to do a presentation in Geneva and invited Feeney, Miller, Parker, and Pilaro to hear their conclusions.

The four owners seethed as they gathered to hear what the consultants had to say. No one had talked to them about how they arrived at their concession bids. "They came with this long complicated presentation, typical McKinsey bullshit of how you solve something," said Alan Parker. "I said to them, 'You know there's sixty-three years of experience around this table of guys who have done bids. Why did you not come and talk to any one of these people?'" Pilaro was enraged "that Adrian could conceivably go out and spend two million bucks of our dough for these goddamn consultants and these people never asked us how *we* approached it. We made a mistake in Hawaii. So what? These 'yo-yos' sat there and talked about decisions in uncertainty, and it was all predicated on oil and how one made a decision to drill for oil when one didn't know if there was oil or how deep it was. I blasted them about the fallacy on oil because usually oil is in quadrants, and you can drill here, and if you don't hit, you can drill sideways, you can drill different blocks. This is duty free. You miss it, you go home. There is no second shot." Feeney listened for a while and then made his own views clear by just getting up and walking out of the room.

The following year, in 1988, even in the wake of the huge bid in Hawaii, the cash dividend paid to the owners from the profits of the duty-free stores was $400 million. Of this, Chuck Feeney's foundation received $155 million. On top of the profits from its own business portfolio, and multi-million-dollar dividends from the Camus agency, the foundation was raking in more than $2 million every five days, in cash. He had worked hard to stay out of the limelight. But this couldn't go unnoticed.

Rich, Ruthless, and Determined

On Friday, October 7, 1988, a colleague handed Chuck Feeney a copy of *Forbes* magazine, folded over at page thirty-six with the headline, "Rich, Ruthless and Determined." "Have you seen this?" he said. "Oh shit!" responded Feeney.

Feeney read with dismay that he had been included in *Forbes* magazine's list of the 400 richest Americans. According to the New York–based journal, Charles F. Feeney was the twenty-third-richest American alive, worth $1.3 billion, richer than Rupert Murdoch, David Rockefeller, or Donald Trump. Paul Hannon's prediction three years earlier that they were getting "too big and interesting" to be ignored by *Forbes* had been borne out.

Bob Miller was not on the rich list, as he had given up his U.S. passport and taken British citizenship, but the magazine estimated that he, too, was a billionaire. As an English national, Alan Parker did not get a rating. Tony Pilaro was on the rich list, coming in at 231st place with an estimated worth of $340 million, though *Forbes* wrongly reported his share of DFS at 10 percent, rather than 2.5 percent.

The *Forbes* article got the whole Feeney family in a tither. Chuck's sisters in New Jersey found the sums "mind-boggling." Danielle called Arlene and told her that Chuck was furious, though she privately thought part of him was quite proud that he was recognized as a successful businessman by his peers. In New Jersey "everybody from St. Mary's went out and bought *Forbes,*" said his school pal Bob Cogan. "We were flabbergasted. We never knew what the hell he did. He could have been in the CIA. He wouldn't tell. Maybe he didn't want anyone to think he was better than us. And here is a guy coming out of nowhere and up there with the Rockefellers."

What concerned Chuck most about the 2,750-word *Forbes* article was that it disclosed that he lived in London with his French wife and had five children and had invested in or established dozens of enterprises in Europe, Asia, and the United States through Bermuda-based General Atlantic Group Ltd.

Harvey Dale moved immediately to limit the damage. He asked the Rockefellers for advice on how to handle the publicity. He suggested that Feeney travel under an assumed name and hire a bodyguard. Feeney did not change his daily routine, but he did heed the advice of Cornell alumnus Jules Kroll, who ran a security firm: "If you are looking for a cab and there is one waiting for you, never take that cab, take the next one."

The title "Rich, Ruthless and Determined" referred to Feeney and Miller. *Forbes* described Feeney as highly strung, fast-talking, fast-thinking, frugal, and a frenetic economy-class traveler who was most content at 36,000 feet, and Miller as an extrovert who wore his silvery hair modishly long and favored bespoke suits. It had an account of Feeney appearing one day at a business meeting in London with a pin holding up his trousers.

"He did that because he liked to show he was a common man," recalled Bonnie Suchet, his office manager in London. Feeney saw the humorous side: He sent associates a note with the *Forbes* article attached by a safety pin.

The *Forbes* reporters, Andrew Tanzer and Marc Beauchamp, knew nothing of Feeney's philanthropy, but they clearly had a good inside source in DFS. They described how DFS had forged close links with Japanese tour groups, evolved complex tactics to get them into their downtown shops, and squeezed suppliers to mark up goods by up to 200 percent. They also knew of the Camus relationship. They quoted Desmond Byrne, who had set himself up in Honolulu as an analyst of the duty-free business. The DFS shareholders guessed that Byrne had soured on them because of his mistake in leaving the company; if he had stayed on as accountant, he could have been Alan Parker. Earlier that year, Byrne had sent a letter to the *Honolulu Star-Bulletin* accusing DFS of greed for seeking special government treatment by organizing a golf tournament for Hawaii legislators.

Forbes estimated that DFS sales the previous year had soared to $1.6 billion. They were close to the mark. A confidential internal memo prepared by the DFS finance department that year for the four partners revealed that in the decade before 1988, annual sales had increased from $278 million to $1.543 billion. It was an astonishing growth rate—almost 19 percent per annum. What only the four owners knew was that during that period, they had received cash dividends of $867 million, of which Chuck Feeney had got $334 million.

In the same edition of *Forbes* that listed him as a billionaire, Feeney noted an editorial by Deputy Managing Editor Lawrence Minard, in which he wrote that the only ways to get off the *Forbes* 400 were to (1) lose your money, (2) give it away, or (3) die. Five days later, Feeney wrote a memo to Harvey Dale. "I have come to the following conclusion," he wrote in his slanting backhand. "For personal and family reasons I do not intend to appear on the *Forbes* list next year. *Forbes* has stated the conditions under which one can get off the list. Option (1) is unlikely. Option (3) is undesirable. That leaves Option (2)." The best thing to do would be "to convince *Forbes* to delist for the future and be cooperative with our desire to minimize foundation exposure."

Feeney suggested that a private meeting be arranged with the vice chairman of *Forbes*, James J. Dunn, to advise him about their need to maintain confidentiality.

Dale and Hannon turned to the public relations firm of Fleishman Hillard in New York for professional advice. Senior Vice President Peter McCue told them bluntly, "There is no way for Chuck to be removed quietly from the *Forbes* list." He advised instead that they prepare for a public announcement on their own terms. "We can ill afford to have it misrepresented by a crusading journalist, eager to ascribe sinister or dubious motivations to Chuck, so that we will be forced into defending what should have been praised in the first place," he warned them. After that, they could arrange a private meeting with *Forbes*.

Over the following weeks, Fleishman Hillard produced voluminous assessments of the prospects for getting Chuck dropped from the *Forbes* list. On November 22, Peter McCue submitted a 2,000-word memorandum saying they could give the true story of Chuck's net worth to a rival journal, hold a press conference to reveal the existence of the Atlantic Foundation, or set up a private meeting between Chuck and Malcolm Forbes, proprietor of

Forbes magazine, at which Chuck would offer proof of the error—that he was a billionaire—in exchange for a correction in his magazine. He ruled out the first option as it would humiliate *Forbes* and the magazine might seek to dig up dirt on Feeney to prove it was right: "Rats don't become more lovable by placing them in a corner." A press conference would similarly embarrass *Forbes*, "swiftly, openly and globally all at once." However, by going to Malcolm Forbes himself, Chuck would be giving him a wonderful Christmas present, "the chance to feel truly good about himself by doing the only honorable thing." (Beside this suggestion, Feeney scrawled "Huh!") If Forbes failed to do the "decent thing," they could fall back on options one or two.

The favored option had one flaw. Feeney would not subject himself to an interview with Malcolm Forbes, as he made clear in a comment on the margin.

Chuck Feeney and Harvey Dale had good reason to be apprehensive about public scrutiny of the still-secret foundation. With a fortune estimated by *Forbes* at $1.3 billion—and it was certainly greater—the Atlantic Foundation, if registered in the United States, would be one of the ten largest American charitable institutions, about the same size as the Mellon Foundation and close behind the bellwether $1.6 billion Rockefeller Foundation. Yet as Paul Hannon pointed out in a memo that he sent to Feeney by courier on November 30, 1988, the Atlantic Foundation's annual giving over the previous three years ranged from $10–$20 million, well under 2 percent of its assets, and it had only five employees. By contrast, the Mellon Foundation had distributed nearly $65 million the previous year. This made the Atlantic Foundation look very stingy, or worse.

Forbes might in fact conclude that the Atlantic Foundation was a tax-efficient method for Feeney to retain control of most of his fortune. Why else would he create a secret offshore foundation over which he had retained effective control, not subject to American laws requiring extensive disclosure and a higher rate of annual giving? American law prohibited large investments in related enterprises, but Feeney, through the foundation, could continue to invest in profitable opportunities without restriction, with income from offshore investments flowing into Bermuda free of U.S. tax. *Forbes* might also claim that as a foreign entity, the foundation paid no capital gains tax on sales of U.S. investments, and Feeney could pay himself from the foundation without interference from the IRS.

"Harvey was very draconian about not trying to get exposure, I shared that view, but the problem was that when you come to the point you are not telling people what you are doing, they suspect, they say, 'What's goin' on here? They must be up to something,'" Feeney recalled.

Hannon suggested that even after a visit to Malcolm Forbes, the magazine might still refuse to remove Feeney from its rich list on the grounds that it could not be certain that Feeney had really given his fortune to charity or that he had simply found a clever way to multiply his millions tax free outside of the clutches of the United States—or both.

After months of mulling it over, Chuck Feeney decided to do nothing. They would let *Forbes* and other magazines with rich lists print what they wanted. The existence of the foundations must be kept secret. Everybody must continue stalling reporters. The culture of *omerta* would remain. Even Feeney bound himself to a code of secrecy. As chairman and chief executive of General Atlantic, he signed a formal contract with the group for his salary, which that year was recorded as only $75,000. It contained a clause stating, "You will not disclose any information acquired by you during your employment." So he had legally obliged himself to remain silent.

Staff working closely with Feeney could not help but know his secret. However, said Bonnie Suchet, "the circle was so devoted to Chuck they wouldn't betray him." New senior recruits continued to be put through rigorous procedures. When David Smith was hired as chief financial officer of InterPacific, the Pacific subsidiary of General Atlantic, he was instructed to meet an official from Fleishman Hillard, who told him not to say anything to anybody about anything, and if in doubt to say, "I don't know." "I had many dinners and lunches with Harvey Dale," recalled Smith, "and each time he would impress on me the need to keep things quiet." Smith got adept at handling questions from financiers. "When I needed to go to a bank to secure borrowings for an investment, there were good questions about where the equity was going to come from, and I had to artfully dodge those questions by just saying that it was from a private individual, and he was going to remain so," he said. "The reaction usually was, 'Oh! That's very good. Can we meet him?' I would say, 'No, you can't.' At the end of the day, they just accepted that this person was not going to be revealed, and they were not going to meet him."

Although *Forbes* identified General Atlantic Group Ltd. as the parent company for Feeney's businesses, it did not make a connection with its highly profitable investment subsidiary, General Atlantic Inc., which had established itself in a leafy suburb of Greenwich, Connecticut, as an engine producing liquid assets for Feeney's charitable foundation. (In 1989, it became independent as General Atlantic Partners, but the philanthropy remained its main client.) One of its most profitable ventures was the creation in July 1981 in Denver, Colorado, of the General Atlantic Energy Corporation as an oil exploration company that they sold to the Presidio Oil Company in December 1988 for over $100 million. A New York publisher, Niall O'Dowd, recalled a Texas businessman saying, "You know, they are all talking about this guy Feeney down here. He got in at the bottom, and he sold at the top of the oil market. They're all saying, 'How the fuck does he know to do that? Who is this guy Chuck Feeney anyway?'"

Ed Cohen, the head of Feeney's investment firm, recruited a friend, David Rumsey, a real estate specialist and owner of one of the world's largest collections of old maps, to negotiate property deals for Feeney in New York and San Francisco. "Chuck Feeney is not your usual businessman," Cohen told Rumsey. "He's a philanthropist. You will be doing real estate business but you will also be helping in that." He told Rumsey they needed to invest the flow of cash coming in from DFS in good strong investments and try to get a mix of real estate, oil and gas, "and something they call software." "What's that?" asked Rumsey. "Oh, it's computer stuff," said Cohen.

The "computer stuff" was providing the Atlantic Foundation with some spectacular successes. A $3-million investment in Morino Associates, a high-flying computer software firm later renamed Legent, was parlayed in 1988 after five years into approximately $52 million in marketable securities that could be liquidated tax free.

Rumsey recalled how he, like Smith, had to convince bankers they were not laundering hot money. "I would go to the bank and say, 'We are General Atlantic,' and the banker would say, 'Oh yes! We've heard about you guys. Can you give me your complete statement?' I would reply, 'Well, we can only go so far up the chain because our principal is a very private person. Going up the chain would show this company is worth hundreds of millions in cash.' At this point the banker would roll his eyes and ask, 'What kind of business are you guys in?'" Rumsey always refused to say.

Rumsey negotiated major property purchases in San Francisco, including the eighteen-story JH Dollar Building and the landmark Humboldt Bank Building, and the most ambitious San Francisco investment Feeney got involved in—the development of an 865-apartment complex of one- and two-bedroom apartments and studios on the Embarcadero in the heart of the

South Beach neighborhood known as Bayside Village. The original site was covered in old pipes and abandoned warehouses, and the neighborhood was run down, but Feeney, who loved San Francisco, saw the potential for reviving the area and providing affordable housing within walking distance of the famous Fisherman's Wharf tourist district.

Feeney formed a partnership with ForestCityRatner to build the complex with $12 million in equity and a bond issue of $80 million. When David Rumsey and Steve Albert from ForestCityRatner brought Jack Masterelli of Bankers Trust, from whom they wanted the $80 million loan, to see the site, he said, "You guys must be out of your mind." They convinced Masterelli the investment would work. Then Delancey Street, a foundation that ran rehabilitation centers for victims of poverty and abuse and former gang members, announced it had acquired a 400,000-square-foot space across the Embarcadero from the apartment site. It was run by cofounder Mimi Silbert as "a Harvard for losers." The prospect "freaked out" the banker. Mimi Silbert sent Feeney a message complaining that his partners were "bad-mouthing" the proposed center as a den of drug abusers, whereas "it is more likely that people will be smoking pot in your place than over here, where the rule is one strike and you are out." Delancey Street had in fact a reputation as a self-sufficient rehabilitation center where those who survived got an education or training in marketable skills. This was right up Feeney's street, in every sense.

Mimi Silbert offered to help placate the banker, so Rumsey brought Masterelli to her Pacific Heights headquarters for a dinner. "So we all went over, you know, a bunch of young suits, with Masterelli, and she charmed everybody," he recalled. Masterelli closed the deal. Bayside Village was completed in three phases from 1986 to 1990, to become the biggest apartment development in the southern part of San Francisco. General Atlantic Group retained a small apartment there that Chuck Feeney could use when in town. It became one of his favorite stopping places on his global travels, and he would dine in the restaurant established by the Delancey Street residents.

In 1989, David Smith negotiated the purchase for InterPacific of Western Athletic Clubs, a San Francisco company that would grow to eleven private health, fitness, and athletic resorts along the U.S. West Coast and employ approximately 2,000 people. Western Athletic Clubs became another "cash cow," for Atlantic Foundation, said Smith years later in San Francisco. "It is a dues-based business so the cash flows are steady, unlike the retail stores in Hawaii, where the income fluctuated from season to season.

We paid $37 million, of which I borrowed $30 million: it's probably worth now $300 million." With Feeney's encouragement, the Western Athletic Clubs set high standards for corporate philanthropy, donating 5 percent of all profits to community charities. "They also put on events and sponsor them to raise money for cancer, things like that," said Feeney. "They call it social responsibility."

Having acquired health clubs and an address in Savile Row, Feeney liked to joke, pointing to the girth that stretched his Hawaiian shirt, that he still managed to be out of shape and shabbily dressed.

InterPacific Group under Feeney's guidance also developed Pacific Islands Club Resort hotels as models of high-end holiday destinations in Guam and Saipan and invested in the exclusive Bali Golf and Country Club (the setting for the 1995 Johnny Walker World Classic of golf), and the elegant Laguna Beach Resort spread out over twenty acres in Phuket, Thailand. Paradoxically, for a frugal person uncomfortable with the trappings of wealth, Feeney devoted much effort to providing luxury vacations for wealthy people. He would stay in the five-star hotels when on business, though he displayed his by now well-established frugal habits. John Green, a former manager of Laguna Beach Resort, recalled sitting down once for a strategy session with Chuck and slipping his Montblanc pen out of sight when he saw that Feeney was using a pencil.

Feeney extended his—or Atlantic's—hotel ownership in Texas and Oklahoma, where he bought a number of upscale hotels that were branded under the name "Medallion," and run by Sidney Willner, a former vice chairman of Hilton, and Feeney's associate, Fred Eydt. The star of the Medallion group was the 322-room Seelbach Hotel in Louisville, Kentucky, which was featured in F. Scott Fitzgerald's *The Great Gatsby*. Feeney sometimes attended the Kentucky Derby with his brother-in-law Jim Fitzpatrick, and this was another fine hotel he liked to frequent. The Oklahoma Medallion was located four blocks from the federal building that was blown up on April 17, 1995, when Timothy McVeigh parked his Ryder truck outside with its freight of 5,000 pounds of homemade explosives. Feeney immediately sent word that the hotel, part of which was closed for renovations, was to open its doors and give free rooms to the injured and rescue workers. Staff were also sent from other Medallion hotels to assist.

In London, Feeney was also opportunistically investing in new business ventures. One day at Heathrow Airport he came across a magazine called

Airport, distributed free by Redwood, a London company that published trade magazines. It looked like a good investment, with advertising revenue that would cover the cost of production. He went to a pay phone and called the co-publisher, Christopher Ward, a former *Daily Express* editor, who, he learned right away, was contemplating shutting the magazine down as it was losing money. Feeney abandoned his travel plans, caught a taxi into London, and bought the magazine. But it failed to recover, and he had to write it off. "We were blindsided," he said. "Having agreed to give publishing rights to this magazine, the airport authority started their own." However, he became a major shareholder in Redwood, helping ensure the survival of the company.

At the end of the 1980s, it was evident to anyone following the news—as Feeney avidly did—that there would soon be opportunities for investment in the disintegrating Eastern Bloc of Communist states. After the Velvet Revolution and the overthrow of the Communist government in Prague in November 1989, Feeney flew there to look at the possibility of developing hotels in what was then Czechoslovakia. He checked into the Art Nouveau–style Palace Hotel near Wenceslas Square in January 1990 and got into conversation with the front-office manager, Jiri Vidim, about what was going on in the newly liberated city. For once, Feeney's cheap watch—he was wearing a plastic Casio—made an impression. "It was a luxury product to us," recalled Vidim, "everyone wanted a Rolex or a Casio!" The Czech hotelier took Feeney around the snow-covered streets, but every hotel was still state-owned and nothing was for sale. Feeney saw, however, that the Czechs were hungry for Western things, just as the Japanese once had a pent-up appetite for luxury goods and spirits. He gave Vidim funds to create a joint venture company with General Atlantic and sent Jim Downey and an Irish colleague, Martin Kinirons, to set up shop in Prague. They refurbished a hairdressing salon in a house off Lesser Town Square, called it New Age Shoppers, and stocked it with TV sets, record players, electronics, watches, jewelry, ties, and cosmetics brought in a forty-foot trailer from Dublin. The shop was besieged when it opened on December 18, 1990, and it took less than sixty seconds to sell the first watch. Two more New Age Shoppers stores followed shortly afterward, but the venture lasted only four years. It was not the duty-free story all over again. Eastern Europeans lacked the hard-currency savings that the Japanese had accumulated. But Feeney was a pioneer. He was the first businessman to open a Western shop in post-Communist Prague.

With his Catholic, Irish American background, Feeney was most pleased, however, that he was able to help rehabilitate an order of nuns struggling to survive in Prague after the fall of communism. In 1950, the Gray Sisters of the Third Order of St. Franciscus, who traditionally looked after the sick, had been ousted by the secret police from their five Prague convents, including a monastery at 9 Bartolomejaska Street in the heart of the historic old city. The Communist government had converted this convent into an interrogation center known as Ruzyne Prison. Its most notable inmate had been Vaclav Havel. After the Velvet Revolution, the 150 surviving nuns were able to return to their convents but many were elderly, and they had no money for renovations.

Chuck Feeney and Jiri Vidim came up with a plan. They traveled to see the seventy-eight-year-old mother superior of the order in Lomec, deep in the pine forests of southern Czechoslovakia, to broker a deal whereby Vidim and a partner would acquire the monastery from the nuns and convert it into an eighty-room budget hotel named the Cloister Inn, with special cloisters set apart for the nuns on the top floor. As an added tourist attraction, guests could stay in Cell No. 6 down below, where Havel had been incarcerated. General Atlantic provided a letter of credit for $800,000 drawn on Chase Manhattan Bank to finance the renovations.

The nuns were delighted with the arrangement and were profuse in their thanks to Chuck Feeney. "They pray for him every day," said Jiri Vidim.

CHAPTER

The Wise Man Cometh

While Chuck Feeney was exploring new ventures in post-Communist Europe, his partners in DFS were ganging up on him. On May 12, 1990, Bob Miller, Alan Parker, and Tony Pilaro filed into the office of the international law firm Allen & Overy, at 40 Bank Street in London, for an extraordinary directors' meeting of DFS. Chuck Feeney was not there. He had long since stopped attending regular DFS board meetings. In his place were George Parker and legal counsel Paul Hannon, and it was they who took their seats around the conference table at the law firm.

There was no small talk. The principals and the lawyers read from scripted legal documents. Miller put on a large pair of spectacles, and, as he recalled, "read the riot act." After thirty minutes, the three shareholders voted to throw Feeney's representatives off the board that managed and controlled DFS's retail activities. They believed they had the legal power to do so. As Tony Pilaro put it, the will of the majority "can and does control."

George Parker and Paul Hannon furiously gathered up their papers and left the room. "It was a searing experience," said Hannon. Chuck Feeney, cofounder, visionary, and owner (through his foundation) of 38.75 percent of DFS, no longer had a voice in the governance of the company.

The four guys in a room had never really been four buddies in a room, but now they were embroiled in a dispute that threatened to break up the partnership. Alan Parker, the least excitable and the most high-minded of the three shareholders, had orchestrated the ousting of Feeney's representatives from the board. It was the culmination of a campaign he and the other two had waged to get Chuck Feeney to stop his independent retail activities in Hawaii, which the co-owners maintained was competing for the same tourist dollars as DFS, and was therefore unethical competition.

"It was awful," said Alan Parker. "I felt very badly about doing this. Chuck was the visionary, the brains behind it, and there we were throwing him off."

The dispute had its origins in Feeney's purchase in 1976 of Andrade, the retail chain in Hawaii that sold ready-to-wear clothes and casual gear such as aloha shirts and muumuus, popular items with tourists. Three years later Feeney had opened a big Andrade store in a new shopping center in the heart of Waikiki, just across the road from the DFS Galleria. In 1985, Feeney acquired three other Hawaiian clothing stores called Carol & Mary and four Honolulu fashion shops purchased from the Japanese trading group Seibu, which he figured "were losing their asses running it." These stores, trading under the name of their Irish immigrant founder, Patrick Michael McInerny, had traditionally provided garments for Honolulu's kings and high-society shoppers. One of the McInerny stores was located at the Royal Hawaiian Shopping Center in Waikiki, only two blocks from the DFS downtown mall. InterPacific, through which the purchases were made, had by 1990 become the second-biggest retailer in Hawaii, after DFS. Grouped together as the Hawaiian Retail Group, it had 600 employees and also held leases in the Royal Hawaiian Shopping Center, which catered to tourists. "Once they got into the Royal Hawaiian, I think that created the issue," said Tony Pilaro. "If the customer is a Japanese who has $100, and you are after that, and we are after that, we are in competition."

Feeney reckoned that he had also gotten up his partners' noses with his 1978 purchase of the 800-room hotel in Guam, where everyone was chasing the Japanese customer. The disagreement had been exacerbated after Feeney hired Paul Slawson, former chairman of the American University in Paris, to run InterPacific, in 1986. Slawson adopted a more aggressive approach to raking in tourist dollars in Waikiki, and Feeney didn't rein him in. Always immaculately dressed and exuding a sense of corporate leadership, Slawson for a time represented Feeney on the DFS board, where his attitude grated on the mild-mannered Alan Parker like sandpaper. "He made himself persona non grata [with DFS directors] because he was clearly competing with them," said Paul Hannon.

Things got so tense that in mid-1988, Paul Hannon initiated discussions with William Norris, a lawyer representing the other three DFS owners, to see if they could resolve the problem. In five months of meetings they got nowhere. Feeney was clearly not going to budge. In January 1989, the co-owners engaged Mark Kaplan, a lawyer from the Skadden, Arps, Slate, Meagher & Flom law firm in New York who had formerly been Tony Pilaro's designated representative on the DFS board and who had a reputation as a rainmaker, to act as intermediary. Kaplan made a swing through Europe, canvassed the views of the three co-owners, and presented their concerns to Feeney through Hannon. He came up with a series of recommendations, but they were never acceptable to all the parties. Miller thought they were "too legalistic."

Parker believed Feeney saw no problem with what he was doing. "The bottom line was that Chuck saw himself making a greater contribution to DFS than anyone else. Therefore he could do on the side whatever he wanted to do. I saw it as morally wrong. Chuck never saw it that way." He also maintained that Feeney's retail business "was increasingly concentrating on selling to Japanese tourists and obtaining supplies from existing or potential DFS suppliers," and he was concerned that Feeney was using his "DFS hat" in dealings with suppliers to gain favorable price terms for his businesses. Feeney said this was simply not true. His retail business was 90 percent for the local and not the Japanese tourist market, and they never advertised for Japanese customers.

Bob Miller didn't see Feeney's actions as unethical or immoral. He saw the situation as "a sort of ego" play between himself and Feeney, of which Andrade was the manifestation. Why else would he want to compete when he was making 100 times more money out of DFS, he wondered. They all knew Andrade wasn't making any real money. When Feeney set up Andrade "right in our front yard in Hawaii," Miller said he told him, "You can't do this, Chuck. For Christ's sake, there are plenty of opportunities where you can invest your money on a noncompetitive basis. Why do you want to crawl up our backside?" But he reckoned he knew the answer. "I always figured that deep down beneath the surface he sort of resented the fact that he didn't own more shares of the company [DFS]. This is my own personal opinion."

Some of Feeney's friends were also critical. "You don't open another store in competition, chasing the same money," said Jean Gentzbourger. "I think basically that is not a fair way of doing business. I wouldn't do it. Chuck should have stopped."

The huge bid of $1.151 billion for the Hawaii concession in 1988 had worsened relations. Parker was "outraged" by having Chuck compete with DFS at this time in Honolulu, Pilaro said.

Adrian Bellamy, who was running DFS for the owners, thought it was a storm in a teacup. He didn't think Andrade was taking money out of their pocket, though it was "pissing in your soup to some degree." He believed Feeney did it because it was what he liked doing. "He has always done various things. Andrade came along and he bought into it. He was fascinated by it." The truth was, Andrade never made any money, except from Ferragamo shoes, said Mike Windsor, who ran InterPacific before Slawson took over, and many of their stores were on the other Hawaiian islands where there was no DFS presence.

Feeney himself was dismissive of their concerns. "There was a period when Bob was living in London, a bid came up for an airport, and Bob and Jean Gentzbourger bid for it themselves outside of DFS. They wanted to operate the concession. Nobody ever bitched about that. That was fair game," he said.

Looking back, Paul Hannon argued that Feeney's business activities were in no way improper. There was no agreement among the DFS shareholders preventing it, and other shareholders had pursued similar private retail operations in the past, he maintained. Moreover, Feeney's Hawaiian retail stores were never important operations and they never made money. His assessment was that Alan Parker genuinely believed that what Chuck was doing was morally wrong, that Miller just saw another opportunity to "get at Chuck," and that Tony didn't really care but that he tried hard to resolve it, as it gave him some control of a major issue among the "big boys."

On the basis of advice from his lawyers that they had a legal right to oust Feeney's representatives from the DFS board, Parker had organized the extraordinary meeting at the Allen & Overy office in London.

"Finally they kicked us off the board," said Hannon. "They thought that would pressure Chuck. It certainly pressured George and me. But Chuck said he didn't believe we were doing anything important on the board anyway. That was sort of insulting to me," he added, laughing. "But there was no pressure at all on Chuck. He couldn't care less."

But he did care. Chuck was very upset by the charge voiced by Miller at the meeting in Allen & Overy that he was "usurping DFS's corporate opportunities to earn profits outside of DFS." "Chuck's view was that the businesses were quite different, and there was no problem, so he didn't agree with Alan," recalled Harvey Dale. "In hindsight it might have been more prudent not to do that [open stores next door to DFS in Hawaii] but the stores were selling things that weren't any important part of DFS business. I can understand why he did it. Remember that of the various passions that moved Chuck, this entrepreneurial thing is embedded in the bone marrow. It's very strong, so he saw an opportunity and he wasn't reflecting on whether it would be provocative or otherwise. It probably never even entered his mind. He thought this is a good thing to do, let's go and do it."

Throwing Chuck's representatives off the board "was a huge overreaction and we obviously couldn't tolerate that," continued Dale. "We were prepared to take legal action and consulted counsel in various countries of the world. We had meeting after meeting after meeting internally to talk about what to do." Litigation would have blown anonymity, "but we were at an impasse and eyeball-to-eyeball and on the cusp of litigation with all of its risks."

Saddam Hussein became the catalyst for resolving the dispute. On August 2, 1990, more than 100,000 Iraqi soldiers backed up by 700 tanks invaded Kuwait in the early hours of the morning. The Iraqi dictator threatened to turn Kuwait City into a "graveyard" if any country dared to challenge him. President George H.W. Bush condemned the attack as "a naked act of aggression." War involving the United States was inevitable. The alarm bells rang throughout DFS. A war would send world tourism into a sharp decline—and with it DFS dividends. Feeney was in Dublin that day and he was told the news by John Healy, whom he met early in the morning. "His face turned absolutely white and he turned around and ran up the stairs and he didn't emerge from the apartment for the rest of the day," said Healy. "He was glued to the television. He spotted immediately the implications of that great event for international travel and particularly the traveling habits of wealthy Japanese tourists and therefore their propensity to buy duty-free goods."

On August 9, George Parker, who maintained good relations with all the owners despite being one of Feeney's close business associates, flew to San Francisco, where he knew Bob Miller was attending a DFS board meeting to discuss the crisis. He waylaid Miller in the lobby of the Park Hyatt Hotel. "Look, this is stupid," he told Miller over a drink in the lobby bar. "We've got to solve this problem. Business is tanking. Let's meet without the lawyers and establish the ground rules on how we all work together." Miller agreed it was worth a try. "We wanted to protect the integrity of the company and not to have a shareholders' dispute that would tear DFS to shreds; it was too valuable an asset to play games with," he recalled. Eight days later, George Parker sent a message to Miller to say Chuck had agreed. Tony Pilaro and Alan Parker fell into line. They all had bigger problems now. DFS cash registers were falling silent. Daily sales counts by the regional DFS president in Hawaii, John Reed, showed that takings in some weeks were down by 50 percent. "We were paying a million dollars a day in concession fees and we had no revenue, nothing coming in the door," recalled Alan Parker.

Miller had acquired a big yacht, and he took George Parker for a sail around the Cape of Good Hope. Feeney's associate came back from the trip believing he had found a way out of the impasse. The proposed solution was arbitration rather than litigation. A "Wise Man" would be appointed to resolve the retail argument and future disputes. "We went back and forth, and George and I worked on it, and we finally got Chuck to agree to it," said Hannon. On Wednesday, February 20, 1991, three days before the U.S.-led coalition forces began their ground offensive against Iraqi troops in Kuwait, the four DFS owners signed what became known as the Wise Man Agreement. "Then we were put back on the board," said Hannon.

Under the Wise Man Agreement, Feeney agreed to sell General Atlantic's Hawaiian Retail Group to an unrelated third party by January 31, 1993. No shareholder would operate any retailing whatsoever in certain "dome" areas, including Hawaii and Guam. The owners would in no case invest in or develop any business interests that would directly and materially compete with either DFS or other DFS interests. They agreed on limitations to doing business with DFS suppliers. All shareholders were prohibited from operating on a worldwide basis any retail business aimed at Asian tourists. All disputes would be resolved by arbitration by the Wise Man. The agreement also mollified Miller by labeling the shareholdings A, B, C, and D. Bob got the A shares, Chuck the B shares, Alan the C shares, and Tony the D shares. Their value stayed the same. His co-owners suspected that Feeney had little intention of selling the Hawaiian Retail Group and would stubbornly hold out as long as he could. Events would prove them right. When challenged about obduracy in his character, he said, "I prefer another word—tenacity."

Tony Pilaro found the Wise Man in the figure of Ira M. Millstein, one of New York's most prominent lawyers. A $500-an-hour senior partner in the prestigious New York law firm Weil, Gotshal & Manges, the then sixty-four-year-old arbitrator with glasses and receding white hair had been called to counsel high-profile boards such as General Motors, Westinghouse, and Walt Disney on issues of corporate governance. He had negotiated the bankruptcy settlement of corporate raiders Drexel Burnham Lambert. Millstein had a peripheral association with DFS going back ten years. Now he sat the four partners down and, as Pilaro recalled it, told them, "You jerks! You have got the greatest thing going. Come on! You have got to get together and find a method of resolving disputes."

Because of the disruption to travel caused by the Gulf War, dividends for the four DFS shareholders plummeted to a mere $12 million in 1991, compared to an average of $272 million a year over the previous four years. DFS had to negotiate with the Hawaiian authorities to defer $103 million in concession payments for two years.

With the fall in DFS sales, Feeney's rating in the *Forbes* rich list went down—from $1.9 billion in 1991 to $0.9 billion in 1992. Chuck Rolles had dinner with him in New York on the day the magazine came out with the new list. As they left the restaurant to return to the Cornell Club located twenty-four blocks away, he turned to Feeney and said, "Do you want to walk or take a cab?" "Well," said Chuck. "*Forbes* just said I lost a billion in the past year so we'd better walk." Which is what they did. In fact, in 1991 Feeney was personally worth less than $1 million, according to an audit by his accountants at Price Waterhouse.

The downturn in the duty-free business was a huge setback for the Atlantic Foundation, which had made charitable pledges it could not now meet. These were legally unenforceable, because of the structure put into place in Bermuda, but they were "morally enforceable," said Harvey Dale. This caused "severe distress to those donees and to us." Dale found it "personally very painful" to inform Cornell president Frank Rhodes that they had hit a big bump and were not going to be able to make their commitment that year. With DFS in the doldrums, General Atlantic Group had to secure a $60-million line of credit from Hanover Trust to guarantee cash commitments. More liquidity was found in 1991 when Feeney sold the Pacific Island Club Hotel in Guam to a Japanese company for $200 million; he had bought it for $80 million.

The tourist trade quickly recovered after the Gulf War, but the crisis, and the split among the DFS owners, reinforced an idea that Feeney had been mulling over for some years. The time was coming to sell Atlantic Foundation's share in the duty-free business. The possibility of selling or going public had arisen before but never in a serious way. There had also been some discussions about splitting the company, with Bob taking Asia and Chuck taking the United States and Guam, but they had come to nothing.

Feeney's emotional ties to the company he had cofounded were also fraying. He was getting complaints about how the company ethos was changing for the worse as it expanded into a huge multinational. One senior executive wrote to Feeney in 1989 warning that the moral fiber of DFS had been corrupted. The owners had never asked DFS executives to do anything contrary to moral standards, and "we all sleep well at night," he wrote, but now it had become like any other business, "insensitive, selfish and greedy."

Feeney asked Paul Hannon to draw up a list of public and private entities with large enough cash reserves to buy DFS. Hannon identified twenty-four cash-rich companies and individuals worldwide that could put up the estimated $2 billion needed, ranging from American Express to the sultan of Brunei, but it was clear to Feeney that in reality only a very few companies, like Louis Vuitton Moët Hennessy (LVMH), the world leader in luxury goods, based in Paris, were capable of buying and operating a giant retail operation stretched across the globe such as DFS.

CHAPTER 19

Stepping Down

By 1991, the Atlantic Foundation and the Atlantic Trust had in secrecy made a total of $122 million in gifts over seven years. This spending was far below the 5 percent of assets required of American charities, but Feeney's operation was unique in that it was top-heavy with businesses and properties, and only a small percentage of assets was in liquid form. Feeney was, however, keen to increase giving substantially. He was approaching sixty years old and wished to get more involved in putting the foundation money to good use. He decided the time had come to think about stepping down as chief executive of General Atlantic Group and devoting himself full time to philanthropy. When he mentioned this to Paul Hannon, his counsel asked, "Do you think you will enjoy that more?" "No," he replied. "It's much harder work because of the people you deal with and because there's no bottom line, but that's what I want to do."

He still desired to do everything anonymously. *Forbes* reporter Paul Klebnikov had been trying to ferret out more information to update the rich list. If anything leaked about the foundation's obsessive secrecy and low level of giving, it could raise suspicions that it was up to no good. A new set of instructions to staff on dealing with the media was circulated by Harvey Dale and Paul Hannon in March 1991. Headed "When the News Media Call," it gave several recommended responses to reporters' questions, starting with "Can I help you?" and ending with "Come on, we're a private company, and we simply don't give out that sort of information to the press. I've got to go. Good-bye!"

In early July 1991, Harvey Dale became alarmed when an unidentified woman phoned his secretary and asked how to contact "Harvey Dale of Exeter." Exeter was the name of an unlisted entity known only to Atlantic insiders that had been used to facilitate the purchase of the foundation's assets from Danielle in 1984. Worried that an exposure was being planned by a media organization, Dale contacted Chuck, who was in London, and suggested that despite their reluctance they should speed up preparations for a controlled "unveiling" and start preparing a press release. Paul Hannon warned in a separate communication, "Our complicated, byzantine tax-efficient structure is a negative, and we should be prepared to answer questions in this regard when we go public."

Several copies of an announcement were drafted in July and August 1991, disclosing the existence of the foundation and the fact that Feeney didn't own it but was planning to administer it full time. One version dated July 22 included a comment from Feeney that his goal was to stimulate the interest of wealthy people in "giving while living," but "I couldn't do that while continuing to be known as a reclusive billionaire with no philanthropic interests." Most drafts included French philosopher Blaise Pascal's observation that "noble deeds that are concealed are most esteemed" and American financier Bernard Baruch's remark that "there's no limit to what you can accomplish if you don't care who gets the credit."

The following month, however, Chuck Feeney decided once again to do nothing. He would allow the misperception that he was "wealthy" to persist to preserve the anonymity of the charity. In any case, it was definitely not a good time for him to face a media firestorm.

In October 1990, Chuck and Danielle had separated over his close relationship with his longtime German assistant Helga Flaiz, who often traveled with him. The separation was a shock to everyone, but not a huge surprise. It was evident that Chuck and Danielle had grown apart during the 1980s. Friends described them as a mismatch in their later years together. They had been leading increasingly separate and different lives, and Danielle had known for some time from her husband's depressed and angry moods at home that her relationship with him was over. Feeney had been spending less and less time at the family houses, and he made a point of never going on board the yacht that Danielle bought. Nor did he set foot in the once run-down family home at Saint-Jean-Cap-Ferrat on the French Riviera after Danielle finally transformed it into an elegant mansion.

The children were immensely saddened by the split. They were close to both parents. The contrast between their mother and father was nevertheless obvious to them. "He had become a frugal, self-flagellating philanthropist who craved anonymity, whereas Danielle had a big yacht and a big personality," said a family intimate.

Feeney told his children—now all young adults—that he would be changing his life, that he would be constantly on the road, living only a few weeks at most in any one place at any one time. He gave each a binder with articles explaining what motivated his giving. One was Carnegie's essay on wealth. Another was about the excesses of the sultan of Brunei, who spent $1 million on a child's birthday. They were his singular way of telling them about himself and his motivations.

The legal aspects of the separation put the future of the foundation in question. Danielle's lawyer, Milton Gould of Shea & Gould, challenged the finality of the 1984 settlement and sought an increase in the compensation for the assets that Danielle had signed over to the Atlantic Foundation and for which she had received $40 million. A new settlement was reached that gave Danielle an additional $60 million from the foundation—the total available in liquid form in the businesses it held at that time, and $40 million more was pledged over five years to a family charitable foundation. Feeney insisted that Danielle get all the family homes, in Paris, London, the south of France, Connecticut, Hawaii, and New York. He wanted them to stay in the family to avoid any bitterness, he said. He took nothing himself from the family property. "Chuck was aghast at the notion that he had a legal right to ask anything of Danielle," said Harvey Dale. In 1995, after a divorce with Danielle was finalized on the basis of two years' separation, Feeney married Helga Flaiz at a small private ceremony in Bermuda.

While this was happening, Feeney was beset by a family tragedy. His sister Arlene's son, James (Jimmy) Fitzpatrick, was diagnosed with terminal cancer. Feeney used every contact in the medical field to get the best treatment for his nephew. But even the specialists from the Cornell medical faculty to whom Feeney appealed for help could offer little hope. The provost for medical affairs, G. Tom Shires, told Feeney to expect the worst. Years later, Feeney could recall his exact words: "Your nephew has got a tall mountain to climb. Do you understand what I am saying?"

His nephew's illness cast a pall over Feeney's life and work. Jimmy was like a son to him, and he had a lot of his uncle's qualities. A graduate of

American University in Washington, he would often stay with Chuck and go jogging with him. One Christmas in San Francisco, Jimmy was hit by an out-of-control fire truck while standing at a bus stop and was seriously injured, and Feeney flew immediately from Honolulu to make sure he got the best hospital treatment in San Francisco. Afterward, he took him to Hawaii to recuperate and gave him a job overseeing the rebuilding of the hotel owned by InterPacific in Guam. Feeney even got involved in Jimmy's personal life, once taking a flight to—successfully—talk him out of marrying a girlfriend he thought unsuitable.

As Jimmy's condition worsened, Feeney gave up much of his world travel to spend time with him. His nephew died in March 1992. Over the years, the untimely death of people he loved made Feeney abnormally sad and depressed, and he found it particularly hard to accept the injustice of it, said a family member. "He was hit very hard by Jimmy's death," recalled Patrick. "My Dad loved his nieces and nephews almost as much as his own kids." As always, unwilling to express his deepest-felt emotions directly, Feeney wrote a moving script that he and Caroleen read at the requiem mass on March 9, 1992, at St. Genevieve's Roman Catholic Church in Elizabeth, in which he played the role of advocate for Jimmy to enter heaven.

"No matter how much money you have, you can't solve the health issues of those you love," reflected Feeney years later. "Here was Jimmy, and I was giving everything I own to try to solve his problem but it wasn't for solving." The tragedy reinforced his determination to focus the Atlantic Foundation on medical and biomedical research in future years.

For the first time in his meteoric business career, said a friend, Chuck "took his eye off the ball." Feeney stood down as chief executive of General Atlantic Group and appointed Paul Slawson to take over. As head of InterPacific, Slawson had been involved in the purchase of Western Athletic Clubs and the development of the Pacific Islands Clubs, and had invested in such sidelines as the market for diapers in Taiwan and in Pizza Huts in Thailand and Beijing. Feeney believed he could bring similar intuition and skills to the management of General Atlantic Group as a whole.

Paul Slawson moved to London to assume his new responsibilities in October 1991. When he called everyone together in Savile Row and asked them what they were interested in, Chris Oechsli, a brilliant young American lawyer hired as assistant counsel to General Atlantic by Paul Hannon, responded, "If there is an opportunity to do more operations I would be glad to do that." Oechsli had extensive travel experience—he was born in Costa Rica and studied Mandarin in China—and had already been peripherally involved in some of Chuck's East European operations.

The next day Slawson called Oechsli into his office and said, "I noticed your interest in operations. I am going to put you in charge of an operation—moving our offices!" Slawson didn't like "funky" buildings and set out to "modernize" General Atlantic. He moved company headquarters to a new office block at 25 Grosvenor Street. The building was contemporary in style, with curved walls and modern art. Slawson installed a £10,000 mock-medieval table in the conference room. "It had the perspective of an international corporate office, unlike the rabbit warren in Savile Row of familial types that kind of pottered about," said Oechsli. "There was a new ethic—from the expenditure to the aesthetics to the gravitas of the people." Feeney kept his own private office in Savile Row and stayed away from Grosvenor Street, where Slawson installed a team of three Americans from the financial world to help run the show.

Slawson began employing highly paid consultants and getting involved in a round of black-tie dinners and receptions. An associate recalled that his team was "very top-heavy, with no expense spared in their offices, their furniture, their decoration or their staff numbers." The Slawson operation became, Oechsli thought, "very un-Chuck-like" with too much bureaucracy.

Slawson moved to repeat the success of Western Athletic Clubs by initiating the purchase of Cannon's Health and Fitness club in London. Located under the viaduct at Cannon Street Railway Station with a swimming pool and squash courts, it was patronized by London's smart set and city types. Its board chairman was an old Etonian, Sir James Harvie-Watt, who was also chairman of the exclusive Queen's Tennis Club in London. Cannon's had a second sports center in Covent Garden and a country club outside London.

The sports club was run by the Australian sporting legend Ron Clarke, then fifty-three, who set nineteen world track records for running in the 1960s and lit the flame at the Melbourne Olympics in 1956. Feeney called Clarke and told him he would come by at about 8:00 AM the next day for a look around before the purchase went through.

"I thought I would have time to have my usual early morning workout before he arrived," recalled Clarke. "Unfortunately he arrived about 7:00 AM and, as he wanted the meeting to be low key, I hadn't told any staff to look out for him. We had a strict ruling that nobody, but nobody, got into the club past the turnstiles without a membership card. By the time I had my shower and was in the office, Chuck had already been waiting an hour. When the girls phoned up to say there was an American gentleman in the foyer who had been waiting for me for so long, I almost died. I thought he would be spitting chips. I was a fan for life when, instead of being angry for being kept waiting, he complimented the girls for being so vigilant, said they had done absolutely the right thing, and was not put out at all." Clarke found Feeney to be "unlike any businessman I had ever met in that he seemed to have little interest in clothes or creating an impression. And when he asked a question, he listened to the answer." Feeney liked what he saw that morning, and General Atlantic Group purchased Cannon's.

After a year, Chris Oechsli wrote a memo to Feeney saying that he didn't feel the new people were acting in his best interest and he was planning to move on. Feeney asked him to stay put. "We're looking into some of this. It doesn't seem right," he agreed. Oechsli stayed and was promoted to general counsel in place of Paul Hannon, who left General Atlantic to become an international industrial arbiter.

Feeney went on a trip around the world and found that there was a lot of discontent throughout the ranks of the companies he had created, General Atlantic Group and its subsidiary, InterPacific. His faith in Slawson unraveled. On his return to London in early summer 1993, he had a list of names written on a legal pad of those people who had left the organization in the previous few months. "I could see the disruption he was causing," recalled Feeney, who measured things in human terms. Harvey Dale concluded in an internal report that overheads had become excessive, major strategic errors had occurred, and morale of staff had suffered. In June, Feeney asked Slawson to stand down, after only two years in the job. He hated confrontation and found the episode upsetting—and expensive, as it involved large compensation payments. Feeney once more took over the running of General Atlantic Group and moved the headquarters back to Savile Row.

After the changeover, Feeney found that one of Cannon's English directors had been paid £12,500 a year for his services before the club was acquired by General Atlantic, but that after the purchase, this had been increased to £12,500 a *month*. It turned out that he had been told in a letter after Slawson took over Cannon's that he would continue as director and be paid the sum of £12,500 *"payable monthly,"* said Chris Oechsli, whereas it should have been *"annually, payable monthly."* Feeney called in the director after Slawson had gone and asked what he was thinking of when he got the letter. The director replied that American firms were known to pay a lot more and he assumed that was the new arrangement. "Chuck didn't buy that, and that was the end of his role," said Oechsli.

Feeney admired people with athletic dedication, and he was impressed by Clarke and his sporting connections. The former runner invited him to a black-tie event in the Grosvenor House Hotel in London on May 6, 1994, to celebrate the fortieth anniversary of Roger Bannister's beating the four-minute mile. Feeney, wearing a dark suit and blue tie, was seated next to Ireland's 1956 gold-medal winner Ron Delaney, at Ron Clarke's table. There was a stellar lineup of the world's great runners, including Chris Chataway, Chris Brasher, John Landy, Herb Elliott, and Sebastian Coe. Roger Bannister, who had become Master of Pembroke College at Oxford, greeted Feeney warmly as the party was breaking up. They had lunched previously at the Athenaeum Club in London, and Chuck had arranged to make donations to Oxford University. Feeney had been to almost every Olympics since Tokyo in 1964 and had seen many of these runners in action. It was a big occasion for Feeney and marked an increasingly close association with Ron Clarke that would continue in Australia some years later.

CHAPTER 20

Show Me the Building

As part of his long-term plan to devote himself more to his philanthropy, Chuck Feeney purchased a building on Molesworth Street in the center of Dublin in 1989, which he named Atlantic House. He recruited John Healy, the director general of the American Ireland Partnership, to set up and run the operation, to be called Tara Consultants. Healy recalled being invited to meet Feeney in London, where he had a "typically meandering, obscure conversation" with Chuck in the course of which he inferred he was being offered some sort of a job in a consulting company. Knowing by then that Feeney was no ordinary American businessman, he had accepted.

Only when he said yes and traveled to New York for a briefing from his new boss, Harvey Dale, did the Irishman learn that he would be working for one of the world's biggest and most secret philanthropic foundations. The lawyer told him that the Atlantic Foundation and the Atlantic Trust were set up so that the money flowed through different "spigots"—a word for "water taps" not used in Ireland—but Healy guessed the meaning. Dale told him that Feeney was about to step up his philanthropy in Ireland, and Chuck had singled him out for his knowledge and contacts. As managing director of Tara Consultants, he would also have responsibility for enforcing a set of rules: Feeney's name should never appear on any press release or on any plaque; he should not be offered, nor would he accept, any honorary degree; and funding would cease if confidentiality was breached. Healy flew on to Ithaca and was briefed by Ray Handlan on how the Foundation Service

Company worked. He learned the scale of the grant making and about Atlantic Foundation's unique combination of convertible and nonconvertible assets, known as "church" and "state."

"At that stage we were deep into confidentiality," explained Feeney. "We would say, 'We want to do this thing but we don't want any credits for it—just give the impression that you raised the money.'" If beneficiaries wanted his attention, he said, all they had to do was to show him the completed building.

The success of his philanthropy at Limerick University inspired Feeney to look at the condition of the other half dozen universities in Ireland, which were all state-funded and lacking capital to expand and modernize. His ambitions for the then-struggling country were growing. Lifting one boat would make little difference to Ireland's higher-education sector as a whole. Helping a number would make a national impact. He set about arranging seemingly accidental meetings with other university presidents across the country, hoping to find the same drive and vision as in Limerick. His opportunistic philanthropy would be most successful if he found the right people to use the funds well. It was not the philanthropist that deserved praise, he believed, but those who had the position, the ability, and the vision to do good things with the funds. He could use the talents that had made him wealthy to identify and help develop worthwhile projects. But so much depended on the personality and drive of those involved to put the money to good use. "When it came down to it, it's always people," he would often say.

His approach to Daniel O'Hare, head of the fledgling Dublin City University, was typically indirect. O'Hare was invited to the annual dinner in Dublin of the peace organization Cooperation North and found himself seated beside "this small American man." Padraig Berry was there, shooing away a photographer. With glass of white wine in hand, Chuck asked O'Hare about university projects for which he needed funding. O'Hare mentioned that he needed IR£1 million for a research building. "If I had only known who I was talking to!" he recalled years later with a laugh. "Would you mind writing up a little piece, and giving it to Padraig Berry," said Feeney, who explained that he might know some people who could help. Berry came to see the Dublin City University president at his office shortly afterward to get the proposal and emphasized the need for secrecy. O'Hare started to think, "Is this funny money? Is it honest money? Oh God, this might be money laundered." He called a friend in an Irish bank with U.S. branches and asked him, "Who is this Chuck Feeney?" The friend called back: "Blue chip!"

Harvey Dale, described only as a friend of Chuck's, then invited O'Hare to visit his New York home when on a trip to the United States. There Dale casually remarked, "We are pleased to help you with your project." From this O'Hare surmised that Dale had a big role in Feeney's operation. O'Hare found the lawyer to be "a frighteningly bright guy who seemed to know everything about everything, very aggressive, very tough-minded, very strong on anonymity." Later, when he asked Harvey Dale whether he would lose $10 million pledged by Atlantic if he didn't get government matching funds, "he looked me in the eye and said, 'You will definitely lose the money,' and the hairs on the back of my neck stood up."

Feeney was taken with O'Hare and became a regular visitor to Dublin City University. The money started to flow in, just as in Limerick, for new buildings and facilities. "Chuck had a particular affection for the underdog, and we were the new kids on the block," said O'Hare, who was extremely conscientious about concealing the source of funding as demanded by the Atlantic Foundation. He once asked his architect, Barry Kehoe, to show a "visiting American" his plans for a sports complex that Atlantic was funding. Feeney examined the blueprint and said, "You could move that from here to here. . . ." Kehoe interrupted, "Oh no, you couldn't." O'Hare kicked him under the table, and the architect took the hint. Afterward, O'Hare told Kehoe in confidence who Chuck Feeney was. "Barry was a former priest, so he was used to the confessional and kept the secret," he recalled gleefully.

Feeney was also impressed with Tom Mitchell, the provost (president) of Trinity College, the oldest university in Ireland, set in the heart of Dublin. John Healy brought Feeney to lunch with Mitchell in September 1991. "All I knew was that he was wealthy, but he was very, very different from any of the really rich American businesspeople I had met," recalled Mitchell. "He was quite reserved and initially shy, and in appearance and the way he talked he bore little resemblance to the stereotype of an Irish American business-man." Although Feeney had been funding Limerick University for four years at this time, the secret of his foundation hadn't leaked out, and Mitchell had no idea how important Feeney could be.

"The thing that stands out from that lunch," recalled Mitchell, "was that he kept saying, 'You have to think big! Don't be afraid to think big.' That never left my mind because the task facing Trinity and Irish universities was very big and the resources to do it were small. You know how dark an era the 1980s was. There was no investment in anything that wasn't desperately needed. Trinity was bursting at the seams. The labs were inadequate and overcrowded. The library was outdated. Classrooms were overcrowded. As an institution we could not aspire to international caliber."

Feeney became personally involved in modernizing the university. "All the things I wanted to do got a major start from Atlantic funding," said Mitchell, but not of course before Harvey Dale appeared on the scene with his dire warnings about confidentiality. Trinity College Dublin got scores of millions of dollars in funding for a student village, a revamped library, and other capital projects and research programs.

Eventually all seven universities in the Republic of Ireland and the two in Northern Ireland received substantial funding from Atlantic, totaling hundreds of millions of dollars. Feeney did not get what he called "good vibes" from all Irish university leaders, but he reached a point where it would have been invidious to discriminate. Universities in Ireland were elevated, in extraordinary secrecy, without even the top education department officials knowing who was behind it, from Second World to First World level over a period of a few years, primarily through Chuck Feeney's intervention. The Irish higher-education system was subsequently better placed to provide graduates and researchers for the emerging Celtic Tiger economy of the late 1990s.

As time passed, the individual university heads began to realize they were all benefiting from one big "anonymous donor" and that the man behind the philanthropy funding rival universities was most likely their own secret benefactor, Chuck Feeney. Danny O'Hare, however, never joined in chitchat in academic circles when talk turned to the "anonymous donor." "I would look on, thinking—you are very naughty children, weren't you all told to keep quiet about these things," he recalled. But it irked him to stay quiet. He read in the *Chronicle of Higher Education* that it was important for the person who received money to be able to talk about it, otherwise it does the person psychological damage. He sent the article to John Healy and Harvey Dale and said, "Look, you are doing psychological damage to me!" "That's OK," they said, "we won't give you any more money!"

Ed Walsh also found the restrictions frustrating and once had a bit of fun at the expense of Atlantic Foundation staff. Chuck and Helga invited Ed

Walsh and his wife, Stephanie, to spend a holiday with them in Thailand. They were picked up by a courtesy Rolls Royce sent by InterPacific's Laguna Beach Resort, and Walsh took a snapshot. On returning home he made a mock-up of the front page of the weekly *Limerick Leader* newspaper on his computer, inserting the photograph and a fictitious article by reporter "Margaret Ryan." Headlined "Feeney's Other Life," it reported that Feeney was spotted in Thailand getting into a Rolls with two blondes and that in contrast to his frugal ways elsewhere, he led an extravagant lifestyle in Thailand in a 145-bedroom residence with 376 staff and a pet elephant. (The blondes were their wives and the "residence" was the hotel.) Walsh sent the mock-up page to the Atlantic Foundation office, where, he happily recalled, "They went totally bananas; they thought it was for real."

Mark Patrick Hederman, a Benedictine monk at Glenstal Abbey in County Limerick, also had a bit of fun getting around the "no publicity" rules imposed by the Atlantic Foundation to acknowledge a $2-million donation for the monastery library. He prefaced his biography* with a poem entitled, "To the Unknown Donor."

> *Clematis grows through creepers round these walls*
> *Hundreds of leaves hide endless blocks of grey*
> *Autumn descends in rainbowlike decay*
> *Rescuing evening from the dread footfalls*
> *Littering planetaria with sound*
> *Edited rows of books envelop us*
> *Shelves full of memories tell us what we found*
> *Fascinating on the transit bus.*
> *Futures are formed by those who read such signs*
> *Ears finely tuned to register beyond*
> *Eyes of a hawk. Magnificence aligns:*
> *Nothing on earth can fail to correspond.*
> *Every minute vibration always links*
> *Yours to the so-called riddle of the sphinx.*

Only a very astute reader would notice that the first letter of each line spelled out the name Charles F. Feeney. "There was no way to thank Chuck

---

*Mark Patrick Hederman, *Walkabout, Life as Holy Spirit* (The Columba Press, 2005).

for his donation to our library," said Hederman, "so I put in a coded dedication to him. It was my secret Da Vinci Code!"

Feeney had already experienced the monk's penchant for poetry. When inquiring about a delay in the funding, Hederman had sent him a long fax in doggerel verse that began:

> *Dear Chuck*
> *we're stuck*
> *without a buck*
> *and several bills to pay*
> *unless you bless*
> *our neediness*
> *this merry month of May . . .*

When he started directing funds to Limerick University in Ireland, Feeney was surprised to find that there was no place for visitors to stay in the locality, except in the city of Limerick some miles away. He had seen the importance of the Statler Hotel on the campus at Cornell. He spotted a chance to do something similar for Limerick University when he had lunch there one day with Ed Walsh and Brendan O'Regan. Over the meal, Walsh complained that a seven-acre field right at the university entrance had been put up for sale and would likely become the site for "a glorified pub and some grotty development."

Feeney suggested they go and take a look. The three tramped through high grass and peered through blackberry brambles at the piece of land. Feeney later showed the site to Padraig Berry. "That's an important field," he said. "That was my cue to acquire the field, which I duly did," recalled Berry. "That was how it worked. I would negotiate the price, ring Bermuda, say I needed a million or ten million, and in came the money, directly, in cash, no systems, no control, no nothing." Once the sale was completed, Feeney donated the seven acres to the university.

About six weeks later, Feeney invited Walsh to breakfast at Ashford Castle. He moved aside the coffee cups and spread out an architectural drawing of a hotel and conference center for the field. It would be called Castletroy Park Hotel. He said his business would buy back two acres of the land on which to build the hotel.

"He gave us money to buy seven acres," said the university's finance officer, John O'Connor, "and then bought back two acres to build the hotel himself." In other words, said O'Connor, he paid twice for the land to build the hotel. "And he would often accuse me, tongue-in-cheek, of profiteering!"

Feeney set up a management company under Padraig Berry to build the hotel and make it a showpiece for the hospitality industry in Ireland. The *Sunday Business Post* in Dublin tried to find out more about the hotel's financial backer but admitted in print that after three weeks of an "international search," it had failed to find a photograph of the mysterious Mr. Feeney.

For all its reputation as a country of "a hundred thousand welcomes," Ireland had a weak hospitality structure. Its biggest hotel chain, the state-owned Great Southern, had nine grand hotels in the south and west of Ireland but they were badly run and inefficient. Feeney had toured the Great Southern Hotels on his earlier visits to Ireland with a view to buying them and concluded everyone had a "fat job" and the management was incompetent. He met the then-minister for labor, Bertie Ahern, in Dublin's Mespil Hotel and told him he wanted to buy the chain and modernize the hotels. Ahern agreed with Feeney's assessment. The company suffered from low morale, the board was in tatters, and staff were leaving, he told the American. But there would be no sale because of SIPTU, the Services, Industrial, Professional and Technical Union, the biggest and most powerful Irish trade union, to which all the hotel workers belonged. SIPTU would never agree to private ownership, said Ahern. (The Great Southern Hotels continued to languish and were eventually sold off in 2006.)

Castletroy Park Hotel, the first modern hotel of its size to be built in Ireland since World War II, was opened to widespread acclaim by Irish president Mary Robinson on May 5, 1991. It had 108 rooms and a combined health and fitness center with a twenty-five-meter pool, a first in Ireland. Soon afterward, it won the Egon Ronay award for the best business hotel in the country and was given four stars. It soon acquired a reputation for paying decent wages compared to other Irish hotels.

"Castletroy was his baby," said Aine McCarthy, junior manager at the time. Feeney would sit in the lobby and watch how people were greeted and checked in, and how luggage was carried. He fussed over the display of cereals, the supply of fresh juice, the softness of the butter, and the type of rashers in the buffet breakfast. Once when he saw a patron carrying a pint of Guinness into the conservatory, he asked McCarthy to go and tell him it was not the place for drinking.

The first two months were plagued with teething problems. Early one morning, Padraig Berry came across Feeney running a vacuum cleaner over the lobby carpet where workmen had been doing repairs. Berry made the mistake of saying, "You can't do this kind of stuff!" He still remembers the sharp rebuke in Feeney's expression. "He would be very fussy, to see that everything was absolutely right," said Berry. "He had incredible attention to detail. It was almost an obsession. The one time he and I had a row, over somebody who should be fired, he said, 'If you are unwilling to do it, why do I need you?' He looked me in the eye, with cold blue eyes like steel."

When he stayed in the hotel Feeney always insisted on a different standard room and never took a suite. No one was allowed to say he was there. Roger Downer, who succeeded Ed Walsh as Limerick University president, remembered a clerk saying, "We have no record of a Mr. Feeney staying here," while he knew Feeney was upstairs.

In Ireland, and especially in his hotel, Feeney was more tempted to let his hair down. After the grand opening of the $25-million foundation building and concert hall at Limerick University, officiated by U.S. ambassador to Ireland Jean Kennedy Smith in September 1993, which he observed discreetly from a spot where he wouldn't be noticed, Feeney joined a celebration dinner for local dignitaries at Castletroy Park Hotel. His philanthropy and his lifestyle were by then an open secret among the invited guests. Ed Walsh joked in an after-dinner speech that the donor was so secretive that he had been relegated to the laundry room. To turn the tables on Walsh, Feeney slipped out and arranged for the hotel's closed circuit television to show him hanging his shirt on a clothesline. Everyone enjoyed the joke. Feeney did in fact often do his own laundry in hotel rooms. His frugality was a talking point on the campus. John O'Connor remembered a conversation at the Castletroy Park Hotel with Feeney and John Healy about multi-million-pound investments, during which Feeney made six calls to Bonnie Suchet, his secretary in London, to get a cheaper air ticket. The message O'Connor got was, "Don't squander money."

As time went by, Ed Walsh became more ambitious. He got Chuck Feeney and his foundation board chairman, Lew Glucksman, together and said: "Look, we need to raise £25 million for the library and I am going out of the room for fifteen minutes and when I come back, I want the two of you to tell me how we are going to build the library." He left the two men in the room. When he came back, they said, "Well, OK, here's how we are going to do it." Both Feeney and Glucksman pledged significant funds, and Glucksman's name went on the building.

The university then came up with a plan to construct a sports arena to house an Olympic-size swimming pool. John Healy was skeptical about the ability of finance officer John O'Connor to procure sufficient government funds, though he considered him "the smartest guy in the field." In an unguarded moment, he promised O'Connor he would come and swim two laps, naked, if the fifty-meter facility was ever constructed. The magnificent pool was completed and was opened in 2002 by Prime Minister Bertie Ahern. Every time he went to the university afterward, Healy was cheerfully reminded of his promise to swim two laps naked. "I did it quietly one night when nobody was there," he protested with a straight face, adding, "I didn't say I would do it in front of an audience."

CHAPTER

Four Guys in a Coffee Shop

In January 1993 Chuck Feeney got a call from a publisher friend, Niall O'Dowd, in New York asking him to meet for dinner. They went to P. J. Clarke's on Third Avenue. With its low ceiling and dimly lit rooms, it was a perfect place for a conspiratorial meeting, which was what O'Dowd had in mind. Part of his friendship with Feeney was that he never, ever, asked him for anything. This would be the first time. Leaning across the little wooden dining table, the publisher came straight to the point. "OK, Chuck," he said. "Here's what I'm doing. I'm putting together a group of Americans to go to Ireland. I think the IRA [Irish Republican Army] will call a cease-fire. I think that they are ready to reach out to America. I think that this is something that is very important you get involved in."

Feeney's reply came without hesitation. "Yeah, definitely," he said. "I feel very strongly about my roots, and I will be very much committed to whatever you want to do."

The two had been friends for about six years. A former schoolteacher from County Tipperary in Ireland, O'Dowd had emigrated to the United States in 1979 and cofounded *Irish America*, a journal that focused on prominent Irish Americans and was unapologetically pro-business and pro-nationalist. After coming across the magazine in 1987, Feeney had called O'Dowd to tell him how much he liked it and invited him to breakfast at Kaplan's on East Fifty-ninth Street, a run-down diner that has since closed. O'Dowd said, "I found this guy sitting there in the corner, very unobtrusive, wearing a Mac, with nobody else around. He told me absolutely nothing about himself. I just assumed he was a businessman. He said he was very happy that somebody was finally chronicling the Irish American community because he felt that Americans had moved on too far from their roots." They talked for most of the morning. After that, Feeney regularly called O'Dowd when he was in town. They would have coffee at Kaplan's or lunch at P. J. Clarke's, and the Irishman would go for weekends to Feeney's house in Connecticut.

"We hit it off because basically he looks at the world as a fairly absurd place and so do I, to a large extent," said O'Dowd. "He has a kind of put-down humor, self-deprecating. He very consciously disdains everything that other people would make a fuss about. And he had this long-running dialogue with the waitress at Kaplan's. They were always having a go at each other about his 'meanness.' She would say, 'I suppose you only want boring tea?' and he would say, 'Just give me a glass of water.' One time when someone at a nearby table started talking on a mobile phone, Chuck pulled out a large toy phone made of plastic and pretended to have a loud conversation."

O'Dowd, who had no idea how rich Feeney was until the October 1988 *Forbes* article, saw in him a product of a distinct, family oriented Irish American community in New Jersey. "There's a whole containment thing there, a whole personality, a very identifiable, separate Irish existence," he said. Feeney became emotional, and was sometimes moved to tears, when talking to O'Dowd about his parents who had passed away and their impact on him. In contrast to other rich Irish-American businessmen O'Dowd knew, who were mostly Republican, he found Feeney leaning to the left of the Democratic Party. "Here was this guy, one of the richest men in the world, a flaming Communist!"

They discussed Irish politics a lot. Feeney was distressed by the violence in Northern Ireland, where the outlawed Irish Republican Army was waging a guerrilla war against British control of the province. The IRA campaign targeted members of the majority Protestant population who had any connection with the British army or the Northern Ireland security forces. On November 8, 1987, an IRA bomb placed at a British war memorial killed eleven people attending a remembrance service in the town of Enniskillen, only a few miles from Feeney's ancestral home. Feeney was in

London. He saw the gruesome aftermath on television. He thought, "This is madness, it has to stop."

"Maybe I was naive at that stage," said Feeney, "but I took the view that this is not the way Irish people react—by blowing up kids at commemoration events." He was particularly moved by the heart-wrenching story of how a nurse, Mary Wilson, died in the rubble holding the hand of her father, Gordon Wilson, saying, "Daddy, I love you very much." Feeney's daughter Leslie remembered him saying after the Enniskillen bombing, "In my lifetime, I want there to be peace, this has to be resolved in my lifetime." "He was always taking these things to heart," she said. "His attitude was— with my wealth I have got to do something."

O'Dowd had good contacts in Ireland, and he received indications that the IRA was ready to move in the direction of peace. But its political wing, Sinn Fein, and its leader, Gerry Adams, were ostracized by the British, Irish, and American governments, and there was stalemate. With the end of the Cold War and the election in 1992 of a Democratic president, Bill Clinton, O'Dowd believed that the United States could form a bridge to bring the Sinn Fein leaders into the political mainstream and nudge a peace process forward. He got the idea of creating a small delegation of respected Irish American figures to act as amateur envoys to help promote a dialogue among the three governments and all the parties in Northern Ireland. To be politically acceptable, the delegation had to include significant figures from corporate Irish America with no history of support for the IRA. Chuck Feeney was the first name that came to his mind.

Feeney's agreement to participate didn't give O'Dowd much leverage when he went to recruit others. "It was no use at all. Nobody knew who he was, that's the truth. Getting Bill Flynn was much bigger." Bill Flynn, head of Mutual of America on Park Avenue, was a pillar of corporate Catholic respectability in Manhattan. He was chairman of the National Committee on American Foreign Policy and a member of countless charitable and educational boards. Trade union executive Joe Jamison and former congressman Bruce Morrison from Connecticut, a hero to the Irish for his success in winning visa concessions, also joined the group, which called itself Americans for a New Irish Agenda. Their first mission was to Arkansas in January 1993 to lobby the incoming Clinton administration.

To show Chuck Feeney that Gerry Adams was serious about ending the violence, O'Dowd arranged for a private meeting between the two men.

Feeney and O'Dowd flew to Dublin and were picked up by Sinn Fein guides at their hotel and taken to a house in a working-class area. At the time, Adams was under constant threat of assassination. On March 14, 1984, loyalist gunmen had fired twenty bullets into his car and he had been seriously injured. The bespectacled, black-bearded Sinn Fein leader was always on his guard and changing his schedule.

Feeney and Adams talked in the cramped living room, one on each side of a tiny fireplace, as burly guards stood outside. "Even though I had been briefed about who this guy was, it was in the middle of one of those mad hectic days when you are meeting a whole lot of people," recalled Adams. "But I was very impressed by him. He didn't pontificate. He was very unprepossessing, very down-to-earth and ordinary. I talked about the ongoing efforts to build a peace process, the importance of dialogue, the importance of trying to get people outside the box to come in. My view at that time was that you don't change the people, you change the political conditions. If it was a contest between Ireland and Britain, the Brits would always win because it was an unequal contest. It could be that people from outside the box could change things."

Feeney had "an innate feeling" about Adams. He was convinced that the Sinn Fein leader was trying to achieve what Irish Americans overwhelmingly wanted, taking the gun out of Irish politics. "Chuck can figure people out," said O'Dowd. "He liked Adams a lot. They were the two smartest men I have ever been with in one room. They had a very good conversation about what America needed to do."

John Healy was worried when he heard about the meeting, as were some members of the board of Atlantic Philanthropies. For Healy, there were serious implications for the founder of a major philanthropic foundation having dealings with the head of an organization regarded as the mouthpiece of a terrorist group by the U.S., British, and Irish governments. Adams was widely reported to be a member of the IRA's army council, though he always denied it. In the ghettos of Belfast he was a folk hero, but he was barred from traveling to Britain and America, and his voice was banned from British and Irish radio and television.

But Feeney was undeterred. A second meeting was arranged to show him conditions in war-ravaged Belfast. O'Dowd was told to bring him to a house in Ballymurphy, a working-class nationalist area of West Belfast. He and Feeney traveled in one of Belfast's old-style black taxis that served the nationalist area. They saw British soldiers patrolling the scorched and rubble-strewn streets with rifles at the ready. They knocked on the door of a two-story row house with a small garden in front. A large man came to the door and eyed the two men with suspicion. "What do youse want?' he asked. "Are youse peelers [police]? Are youse collection men? Are youse here to fucking get me? Get the fuck out of here! Get away from my house!"

O'Dowd had gotten the address wrong. The pair ran down the little garden path with the householder in pursuit. "I was petrified at this stage," said the publisher. "Then the completely insane thing is, we're out on the street, who comes by in a big reinforced armored taxi but Gerry Adams on his way to meet us at a totally different address." The doors of the taxi opened from the inside and they climbed in and sped off. "We were in fits laughing," said O'Dowd. "Here was one of the richest men in the world being chased as a debt collector." Feeney was taken with the fact that the door of the armored taxi could not be opened from the outside, as a precaution against being ambushed.

Back in New York, the Irish American group arranged to visit Ireland for a round of public meetings with all parties, including Sinn Fein, as a way of bringing them in from the cold. They asked for a brief cease-fire from the IRA to establish the credibility of the Irish American group with the Clinton administration. It took some months to organize, but at last the message went out secretly to IRA commanders: No attacks should be staged for one week in early September 1993. There would be no announcement. Only the White House and the Irish American delegation would know.

On Monday, September 6, 1993, Feeney, O'Dowd, Bruce Morrison, and Bill Flynn met in the coffee shop of the Westbury Hotel in Dublin to discuss their strategy. Feeney looked like a vacationer in a zipped jerkin and black slacks. O'Dowd passed around a document in which the IRA pledged to conduct a weeklong cease-fire, starting at midnight the previous Friday. It had already been in effect for forty-eight hours. Ireland was at peace, if only for a few days, and it had been achieved by the four guys in the coffee shop. O'Dowd then destroyed the document, in keeping with his promise to Sinn Fein that it would remain strictly confidential.

Feeney experienced on this trip a level of secrecy that would have impressed Harvey Dale. Everyone had a code name for telephone conversations. Gerry Adams was the Chairman of the Board and the IRA, the Football Team. The Irish Americans were known as the Connolly House

Group because they met Adams in the Belfast Sinn Fein headquarters, named after James Connolly, a leader of the 1916 Rising in Ireland. The U.S. ambassador to Ireland, Jean Kennedy Smith, was known as *speirbhean* (visionary woman). Chuck Feeney was referred to—with a distinct lack of imagination—as CF. When traveling around in a hired car, they communicated only through scribbled notes in case the driver was spying on them.

The group went first to meet the Irish prime minister, Albert Reynolds, who was heavily engaged in backdoor diplomacy himself. "Albert just threw everyone else out of the office and conducted a two-hour seminar with us," said O'Dowd. They visited *speir-bhean* at the American embassy. They then drove the 100 miles to Belfast and met the Northern Ireland secretary, the British government's pro-consul, Sir Patrick Mayhew, in Stormont Castle and embarked on a round of all the political parties. The Reverend Ian Paisley, leader of the pro-British Democratic Unionist Party, which was fiercely opposed to Sinn Fein and deeply suspicious of Irish Americans, said to Feeney, "We know where you are coming from." "How so?" asked Feeney. He said, "You are an Irish American." "Yes," responded Feeney, "but it doesn't preclude me from helping." The climax of their visit was an intensive session with Adams and his colleagues at the heavily fortified Connolly House. They came away convinced that the militants on both sides were looking for a way out of the impasse.

The secret IRA cease-fire ended on Monday, September 13, after Feeney, O'Dowd, Flynn, and Morrison were safely out of the country, with a powerful explosion that wrecked the Stormont Hotel in Belfast.

The group made several more trips to Ireland. Once, in Belfast, Feeney went off to hire a car to drive them to Derry and returned with a bargain-price economy model into which the Irish Americans, including the towering figure of Bill Flynn, had to squeeze for the 128-mile round trip. Adams recalled that in their meetings Feeney said little, but when he did speak it was usually incisive and straightforward. "Sometimes people come and they have their advisers, and they have their line, and if they are running for public office they are influenced by all of that," he said at Sinn Fein's office in Belfast. "Other people come who are quite powerful and they have their little touches of egotism and expect to be treated in a certain way. Chuck didn't come with any of that. All the time I have known him it was exactly the same. I never saw him as being secretive. I saw him as being ordinary. He

190 II The Billionaire Who Wasn't

has taken biscuits out of his coat pocket that he had picked up from the
hotel bedroom—custard creams," he said laughing. "I wouldn't call that frugality. He's paying for the hotel. I also think he likes to take a rise out of
people in that regard." What was extraordinary to Adams was the traveling
that Feeney did. "He would come in here having come from Australia on his
way to San Francisco, and we would ask, 'When will we meet again?' and he
would say, 'Well, I'm going back to Australia, then I am going to Hong
Kong, then Limerick.'"

A secret back channel of communication was established linking Adams
and President Clinton, going through Ted Howell of Sinn Fein in Belfast to
Niall O'Dowd in New York, Trina Vargo in Senator Edward Kennedy's office on Capitol Hill, and Nancy Soderberg in the National Security Council in the White House. It was used to allow Adams to provide President
Clinton with the assurances that he needed to give him a forty-eight-hour
visa waiver in January 1994 to attend a Northern Ireland peace conference
at New York's Waldorf Astoria Hotel. Adams's visit was a media sensation.
The British government was outraged. Feeney was delighted.

President Clinton, wearing a tuxedo and a green bow tie, held a St.
Patrick's Day party at the White House six weeks later, to which Feeney and
the other members of the Irish American group were invited. The buffet included green chocolate bowler hats, Blarney cheese, and Irish coffee cake.
Feeney and O'Dowd chatted with Senators Edward Kennedy, Christopher
Dodd, and George Mitchell in the crowded East Room, where guests min-
gled with Hollywood celebrities such as Paul Newman and Richard Harris.
O'Dowd recalled Feeney quietly talking to one of his heroes, eighty-seven-
year-old civil rights activist Paul O'Dwyer of New York. The evening ended
with Bill Clinton and Northern Ireland politician John Hume singing
"When Irish Eyes Are Smiling."

Feeney was in Australia in August 1994 when he got an urgent message
from O'Dowd. He was needed in Belfast, as dramatic events were about to
take place. "He jumped on a plane, flew to L.A., from L.A. to New York and
met me at Kennedy, and we went over to Ireland, it was that important to
him," said O'Dowd. The IRA was on the brink of a cease-fire. Sinn Fein
needed reassurances in person from the Irish American peacemakers that
this would produce a political dividend in the United States. Chuck
Feeney's presence was essential. He had made a commitment that he would
put up money for a Sinn Fein lobbying office in Washington, D.C. Such

Irish American support for the peace strategy of Sinn Fein would make the possibility of a dangerous split among IRA supporters in America less likely.

Feeney joined the amateur emissaries once more in Dublin on August 25, 1994. The group went first to see Albert Reynolds at his office in Dublin. The prime minister surprised them by vehemently rejecting anything other than a permanent cease-fire. "They were leaving to go to Belfast and I told them straight out—if you go to Belfast, I said, and you come out talking about a three- or six-month cease-fire, I'm not with you. It's not acceptable. It's either all or nothing," he recalled years later over coffee in a Dublin hotel. "And I could see all their faces looking at me around the table. And Bill Flynn said nothing. And Chuck Feeney said nothing. O'Dowd and Bruce Morrison, I think, were a bit taken aback."

The next day in Belfast the group, now including Joe Jamison and Bill Lenihan, representing the U.S. labor movement, tried to figure out over breakfast at the Wellington Park Hotel whether the cease-fire would be declared permanent. Feeney predicted confidently it would be. "Chuck was the only one who said exactly how it would play out. He read Sinn Fein perfectly," said O'Dowd.

Inside Connolly House, Adams calmly told the group, "We're talking about a complete cessation." They emerged into the media scrum. Feeney had previously managed to dodge the cameras, but this time he was too late. A freelance photographer climbed onto a railing and took a picture from above as he hung back behind the others. Feeney, a small figure in suit and tie behind Adams, was clearly identifiable in the picture that appeared in the Dublin newspaper, *The Irish Times*, the next day, though his name was not in the caption.

Shortly afterward, the IRA declared a "complete cessation of military operations," starting at midnight on Wednesday, August 31. Six weeks later, on October 13, the loyalist paramilitary groups also announced they were going on cease-fire.

Chuck Feeney negotiated directly with Sinn Fein officials on the funding for an office in Washington to promote a political alternative. "We gave $20,000 a month for thirty-six months to Sinn Fein—a total of $720,000, and there were dollops on top of that," said Feeney years later. "It was the right thing to do. It proved you can bring people around to your thinking." A British barrister sympathetic to Sinn Fein, Richard Harvey from the Haldane Society of Socialist Lawyers in London, negotiated the figure and the drawdown arrangement, said Sinn Fein official Ted Howell. The money would go by wire transfer to a body set up in New York called Friends of Sinn Fein, presided over by lawyer Larry Downes. "We met and went over everything over a soda," said Downes. "He made it clear from the start that this money would be for a democratic process, exclusive of any violence." All accounts were submitted to the Department of Justice in Washington. Adams said that "not one penny" of Feeney's money went to the IRA. Feeney emphasized that it was an "absolutely personal" donation from his own funds. At the time, he was officially taking a salary as chief executive of General Atlantic Group of $500,000 a year. The matter was too political to be linked publicly to the work of the Atlantic Foundation and its directors.

Feeney's initiative was applauded by the White House. "Our whole approach on this was that the more interaction and engagement with them [Sinn Fein], the more moderate they would become," said Nancy Soderberg about his funding for the Sinn Fein office—a prediction that was to come true as time passed. Feeney took a personal interest in the location and furnishing of the office in a modern building near Du Pont Circle in Washington. Gerry Adams formally declared the office open at a reception in a Washington hotel in March 1995, grandly referring to it as Sinn Fein's "diplomatic mission." There was hilarity when an English reporter, Peter Hitchens, asked if it would have a military attaché.

Feeney later gave $200,000 to Gary McMichael, a political representative of the loyalist paramilitary Ulster Defence Association, which had carried out many murders of Catholics in Northern Ireland, in order, he said, to balance things. He thought McMichael was like Adams, a person who genuinely wanted to achieve peace.

There were setbacks. On February 2, 1996, Feeney was in his San Francisco office when someone called him to say that the IRA had ended its cease-fire in protest against the lack of political progress. It had exploded a massive bomb at a large business development in London known as Canary Wharf, killing two men and injuring thirty-eight people, and causing damage estimated at $150 million. Aine McCarthy, then Feeney's project manager, glanced over at him after he replaced the receiver. Tears were running down his cheeks.

The cease-fire was renewed on July 20, 1997, and on April 10, 1998, the main parties in Northern Ireland and the British and Irish governments signed on to what became known as the Good Friday Agreement, setting out a plan for devolved government, the early release of paramilitary prisoners, the decommissioning of paramilitary weapons, reform of the police and criminal justice system, and new relationships between Northern Ireland and the Republic of Ireland.

In the following five years, as the political process played out, Feeney directed a total of $30 million through Atlantic Foundation to worthy projects in Northern Ireland, including $2.5 million to community groups to help Republican and Loyalist ex-prisoners move into "positive politics." Atlantic Foundation provided funds to help such people become involved in community development and to provide nonviolent alternatives for justice in areas where policing was still a problem. In 2006, the IRA finished a process of decommissioning, that is, destroying, its weapons, which included tons of explosives, rocket launchers, and heavy machine guns, and in 2007, it took the final step of supporting the reformed police force. Chuck Feeney was invited to witness the formal launch on May 8, 2007, in Belfast of a power-sharing administration, including Sinn Fein and Ian Paisley's Democratic Unionist Party. The week before Feeney was in New York where he fell and required several days' hospital treatment for his knee. However, the philanthropist, who had just turned seventy-six, insisted on flying across the Atlantic for the highly-emotive event in the Northern Ireland Parliament Building, known as Stormont, attended by the British and Irish prime ministers and scores of political and community figures. He arrived unshaven and in an open-neck shirt and hung around the back of the crowd of VIPs in the main hall, leaning on a walking stick. "It's rare in life you get to write 'finish' to a major undertaking in such a satisfactory way," he said. "Today is that day." Atlantic continues to pour money into Northern Ireland to underpin the peace.

Gerry Adams reflected that the intervention of the Irish American peacemakers and President Bill Clinton brought the cease-fire forward by about a year and that scores of lives were saved. "It was key to the timing and the development of the breakthroughs which came, and it was key to us being able in many ways to argue [to the IRA] that there was an alternative way forward, and part of the alternative way forward in helping our struggle was the international community." It was crucial to Sinn Fein to get the commitments from the White House on access and visas, the right to raise funds in the United States, and promises that Sinn Fein would be treated like other parties.

Another important factor was the opening of a Sinn Fein office in Washington. "Chuck was the person who signed up to do that," Adams said. "From that first meeting, he was the guy that delivered. All of the group played a huge role in delivering, but Chuck was the guy at the end of it all, when we were putting forward a proposition, who did it, in an understated way. I have learned since that when he was coming in to play a role, he researched and checked out and explored and investigated and cross-checked. He is extremely well-informed. He had informed judgments. To say that he is naive is totally untrue. The Irish peace process is the most successful U.S. foreign policy issue and those in at the birth of that have been validated and vindicated, and Chuck more so in that he put up hard cash, he put money where his mouth is. The investment he made to the peace process was pivotal. It was a brilliant investment. I am a huge fan of his. Even if he had never come near the Irish peace process, I think he is one of the most decent people I have ever met. He represents the very, very best of America where you can actually use power and influence in a very positive way for humanity, and I am lavish in my admiration."

PART THREE

BREAKING UP

CHAPTER

The French Connection

The travel business recovered quickly after the end of the Gulf War, and Atlantic Foundation's share of the cash dividends from DFS improved to $57 million in 1993 and $120 million in 1994. But the painful experience of reneging on charitable pledges convinced Feeney more than ever that the time had come to sell his holding in the company to put the philanthropy on a more reliable basis. "I wanted to make sure that we could see a long-term flow of money for our charitable giving," he said.

"We knew that we had a huge asset which was completely illiquid and nondiversified, so we had the worst portfolio you could possibly have," recalled Dale, who estimated in his 1994 president's report that Atlantic Foundation's assets were worth $2 billion, $1 billion represented by the stake in DFS and $500,000 each in the businesses and the investment portfolio. "DFS could have gone into bankruptcy, or we could have another year without dividends. Who knows? Life's complicated. We had known for years that a sale was very desirable. It became much more clear in the pain of the closing down of the dividend at the time of the Gulf War. We just couldn't keep punishing our beneficiaries in that way. We needed to exit at some juncture."

Feeney was also convinced that DFS was a mature business, and it was time to sell for business reasons alone. New patterns in tourism worried

197

him. "At one time I could stand at the airport and tell you if I saw 100 Japanese come in what was the average spend," he said. "Then all of a sudden they started showing up in tattered shorts and all that, and I said—these aren't the same Japanese that we sold to all these years."

The changing trends were most obvious in the DFS stores in Hawaii. John Reed observed that value had replaced status in the Japanese market, and the new Japanese tourists had less disposable income than those who propelled DFS sales in the early days. "They have become younger, less affluent, more demanding and unmindful of the gift-giving and other traditions that bound their predecessors," Reed told *Pacific Business News*. There were no longer any shortages in Tokyo, and the prices in Japan had gone down. The decline of the Japanese yen against the dollar and credit restrictions in Japan also drove down spending levels. Japanese tourists were more inclined to buy single items for their own consumption.

After stepping down as DFS chief executive in January 1995, Adrian Bellamy, in a confidential report he wrote for his successor, Myron E. Ullman, offered a similar downbeat assessment. DFS was a huge financial success, and it had the most effective marketing system in the world, but there were ominous portents, he warned. There were tough times ahead for the concessions on which the business relied. The historic formula of escorting Japanese tourists straight to DFS stores was looking jaded as travelers from Japan were becoming more independent. Items sold at DFS stores offered customers substantial savings but not because DFS paid no duty—this was eaten up by concession fees—but because of the vast difference between home market prices in Japan, Korea, Taiwan, and elsewhere, versus DFS prices. This was due to the inefficiency of the distribution structures in those countries. "Unfortunately for us this unique advantage which we conveniently tucked under the banner of duty free is fast collapsing." It had collapsed in liquor in 1987, was now collapsing in cosmetics and perfume, and there would be global prices in a 10-percent range by the end of the 1990s. Bellamy added that DFS was too decentralized, that if it did not modernize it would be "soundly beaten by competition"; that in Hong Kong the shops were shoddy and an embarrassment to vendors; that DFS was "great in our paternalism but not in our empowerment"; and that if the management system of "kick ass and take notes" did not change, they were in trouble.

Bellamy also advised his successor that DFS was "truly somewhat arrogant" with customers in the way it got staff to push Camus cognac. He claimed the DFS-owned distribution company, Camus Overseas Ltd. was dysfunctional and "we are dealing with a very, very sick category of merchandise which doesn't seem to me to have much upside." The outgoing chief executive had never been happy with the Camus arrangement, which was managed by Jean Gentzbourger from 1972 until 1985—when he had stepped down and sold his shareholding for $3.6 million—and which he took over again in 1992 after his successor had left. Gentzbourger calculated that over a period of twenty-five years, the Camus arrangement on its own made between $600 to $700 million in dividends for the four DFS owners. The dividends were diminishing, however, as the purchase obligations were becoming more onerous compared to the opportunity for sales, and the partners were becoming increasingly unhappy with the way Michel Camus's successors were doing business.

Nonetheless, DFS was still perceived as a phenomenal success story, and in the early 1990s there was no shortage of suitors. "We would get a letter every three months saying, 'Gee, you people have a wonderful business, and we'd like to talk to you about buying it,'" said Feeney. "They would say in a letter, 'Let's put something together.' When you talked to them they would say, 'Here's how we will do it. We will give you 10 percent and pay the rest later.' It doesn't work that way, folks. So depending on the letterhead, we would get back and say, 'Well, it is a good business and we've been operating it for a long time, and by the way it's a cash transaction, and the cash involved would be $3 or $4 billion dollars.' That chased away the walkers, talkers, and gawkers."

Then in July 1994, Harvey Dale got a call in his New York office from an old acquaintance, George T. Lowy, a partner in Cravath, Swaine & Moore, one of the law firms Feeney used. Lowy had contacts in Paris and spoke fluent French. "I have somebody who might be interested in buying DFS," Lowy said. He couldn't give a name but asked, "Would you be interested in talking?" "You will have to get permission to give me the name, and I will have to go and talk to Chuck and we will respond," replied Dale. Lowy called back the next day. His informant was the chairman of Lazard, the New York and Paris–based investment banking firm that specialized in mergers and acquisitions. Lazard managing partner Antoine Bernheim was a personal friend and patron of Bernard Arnault, the head of Louis Vuitton Moët Hennessy in Paris; he boasted once that he carried Arnault "to the baptismal font of finance."

Dale knew immediately that if LVMH was behind the approach, it was serious. With annual sales of nearly $6 billion, the huge Paris-based company was perhaps the only retailer in the world at that time that could buy the duty-free business outright for cash. Arnault, then forty-five and on his way to becoming one of the world's richest people, had taken over LVMH after the merger of Louis Vuitton and Moët Hennessy. In a bitter power struggle four years earlier, he had ousted Henri Racamier, the former chairman of Louis Vuitton, to gain absolute control. He was in the process of building an empire of high-end brands that already included Louis Vuitton, Christian Dior, Givenchy, Celine, Christian Lacroix, Kenzo, Loewe, Fred, Veuve Clicquot Ponsardin, Hennessy, Moët & Chandon, Dom Pérignon, and Pommery. He had also acquired a famous department store, Le Bon Marché.

He had, it emerged later, been eyeing DFS for some years. He liked the potential synergy of acquiring DFS's network of 180 stores. LVMH was the biggest supplier of designer goods to DFS. Arnault was also seeking to expand into Asia, the source of the world's new money, where DFS was already entrenched.

Feeney was intrigued. On August 10, 1994, he and his legal counsel Chris Oechsli flew from London to Paris and took a taxi to Avenue Montaigne, the tree-lined boulevard off the Avenue des Champs-Élysées lined by the elegant fashion houses of Gucci, Jill Sander, Chanel, Chloé, Celine, Escada, and many other brand leaders. Arnault greeted his visitors in a reception room at Dior headquarters at 30 Avenue Montaigne, furnished with large white couches and a portrait of Christian Dior. They spoke in French. Feeney thought the slender Frenchman with elf-like features was a gentleman. They related well. The two had a lot in common. Both dressed modestly and avoided the limelight. Neither liked attending celebrity events. They were obsessive about the detail of retailing. Feeney was known to check if there was ink in the display pens in DFS stores, and Arnault was once able to tell that Givenchy's cosmetic counter in a New York store had expanded by a couple of feet at the expense of a sister company since his previous visit.

Feeney was elliptical with Arnault except on one point. "We are not talking about trading paper, we are talking about cash, serious cash," he said. The French fashion magnate did not blink. He asked for some financial information to put a price on DFS equity. Feeney told him that sales had reached $3 billion a year. They parted with an undertaking to begin negotiations for Arnault to buy a portion of Feeney's shareholding in DFS as a first step. After the flight back to London, Feeney told Oechsli, "I want you to run with this."

"Chuck was open to a lot of angles," recalled Oechsli. "He did not give the impression that he was thinking: Here is an opportunity to divest. Quite the opposite. His tactic was: First we will let you see some rough information, just a sense of what's there, but we don't want to give you too much because we are concerned about exposure to our partners and what they can see."

Arnault discussed Feeney's visit with his confidant, Robert Leon, when they met for their ritual Saturday morning coffee in a Paris café. There were better uses for LVMH's cash, suggested Leon. But Arnault was attracted to the idea of buying into the first truly successful global retailer. The duty-free business absorbed 20 percent of the production of the French luxury market, and the more he controlled distribution, the more he was master of his own fate.

The following month, Arnault and Feeney entered into formal negotiations for LVMH to buy 8.5 percent of DFS as a first step to possibly acquiring the whole company. It was small enough not to tilt the balance among the four shareholders, but big enough to allow Arnault to come in and participate in the business.

Feeney contacted the others to tell them what he was doing. "I think we have an opportunity to sell now, I think we should do so," he told Bob Miller. "This is a live one. This is someone who will look you in the eye and say we are not talking about trading paper, we are talking about cash, about serious cash." Miller replied, "That's interesting. I wonder what they have in mind." He was, however, deeply troubled. He recalled thinking, "DFS is our baby: I was concerned about his [Arnault's] reputation and that he might buy our company and then just 'flip' it. Would he destroy the company or sell it on?" Arnault had a reputation as a corporate raider. Pierre Bergé of Yves Saint Laurent once described him as a "bird of prey." His "cold stare" was described in a *Forbes* magazine article as rivaling that of the old widow Clicquot on the label of Champagne Veuve Clicquot.

Feeney sought out Tony Pilaro in an investment office his partner had established in Dublin. "He sat right here," said Pilaro in a high-ceilinged room lined with bound DFS records. "He said, 'I'm selling 8.5 percent of my interest to LVMH.' He wanted my backing and support." Pilaro subsequently

202 || The Billionaire Who Wasn't

called Harvey Dale and, according to Dale, told him "with great excitement" that he thought a sale to LVMH would be lucrative to the four
shareholders and increase DFS's revenues substantially. His enthusiasm
stemmed from an assumption that Arnault would at last allow DFS to sell
its most expensive top-of-the-line merchandise. LVMH's largest retailer,
Louis Vuitton, sold its luxury leather goods only through Louis Vuitton
stores. If LVMH bought DFS and ended the ban, it could boost DFS annual sales by an estimated $150 million a year.

Miller, Pilaro, and Parker asked for a face-to-face meeting with Arnault
to see what he had in mind. The three non-Feeney owners took their turn
on the white divans of Arnault's reception room in Paris on October 13,
1994. The following day, Pilaro wrote to Arnault, saying that the synergies
between LVMH and DFS were obvious and his effort to buy a minority
stake "warranted serious consideration by all parties." But he added, "The
price will have to be compelling." He made clear that their agreement to
Chuck selling 8.5 percent of the equity would depend on LVMH allowing
DFS to sell Louis Vuitton merchandise. Arnault would not accept such a
condition and did not bother to reply. On January 23, 1995, Pilaro wrote
again to the LVMH chairman. This time he said that he, Miller, and Parker
had no interest in selling any of their holdings to LVMH.

Six months passed, with Chris Oechsli and Jim Downey commuting
back and forth to Paris to negotiate with the LVMH lawyers before Feeney
formally proposed, on July 20, 1995, selling Arnault an 8.5-percent interest
in DFS, as a first step in acquiring Feeney's total shareholding, assuming a
capital value for DFS of $3.5 billion. It was another four months before Ar-
nault responded. On November 13, 1995, he accepted the two-step purchase deal, while indicating his desire to buy up the other shareholders'
interests in DFS. Two weeks later, on November 29, Feeney wrote to his co-
owners, informing them of the agreement and of his view that not only was
LVMH the only company capable of buying DFS but that Arnault was willing to go all the way. He disclosed that he had obtained assurances from Arnault that he would respect and maintain an "arm's-length commercial
relationship" between LVMH's subsidiaries and DFS.

Pilaro wrote to Feeney, saying he and Parker would meet Arnault again in
Paris on January 9, 1996, and that he would inform him that the other
shareholders were willing to consider an offer for all their equity in DFS, but
only if the price was higher than the suggested $3.5 billion capitalization.

Their primary objective, Pilaro said, was "to extract the highest possible price for the company." The meeting with Arnault did not go well.

"I tried to extract from Arnault, 'What is your strategy? What do you want to do?' But he was not very forthcoming," recalled Pilaro. "I specifically said, 'If your strategy is to improve the profitability of both companies, let me give you a little secret. There is a very simple way of doing this. You should sell your [Louis Vuitton] merchandise to us to resell.'"

The Brooklyn-born lawyer's next step was to propose to Miller and Parker that if Feeney was keen to sell, then they three, and not Arnault, should buy him out. They drew up a formal proposition to acquire Feeney's 38.75 percent holding in DFS, plus his interests in the Camus distribution business and the retail stores Feeney had acquired in Hawaii—collectively known as the Hawaiian Retail Group—based on a total capital valuation for the whole duty-free business of $2.3 billion, which was more than a billion less than Arnault's valuation.

The Wise Man now got caught up in the affair. Since the dispute over Feeney's retail activities in Hawaii, the owners had a mechanism for coping with their differences, and at this point they contacted Ira Millstein at his Manhattan office and asked him to relay their offer to Feeney. Millstein did so on February 23. Feeney didn't bother to respond. He found the offer "somewhat confusing and clearly inequitable," given that LVMH had just made a much higher offer without asking for the Hawaiian stores to be thrown in. Shortly afterward, Ira Millstein told Feeney, "Tony's miffed that you didn't respond." Feeney replied, "I don't respond to an offer like that."

Millstein then accompanied Miller, Parker, and Pilaro to a meeting with LVMH in Paris on May 6 to see if Arnault would up the ante. Arnault said he would raise his price on the basis of a capital value of DFS of $4 billion if he was able to acquire a majority shareholding. Millstein invited Arnault to come to New York a month later for a one-to-one meeting at which he would convey the response of the shareholders. Miller warned the Wise Man before the meeting that he would not consider a sale at the price Arnault was offering. Arnault flew from Paris to New York, and on June 13 presented Millstein with a formal proposal—to buy a majority holding in DFS based on a capital value of at least $4 billion, or a minority holding based on a valuation of $3.5 billion. The French luxury goods mogul told the Wise Man that he believed there was a unique synergy between the two companies, and that was why he could pay more than anyone else.

After the Arnault-Millstein meeting in New York, Feeney took Parker to dinner to urge him to think about joining him in selling their combined shareholding to LVMH. He sensed that Parker was wavering. The two had always maintained cordial relations, even during the split over Feeney's independent retail activities. Parker was never *emotional* about that, Tony Pilaro recalled. Together Feeney and Parker owned 58.75 percent of the equity; if they sold together, it would give Arnault control of the duty-free empire and guarantee a valuation of at least $4 billion.

Parker felt that he was the "piggy in the middle." His arm was being bent by Feeney on one side and Tony on the other. But the Arnault offer was looking very attractive. The LVMH head was valuing DFS at 33 percent more than its estimated annual sales of $3 billion, which was a hefty premium even in the bull market for high-end retailers in the mid-1990s. Feeney stood to get something approaching $1.6 billion and Parker over $800 million. The payments would be in cash. "I started thinking about it," said Parker. "It was a staggering amount of money."

The tipping point for Parker was a commitment that Feeney extracted from Arnault that if Feeney and Parker sold, the other two DFS owners could take up the offer on the same terms up to sixty days after the closing. "We made an undertaking that nobody would be hung out to dry," said Feeney.

Parker decided to throw in his lot with Feeney. "Alan is pragmatic, he's a good bean counter and a good financial investor," said Feeney. "He agreed to sell."

Miller had to be told. They set up a conference call. "Bob was terribly distressed," said Feeney. "He was shocked that Alan would come to our side. He accused Alan of selling out. There was an abrupt end to the conversation."

At this stage Tony Pilaro pushed the idea of floating the company on the stock market, and he got investment bankers Morgan Stanley to draw up a proposal for going public. "Tony was always a market guy, his idea was always to go public," recalled Parker. A meeting of the owners, without Feeney, was set up in Ira Millstein's office at 767 Fifth Avenue to hear what Morgan Stanley had to say. The investment bankers, with backing from Chase Manhattan Bank, told them that they could get between $5 and $7 billion in an initial public offering (IPO), but the market wasn't ripe enough and they would have to wait six months. The choice facing them, recalled Parker, was between a potential $6 billion from the IPO "and the bullshit from Morgan Stanley that it would be a lot more than that," and a share of a guaranteed $4 billion from Arnault. Six billion sounded very good, but it was normal that only 20 percent would be offered initially as investors would want to see them stay in charge.

"Chuck Feeney wasn't convinced that an IPO could be done or that it would be the appropriate thing to do," said Chris Oechsli, "but Tony kept badgering Bob, and Bob was kind of taking his cues from Tony." "Bob was totally in Tony's pocket," declared Parker.

At another meeting of the shareholders and their lawyers with the Wise Man in New York, Pilaro made allegations about Chuck giving confidential information to a competitor. Harvey Dale countered sharply that in having Morgan Stanley evaluate DFS for an IPO, Pilaro had provided at least as much information to bankers.

The action moved back to Paris. On June 26, Ira Millstein and the four DFS shareholders rented a conference room at the Ritz on Place Vendôme, a short walk from Avenue Montaigne, to examine all the variations on the table and then go to see Arnault. ("I still can't get over the cost of the room for the meeting," said Parker years later.) Just as they settled down, however, Miller and Pilaro came up with a surprise of their own. They presented Feeney and Parker with an offer to buy them out, based on a valuation of DFS at $4 billion, including the Camus business and Feeney's retail operation in Hawaii. They argued that the least they could do was allow them to buy DFS at the same price Arnault was offering—though the LVMH chief had not asked for the Hawaiian Retail Group to be included. Feeney and Parker asked for time to think about it. They broke up in less than a hour, and the meeting with Arnault was put off.

The atmosphere between the two camps grew distinctly hostile. Miller and Pilaro arranged for their bankers to visit DFS stores to do due diligence before putting up the finance for a possible buyout. "Bob and Tony were going to have DFS pay for the bankers' trip by charter aircraft, which I found out about and said, 'No way! This is a shareholder transaction, this isn't company expense,'" said Parker. "Things got pretty hairy after that. There was not a lot of friendliness. It was an awful thing having been in business with them for thirty years. I mean, the animosity between Chuck and Bob was pretty bad. I had been pretty friendly with everybody, and now I was surely on Chuck's side."

Parker was never convinced that Miller and Pilaro had the financing lined up to buy them out. Feeney was even more skeptical. "Miller tried to prevent us from selling to Arnault because he wanted to buy it himself," he said, "but he couldn't. He didn't have the money. It was an equity investment, a high, substantial-risk investment, and he had to put up big money." Tony Pilaro insisted that they did have the banks' support. "We had it," he said. "I had the letter. It said, 'Tony Pilaro, Bob Miller, you have got a $3.75 billion credit line, all you have got to do is pay us an up-front fee of $20 million for the commitment.' The next day we get another letter. It said, 'And by the way Tony, if you need another $500 million for working capital [you can get it].' Maybe Chuck didn't feel that that was real. But we did have the money."

CHAPTER 23

Musical Chairs

On July 3, 1996, a week after Bob Miller and Tony Pilaro presented Chuck Feeney and Alan Parker with an offer to buy them out of DFS, the four came together in Cannes on the French Riviera for the wedding of Jean Gentzbourger's son Marco. All the families were invited. Chuck's former wife, Danielle, and their children were among the wedding guests. Miller was accompanied by his wife, Chantal, and his daughters and his bodyguard. It was a rare social get-together of the DFS owners, and it came at the height of the biggest crisis in their thirty-year relationship. Typically, Chuck lodged in a small downtown hotel, the three-star L'Olivier on Rue des Tambourinaires, while the others checked into Les Muscadin, a four-star town-house hotel with sweeping views of the Bay of Cannes once favored by Picasso.

Feeney and Parker had already decided to reject the offer made by their partners unless Miller and Pilaro raised their price and produced the money by September 1, after which they would proceed with a sale of their shareholdings to LVMH. They expressed their concern that the Hawaii bid was coming up again in the autumn, and if DFS lost it, the value of the company would fall, and they wanted to move before that.

However, the wedding gave Feeney and Parker an opportunity to pull Miller aside on his own and persuade him to go along with the sale to LVMH, or at least not try to block it. They met him discreetly in a large waterfront hotel on the Croisette. They went over everything again, pointing out that they had protected Miller in the agreement with Arnault as it in-cluded a sixty-day window for him to sell on the same terms. Parker thought they had Bob convinced.

But not for long. The next morning, recalled Parker, "I got a call from Tony—would I go to the wedding in the car with Linda, his wife at the time. I thought it odd but I said, no problem. I guess Tony had got some whiff of what was going on, and he needed to occupy me. He then shot off to see Bob. The next car was Bob and Tony. By the time Bob got to the wed-ding, he said, 'I'm not going to do the deal, it's not going to work.'"

Pilaro dismissed the suggestion that he connived to get in the car with Bob. "I'm not that devious, believe me, I certainly wasn't playing musical chairs," he said. He protested that he could influence Miller on *how* to do something but not *whether* to do it. "To think otherwise is an overstatement of the power of Pilaro's logic!"

Miller would later conclude that "Tony was probably more of a hindrance to me than anything else, because he was pushing for me to buy out Chuck. Tony had a certain way of hyping things up."

The colloquy continued at a reception under the lemon trees in the garden of Gentzbourger's elegant villa on the Avenue de la Croix des Gardes over-looking Cannes. "I knew something was going on," recalled Gentzbourger. "They were talking, and they didn't look very happy. Tony was jumping all around from one to the other trying to activate something." He joked with Feeney later that he should get a commission for providing his garden for such high-level negotiations.

The young Feeneys posed for pictures with the Millers, but the tension between their parents spoiled the atmosphere. They felt the Miller sisters saw them as the bad guys whose dad was being horrible to their dad, with-out any appreciation that perhaps Bob Miller was making a big mistake. Danielle had remained for years on cordial terms with the Millers, and she had liked Bob when they all lived in Hong Kong. But the friendship had been fraying over the years and she now saw Bob's opposition to her former husband as akin to treason.

Miller, too, was deeply unhappy about the turn of events. "It was really tough for me—my whole life has been spent building this business, and now everybody was moving too quickly and what with the high cost of mezza-nine debt, the possibility of an IPO, or selling to Arnault, it was very diffi-cult to think clearly. Tony was pushing a plan that maybe we could buy out

Chuck. We actually had the bankers lined up to raise $2 billion in cash for us, but I was unhappy with the high interest costs. It was a very difficult and tormenting time for me."

Chuck Feeney showed few signs of strain. Oechsli recalled going into his office in London at the height of the fraught negotiations and seeing plans for a restaurant in San Francisco's Bayside Village called Pizza Prego at the top of the pile of papers on his desk. "He would be more interested in the pizza menus than he would be in discussions about a $4-billion sale!"

But even Feeney began to have second thoughts, recalled Oechsli. "He felt almost an obligation to Arnault that he wasn't going to hand him a business with feuding partners, and at one point, after Alan Parker came on board, he was just prepared to not do it. It was consistent with his avoidance of conflict. I remember going down to my office, and just typing out a memo saying, 'This is it. You might never have this opportunity again. These are big boys and they all know what they are getting into.' I was worn out at this stage," said Oechsli. "We had been at this for two years. We had to do it."

As the summer dragged on, nothing got resolved. The Wise Man expressed his frustration with the impasse in a letter delivered to each of the DFS owners: "Two people want to diversify, two do not. This has happened before in the history of the world, and people have worked it out. It doesn't require a rocket scientist, only a recognition of reality." A protracted legal wrangle could expose DFS's "dirty linen," he warned, and if he were forced to arbitrate, the inner workings of one of the most secretive companies in the world would be revealed. "So far the world isn't aware of your respective holdings, interests, etc. Nasty litigation will bring it all out."

His words had no effect. The final split came on August 30, 1996. On that day Arnault had been invited to make a presentation to the four owners at Ira Millstein's office in New York. He had already sent word through a back channel that he would pay Miller and Pilaro a premium—a little extra to save face—if they agreed to sell. Getting more than Chuck would surely satisfy Bob's pride.

Before Arnault arrived, the four faced the Wise Man across a table, their lawyers behind them. Bob Miller protested to Ira, "This is my company, I want to buy the company," recalled Pilaro. Millstein retorted, "Listen, Arnault will pay you more, you guys will get a higher price, and these guys, Alan and Chuck, won't care."

Feeney and Parker reiterated that they intended to sell to Arnault by September 30, and that they weren't convinced that Bob and Tony had the wherewithal to buy them out. They were concerned that Arnault's patience was running out.

At this point Miller and Pilaro got up and walked out. "We left in a huff," said Pilaro. Feeney recalled that Miller "went storming out." It was the last occasion that the four guys who had presided for three decades over one of the most successful retail operations in the twentieth century would meet together in one room.

Miller and Pilaro took the elevator to the ground floor. As they stepped out, Bernard Arnault was waiting to get into the elevator to go up. The Frenchman looked in astonishment as Miller and Pilaro emerged and walked past him. Pilaro said, "Hello!" but didn't stop. He and Miller walked out onto Fifth Avenue. "He was probably thinking he was coming to the birthday party, and he was going to buy the whole company, and he sees two guys walking out," said Pilaro. The meeting in Ira Millstein's office was abandoned.

But Miller was still conflicted. He called Feeney after the walkout and suggested they meet one more time back in London. Miller, Feeney, and Parker had flown back to England immediately after the fiasco in Millstein's office, while Pilaro stayed behind in New York. On Sunday morning, September 1, they met around a table in a ground-floor room of Atlantic Group's headquarters at 17 Savile Row. The building was otherwise deserted. Feeney brought Chris Oechsli along to provide technical and financial data so that the three could work out a new proposal. Miller said he was willing to consider selling to Arnault after all, but at a higher price if possible. As they worked their way through financing issues, Chris would dash upstairs and telephone Jim Downey at his home in a Dublin suburb and Downey would come up with new formulations on his Toshiba laptop.

Oechsli noted that the three shareholders, who had come through so much together, seemed to have little to say to each other while waiting for him to bring each new set of figures. "They didn't talk very much, they kind of looked down," he said. There was a surreal element to the few words the shareholders did exchange. They spoke in shorthand: "two point eight," "three point four," meaning $2.8 billion or $3.4 billion. After an hour and a half, they arrived at a formula for a phased sale by all four shareholders to LVMH. They would each sell just under half of their holdings to Arnault on the basis of a capital value of $4.2 billion for the company, while giving LVMH the right to buy the remaining shares after eighteen months. Miller initialed the deal.

"We actually had the initials on a piece of paper that they were all going to agree to," said Oechsli. "I went upstairs to Chuck's office after they had gone and said, 'This is pretty positive, isn't it?' And Chuck said, 'No, Bob is going to change his mind tomorrow.'" Parker, too, was dubious. Miller, he recalled, said only that he was "pretty sure" he would do it. He had seen over the years that Miller would sometimes not stand up to Feeney in person and later would change his mind.

Tony Pilaro realized something was going on when he got a call that Sunday at the Carlyle Hotel on Madison Avenue from Ira Millstein, saying that Alan Parker's investment banker from Goldman Sachs was trying to contact Miller and did he know where he was? This could only mean one thing—that the other two had gotten to Bob. Pilaro dashed to the airport and got the pilots of his private Gulfstream III to fly him to London immediately. He took a car straight to Miller's mews residence in central London. He wanted to be there because "maybe the banker would influence Bob one way or another." Shortly after he arrived, the Goldman Sachs banker knocked on the door. "He was stunned that I was there," said Pilaro.

Pilaro and Miller came up with a revised proposal of their own. They would go along with a sale of DFS by all four owners, but only if LVMH agreed to pay the tax burden that would arise because of the way Miller and Pilaro had restructured their interests in DFS during the "Big Bang" in 1986. The idea was conveyed to Paris, but Arnault was not interested. On September 18, Miller wrote to Feeney and Parker to say he had, after all, changed his mind about the agreement he had initialed. He suggested wistfully that they should all "quiet down now and let DFS get on with its business of making money."

Miller's reluctance to break his lifelong link with DFS was clearly a major factor in his decision. Feeney saw this as a line Miller could not cross. "I did an analysis once and figured you were never going to get Bob. He would lose face. Bob was Mr. Duty Free. He liked to play the role. He kept coming back saying, 'Duty Free is my baby.'"

Feeney and Parker returned to New York at the end of September to finalize their deal with LVMH, a complicated procedure that required a team of lawyers from both sides working flat out for most of a week to draw up the terms. "There would have been twenty lawyers in the room and Chuck, myself, and Harvey in a side room where they would consult us on issues," recalled Parker. One of the lawyers, David Gruenstein from Watchell, Lipton, Rosen & Katz, made a deep impression on Parker. "Tremendous. Tough as nails. I've never come across anyone like him in my life. When we were closing, he worked three days without going to bed."

On Tuesday, October 1, everything was ready for Feeney and Parker to sign. Feeney abandoned his casual gear and turned up wearing a suit, button-down shirt, and blue silk tie, though with his trademark black plastic watch. With lawyers in shirtsleeves and gold watches hovering behind them, they signed a series of legal documents with red seals, laid out on a long glass table. It was done at last. Feeney and Parker had signed away their share-holdings in DFS to LVMH on the basis of a capital value for the whole company of $4.2 billion.

Looking up over his reading glasses, Feeney allowed himself a satisfied smile. An assistant handed him a glass of champagne. Feeney got up and posed for photographs, glass of bubbly in hand, with Harvey Dale, Jim Downey, and Chris Oechsli. Feeney and Parker then retired, exhausted, with a couple of the lawyers to celebrate their multi-billion-dollar deal in typical Feeney style, in a nondescript New York restaurant.

The deal had a "drop-dead" date of December 31, 1996 (later revised to January 15, 1997). Miller and Pilaro could sell on the same terms, up to that date, if they changed their minds. LVMH got in touch with Miller and Pilaro to say the offer could be taken up right away. They refused. Miller was furious. He complained bitterly that Feeney and Parker had "snubbed their partners of half a lifetime."

CHAPTER 24

Cutting the Baby in Half

Three weeks later Bob Miller and Tony Pilaro threw down the gauntlet. On Thursday, October 24, 1996, motorcycle messengers brought two letters to Ira Millstein at his Manhattan law firm, Weil, Gotshal & Manges, one each from lawyers representing Miller and Pilaro. The letters reminded Millstein that the Wise Man Agreement stipulated that any dispute or controversy relating to the agreement should be resolved by arbitration before him. They claimed that the proposed sale by Chuck Feeney and Alan Parker of their shareholding in DFS to Bernard Arnault breached the Wise Man Agreement. They requested that Millstein rule that it could not go ahead.

The following day, lawyers for Miller and Pilaro filed Case Number 96605345 in the New York Supreme Court, on Centre Street in downtown Manhattan. The 200-page document called for an injunction to prevent the sale of DFS holdings by Feeney and Parker from going ahead, on the grounds that it would substantially undermine DFS Group's ability to compete with LVMH. It also accused them of divulging confidential information to a competitor. Judge Beatrice Shainswit, a twenty-year veteran of the New York Supreme Court, ruled the same day that Feeney and Parker must show the court by November 25, 1996, why an injunction should not be issued.

Up to this point, the fight for the future of DFS had escaped media attention. The lodging of court documents changed that. DFS was forced to issue a press release on October 30 giving details of the proposed sale of Feeney's and Parker's holdings to LVMH. The *New York Times* reported that "high-flying billionaire" Robert Miller was seeking to block the sale by Chuck Feeney and Alan Parker, as he and Mr. Pilaro "do not want to be the minority shareholder in a company controlled by DFS's largest supplier and a major competitor." Quoting people "familiar with his far-flung interests," it described Feeney as a billionaire whose estimated net worth was "much more" than the $975 million cited in the most recent *Forbes* magazine rich list. The *Wall Street Journal* and *The Financial Times* also reported the dispute. A spokesman for Arnault was quoted as saying Miller and Pilaro were just holding out to get a better price.

The day the story appeared, Caroleen Feeney was walking along Columbus Avenue in New York when she saw Andrew Pilaro coming in the opposite direction. They had been friends since childhood, when the Feeney and Pilaro kids went out in the company junk in Hong Kong on weekends. Instead of avoiding each other, however, they hugged. "This has nothing to do with us, it's between our parents," Caroleen remembered Andrew saying.

The news that DFS was for sale brought the barbarian to the gate. Henry R. Kravis, of Kohlberg Kravis Roberts & Co. (KKR), whose 1988 leveraged buyout of RJR Nabisco had been dramatized in the book *Barbarians at the Gate*,* wrote to Ira Millstein, expressing his interest in buying out DFS for a price higher than that offered by LVMH. The corporate raider, who had a reputation for buying companies, restructuring them, selling off selected assets, and then getting rid of the company at a profit, and who had bought and sold such American brand names as Gillette, Texaco, Samsonite, and Safeway, said he could back his bid with more than $5 billion in equity capital. "We believe that KKR is uniquely positioned to facilitate a transaction in a timely manner," he wrote.

LVMH brushed off the Kravis bid. Such an offer wasn't permissible under the terms of the agreement to purchase signed with Feeney and Parker, a spokesman said. None of the four owners of DFS took it seriously.

The Wise Man invited the legal representatives of the owners to come to his office at 10:00 AM on November 6 to begin his arbitration. Eleven

---

*Bryan Burrough and John Helyar, *Barbarians at the Gate* (HarperCollins, 1990).

highly paid New York lawyers crowded into the room. Chuck Feeney's team was headed by Frederick A.O. "Fritz" Schwarz of Cravath, Swaine & Moore, who in 1975 was general counsel to Senator Frank Church's Senate committee that investigated U.S. intelligence agencies. Bob Miller was represented by Peter Fleming, who had appeared for former attorney general John N. Mitchell in the Watergate hearings, and by William Brickern, both from Curtis, Mallet-Prevost, Colt & Mosle. Pilaro had two teams, one headed by Thomas J. Schwarz from Skadden, Arps, Slate, Meagher & Flom, the other by Anthony Genovese of Robinson, Brog, Leinwand, Greene, Genovese & Gluck. Alan Parker was represented by Bernard Nussbaum of Wachtell, Lipton, Rosen & Katz, who until two years previously had been President Bill Clinton's White House counsel.

Ira Millstein spoke with some weariness. The four shareholders were his friends, he said. He had tried everything to avoid arbitration. "I've been discussing the various proposals for sales to LVMH from day one, starting with Chuck's desire to sell by himself, and continuing on through the various confederations thereafter, with some selling and some not selling, and some agreeing and some not agreeing. I've been involved in every one of these discussions with every single one of the partners. Chuck has come to see me alone. Bob has come to see me alone. Tony has come to see me alone. I've met them together and separately and in every combination known to man." He had also had "untold" numbers of discussions with Bernard Arnault, asking him to help get a deal on track with one, two, or three, or all four of the owners. Nothing had worked. "I am a totally unsuccessful arbitrator or Wise Man or whatever in trying to get them to agree to do this together," he said. "I flunked." Now, he went on, he would listen to their arguments and then go off into a corner and make his own mind up.

"I have to find a way to cut the baby in half," he said, "and somebody is going to be very unhappy."

When Miller's lawyer sought a delay to consider whether or not to give Millstein a waiver for any conflicts of interest in past dealings with individual DFS owners, the Wise Man responded with exasperation. His seventieth birthday was coming up in two days' time, on Friday, he told them. He was planning a weekend away with his family. He would not be back until the following Wednesday. Without a waiver, "I'm out of here," he said, and they would have to pick another arbitrator very quickly. He had

a nice career, and he wanted to keep it that way, so he did not want anyone accusing him later of conflict of interest. The Miller lawyers went into
a huddle. Fleming came back to say, "Mr. Miller waives."

Millstein requested that both sides file briefs and responses by December
4, after which he would make his ruling. Until then the deal signed by
Feeney and Parker was on hold. One other thing, he said, as the lawyers
stuffed files back into their briefcases. He wanted any outstanding bills due
to him settled right away so there was no question of seeming bias. The
Wise Man, who charged $500 an hour as a senior partner in his firm, also
asked for a check for $250,000 against his fees.

In the following days, claims and counter claims piled up on the Wise
Man's desk. From Paris, Bernard Arnault sent a sworn declaration that he
would maintain DFS as an independent business. He pointed to the experience of Le Bon Marché, the French department-store chain that LVMH
had acquired in 1988 and which he claimed was left to its own devices. He
enclosed a floor plan to show that competing boutiques were located as
prominently in the Le Bon Marché stores as LVMH affiliates.

In their depositions, Miller and Pilaro argued that the Wise Man Agreement prohibited a transaction of the sort contemplated by Feeney and
Parker. They claimed the sale would hurt DFS because it would damage relations with other luxury goods houses. They produced correspondence and
memos purporting to show, inter alia, that Feeney had recognized the right
of the other shareholders to approve or disapprove a sale of his holdings.
Feeney and Parker responded with eight affidavits and boxes of correspondence. They argued that the Wise Man Agreement did not restrain a shareholder from selling and that it would not be in LVMH's interests to run
DFS as anything other than an independent company. They pleaded that if
the sale were blocked, they might never be able to find another buyer. They
also threw back at Pilaro the statement he made at the board meeting in
1990, when Chuck's representatives were thrown out, that the will of the
majority "can and does control."

When Fleming, acting for Miller, again asked for a delay, pointing out
that his client had to read through the affidavits, "a chore which unfortunately takes some period of time," Nussbaum responded sharply: "Messrs
Miller and Pilaro can complete this chore in a few hours if they sit down to
read the affidavits." As tempers frayed, Fritz Schwarz accused Miller and Pilaro of just wanting to continue their personal lifestyles.

On November 18, Chuck Feeney submitted an affidavit, sworn before U.S. Counsel Robert Dolce in London, that the assets of his General Atlantic Group, including the entire 38.75 percent interest in DFS, had been transferred irrevocably to the Atlantic Foundation in 1984, and later in part to the Atlantic Trust, "exclusively for charitable and philanthropic purposes." This, he argued, underscored the point that they "would never have consented to any restraint" on their ability to sell the shareholding in DFS. The Atlantic Foundation had up to that point committed in excess of half a billion dollars in grants and was one of the world's largest international charitable institutions, Feeney disclosed. Satisfying the charities' commitments required that its holdings remain freely transferable so that return on investment would have an acceptable level of risk and volatility.

Only Feeney's own counsel had prior knowledge that Feeney had given everything away: Fritz Schwarz had for some time been on the board of his foundation. All the lawyers and their clients had access to his deposition, but this bombshell did not leak to the media. However, Feeney's statement was included in the documents filed before Judge Beatrice Shainswit, who was expected to issue her decision after the Wise Man ruled. It was now only a matter of time before it became public knowledge.

In an attempt to persuade Ira Millstein that Bernard Arnault was not an acceptable buyer, Bob Miller's lawyer, Peter Fleming, launched a strong attack on Arnault's business ethics in a submission to the Wise Man in early December. The French businessman could hardly be trusted, argued Fleming. The *Sunday Times* had described Arnault's four-year campaign to take over LVMH as "the most vicious corporate battle ever seen in France" and the *Mail on Sunday* had charged that Arnault raised cash for LVMH by ensuring that Christian Dior and Le Bon Marché, both of which had minority shareholders, took on large amounts of debt. He demanded that Arnault sign a tough cooperation and noninterference agreement to protect Miller's and Pilaro's interests if they became minority shareholders.

Parker was shocked when he read it. "They filed all sorts of documents about Mr. Arnault and what a bad guy he was; I was horrified to hear that in a private case such documents could be available to the public," he said.

The antagonism between Arnault and Miller led to a minor crisis in New York's fashionable society. Miller's daughter Marie-Chantal, who had married Crown Prince Pavlos of Greece and was living in Manhattan, withdrew as cochairman of the Metropolitan Museum of Art Costume Institute

Ball—the most glittering event of Manhattan's black-tie season—on December 9 because Bernard Arnault was a guest of honor.

On December 12, the Wise Man received a letter and a box of documents from Arnault to provide reassurances to him that Miller and Pilaro would have their status as minority shareholders protected. The box contained copies of highly confidential investment bankers' reports and internal memoranda for the Wise Man's eyes only. The lawyers argued all morning over whether Millstein should read them or not and finally agreed that he should go through them in camera. Only when Millstein started poking through the LVMH documents did he realize that they were all in French, and he had to get a French-speaking colleague to help him out.

The session ended on a sour note, with Nussbaum accusing Miller and Pilaro of putting their heads in the sand. It was a good deal, he said. "Miller knows it. Pilaro knows it. They know it. They know they will be benefited by this transaction. But it's not going to be theirs anymore. It's not going to be 'my company' anymore, as Miller tends to say. It's not going to be 'my baby.' That's what this is about. This is not about economics and harm; this is about ego and prestige." Fleming was outraged: "Take that back, Bernie, strike that," he said. The Wise Man intervened to say, "It's an argument, but I promise you it's not going to be the basis of my decision."

At this point, Tony Pilaro tried to strengthen his and Miller's case by raising doubts about the future of DFS's license in Honolulu. The Hawaiian authorities could withdraw the duty-free concession if DFS changed hands. The issue was on the agenda for a meeting of the Board of Land and Natural Resources in Honolulu on December 13. The eight-member board was expected to go along with any new ownership arrangement, but at 5:30 AM Hawaii time, Tony Pilaro telephoned John Reed, the head of DFS in Honolulu, and pleaded with him to get approval of the sale taken off the agenda until the new year. Reed reported the request to DFS headquarters in San Francisco and was advised that it would be inappropriate to intervene. DFS chairman Myron Ullman in turn informed Ira Millstein confidentially about what was going on.

When the eight members of the Board of Land convened at their office on Punchbowl Street, Honolulu, on December 12, one of the them asked Reed why they should be involved in a dispute among the DFS owners. Reed replied, "I'll tell you what this is all about. We have minority owners that are now big fish in a big pond, and if this transfer goes through, they will be little fish in a big pond. Secondly, if this transfer goes through, the minority owners will not receive any dividends for five years." According to Anthony Takitani, a lawyer representing Miller and Pilaro at the meeting, Reed went on to claim that the dividend money would be used instead for LVMH's debt service. The board made clear that the sale of DFS would cause no problems.

Bernard Arnault had in fact already told Millstein two days earlier that while LVMH could not continue to pay 90 percent of the dividends to the shareholders as had been the case historically, it would pay "a more customary minimum 50 percent."

Tony Pilaro then made a direct appeal to Millstein, quoting what Reed had said. "The clarion bells are ringing, Ira," he wrote on December 14. "Bob and I are not protected. We have close to $2 billion at risk. . . ." If they became minority shareholders to Arnault, he and Miller would not get any dividends because Arnault was going to have to pay off his debts and the Wise Man should protect them. He enclosed records showing DFS dividends had gone up from $34 million in 1977 to $309 million in 1995. In just under two decades, $2.85 billion in cash had flowed into the accounts of the four owners. These were the stakes involved in the Wise Man's decision. "You can, you should, and I pray you will protect us," wrote Pilaro, concluding with a request to the Wise Man to either stop the sale or order Feeney and Parker to sell them 9 percent of the shareholding to give them majority control over LVMH.

As he drafted his arbitration, the Wise Man received a final appeal on December 15 from Peter Fleming, in which he attacked Arnault for his "basic disdain of minority shareholders" and accused Alan Parker of "shamelessly" seeking to avoid his obligations under the Wise Man Agreement. He enclosed a letter from Miller's eighty-year-old nominee on the DFS board, Lawrence Lachman, who as head of Bloomingdale's had transformed it from a New York department store into a national chain. Lachman warned of the damage a great company could suffer from combining a retailing and a manufacturing operation. Bloomingdale's succeeded, he said, because he had gotten rid of an in-house manufacturing company for drugs and cosmetics that was losing money.

On getting copies of the letters, Nussbaum wrote to accuse Miller of seeking delay through Lachman, and said Reed could not possibly know about LVMH plans for dividends.

The Wise Man was finally ready to issue his decision on Tuesday, December 17. Feeney walked through the chilly streets—snow was forecast—to the offices of Cravath, Swaine & Moore, at the Worldwide Plaza on Eighth Avenue and Fiftieth Street, to await the ruling. If it was in his favor, the sale would be confirmed and the ownership transferred right away.

About thirty lawyers, investment bankers, bank officials, signatories, and assistants gathered in a conference room in the firm's elegant premises, decorated in Italian green-and-crimson marble and German wood. Papers were laid out on the table for signatures. Someone carried in a fax machine and plugged it into a socket. The LVMH lawyer arrived. He had been walking around for days with checks for hundreds of millions in his pocket, recalled Alan Parker. Letters, legal documents, and deposit slips were laid out on the table. An official from J. P. Morgan turned up wearing sneakers so he could run to the bank with the checks and deposit slips: He wouldn't even try to find a taxi in the pre-Christmas gridlock on the Manhattan streets. The money would have to be lodged immediately: A billion dollars for one overnight was worth tens of thousands of dollars. Another bank in New Jersey was on standby to keep its clearing operation open if Millstein ruled in their favor after bank closing hours. Everyone waited, sipping cups of coffee.

"If the decision went in our favor, we would have to close within minutes because there was the risk that the losing party would immediately go to court and enjoin the arbitral provision, thereby making this whole litigation public and slowing things down," said Harvey Dale. "But the courts will never reverse a closing if it has already occurred. So a lot of things had to happen very fast, and this was a complex closing. A lot of moving parts had to be brought together."

At 3:30 PM, the fax machine rang. Eleven pages of Millstein's decision spilled out before the words "the sale may proceed" appeared. The Wise Man made one condition—that the minority partners be protected and LVMH sign a specified cooperation agreement to allow DFS to continue independent operations, something to which Arnault had already agreed.

Somebody said, "Let's go!" and the room suddenly stirred into life. The purchase checks were signed, "$700 million here and $400 million there," said Chris Oechsli with a laugh. The man in sneakers from J. P. Morgan set off at a run. The LVMH lawyer signed the cooperation agreement and a copy was rushed by messenger to Ira Millstein's office seventeen blocks away on Fifth Avenue. A letter was faxed to the New York Supreme Court, signed by Chuck's lawyer, Fritz Schwarz, asking that if Miller and Pilaro applied for an injunction, Feeney should be given an opportunity to oppose it. It wasn't necessary. "After the ruling, we fully anticipated that they would try to file an injunction to stop the checks clearing, but they didn't," said Parker. It was 8:00 PM before the final document was signed and witnessed and the checks cleared by J. P. Morgan.

Chuck Feeney received $1.6275 billion in cash from Bernard Arnault for his foundation. Alan Parker received $840 million.

Miller and Pilaro were half expecting to lose. "Ira came down with his decision at 3 o'clock," Pilaro recalled. "Immediately thereafter the transaction closed with Chuck and Alan. Immediately! So clearly, all their lawyers were well aware in advance that the decision would be positive to them, and the closing was held."

Chuck Feeney, Alan Parker, and a dozen of the lawyers held a celebration champagne dinner that evening in an alcove at Lattanzi's, a family-owned restaurant on West Forty-sixth Street famous for its Roman-Jewish cuisine. Among the guests were two senior members of the team employed by LVMH—the producers of Moët & Chandon—though as Oechsli noted, it was the DFS sellers who paid for the champagne. They could afford it.

CHAPTER

Erreur Stratégique

B ob Miller and Tony Pilaro had not given up. Though they failed to seek an immediate injunction to stop the sale on the day of the Wise Man's ruling, they returned to New York Supreme Court after the new year and asked Judge Shainswit to rule that the Wise Man had exceeded his author- ity, and that his decision to allow the sale should be voided. Said Pilaro, "We were seeking some very rapid action." On Friday, January 10, 1997, the judge ordered Chuck Feeney and Alan Parker to show cause within one month why the Wise Man decision should not be overturned.

But the following morning, LVMH assumed control over DFS as a thirty- day antitrust period expired. The shares and the funds were transferred and the operation completed. Arnault had succeeded in winning control, though the market hammered LVMH stock price on fears that the DFS purchase might impact on the profitability of the French fashion empire.

Pilaro also sought to take an action against Ira Millstein personally for ig- noring the "clarion bells" and allegedly breaching the "power in trust" in him by allowing a sale to a competitor. His law firm, Skadden, Arps, Slate, Meagher & Flom, declined to take the case, however, and he let the matter drop.

Pilaro had one more card to play. He revived the unresolved and con- tentious dispute over the retail stores in Hawaii. The Wise Man Agreement of February 20, 1991, stipulated that Feeney cede control of his Hawaiian Retail Group to a third party by January 31, 1993. He had done nothing, however, and had gotten the deadline extended to January 31, 1994. Again nothing had happened. After further false starts and delays, Pilaro had asked the Wise Man in January 1996 to direct General Atlantic to transfer its interest in the Hawaiian Retail Group to DFS. Feeney responded by signing an agreement in principle on March 25, 1996, to sell the Hawaiian Retail Group to an entity owned by the four DFS shareholders. But ten months had passed since then, again without anything happening.

"From day one, Chuck simply ignored that part of the Wise Man Agreement," said Chris Oechsli. "It just dragged on and on. We spent many, many hours on how the retail group would be restructured—and we never did it. We were very clever. I remember doing lots of machinations that ultimately didn't go anywhere."

Mike Windsor, who ran the Hawaiian Retail Group from 1996, recalled that Feeney offered at one point to give the group to a special charity of the DFS owners' choosing. "But they turned us down. They wanted to rub Chuck's nose in this; the other three wanted to win, rather than a rational solution. We never did sell the Hawaiian Retail Group because he didn't want to. And I always asked Chuck, when this fight was going on, 'Look, we're not making any money out of the retail stuff. It's not worth it. Why don't we get rid of them?' And he said, 'They've got my Irish up, I'm not going to give in.'"

On January 2, 1997, Pilaro instructed Anthony Genovese of his second legal team to write to Ira Millstein, demanding that he force Feeney to transfer the Hawaii stores to the four DFS shareholders or face a fine of $50,000 a day, retroactive to March 25, 1996, if he did not transfer the retail stores as a going concern within two weeks. Miller followed Pilaro's lead, making the same demands in a letter the following day. Feeney told Oechsli to set up a meeting with a representative of Pilaro and Miller before January 17 to implement the transfer. This time, he said, there would be no problem.

This sideshow was soon overtaken by more dramatic events. Pilaro flew to London, booked into Claridge's and on Wednesday, January 15, the day when Arnault's offer to buy them out would expire, invited Miller to lunch. They went to Mark's Club, just off Berkeley Square, a private dining club where Pilaro was a member, and were joined by Pilaro's nominated director on the DFS board, Rick Braddock.

As they worked their way through the main course, at an antique table overhung by oil paintings on fabric-covered walls, Tony Pilaro told Miller he had decided after all to accept Bernard Arnault's offer for his 2.5 percent shareholding, which in his case amounted to $110 million cash. Miller was stunned. "You have to do what you've got to do" was all he could say.

"Right in the middle of the lunch, Tony said, 'Bob, I am going to sell,'" Miller recalled. His mind went back to the day thirty-two years earlier when Pilaro had left the company, thinking it was going bankrupt. "Unfortunately, this is Tony's way of doing things: He gets all excited and then at the last moment can change his mind completely," he said.

Pilaro urged Bob to sell as well. He had been the "pit bull" fighting Arnault, he pointed out. Was he sure he wanted to stay? They might also get more for their shares than Feeney and Parker. Arnault had talked about adding on a premium if they made the jump. "Let's call him up and see if the premium is still around," he said.

They finished their lunch and went to the offices of Morgan Stanley on Cabot Square to make the call to Arnault. With so much at stake, an office room was provided, and Anthony J. Tennant, a senior adviser at Morgan Stanley, was recruited to make the call on their behalf. Tennant had been a director of Christie's International PLC and would later be charged in a U.S. court with conspiring to fix auction commission rates with A. Alfred Taubman, chairman of the board of directors of Sotheby's: Taubman was convicted but Tennant, who denied the charges, could not be extradited and avoided trial.

"Tennant calls up," said Pilaro. "He says, 'I have Mr. Pilaro and Mr. Miller here. And they have got some questions. They would like to know about the premium that you offered them. Is there a premium?' Mr. Arnault said, 'I understand the significance of the premium.' Tennant said, 'Will there be a premium?' He said, 'I cannot answer that at this time.' I said to Tennant, 'Ask him when you will be able to answer that.' And Mr. Arnault said, 'Friday.' It was Wednesday. Our put was expiring that day. I said, 'Mr. Tennant, will you ask Mr. Arnault if he will extend the deadline of our put to Friday.' Arnault said, 'No.' I said, 'Tell Mr. Arnault I'm exercising my put today, and he will hear from my lawyer.'"

Arnault was overheard to remark, "At least we got one of them." Pilaro interpreted that to mean "At least we got Pilaro to sell," but later he thought he may have meant, "At least we got Miller to stay, and I don't have to spend another billion six to get control."

Miller that day was "very to himself, very oriental, not an easy read," recalled Pilaro. "He may have thought Arnault disliked me so much that maybe with me gone, there would be a more friendly relationship between the two." Pilaro offered to sell him his 2.5 percent for $110 million, but Miller wasn't interested.

He was subsequently asked by LVMH to sign a non-compete agreement. "I said, 'Jesus Christ, I'll sign anything.' I washed my hands of Duty Free."

The day Pilaro sold, Chuck Feeney and Alan Parker were in Paris for a celebration dinner with Arnault in one of the city's top restaurants. Before the dinner, the pair stopped at Arnault's office. A banker from Lazard came hurrying down the stairs to say, "You won't believe what has just happened. Tony has just signed."

The mood at the dinner, attended by about twenty people, was euphoric. Feeney sat in the place of honor, between Arnault and his slim, blonde wife, Hélène Mercier, a Canadian-born concert pianist.

Harvey Dale got word almost immediately of Pilaro's decision to exercise his put. "I couldn't believe it, he had bad-mouthed the deal," he recalled. Dale phoned Ira Millstein. The Wise Man was at a meeting, but the lawyer insisted that he take the call. Millstein came on the line. "Tony 'put'!" said Harvey Dale. "The fuck!" said Millstein.

There was never a question in his mind about staying in DFS, Pilaro recalled one spring day over coffee at his chalet in Gstaad, Switzerland. "When the deal was done, why would I want to be a minority partner to Bernard? He had control." Pilaro was aware that Arnault regarded him as a troublemaker. He conceded that he had been wrong to oppose the sale all along. "Chuck was a genius on timing. He had a great sense of the unknown, a feel that something wasn't right somewhere. It happened more than once in our company that he came in and said, 'Let's do something,' and we took a different tack, and he was right."

The relationship between Miller and Pilaro never recovered. "To say the least, I was disappointed with Tony and I haven't really spoken to him since," said Miller. The friendship between Pilaro and the Wise Man also came to an end. Several years later, Millstein wrote to Pilaro to say that while he had never done any work for Arnault, he wanted to inform him that the LVMH chairman had now asked him to represent him in a legal matter. Pilaro said he replied along the lines of, "We are big guys, we have known each other for long enough, let me tell you, I do believe that what you did [allowing the DFS sale] violated the power in trust that you owed to me." They never communicated after that.

In New York that same day, Chris Oechsli met Pilaro's lawyer, Craig Leonard, to negotiate the sale of Feeney's Hawaii stores. "Then we heard that Tony had just decided to sell and from that moment on, we did virtually nothing on the Hawaiian Retail Group," said Oechsli. Nobody was interested any more. The Hawaiian stores stayed in the possession of General Atlantic.

With Pilaro gone and Arnault in effective ownership of DFS, Miller and Pilaro's court case went nowhere. When it came up for hearing in February, Pilaro's name was deleted from the appeal "with prejudice." It was adjourned to March 27, when Miller's lawyers told the court he would not pursue the action any further.

Miller meanwhile pressed Arnault for a higher price for his 38.75 percent, and thought he had a deal at one point but the LVMH boss turned it down. There was no premium after all. He resigned himself to his status as minority shareholder.

"The whole issue affected me quite traumatically," reflected Miller years later at his shooting lodge in Yorkshire, England. "My health suffered, I got the shingles, I guess as a result of the emotional turmoil I suffered at the time." He worried whether he had done the right thing, and how he would relate to Bernard Arnault, whose business practices his lawyers had excoriated. He realized that "once Alan decided to sell, then the game was pretty well over," and Tony had left him in the cold. He said he stayed on because he did not want to break his connection with DFS and because he thought he could get a higher price out of Arnault.

The *Wall Street Journal* reported that Miller had been left "a disgruntled minority shareholder openly at odds with a large supplier and controlling shareholder." French economics writer Airy Routier wrote that Arnault "flipped the amiable Robert Miller like a pancake," and that Miller decided to remain a shareholder "to his own discomfort."*

But some felt that Arnault himself had been turned over like *un bleu*—a rookie—by Chuck Feeney, reported Routier, citing one prominent businessman whose opinion it was that the French fashion mogul made a veritable *erreur stratégique* by buying DFS just before the Asian financial crisis of 1996–1997.

Arnault had in fact acquired a declining asset. In the eighteen months while the sale was being negotiated, DFS sales dropped from $3 billion to $1.5 billion. With Japan's recession, Asia's economic downturn, and the weakening of European currencies, the core DFS customers were spending less.

---

*Airy Routier, *L'ange exterminateur: La vraie vie de Bernard Arnault* (Éditions Albin Michel S.A., 2003).

Conor O'Clery || 227

Dividends dried up. A year after the sale, 320 staff were laid off, and Hong Kong had its first ever loss. Sales in the DFS mother ship in Hawaii dropped from $426 million in 1995–1996 to $229 million in 1999–2000. By 2000, quarterly profits were reported to be running at less than $20 million, despite the installation of Louis Vuitton and Celine boutiques in the DFS Gallerias.

On the plus side for Miller, he had significant veto checks over Arnault. The Wise Man had ensured that LVMH would not interfere with DFS for ten years. Nor could the French company take on major new strategies or debt without Miller's consent. Miller took the attitude that he and his new partner were in bed together, and they might as well make the best of it. He told Bernard Arnault that he would do whatever he could to ensure that the price he paid was justified one day. It was in his interest to do so as well. They now worked well together, he said.

As for his relationship with Chuck Feeney, the split had little bearing on him. "We were distant at that time in any case. I really haven't seen Chuck since 1996. All partnerships break up at some stage, even the Beatles. Arguments start about who contributed most to the success of the partnerships. And then the wives get involved, and it gets extremely complicated. We've got more money than we know what to do with. So everybody's happy. Forget it. It's not worth worrying about. LVMH bought out Chuck and Alan at a very good price. God bless them if they are happy with their monies. Do I regret not selling out at the same time? I don't know. I have thought about it a lot. I don't know if all that money in a lump sum would have made me any happier than I am now. I really love DFS and the company. But all the legal things we did with the Wise Man, Ira Millstein, to be quite frank, all of that was pure bullshit. We didn't really need all that fancy legal stuff. The lawyers have a way of dragging you in and making things more complicated than they are. We were paying huge legal bills at that time, and I don't think any of that would have affected the outcome. When the dust settles, you find out it was all just a huge waste of time, energy, and money."

The success of DFS arose from the fact that they were in the right place at the right time, reflected Alan Parker at his mansion on the shores of Lake Geneva. "Nobody ever put a penny in the business: We took out $8 billion or whatever it was. Nobody is that smart. You have just got to have a lot of things going your way." It was Chuck's foresight in seeing the downturn that led to the greatest decision of the lot, he believed. The best thing they did was to sell DFS before it contracted and layoffs became inevitable.

"It would have been an awful experience for us to have gone through, and we wouldn't have done any better. It would really have got to me and to Chuck to lay off thousands of people. They have laid off probably 5,000 people since 1997. It would have to have been a disaster, particularly for people who have been generous like we have been. I think it would have had a very dramatic effect on Chuck."

"I always thought the most fascinating thing about Chuck was how he came to decisions about things," reflected Adrian Bellamy, looking back years later in London where he was executive chairman of The Body Shop. "If you analyze Chuck, there seems to be no coherent way that he comes at a particular decision, in the sense of the way most of us come to a decision, talking it through with people in a fairly rational sort of way. He would ask a tremendous number of questions of a tremendous number of people. You would have no idea where he was ending up. All of a sudden he would be in that space. The most interesting one—how he got to the position of believing he should sell the company, and how he managed the LVMH situation—that wasn't a case of 'Let's sit down in the room, guys, and decide if we should sell.' He was down the road long before most of the others. How did Chuck think that through? I have come to the conclusion that somewhere in his intuition is a brilliance that we don't see easily. Because it is not transparent, and yet it is very, very sure-footed. He had this capacity to push the right buttons at the right time without coming to it in a normal intellectual way."

"Everybody says it was pure genius on my part to have done this transaction at the price we did at the time we did," said Feeney over lunch one day in P. J. Clarke's crowded back room. "No genius! We would have done it sooner, and probably for less money." And he insisted that it was "dumb luck" that he made so much money in the first place, rather than anything that made him different. He often wondered "whether Bob's position didn't help us in the end to get the best price." He reckoned that Miller really regretted not selling. In 2005, DFS was estimated to be worth around $1 billion, making Miller's stake worth $400 million, one-fourth of the price he could have gotten without taking into account added value over the years.

Tony Pilaro maintained that he provided the competition that forced Arnault to pay such a high price, and he would say to Chuck, "Don't underestimate the fact that there was competition, and competition has a tendency to preserve value."

The profitable side business the four owners had, that of distributing Camus cognac and armagnac worldwide through their company, Camus Overseas Ltd. (COL), also came to a fractious end. During the sale negotiations, Jean-Paul Camus sent a handwritten letter to the DFS owners asking what would happen to the special deal he had with them if they sold. Camus was still getting most-favored-cognac treatment: In the previous four years, DFS had sold $242 million worth of Camus cognac compared to $50 million of Hennessy brandy. Would Arnault, who owned Hennessy, not reverse this? In response, Arnault gave an assurance that he would not interfere with the long-standing arrangement. But Camus had other problems. It produced only a small percentage of its own "juice" and bought the bulk from outsiders, which required massive borrowings. It was near bankruptcy, and the bank looked for somebody to lay off their loans. Feeney and Parker were asked to attend a meeting at a bank in Paris. There were ten to fifteen French bankers there, recalled Parker. The bankers said, "You guys have made a ton out of Camus, it's your problem, not ours." He retorted, "We have our commitments to Camus, and we will meet those commitments and we will buy the cognac we have committed to buy, and that's all, and the rest is your problem." Feeney and Parker walked out of the bank. Morgan Stanley valued COL at $600 million, but "eventually we gave the whole thing back to Camus for nothing, the distribution rights on a worldwide basis, in return for being let off the hook," said Parker.

Lee Sterling and Jeff Mahlstedt, who left DFS in 1965 to pursue their own business interests, reflected on the wisdom of their career move when they heard about the multi-billion-dollar sale of the company which they once partly owned. "I think I left a few years too early," said Sterling. "I don't regret it, but it sure would have been nice to stay on!" "Was I sorry?" said Mahlstedt. "Anybody in their right mind would have to say, 'Of course!'"

After the DFS sale, Chuck Feeney and Alan Parker arranged for checks to be sent from the proceeds to 2,400 long-term employees at the duty-free stores. Feeney set aside $26 million for this, and Parker $13.5 million. Those who qualified were managers with five years' service, employees with ten years, and retired staff with fifteen years who had left in the previous five years. In an accompanying letter, Feeney described the payments as a gift "by which we intend to show our goodwill, esteem, and kindliness."

It was an almost unheard-of act of generosity in the corporate world. Feeney and Parker got hundreds of letters from grateful workers who had no idea the checks were coming. A production manager in Honolulu described how when the staff opened their envelopes, there were "whoops of joy, tears, some had to sit down due to nervousness—all the emotions of having received a generous gift." A woman in the Waikiki duty-free shop told Alan Parker that when she was informed she would get a gift, she had expected a watch or a purse. "Then the next day when I came to work and was handed the two letters, I opened your letter first, my heart stopped a bit, I couldn't think and went into shock. I cried and cried, I just couldn't believe it. Then I opened Mr. Feeney's letter! One of the managers had to comfort me before I started my shift."

There is much nostalgia in DFS for the time when Chuck Feeney and Alan Parker were owners. Both—especially Feeney—had inculcated a caring culture in DFS, said Bellamy. "Chuck was always for the little person, the salesladies and their families." DFS had once been a happy company and people loved it from top to bottom. "We always had parties at year's end, and management would dress up in funny clothes up on the stage telling the salesladies how good they were. We paid people well and gave them good benefits. That undoubtedly came as much as anybody from Chuck."

In Waikiki in January 2006, staff members openly expressed their despondency at the erosion of their benefits and working conditions since the sale. The level of health care, scholarships, and bonuses that the original owners had introduced was a thing of the past, they said. There were rumors of more layoffs at the DFS Galleria, where staff had been cut back again after the 9/11 attacks hit air travel.

"The Japanese visitor to Hawaii is younger now and has been here a number of times," said Phil Fong, DFS Hawaii's former inventory controller, at the Honolulu warehouse where he today runs a jeans business. "The focus now in DFS is more on cost savings and efficiency. It is 100 percent different culture from before the sale." He related that in 1998, he was asked to tell the thirty staff in the DFS Honolulu accounts department that they were all being let go. As soon as he had completed this unpleasant task, he was told his own job was being eliminated and that he must leave immediately.

In January 2006 in the Waikiki DFS Galleria in Hawaii, the eyes of an elderly Japanese sales assistant crinkled up in delight at mention of Chuck Feeney's name. She clasped her hands. "Oh! I remember Feeney-*san*. Very nice man. He gave me $10,000. Mr. Parker gave me $2,500. When I got the checks my husband said, 'Count the naughts!' We were so full of thanks!"

PART FOUR

GIVING IT AWAY

CHAPTER

"A Great Op."

The sale by Chuck Feeney of his foundation's share in DFS meant that his days of anonymity were about to end. Submissions made to the Wise Man and to the New York Supreme Court disclosing that he had secretly transferred his ownership of the duty-free empire to his charitable foundation might be accessed by the media at any time. With the injection of $1.6 billion from the DFS sale on top of an already overflowing treasure chest of investments and properties, his foundation had surely become too big to escape notice for much longer.

Harvey Dale worried that without proper management of the publicity, people would suspect the money in the foundation was tainted. Two years earlier, the pretense of anonymous giving was used to perpetrate the biggest scam in the history of American charities, when the Foundation for New Era Philanthropy, founded by Philadelphia-area Christian businessman John G. Bennett Jr., defrauded donors of $135 million by inviting them to contribute large sums to his foundation for fixed periods that would be matched by secret donors—who did not exist.

Atlantic Foundation put its strategy for the "unveiling" of its secret existence into motion on January 13, 1997. That day, the president of the Atlantic Foundation's service company, Joel Fleishman, called *New York Times* publisher Arthur (Punch) Sulzberger and asked for an urgent meeting. They had been friends for years, but Fleishman, a professor of law and public policy at Duke University and onetime wine columnist for *Vanity Fair*, had never told Sulzberger that he was secretly running the service arm of a major world philanthropy.

Sulzberger was suffering from a cold, and he invited Fleishman to drop by his apartment on Fifth Avenue. There the Duke professor told him, "Well, Punch, I've never been able to tell you what I really do. I have always been a bit obscure in my answers to your questions. Now I can tell you what I do, and this is it, and we are going to announce the existence of this organization in ten days' time, and the *New York Times* can have an exclusive."

The publication of the story was set for Thursday, January 23. *New York Times* senior executive Michael Oreskes assigned reporters Judith Miller and David Cay Johnston to check everything out. They established that Feeney's giving and his passion for secrecy were indeed unique. When they called Thomas A. Troyer, a specialist in philanthropic law from Caplin & Drysdale in Washington, he assured them, "I've never heard of anything like this." David Cay Johnston did not need to be told how important the disclosure was. For years he had been aware of a huge presence in the world of philanthropy, a personage who regularly funded universities and nonprofit organizations, and was known only as "Anonymous."

On January 22, Harvey Dale told three academic colleagues in a midtown restaurant that the next day the *New York Times* would reveal that he was the head of one of the world's biggest private philanthropies. None of his close circle knew about his secret life. Dale had become director of the National Center on Philanthropy and the Law at New York University Law School but had never told members of the board where their funding was coming from. In his mind it was the right thing to do, to go public, he now told them, but in his heart he would miss being a private person.

That same day, with jet engines screaming in the background, Feeney lifted a pay phone in San Francisco airport and by prior arrangement called the *New York Times*. He told Judith Miller he was prepared to reveal his secret to the world, that he was not a billionaire, as he was usually referred to in the business pages, and that he had long ago given everything, including his DFS shares and his businesses, to his two philanthropic foundations, the Atlantic Foundation and the Atlantic Trust, based in Bermuda. He was personally worth less than $2 million, a fact known only to a tight circle of family and friends. In the last fifteen years he—or rather, his charities—had given $600 million to good causes in the United States and elsewhere across the world. He now planned to set about giving away the remainder—which after the DFS sale amounted to some $3.5 billion.

"I simply decided I had enough money. It doesn't drive my life. I'm a what-you-see-is-what-you-get kind of guy," Feeney told Miller. "Money has an attraction for some people, but you can't wear two pairs of shoes at one time." He divulged a few details of his private lifestyle. Yes, it was true what his friends said about him, he said, he flew economy class and he wore a $15 watch.

The newspaper splashed the story as its lead the next day under the headline "He Gave Away $600 Million and No One Knew." Judith Miller's 1,800-word report was hugely positive. It described how over the previous fifteen years, the businessman from New Jersey had given immense sums to universities, medical centers, and other beneficiaries—but with such secrecy that "most recipients never learned who their benefactor was." The donor, Charles F. Feeney, covered his tracks so well, she reported, that business magazines had for years estimated his net worth in billions, not realizing he had given everything away. Her story went on to quote several beneficiaries who had been released for the occasion from their vows of secrecy and were effusive in their praise for his style of giving, and what it had enabled them to do.

Although prepared to talk to the *New York Times*, Feeney still did not consent to his picture being taken. He was happy that the only photograph the paper could find of him was taken when he was seventeen years younger.

The carefully planned unveiling operation did not go entirely smoothly. Jim Dwyer of the *New York Daily News* also had the story that day. "He got a leak. He was all over me on the phone," remembered Dale, who refused to take his calls. Dwyer, too, was extremely positive about Feeney. "I was intrigued by him," recalled the reporter, who had encountered Feeney in Ireland when writing about the peace process. "He is the opposite of the grotesque consumption and excess that has been coursing through American society for decades, where ostentatious wealth is not something to be ashamed of but flattered. He turned that extravagance on its head to defy all the lurid conventions of our society."

"Chuck Feeney," he wrote in the *Daily News*, "is what Donald Trump would be if he lived his entire existence backward."

When Feeney's sister Arlene called him from New Jersey to say he was on the front page of the *New York Times*, Chuck pretended to be surprised.

She told him to go out and buy the newspaper "and not wait until it was in the public library in a few days' time." An old acquaintance called Feeney's office from Hawaii to sympathize with his secretary, thinking Feeney had died.

The day of the unveiling, Harvey Dale released a twenty-three-page statement to the media designed to allay any suspicions that locating the foundations in Bermuda was for shady purposes. He revealed that the board of Feeney's foundation was a blue-ribbon "who's who" from the American philanthropic and educational establishment.

Up to the mid-1990s, there had been only four directors, Chuck Feeney, Harvey Dale, Frank Mutch, and Cummings Zuill, but the board had been expanded after Mutch had warned, "It will look as if there really is some ulterior motive if it's just Chuck Feeney and two lawyers and a banker with all of this money." Sometime before the DFS sale, the Atlantic Foundation had recruited as directors Elizabeth McCormack, adviser to the Rockefeller family and vice chairman of the MacArthur Foundation; Christine V. Downton, a founding partner of Pareto Partners in the United Kingdom and a governor of the London School of Economics and of Kingston University; Fritz Schwarz, chairman of several prestigious bodies, and Feeney's lead attorney during the battle over DFS; Frank Rhodes, who had stepped down as president of Cornell; and Michael Sovern, president emeritus of Columbia University.

The statement also disclosed that of the $610 million paid out in 1,500 grants since 1982, $291 million had gone to higher education, $89 million to children and youth, $48 million to the nonprofit sector, and $23.5 million to aging and health. Another $148 million had been given to overseas charities. The single biggest beneficiary was Cornell University. The document listed twenty-seven "representative" grant recipients who had been authorized to confirm that they had received funding for worthy projects. It said Price Waterhouse would assure reporters that they had certified the accounts of the Atlantic Foundation and the Atlantic Trust throughout the years they had operated in secrecy.

Harvey Dale's chief of staff, Chris Pendry, simultaneously sent "blast faxes" to the hundreds of beneficiaries who had previously been told only that the money came from a New York consulting firm that acted for a number of anonymous donors. They were informed now that this had been a fiction. There was really only one anonymous donor, Chuck Feeney.

The world of philanthropy in America was set alight with the news that in its midst was a previously unknown and active foundation, that if based in the United States, would be the fourth-largest of America's grant-making foundations. Only the Ford, Kellogg, and Robert Wood Johnson foundations had greater assets. Atlantic was bigger than the Pew, Lilly, MacArthur, Rockefeller, and Mellon foundations, and it operated with a tiny staff of a few dozen professionals in the United States and overseas.

The positive tone of Judith Miller's report set the agenda for everyone else. The print and electronic media enthused about the secret giver, who was so little known that one network put up the wrong photograph on the television screen. All across the United States, newspapers carried a glowing *Associated Press* story that produced headlines like that in the *Star-Ledger* in Newark, New Jersey, the newspaper read by Feeney's family and childhood friends: "Tycoon's watch might be cheap, but his charitable heart is solid gold." The *Royal Gazette* in Bermuda delightedly pointed out that "Bermuda's discreet banking laws provided perfect cover for his clandestine giving."

In the *Washington Post*, playwright Jane Stanton Hitchcock suggested that Chuck Feeney had restored the good name of Anonymous, and she advocated the creation in his honor of a "Room of the Unknown Donor," where people could contemplate doing something "both satisfying and legal that no one would find out about." Another public accolade came from *Time* magazine, which listed Feeney, Princess Diana, and Alan Greenspan, as runners-up for the title of 1997 Man of the Year to Andrew Grove, chairman and CEO of Intel and the champion of the microchip. "Feeney's beneficence already ranks among the grandest of any living American and may someday make him the most generous American philanthropist of all time," declared *Time*. In an age of aggrandizement, "Feeney showed that humble hearts still beat. In many ways, that is a revelation even more gratifying than the sums he has given away."

The news of Feeney's beneficence delighted Tom Harville, who had walked out of DFS in 1977 because of his distaste for the way the DFS owners were accumulating money, and who later became CEO of Le Bon Marché. "When I first read the story about Chuck's anonymous and hugely generous philanthropy, I was instantly reminded of my reasons for leaving DFS and how thoroughly I had misjudged him," he said.

Feeney received hundreds of letters from Cornellians, Irish Americans, business contacts, beneficiaries, and old school friends in Elizabeth, New

Jersey, full of warmth, pride, and praise for what he had done. Don Keough, former head of Coca-Cola, wrote to Feeney, saying, "You are a model for all of us." Feeney's early partner in the duty-free business, Harry Adler, wrote complimenting him for reaching the top level of *tzedakah,* or charity, in the Jewish faith, giving anonymously to enable the recipient to become self-reliant. Fred Antil, his friend and Cornell alumus, sent Feeney a note saying the *New York Times* had missed the point—that his greatest contribution to mankind had been introducing him to his wife, Ann. Feeney responded: "Delighted to know this. But I don't think you read the small print. Matrimonial introductions ten percent of lifetime earnings. PS. If it doesn't work out, you get a ten-percent rebate." One of his former sandwich makers at Cornell, Tass Dueland, then a veterinarian professor living in Madison, Wisconsin, recalled his delight at the news. "Ask him, by the way, since I was his first employee, when is my pension going to come?"

Judith Miller, who often reported on terrorism (and who later would go to jail for not revealing the source of a leak from the Bush White House), made only passing reference to Feeney's support for the IRA's political wing, Sinn Fein. Most Americans knew little of the conflict in Northern Ireland. Among leading Irish Americans in the know, Feeney was highly regarded, even revered, for what he had done for peace on the island of their ancestry. Only one critical letter appeared in the *New York Times*, from Thomas J. Flynn of Fairfield, Connecticut, wondering how Feeney could "be so taken in by the myth of Irish nationalism that he thinks his donations to Sinn Fein supported only nonviolent activities."

In Ireland, further public approval followed. *The Irish Times*, Dublin's leading daily newspaper, focused on the revelations about Feeney's massive gifts to Irish universities, comparing his philanthropy to that of one of Ireland's richest businessmen, Anthony O'Reilly. "The main difference between the two men's actions is obvious," wrote Bernice Harrison in *The Irish Times*. "Mr. Feeney mostly gave anonymously . . . Dr. O'Reilly's donations are very public and as such perhaps buy the businessman a kind of immortality."

Coverage of Feeney in the British tabloid press was generally positive. But the *Mirror,* under the headline "Fury over Sinn Fein $4 billion man," alleged that the gift to Sinn Fein by the "elderly eccentric" billionaire had attracted flak "from furious peace groups and Protestants." The "furious peace groups and Protestants" it cited were two people associated with a pressure group called Families Against Intimidation and Terror in Northern Ireland, which campaigned against the paramilitary practice of knee-capping victims, and which received funding from an Irish American with unionist sympathies. One of its founding members, Nancy Gracey, complained to the paper that Feeney was "giving blood money to the very people causing all the hurt and pain." But the *Mirror* also noted that Feeney was "no sectarian benefactor," having contributed to both sides in Northern Ireland. In an editorial headlined "Chuck's Got a Heart of Gold," it concluded that in a world dominated by greed, Mr. Feeney's secret philanthropy "is as refreshing as it is extraordinary."

Peace groups were in fact far from furious with Chuck Feeney. The leading cross-community peace group, Cooperation North, later renamed Cooperation Ireland, alone had received $10 million from the Atlantic Foundation. Many such nonprofit bodies depended on Feeney and Atlantic for their existence. "Reconciliation and human rights were important areas that needed funding in Ireland and we wanted to see the potential of funding such organizations," said Feeney. "In the press they say that half the people I fund in Northern Ireland are Republicans: the logic of that is that the other half must be Loyalists."

John Healy had been apprehensive about the safety of Atlantic staff in Belfast in case a "loyalist bomb-tosser" misunderstood Feeney's contributions to peace, so he consulted an international security firm, Risk Management International, for advice. "Our worries were unfounded. We didn't get a single phone call in Belfast from anybody. We lived a charmed life in Belfast. In the Republic, we got a cascade of applications."

The DFS sale did result in one assessment of Feeney's role in Ireland that upset him deeply. It came in the book by Airy Routier about Bernard Arnault that was published in France. "Opposed to the idea of inheritance . . . Chuck Feeney gives his money for diverse humanitarian causes but also for the IRA, the secret Irish army, of which he is one of the financiers," Routier wrote. "Chuck promised Bernard that the sale of DFS would allow him to finance medical research. But only the God of Catholics and Chuck Feeney know how he will use the money of LVMH!"

Many people in France knew Feeney from the time he lived there and would be exposed to this libel. Two of his children, Juliette and Patrick, lived in France and friends asked them, "Is your father supporting the IRA?" They saw how hurt their father was. "It totally sucked," said his daughter Leslie. "He is such a pacifist, a humanist; the insinuations were totally unfair. The book really pissed him off."

Years later, a Liberal Party member of the Victoria Parliament in Australia, Phillip Honeywood of Warrandyte constituency, alleged in a parliamentary debate that funding for the Melbourne Institute of Technology had come from "a Bermuda-based entity, Mr. Charles Feeney, who is a longstanding major donor to the Irish Republican Army." The Melbourne *Age* reported the comment the next day under a headline that read, "Uni[versity] Benefactor Has IRA Ties, says MP." Feeney was also "pissed off" by this comment, from a minor politician who "couldn't get press any other way but for some reason wanted to get up our nose." The article caused momentary panic among some Australian beneficiaries of his foundation until they checked with contacts in Ireland and got the full picture.

As the dust settled and the media attention faded, Harvey Dale congratulated everyone in the foundation for the success of the unveiling. "The *New York Times* story and virtually all the ensuing international media coverage was very favorable to us," he wrote in a report to directors about the "most significant event" in their history. "None of our worst fears of distortion or unfavorable 'spin' were realized." In fact, he boasted, one of his "spook" friends, who served on President Clinton's Foreign Intelligence Advisory Board, had described the unveiling of Chuck Feeney as "a Great Op."

Despite everything, Chuck Feeney and Harvey Dale were still not prepared to give up the culture of secrecy. The Atlantic Foundation and the Atlantic Trust, which in the wake of the sale were brought together under a single title, The Atlantic Philanthropies, went underground again. Anonymous giving had allowed them to avoid the "crowding out" effect, where other potential benefactors were deterred by funding from a highly visible person with a great fortune, argued Dale in his post-sale report. "We still adhere to two long-standing attributes of our style of grant-making: we don't accept unsolicited proposals, and we insist that our donees keep the source of their gifts confidential."

Atlantic sent a message to all beneficiaries, stating in bold-faced type that they had not been released from their pledges of confidentiality unless specifically authorized. "Our conditions that you not identify the source of the gift remain in force," it proclaimed. "Please let the appropriate individual in your organization know of this continued requirement." Other rules stayed in place: No announcements of awards would be allowed, and recipients would still have to sign confidentiality documents and promise not to seek contact with the donor.

While the focus was on the DFS sale, Feeney's investments were bringing in more huge sums. In 1996, investments in companies such as Priceline.com Inc., E*Trade Group Inc., Sierra Online, and Baan Co. produced a capital return of $403 million. The sale of a stake in Legent Corporation to Computer Associates in 1995 brought in another $173 million.

Of the overall assets of $4 billion, $1 billion was now tied up in "state," or businesses and property, and the rest was in "church." When the Atlantic Foundation was first launched, 90 percent of the assets were in "state" and only 10 percent in liquid form. The proportion in cash now shot up to 75 percent. It would continue to rise. After some twenty years of acquisitions and expansion, Chuck Feeney would now wind down his multinational conglomerate, or as Dale put it in his report to directors, bring General Atlantic Group's various businesses "to ripeness for harvesting."

There was a "tipping point" in favor of the foundation over GAGL, recalled Chris Oechsli, and from then on "we were on a trajectory to divest ourselves of the operating assets." They had already started the process with the sale of Cannon's sports club in London to Vardon, the owner of the London Dungeons, for $40 million and of the Medallion Hotels in Texas and Oklahoma, which in January 1998 brought in a further $150 million.

Harvey Dale noted in his report that in the early 1990s, their liquidity had been so constrained that it had caused "extreme distress both to the donees and to us"—a reference to the drying up of DFS dividends at the time of the Gulf War. Now they need no longer worry about dividends drying up. In the post-sale landscape, Atlantic Philanthropies could spend more than 5 percent of the asset base, "even if that shrinks the value of our portfolio over time." A 5-percent spend rate would be about $200 million a year. In their previous year, they had given grants totaling $140 million. They could now go far beyond that.

Chuck Feeney was much in demand after he was outed by the *New York Times*. The U.S. networks clamored for interviews. However, following his call from the airport, Feeney did not give another media interview for several years, and his foundation ignored regular requests from CBS *60 Minutes* producers to appear on their program. After he gave his interview with

Judith Miller on the pay phone in the San Francisco airport, he flew out of the country on one of his frequent around-the-world trips. Having featured in public through circumstances beyond his control, he resolved to disappear again and revert to the anonymity in which he had always taken refuge. Harvey Dale advised him how to react if confronted by paparazzi on his travels. The lawyer had hired a professional photographer to demonstrate how to prevent a cameraman from getting a recognizable picture of a targeted person. He passed on the advice to Feeney: Close your eyes as a photographer raises his camera, or put a hand over your nose and mouth.

Feeney made one or two exceptions that showed his favoritism to the Irish. When he was recognized and approached in a San Francisco restaurant by Irishman Gerry Mullins, who wanted support for a documentary about photographs taken in Ireland by famed photographer Dorothea Lange, he responded enthusiastically, and the result was an award-winning documentary *Photos to Send*, coproduced by Mullins and Irish American Deirdre Lynch.

Then he stunned his friend Niall O'Dowd by agreeing to accept in person the 1997 award of Irish American of the Year, presented by *Irish America* magazine. Feeney abhorred self-congratulatory events, but he liked O'Dowd and promised to turn up for the lunchtime presentation at the 21 Club on West Fifty-second Street. O'Dowd tipped off two national media friends, *New York Times* columnist Maureen Dowd, and Jim Dwyer of the *Daily News*. At the event, Feeney told the two columnists that when he was a student at Cornell University, he filled in a questionnaire on money and banking and got a note from the professor saying: "You have a flair for writing, but no knowledge of the subject matter. Try journalism." Maureen Dowd asked Feeney if he was nervous at making his first public appearance. "Well, they promised me $20 to make the speech," he quipped. "Chuck Feeney's desire for anonymity is startling in an age when people stamp their names on every available surface," she wrote in her *New York Times* column. "Here was the real-life John Beresford Tipton on the old television show *The Millionaire*, whose face was never seen as he instructed his personal secretary to give some unsuspecting person a check for $1 million, on the condition that the Samaritan never be revealed."

Jim Dwyer recalled that his speech was like a toast given by an unprepared uncle at a wedding and that Feeney concluded his talk in style, saying, "That's it, I'm not doing this again."

One of Feeney's concerns about exposure was that his life would never be the same. But after the lunch, Maureen Dowd noticed him tramping off on foot in an old gray raincoat and tweed cap, unnoticed by passers-by, as other corporate figures climbed into their limousines. Feeney was in fact able to retreat back into semi-anonymity after his unveiling, unrecognized while hailing a taxi in New York or dining at a back table at P. J. Clarke's, where the waiters pretended they didn't know who he was. His wide range of friends and acquaintances around the world—academics, architects, medical professionals, writers, artists, and lawyers—protected his privacy out of loyalty and gratitude.

"Harvey Dale had scared Chuck into believing his life would change enormously if he went public, so Harvey ran it like the CIA," said Feeney's former legal counsel Paul Hannon. "But I think Chuck found out that it didn't change his life at all. He didn't get better service at P. J. Clarke's."

CHAPTER 27

Golden Heart

On April 27, 1997, four months after the sale of DFS, Chuck Feeney spotted a single-column story on an inside page of the *San Francisco Examiner* as he waited for a flight at the San Francisco airport. It was headed "U.S. Foundation Last Hope for Many of Vietnam's Poor." The writer, Sandra Ann Harris, told the story of a mother of seven children who lived in a one-room hut in Vietnam without doors or windows. She did not have the means to feed her children and was relying on a humanitarian organization called East Meets West Foundation, based in Los Angeles, for subsistence. But the organization's Vietnam director, Mark Conroy, was quoted as saying that they likely could not continue helping people like that if the foundation didn't get new funding when their five-year $400,000 grant from the U.S. Agency for International Development ran out in five months.

Feeney tore out the article. When he returned to San Francisco, he asked Gail Vincenzi Bianchi, the administration manager of the InterPacific office, to find out what she could about East Meets West.

Although he had turned sixty-six, Chuck Feeney was not contemplating retirement. Far from it. Not for him the three Gs—golf, grandchildren, and gardening—he told his family. His days of investing in new businesses were behind him, but he was determined to devote all his time to philanthropy. He was becoming more fixated on the merits of giving while living. "The world changed when we sold DFS," recalled Feeney. "Our coffers were full from the $1.6 billion transaction. I sort of felt we could do more good by taking that money and putting it into things, but the challenge was, where do you put it?" His philanthropy was opportunistic, but he didn't give randomly. He investigated and scrutinized, and sometimes tested the people involved with small initial grants. And it always came down to his instincts about the quality of the people involved.

The East Meets West Foundation, he learned, was set up by Le Ly Hayslip, a Vietnamese woman whose life as a victim of the war was chronicled in Oliver Stone's 1993 movie *Heaven and Earth*. Born Phung Thi Le Ly, in the Buddhist village of Ky La near Da Nang in central Vietnam, Le Ly was recruited as a child by the Vietcong and at age fifteen was tortured by South Vietnamese forces, but then wrongfully condemned as a traitor by the Vietcong and forced to flee her home. She lived on her wits, and was for a time a prostitute at an American base, but in 1969 she married a U.S. citizen who arranged for her to come to the United States. He died four years later, and she married another American, Dennis Hayslip, who passed away in 1982, leaving Le Ly a trust fund that enabled her to invest and become wealthy. She wrote two books narrating her life.* In 1987, she founded the East Meets West Foundation as a charitable group dedicated to improving the health and welfare of the poorest Vietnamese and to promoting self-sufficiency by building schools and providing safe drinking water.

The story had a strong appeal for Feeney, who believed that helping people was all about helping them to help themselves. He also thought that the Vietnamese had gotten a raw deal from the United States. "I read a lot of books about the American war in Vietnam," he said. "It was a war America was not going to win. One of the things that got to me about Vietnam was that it seemed to me the whole concept was wrong . . . going into a village and killing peasant families. After starting a war with people whom we were not going to defeat, General Curtis LeMay said, 'We're going to bomb them into the Stone Age.' We then put an embargo on trade. Frankly, if you don't trade with the U.S. you don't trade with anybody. It was punitive. Now America is out there trading, and I think that is the right thing to do. We owe it to the Vietnamese after the way we treated them."

Feeney asked the East Meets West executive director, Mark Stewart, an ex-marine who was severely wounded in Da Nang, to meet him in San Francisco

---

*Le Ly Hayslip, *When Heaven and Earth Changed Places* (Doubleday, 1989), and *Child of War, Woman of Peace* (Doubleday, 1993).

for a chat. "He may not have been pretty excited when he went in but he came out of there pretty excited, because Chuck said to him, 'Here, I'll give you a hundred thousand dollars, and you go out and see what you can do with that,'" recalled Mark Conroy. Feeney in effect told Stewart, "Come back and tell me what you did with it. If I like it, well, I have some deep pockets, and maybe we will do some more." East Meets West took the $100,000 to build and renovate some elementary schools and kindergartens and install some fresh-water systems. Stewart gave Feeney an account of what they did, and Feeney promptly made a second gift of $200,000. It was Feeney's style to see how an initial grant would be used before making a major commitment. Feeney also liked to get trusted friends from the past to check things out for him. He called up Bob Matousek, then living in Tiburon just outside San Francisco, and suggested that he take a trip to Vietnam to assess the quality of the people with the foundation and the type of work that they were doing and whether the Communist government interfered.

Matousek flew to Ho Chi Minh City, formerly Saigon, in early 1998—the first of a dozen trips he would make to Vietnam—and then on to Da Nang, where he introduced himself to Mark Conroy. The Vietnam director spent a week showing him different projects. Matousek was moved by the distress of rural parents unable to look after their children properly. Conroy, who regularly traveled around the rice paddies on a motorcycle to meet with peasants, showed him "compassion homes" they had built outside Da Nang: small, dry, brick structures with toilets that could be put up for a little over $1,000. Many homes in Vietnam were made from tarps: They leaked and had no toilet or cooking facilities.

Matousek reported back to Feeney that he was impressed with the people and the work they were doing, and that there was no sign of interference from the government or of officials looking for kickbacks. There would also be no restrictions on money transfers from Bermuda into Vietnam.

In October 1998, Chuck Feeney flew to Vietnam, taking with him Sandra Harris, the author of the *San Francisco Examiner* article. He flew from Ho Chi Minh City to Da Nang on the east coast to see East Meets West operations for himself.

"Chuck came in and sat down in my old office, which people used to call the cave," recalled Conroy. "We had snakes and rats and everything you could think of in there. He came back into the kitchen. He talked for about two hours. Looking back today, I'm a bit embarrassed about it because I was grilling Chuck about what his intentions were, and about his interests in the organization. By then the directors of East Meets West had found out who Chuck was and were asking, 'What's going on? Who's this very rich guy? What's his interest in our little tiny organization?' There was concern that Chuck was going to come in and take the organization over and do what he wanted to do with it. I caught wind of that. I asked him, 'Chuck, why are you coming to Vietnam? What is it that you want to do here?' He said, 'I just thought Vietnam got a bad deal, and I'd like to help out.' He didn't really have to say much more."

Feeney's arrival could not have come at a more propitious time for Conroy, who did not have the funds to do more than manage an orphanage and a primary health care center in Da Nang and do a little irrigation and microcredit. Money was so tight he was reduced to meeting tour boats coming into Da Nang and soliciting money by making presentations to groups of Western tourists.

As they talked in the "cave," Conroy became aware that Feeney was interested in larger projects that could make a big improvement in people's lives and would absorb a lot more money. "He didn't seem as interested in the grass-roots stuff. He could do so much more at the level he is at. He wanted to make a bigger impact. He was convinced that if you educate people, they would develop their own country. We were looking at it from the bottom up as a small organization, trying to keep kids alive, get them educated, while Chuck was thinking top down. It was a pretty good fit."

He took the American visitor to the hospital in Da Nang, where he knew they badly needed a new burns center. At the hospital Feeney asked the directors what their next-most-urgent need was. They said they would really love to renovate the pediatric center, which was in pretty bad shape. Feeney said, "Why don't we do both?"

As they left the hospital, Feeney asked, "What do you think that's going to cost, Mark?" Conroy replied, "Maybe around $300,000." Back in the cave, Feeney gave him contact details for "a Mr. Harvey Dale," and asked him to write a proposal for the two projects. "I wrote a bunch of stuff up on three quarters of a sheet of paper," said Conroy. "Chuck says, 'That looks good,' and signs it and faxes it off to Harvey. The money came a month later."

From then on Chuck Feeney became a regular visitor to Vietnam. In Da Nang, Vietnam's fourth-largest city, he stayed in a $25-a-night hotel, making expeditions to hospitals and schools through streets filled with cyclos, motorbike taxis, and schoolgirls in flowing white dresses riding bicycles. He made sure that the East Meets West Foundation got the money to continue work on water purification, schools, kindergartens, and compassion homes, but "he did not take over the organization in any way," said Conroy. Said Feeney, "They would say, 'OK, this month we're going to make a push on elementary schools, or kindergartens,' and we would support it." In the second half of the 1990s, East Meets West could build only two dozen schools, but with their new patron, they were able to build forty-eight schools in 2001 alone.

Feeney began serious investigation of the education and health needs in Vietnam. He studied surveys and analyses. He got Sandra Harris to work with Conroy for six months to produce a paper on schooling in Vietnam, "Education Under Siege." He got back copies of Vietnam's English-language newspapers to see what he could glean about the state of the country.

Just as he had done in practically every university in Ireland, Feeney dropped by the director's office at Da Nang University to ask him about his plans for the future. The most urgent need was a new library, but the university couldn't afford to build one. Feeney organized the required funding of $700,000 and channeled it through East Meets West. Conroy got a call one day to meet Feeney at the Rex Hotel in Ho Chi Minh City. "He told me, 'That library needs a good elevator. I have spent two days looking at elevators. Otis here are not making good ones, just wrapping parts together, the only good one I can find is Schindler.'" He brought Conroy to the Schindler people and said to them, "This is the guy I want you to work with." A thought struck Conroy. Feeney was planning to buy a lot of elevators. The library was only a first.

"He had a proclivity for construction projects, working with good institutions and good leaders, and building facilities to support their programs: He liked creating tangible assets and institutions to use like major tools," said Chris Oechsli. "I remember Chuck showing me the article from the *Examiner*. He wasn't showing it as a way of saying anything. It's Chuck's indirect style. You only realize this afterwards. He gives people papers, out of the blue, without any background, sometimes totally unrelated to anything you are aware of. You can't tell if this is a precursor to something he wants you to do or this is just something he wants to get off his desk. There's a lot of ambiguity. These kinds of things happen." Feeney also for a brief period got John Joyce, an Irish student in Vietnam, and Steve Reynolds, who had retired from General Atlantic Partners, to act as his representatives in Vietnam, and he started bringing members of the Atlantic Philanthropies board to see for themselves the opportunities there.

Feeney also dipped into the reservoir of goodwill that he had created with his earlier philanthropy. He invited Dr. Walter Bortz, past president of the American Geriatrics Society, who wrote the best-selling books *Dare to Be 100* and *Living Longer for Dummies* and who had been generously funded by Atlantic, to come to Hanoi on a fact-finding trip. He got two Irish university presidents, Danny O'Hare and Ed Walsh, to accompany him to Da Nang and Hue to look at higher-education needs. "People come in and none are aware there is an agenda or a plan, at least in Chuck's thinking, and all of a sudden they tend to meet up in the stew pot of bubbling ideas and possibilities," said Oechsli, who became director of country and health programs in Vietnam for Atlantic Philanthropies.

"Chuck was attracted to Vietnam like a moth to a flame," said Matousek. "He realized Vietnam was the greatest bang for the buck, and he took a real keen personal interest. He would walk through run-down hospitals and schools and say, 'I think we can renovate this and rebuild that.' He would come back six months later, and they would be finished, and the people would show in their expressions the appreciation of the fact that it was his dollars that achieved this. It was, I think, a tremendous feeling for him to see on the faces of educators and doctors the results of making the call on the spot, and seeing the good that has been done: more patients processed through a hospital, more children through a school."

In Hanoi, a thirty-three-year-old Vietnamese American doctor, Dr. Le Nhan Phuong, who was working with Dr. Michael Linnan, the medical attaché to U.S. ambassador Pete Peterson, on a public health program, encountered Feeney and other members of Atlantic Philanthropies at a public-health seminar. "Who are these guys, Michael?" he asked. Linnan replied, "You should take these guys very seriously, as they have the potential to do a lot for Vietnam."

Shortly afterward, when Atlantic decided it needed an in-country director with a medical background, it recruited Phuong—just as he was about to accept a Fulbright scholarship to go back to the United States—and persuaded him to stay and supervise projects funded by Atlantic Philanthropies instead.

Le Nhan Phuong was ten when the North Vietnamese army swept down on Saigon in 1975. There was widespread panic at that time among people connected with the South Vietnamese regime, who included Phuong's parents. His mother, Le Thi Hang, placed him and his sister in an orphanage, in the hope that they would be evacuated in Operation Babylift, a U.S.-government-backed effort to fly out tens of thousands of Vietnamese orphans. To hide their ties with the family, the two children were given different birth certificates and names. The airlift started on April 4, 1975. Two weeks later, Phuong's mother returned to the orphanage to collect the children, having found passage for them on a plane leaving Saigon airport and was mistakenly told they had already been evacuated. A week later, on April 27, Phuong and his sister were among over 7,000 Vietnamese refugees flown out in the biggest one-day evacuation of the war. Phuong and Le Mong Hoang were transferred to Clark Air Base in the Philippines, then Guam, then San Francisco, then Portland, Oregon, where they spent a year in different foster homes. They had no way of knowing where their mother was. A social worker in Portland took away from Phuong the picture he carried of his parents, the only connection with his family. He despaired of seeing them again. A Portland couple with four children applied to adopt them. Three days before the papers were to be signed, their mother arrived on their doorstep in Portland to reclaim her lost children. She and her husband, Pham The Truyen, had gotten out of Vietnam and had been placed in a refugee camp in Little Rock, Arkansas, and then moved to Atlanta. She had undertaken a desperate search for her missing children, going to church and refugee groups, showing their photographs. At last someone recognized them. Phuong and his sister were reunited in Atlanta with their parents.

Phuong trained as a doctor and obtained a master's degree in public health at Johns Hopkins University in Baltimore, Maryland. Although he began practicing as a physician in the United States, he felt himself drawn back to Vietnam. "On the one hand I was trying to fit in as an American; on the other I felt this calling, what I needed to do," he said. In 1998, he went with a group of American Vietnamese doctors to Hanoi, and Dr. Linnan, health attaché of the U.S. embassy in Hanoi, offered him a job helping to develop public health in Hanoi schools at $300 a month. He returned to the United States, gave up his $10,000-per-month job, sold his house and his Mustang convertible—"That was hard," he said with a laugh—and returned to live and work in Vietnam. "It was the most wonderful feeling of freedom," he said.

Like others before him, Le Nhan Phuong came to regard Chuck Feeney as a father figure. He became Vietnam country manager and program executive for Atlantic and accompanied Feeney on visits as guide and interpreter, sharing his jokes and keeping up with his evening consumption of white wine. "He pays attention to individuals," he said. "He told me I should pay attention to my parents and call them often. I never forgot that. We work our hearts out to fulfill his vision."

Because of Feeney's personal involvement, hospital and university directors in Vietnam got to know him and to appreciate that he was the visionary and moving force behind the philanthropy. They reluctantly respected his wishes to remain anonymous. "They pestered us about putting plaques up, but Chuck doesn't want any, so we just don't do it," said Conroy. However, some plaques appeared in Vietnam indirectly honoring Feeney, like that on Tupi Hoa School, opened in 1998, which declared, "Funded by Golden Heart." "Often I would be asked to write a thank-you letter for the donors and some poor uneducated people used that term," said Conroy. "There are probably a dozen 'Golden Heart' plaques out there. Chuck never said anything to me, but Bob Matousek said there should be no more."

One isolated school in Thang Binh, deep in the heart of rural Vietnam, didn't get the message about anonymity. Its director erected a plaque saying, "Funding provided by Feeney." It is almost certainly the only public recognition of Chuck Feeney by name on a building anywhere in the world.

The directors of Da Nang Hospital did find a way of mischievously honoring "Golden Heart" after Feeney organized funding for an engineering and diagnostic center with a helipad on top. When he came by in November 2005 to see the completed building, the director said proudly, "Look at the color!" He had had the six-story building painted green, in honor of Feeney's Irishness. Later over lunch in the little boardroom with a bust of Ho Chi Minh in the corner, Feeney explained to top hospital staff why he resisted the temptation to take any credit. "The truth is all the credit for this is yours. We have carried out our side, but that was the easy side. The real work was on your side. Atlantic is proud to be associated with high-quality people doing what they say they will do." The director pointed out that the high standards that Feeney made possible in turn attracted more funding from other foreign foundations.

Feeney rarely encountered evidence of government interference, though at the Da Nang Learning Resource Center in the College of Education and

Foreign Languages, he was quietly told that the man wandering around the computer terminals where students were accessing the Internet was a Communist Party censor known as the "human firewall."

Feeney was most at ease with the students. On that visit to Da Nang, he abandoned his no-photographs rule and stood beaming with different groups, his arms around them as they took pictures. He told them, "There are lots of people in the world who need help and if you help, then you are a better person."

As a doctor, Phuong used his position with Atlantic to conduct a personal campaign against smoking in Vietnam, where at least 40,000 people die from smoking-related diseases each year. Instead of plaques honoring the giver, he insisted that No Smoking signs were put up everywhere, and that the rule was rigidly enforced. "A No Smoking sign is Vietnamese for Funding by Atlantic," joked a hospital official in Hue.

Feeney's low profile allowed him to sustain his anonymity outside the small number of hospital and university directors who got to know him. Sometimes people knew he was in the room but couldn't pick him out from other Westerners. In Vietnam, he generally wore his aloha shirt, looking like an amiable American tourist on a budget. The Australian ambassador to Vietnam, Michael Mann, held a dinner in Hanoi for Feeney and members of the board of Atlantic who were touring the foundation's projects. "I knew who he was, and the background, but very few people knew because it was all kept very confidential," said Mann. "He came in with a very distinguished group of people, but Chuck was the most unassuming. He was sitting off in the corner with my eight-year-old daughter Alexandra chatting, and he was not involved in the general discussion." At dinner he put Feeney sitting beside his wife, Monique, knowing that both spoke French. She was charmed by him. He told her about his five children and how they had all gone through college, and what they were doing. After dinner she asked her husband, "Who was that nice old guy sitting next to me at dinner?" He replied, "That was Chuck Feeney you were sitting next to, mate!" She had assumed that the important-looking American sitting next to her husband was the "billionaire." Harvey Dale recalled that he was sitting next to Mann. "Chuck would have enjoyed that," he chuckled, when told the story.

"The impact of Atlantic on Vietnam is enormous," said Le Nhan Phuong, looking back seven years after Feeney's first visit. "It is so unlike any other philanthropy group operating in Vietnam. Chuck is not one to give orders. He will steer us now and again to what he is interested in. He identified where and when Atlantic should take action. And when we do, we mean business. Once we identify something, we get there speedily."

The success in Vietnam reflected the remarkable flexibility of Atlantic Philanthropies, which was able to accommodate Feeney's inspired methods of bold problem solving. Oechsli recalled that "Chuck's initiatives sometimes went through the foundation in a perfunctory fashion, sometimes coming in at the last minute before a board meeting and getting a rubber stamp with little documentation. Chuck wanted to 'do' Vietnam, so the rubber stamp was used freely, and we managed to do a lot of low-cost major construction." Later, a strategic plan evolved for Vietnam that focused on health and education.

From 1998 to 2006, Atlantic Philanthropies provided $220 million for a series of building and scholarship projects and health initiatives in Vietnam. This included the construction and equipping of what are now the most modern libraries in the country, designated as learning resource centers, at four major regional universities: Can Tho, Hue, Da Nang, and Thai Nguyen. It also included the building of dormitories, student centers, and sports facilities at the universities of Da Nang, Hue, and Thai Nguyen. Atlantic also supported the establishment of an English Language Institute at Da Nang University to improve English training in the central region. Feeney strongly believed this was vital for the students in central Vietnam eager to get on in the world. "Not to be chauvinistic, but good English is very important," he said.

Almost half of the money was plowed into health programs. Da Nang General Hospital was modernized with the building and renovation of most of its departments, including obstetrics and gynecology, burns, pediatrics, internal medicine, surgery, emergency, tropical medicine, oncology, morgue, and waste management. Atlantic funded new construction and renovations at Quang Tri Provincial Hospital, including pediatrics and surgery, and buildings and equipment for Hue Central Hospital's pediatrics department and cardiovascular center—the only one in central Vietnam. It also paid for new equipment for the catheterization laboratory for the Heart Institute in Ho Chi Minh City and provided money for the first phase of construction of the National Hospital of Pediatrics in Hanoi and a new campus for the Hanoi School of Public Health. "We started putting a lot of money into being the driving force in the creation of the public health system in Vietnam," said

Feeney. Atlantic also provided funding for a wheelchair manufacturing unit, overseen by Bob Matousek and opened in 2007.

The Da Nang Eye Hospital provided Feeney with direct evidence of the effect his philanthropy had on poor, rural Vietnamese who suffered from blindness caused by cataracts. Wearing a green surgical mask and gown, he watched for himself as the surgeon—one of eight trained in Thailand with Atlantic support—used ultramodern equipment to restore the sight of an elderly Vietnamese farmer. The Da Nang Eye Hospital, renovated and equipped by Atlantic Philanthropies, today treats 3,500 people a year for cataracts.

As always, Feeney sought to get leverage for his initiatives. When his foundation, which in 2000 began operating independently from the East Meets West Foundation, funded a health system reform program in Da Nang and Khanh Hoa Province that directly benefited over 2 million people, the respective provincial governments contributed up to 30 percent of the total infrastructure and equipment cost for commune health centers. With Atlantic's help, Dr. Truong Tan Minh, director of the Khanh Hoa provincial health department, was able to make Khanh Hoa a national model for the reform of Vietnam's health care system.

The most ambitious single project for which Chuck Feeney was responsible in Vietnam was a $33.6 million state-of-the-art university in the Saigon South New Urban Area of Ho Chi Minh City, which became the first foreign-owned university in the Communist country. It was sponsored by the Royal Institute of Technology Melbourne (RMIT) with 50-percent cash funding from Atlantic. After a twenty-five-year career as a top diplomat, Michael Mann resigned to become the university's founding president.

"The university asked me to get involved and I said, with people like Chuck Feeney backing it, this is very safe," he remarked, walking among the palm trees planted on the lawns around the main four-level edifice. "Without him we would not have this university in Vietnam, without him these buildings would not be here," he said, gesturing toward the Norman Day–designed campus structures. Because of the equity provided by Atlantic in June 2002, RMIT was able to secure loans totaling $14.5 million from the International Finance Corporation and the Asian Development Bank to build the university and provide it with banks of Compaq workstations. The university in 2006 had a student population of 1,400 and provided young Vietnamese with an internationally recognized Australian degree at less than half the cost in Melbourne. Vietnam's prime minister, Phan Van Khai, told Mann that he wanted the university to be a model for other universities in Vietnam. Mann also planned to make it the number one "tennis university" in Asia. "Getting to know Chuck Feeney has been one of the highlights of my life," said Mann. "He is so low key, but he is dynamic; his mind races at 100 miles an hour."

Mark Conroy, too, came to regard Feeney as one of "the best and most thoughtful people" he had ever encountered in his life. "We are all going to be put in a box at the end of the day," he said. "You can't really wrap yourself in money. A lot of people think they can. They seek to accumulate wealth. They are pretty aimless. When you come into this kind of work, you don't think of money except to help people. People say, 'I have only $200; I'd like to help, but I can't give like rich people.' I say to them, 'You know what, that person with the burned face who benefited from the $200 doesn't think that way.' It's about helping people so that they can help themselves, hoping someday people can get educated and see big enough opportunities to share the planet with each other."

CHAPTER

Bowerbird

Chuck Feeney likes to tell an anecdote about his first encounter with an Australian immigration official in the 1970s, when on a DFS business trip. "I was asked if I had a police record. I said, 'I didn't know that was still a requirement!' The guy went ballistic."

He started visiting Australia regularly after 1993 when his friend Ken Fletcher, the former Australian tennis player, complained one day in London, "I've had it, I want to go back to Australia," and Feeney had replied, "Fine, I'll go along with you." They flew to Sydney and from there north to Fletcher's hometown of Brisbane, the capital of the State of Queensland, a fast-growing city with street cafés, riverside paths, water taxis, and a pleasant semitropical climate on the Pacific coast.

As in Ireland and Vietnam, Feeney relied on a personal connection to introduce him to the country. In Australia it was Ken Fletcher, one of the heroes of Australia's golden tennis era, who won ten major doubles titles in the 1960s, including a mixed doubles grand slam at Wimbledon with champion Margaret Smith Court. Fletcher moved to Hong Kong when at his prime to play professional tennis and gained a reputation as something of a *larrikin*—someone who disdained authority and enjoyed life. He became friends with the Feeneys there and occasionally gave them tennis lessons at the Ladies' Recreation Club. Years later they met again in London, where Fletcher had ended up in a dead-end job running a suburban tennis center, and Feeney, who admired sporting legends, took him on as a consultant on sports and real-estate investments.

In Brisbane, Feeney set up Fletcher in a riverside apartment with a brief to be his eyes and ears, and provided him with a car. "We gave him a job as a kind of a spotter to look for opportunities and bring them to our attention," he said. An old buddy of Fletcher's, retired journalist Hugh Lunn, who lived in Brisbane, arranged to buy a "perch" in Dockside Apartments Hotel and rent it to InterPacific so that Chuck and Helga would have somewhere to stay when visiting.

The two Aussies soon learned about Chuck's close attention to expenditure. "One time when Chuck came out, Hughie presented him with a telephone bill—minor stuff—and Chuck went through it, and I said, 'Hughie, take note of this, here is a multi-billionaire arguing over a two-bob telephone call,'" recalled Fletcher. "I think his frugality comes from the fact that he is a born and bred retailer. Walking down the street, he would be pushing me into the shop windows, a billionaire checking the price of Casio watches. He would say, 'If we could buy those at $1 and sell them for $10, that's my sort of profit.' He never ordered a limo to get around. I drove him. And he hated anybody to think that the big yacht parked outside his apartment block might be his! But he could be generous, too. He once took me to buy a pair of Mephisto shoes, and they're bloody expensive."

After the DFS sale, encouraged by the success of his model for giving in Ireland and Vietnam, Feeney began to look for similar philanthropic opportunities in Australia. In March 1998, he and Fletcher went to see Brisbane mayor Jim Soorley to ask his help in setting up a meeting with university heads. Soorley, a former priest in the Marist order who had been running the city since 1991, organized a dinner in the city's Irish Club with two leading academics, Professor John Hay, the vice chancellor (president) of the University of Queensland, and Professor Laurie Powell, director of the Queensland Institute of Medical Research. He tipped them off to be on their toes, as Feeney might be able to help them with any projects they had in hand.

At the dinner in the President's Room of the Irish Club, beneath a framed copy of a letter written by Michael Collins during the Irish War of Independence, Hay and Powell told Feeney that their plans for development were constantly thwarted by lack of money and their institutions were seriously underperforming. It was the same story as in Ireland. Australia's higher-education institutions relied on fees and government grants to keep going, and there was no tradition of philanthropic funding by businesses or wealthy alumni.

Feeney wasted little time. The next day he called to see Hay, a young, high-achieving administrator, on his Queensland University campus. Hay had an ambitious plan to create an institute of molecular bioscience. Within weeks Feeney arranged for Atlantic to put up AU$10 million (US$7.5 million) seed money for the project. The State of Queensland government agreed to put up AU$15 million, the federal government in Canberra another AU$15 million, and the university a further AU$15 million from the university budget. Hay now had AU$55 million for the institute. "So all of a sudden it was a big project," he recalled. As it got under way, Harvey Dale arrived from the United States and made clear to Hay that the source of the Atlantic funds was to be a strict secret.

A Labor Party premier, Peter Beattie, was elected in Queensland shortly afterward, and he approved of the idea so much he subsequently put in another AU$80 million. "We've since added a lot of money through competitive research grants, so the whole thing is several hundred million dollars," said Hay. "It's one of the most exciting scientific university-based research institutes in Australia."

The project—a model of Feeney's policy of using matching grants to multiply an investment—led to a series of other initiatives. Hay was able to create the Australian Institute for Bioengineering and Nanotechnology when Atlantic put in one-third of the AU$70 million cost and Queensland and the university another one-third each. By 2006, Feeney had directed a total of AU$125 million to the university. "Because of our visibility we are now getting grants from other American organizations and are joint recipients with Harvard of a major grant from the Gates Foundation," said Hay. "Without Chuck Feeney this would not have happened. Without a shadow of doubt Chuck Feeney is the reason I have stayed in Brisbane."

Feeney learned with some amusement the story of the only other major donor in the history of the University of Queensland, who was also of Irish origin. In 1926, James O'Neill Mayne donated the 270 acres of land on which the university was built. He had bought it with money inherited from his father, Patrick Mayne, a young immigrant from County Tyrone who became mysteriously wealthy after a drunken out-of-town stranger was robbed and killed. Patrick Mayne confessed on his deathbed to the murder. The University of Queensland senate was unhappy about the origin of the Mayne fortune and agreed to accept the gift by only one vote. The biggest hall at the university was named Mayne Hall, and Feeney provided AU$7.5

million to transform it into an art museum with a gallery of self-portraits provided free by Australian artists, an idea Ed Walsh had pioneered at Limerick. "It was a no-brainer," said Feeney, explaining that by getting artists to contribute self-portraits and then letting people buy them and keep them on the walls, the university made money. "There are a lot of high-quality artists who like the prestige of having one of their paintings in the collection." "Getting pictures for nothing appealed to Chuck," said Hugh Lunn.

At the opening of the gallery, a photographer came up and asked the philanthropist, "Are you Chuck Feeney?" Feeney said, "No, that's him over there." The photographer came over and said to Hugh Lunn, "I'd like to shake your hand for what you have done for science in Brisbane." "I shook hands, embarrassed," said Lunn. "The photographer left and didn't even take a picture."

Feeney's arrival on the scene coincided with a plan by Peter Beattie to upgrade the state, which up to then many Australians saw as a version of America's Deep South. The fifty-three-year-old Labor Party leader had an agenda to transform Queensland into a "Smart State," promoting knowledge, creation, and innovation, partly to stop its brightest inhabitants from leaving. He wanted to change the image of Brisbane from "Brisvegas"—a gambling city at the center of a strip of casinos—into the capital of high tech. He had the words "Smart State" imprinted on car license plates. At the top of his agenda was restructuring the education system and encouraging research and development in information technology and biotechnology.

Feeney thoroughly approved of the idea. "The smarter you are, the smarter you get," he said, adding that "it was evident that there was an availability of smart, bright young people in Queensland." Feeney became a key partner in establishing the "Smart State," said Beattie.

Professor Laurie Powell also found his institution transformed after the dinner at the Irish Club. Feeney provided initial funding for the AU$60-million Cancer Research Centre at the Queensland Institute of Medical Research, the first cancer research facility of its kind in the Southern Hemisphere. When it was nearing completion and needed a further AU$5 million, Feeney advised Powell to sell the naming rights. Clive Berghofer, a wealthy Queensland property developer, stepped forward with a donation of AU$5 million—a major act of philanthropy by Australian standards. "I've got nothing leased, nothing on hire purchase, nothing rented, and nothing borrowed," Berghofer said when presenting the check. "What's mine is mine, and it is with great pleasure that I can give back to the community for what is now the Berghofer Cancer Research Centre." Feeney was pleased. He didn't like it when subsequently Fletcher commented about "that fool's name up there" as they drove by a huge red neon sign for the Clive Berghofer Cancer Research Centre. "Chuck jumped down my throat. 'He's no fool!' he said. I said, 'I don't mean it like that; it is just that you are so good. You are the bloke who built the building." Feeney said once he took the attitude on naming rights for buildings that "it doesn't matter whose name is on a library as long as there is a library there for people."

"The effect of Chuck's giving in Queensland is enormous," said Hugh Lunn. "One thousand people turned up for a lecture by Dr. Brent Reynolds of the Queensland Brain Institute, which received $20 million from Atlantic, on getting stem cells out of human brains. That is the sort of awareness Chuck has created in Brisbane—one thousand people turning up for a lecture on the brain!"

Almost every single grant in Australia "was just one-third of the amount of money needed," Feeney said with some satisfaction. "One-third from us, one-third from the institution, and one-third from the government." He leveraged more than half a billion Australian dollars on donations from Atlantic Philanthropies.

Feeney leveraged cooperation as well as money. His attitude, he said, was "we can help you, but you have to help someone else." He incorporated Australia's universities into his growing world network, using what Frank Rhodes called the "classic example" of the original template of Cornell helping Limerick. American, Irish, Australian, and later South African and Vietnamese university heads, academics, and scientists found themselves urged on by Feeney and Atlantic Philanthropies to cooperate and help each other.

"Chuck used Australia as a platform of knowledge and technology for Vietnam," said Le Nhan Phuong. Atlantic funded a program to bring Vietnamese students to the University in Queensland. Feeney met some of them on the Brisbane campus one day in November 2005. He arrived dressed in Hawaiian shirt, slacks, and a droopy fawn cardigan and looked anything but a munificent benefactor. The students sensed that Feeney was somehow responsible for them being there, and crowded around him to take photographs, something the university heads were not permitted to do. The group included some striking teenage girls. Feeney told them, "Study hard, beauty won't be enough. We will be successful if you will be successful. Do what you can. Vietnam wants you to come back and help."

As in every country where he spent time, Feeney endeared himself to his new friends with his mild manner and sociability, and his idiosyncrasies. "I think he is unique. He is a great man. He has almost no vanity at all," said John Hay. "He kept bringing me heaps and heaps of papers and articles that I should read and these sometimes became quite mountainous. 'The last time it was only two inches deep,' I said. 'You're slacking off, Chuck!'" Peter Coaldrake, vice chancellor of Queensland University of Technology, found himself looking forward to Chuck's visits to discuss a common passion—American politics. "He would come with a plastic bag and give me cuttings and the latest books. He is an incredible bowerbird. Look at my desk, I'm a bowerbird," he said, pointing to a desk littered with papers and explaining that a bowerbird is an Australian bird that collects all sorts of odds and ends to make its nest.

While Feeney's philanthropy achieved brilliant success in Australia, his one major business venture there was more problematic. This had its origins in the 1989 purchase by the then head of InterPacific, Paul Slawson, of part of South Stradbroke Island off the Queensland coast, as a potential site for a Club Med–type resort that would attract Japanese tourists. The fourteen-mile-long island, just south of the Brisbane suburbs, had ocean beaches, sand dunes, and tropical palms, as well as the golden wallaby, found nowhere else in the world.

"We found this piece of property on this island and were smitten by it," said Dave Smith, then chief financial officer of InterPacific. "It has the ocean on one side for deep-sea fishing and the bay on the other for wind-surfing, etc. Then we started running the numbers. We realized eventually it was not going to work. You have to have a facility on the mainland to park people and dock your ferries and take them over to the island after a flight to Sydney and on to Brisbane. Everything we needed on the island would have to be shipped there. Then there was the problem of garbage disposal. We sort of considered it to be a rather bad idea. We let it sit."

Feeney and Ken Fletcher took the forty-minute ferry ride to the island to have a look on their first visit in 1993. They were doubtful about its suitability for a resort, recalled Fletcher. Instead, they arranged with the state government to swap the island property for a thirty-one-acre site on the mainland where InterPacific could develop a sports and fitness center and donate the profits to the city. That fell through, however, when the government asked for

262 | The Billionaire Who Wasn't

AU$3 million extra. Feeney refused. He was frustrated by the failure of Brisbane officials to realize the seriousness of his effort to provide the city with a super sports center, said Fletcher. "He can be stubborn, can Chuck."

Ron Clarke, manager of Cannon's fitness club in London, went to see the island when on a Christmas visit to Australia in 1994. He found it "breathtakingly beautiful" and returned to London in some excitement with architect's sketches and photographs to show to Feeney. He recommended Couran Cove in the northeast of the island as the "perfect setting for an environmentally based family resort" and persuaded Feeney to let him return to Australia to develop a resort there for InterPacific. Clarke was just as homesick as Ken Fletcher had been. After thirteen years managing Cannon's, he was ready to do something new. Feeney agreed.

The directors of InterPacific were taken aback. They pushed against the idea of giving the former runner carte blanche to build a resort. Chris Oechsli sent a note to Chuck saying Clarke needed oversight. Jim Soorley said he told Chuck, "Don't go there, you will lose your ass." He believed that Feeney's anger at the state government over the failed land swap might have been a factor in his deciding to build the resort despite the advice he was getting. "Chuck is a bit like myself, a pigheaded Irishman." But Feeney saw Clarke as a shirtsleeve kind of operator and a great athlete, and he respected what he had achieved at Cannon's, recalled Jim Downey.

Fletcher bitterly resented the intrusion of Ron Clarke into his territory. He sensed that Chuck "went cool" toward him because he opposed the Couran Cove development and knew he did not like Clarke. Oechsli was critical of the fact that Clarke "took off on his own, like a solo runner" and began the development without providing InterPacific with a proper business plan. He recalled that there were inadequate feasibility studies, an incremental approach taken to the development, and little accountability. Distracted by the drama over the sale of DFS, Feeney had little time to make his own assessment of what was going on.

The problems of developing an eco-resort on a Pacific island were formidable. Some 225,000 tons of acid sulfate soil had to be shifted and a swamp dredged to create a natural lagoon. As it would be on an island with no power links to the mainland, the resort would have to generate its own power, purify the water, and get rid of waste.

The cost of the resort was originally estimated at AU$30 million, "but the next thing we knew, it was AU$60 million dollars and everything just kept escalating," said Chris Oechsli. It rose to AU$90 million and then by the time of its completion in September 1998, to a staggering AU$185, making it one of the most expensive holiday resorts ever built in the world. The figures would have broken many developers, but General Atlantic Group Ltd., the parent company of InterPacific, showed a return on investments that year approaching US$1 billion. Fletcher was scathing about the cost overruns. "How Chuck allowed Clarke to run up the expenses, I will never know. Chuck is such a good man."

"Detailed cost reports during construction were sent back to the U.S.A. on a monthly basis and were controlled by their accounting people, and explanations were provided for all variations," said Clarke in an e-mail response to questions about how the costs escalated. "The major issue was the acid sulfate soils that inundated the area to a much higher degree than original surveys revealed and resulted in entirely new techniques in dealing with them having to be developed by the local university. Then the local government regulations added considerably to the infrastructure with their insistence on tertiary treatment of all sewerage with new treatment plants and stricter hydrological systems for the daily clearance of the lagoon."

Couran Cove Island Resort opened in September 1998. More than 400 VIPs, including several Olympic runners and national figures, dined on a boardwalk terrace. The media hailed Clarke as a development visionary. Couran Cove won fifteen national awards for environment, design, architecture, and engineering. It had the greatest range of recreational and sporting facilities of any spa resort in the world. They included a 150-meter three-lane sprint track with advanced laser technology on which runners could race against lights five meters apart and break a laser beam to record their times. It had a heated twenty-five-meter swimming pool, tennis courts, basketball courts, climbing walls, high and low rope courses, bicycle track, outdoor gymnasium, shuffleboard courts, and baseball cage. There were nature cabins integrated into the forest, waterfront lodges, restaurants, an eighty-four-berth marina, a rain-forest boardwalk, an artist's studio, a store, and even a wedding chapel.

The resort, however, did not make any money. It returned losses year after year, and in May 2006, 100 permanent and casual staff, about one-third of the workforce, were told they would be laid off in a "workplace restructure." Feeney's attitude was that they mustn't expect profit every year and that there would be a right time to sell it. The problem, he said, was that "we have all the costs of a five-star hotel and the income from an eco-resort."

Feeney remained loyal to Clarke and gave him another project, overseeing the construction of a state-of-the-art sports center to be financed by InterPacific on land Clarke selected at Runaway Bay in Brisbane. The center was equipped with a Mondo running track, gymnasium, swimming pool, sports medicine facilities, and accommodation for athletes. Feeney intended that the profits be shared with the city council for more sports facilities and a charity called Children in Need. The costs similarly went up, from AU$10 million to AU$20 million to AU$30 million, said Oechsli.

When it was completed, Feeney backed Clarke's proposal to go to his home state of Victoria in southern Australia to set up and run the Council for the Encouragement of Philanthropy in Australia. Atlantic Philanthropies provided an initial AU$2 million of a three-year grant of AU$7.5 million. Clarke moved to the Victoria capital, Melbourne, where he launched the council in September 2001. He became a strong critic of the lack of a culture of philanthropy in Australia. "It is astonishing to me that we are lagging behind any country in our charitable donations," he said.

Feeney had begun funding major university projects in Victoria, and Clarke recalled the American donor arriving from Brisbane early one morning and spending the day with him visiting a number of major beneficiaries, including the Royal Melbourne Hospital, the Walter & Eliza Institute, the Alfred Hospital, and Melbourne University, which collectively were receiving AU$125 million from Atlantic. "As we walked out of the university I turned right to hail a cab," Clarke said. "Chuck asked, wasn't the way to the tram in the opposite direction? It was, and so we went left, jumped on a tram for the cross-city journey. I thought it ironic, $125 million given in gifts and $10 saved by not using a taxi."

Clarke's relations with Atlantic Philanthropies frayed after a brief article appeared in the Melbourne *Age* on Sunday, April 1, 2001, which referred erroneously to Clarke as a "representative for the Atlantic Foundation and Trust" who had "helped raise AU$163 million of anonymous donations for a variety of Australian projects." Harvey Dale suspected that Clarke was the source. "I was quite insulted, frankly, by him daring to think I had breached any confidences," recalled Clarke. The relationship wasn't helped by a similar article on October 6, 2002, in the Queensland *Sunday Mail*, saying that "when the American altruist wanted advice on grant recipients in Australia, Clarke became his eyes and ears . . . They had arranged close to $200 million in donations in Australia before the latest grants, last month."

The friendship between Chuck Feeney and Ron Clarke deteriorated in 2003 over a lawsuit Clarke and Runaway Bay lodged against ABC television. In November 1999, ABC claimed in its prime-time *7:30 Report* program that Runaway Bay Sports Super Centre had been built on a toxic landfill and was "one of the worst development scandals in Queensland history." Clarke wanted to initiate a defamation suit in Brisbane, but InterPacific lawyers were opposed on the basis that it was difficult to demonstrate economic loss. Clarke pursued defamation action in Melbourne instead, demanding an apology and legal costs on the grounds that it was untrue. The sixty-four-year-old former runner was reported "close to tears" as he testified in Victoria Supreme Court on June 15, 2001, with trembling voice, that he had been depicted as an environmental vandal. On July 4, the six-person jury awarded the former runner AU$710,700 damages and Runaway Bay Centre AU$386,250 damages, ordering ABC to pay the court costs. It was the biggest defamation award ever granted in the State of Victoria.

ABC appealed, and the case was listed for hearing before a three-judge Victoria appeals court in June 2003. Clarke and Werner Graef, who was representing the sports center, agreed out of court to settle for a lesser sum: AU$405,000 for Clarke and AU$81,000 for Runaway Bay. Chuck Feeney insisted that the damages awarded should be held by the sports club, said Clarke, who initiated another legal action to establish his right to the compensation. On Chuck's advice, the suit was settled privately. "I made certain all the cash received went to charity," said Clarke.

"It was the first time I have ever been sued by anyone in my life," said Feeney. The episode marked the end of his relationship with the former runner.

Atlantic Philanthropies ceased funding the Council for the Encouragement of Philanthropy in 2003 at the end of the initial three-year contract period. It had attracted donated funds of just AU$1 million a year. There was little evidence that Clarke could persuade Australian philanthropists to match their American counterparts. Feeney was by far Australia's biggest philanthropist ever. Australia's richest person, publishing tycoon Kerry Packer, with a net worth of over US$4 billion, did not have a philanthropic foundation at the time of his death in 2006. Ron Clarke blamed a culture of meanness among the rich in Australia. "I hate to say it, but I feel our business community leaders remain as selfish as they have always been despite

Chuck's fantastic example, and the growing number of businesspeople around the world doing more for the community," he said.

Feeney did not join in any recriminations over the failure of the Council for the Encouragement of Philanthropy. "A failed effort is still an effort," he said. On a visit to Brisbane in March 2007, he noted that the 200 richest people in Australia had wealth of AU$100 billion in 2006. They had yet to discover the satisfaction of philanthropy, he said, and called on them for leadership.

Ron Clarke returned to Queensland, where in March 2004 he was elected mayor of Gold Coast, a resort city south of Brisbane renowned for its beaches and tourist attractions.

Sitting at a pavement café in Dockside, Brisbane, one sunny morning in November 2005, Ken Fletcher reflected on Chuck's generosity to Australia and to him personally. Only that morning, Feeney had arranged for Ken to see the top cancer specialist in Brisbane to check out his prostate condition. The specialist hadn't offered much hope. Fletcher wondered, half seriously, why Chuck had not just written out a check for a million dollars for him so he could have a decent life. "I don't understand, I am so loyal to him," he said, adding with a grin, "If he had done that I could have taken all my friends on a cruise!"

Fletcher died three months later, on February 11, 2006. At a memorial service in Brisbane, there were many references to his legendary tennis prowess, but the highest praise given to Ken Fletcher in all the eulogies was that he had brought Chuck Feeney to Australia.

After the funeral, Feeney made a rare exception and gave his first television interview ever to Australian television to honor his friend. By then, despite the anonymity rule, he was becoming something of a cult figure in Australia. On October 23, 2006, he appeared with Queensland premier Peter Beattie at the opening of the Australian Institute for Bioengineering and Nanotechnology. The Brisbane *Courier Mail* managed to get a photograph of Feeney and Beattie laughing uproariously together. Reporter Tess Livingstone wrote, "Take a look at these two men. One is humble, shy and deserves much of the credit for recasting Queensland as the Smart State. The other is the premier."

CHAPTER 29

A Nation Transformed

As Chuck Feeney expanded his giving in other countries, he was gearing up for bigger things in Ireland. What would become perhaps his most notable philanthropic endeavor got under way at a dinner organized by John Healy for the board members of Atlantic Philanthropies during a visit they made to Dublin on October 21, 1997.

One of those invited to the dinner was Don Thornhill, Ireland's top education official. As secretary general of the Department of Education and Science, Thornhill received many invitations to functions, and turned most of them down. He didn't know much about Atlantic Philanthropies, but he had heard rumors about a mysterious philanthropy that was giving millions of dollars to Irish universities, and his instincts told him that this might be a significant occasion.

On arriving for the dinner at Heritage House, an elegant Georgian building on St. Stephen's Green owned by General Atlantic Group, the trim, bearded education official found himself placed at the top table with Ireland's Nobel Prize–winning poet, Seamus Heaney; his wife, the writer Marie Heaney; and two Americans, one tall and bald with a commanding presence who introduced himself as Harvey Dale, a lawyer from New York University, and the other a short and genial businessman who said his name was Chuck Feeney. The name Feeney rang a bell with Thornhill: He had read something about the Irish American's involvement in the Northern Ireland peace process.

Healy had invited Seamus Heaney to the dinner, as he wanted someone of note in Ireland to grace the occasion of the directors' visit. He had driven to Heaney's home on the seafront in Dublin and told him in confidence about the hundreds of millions of dollars that Chuck Feeney had given anonymously to Ireland, north and south.

Seamus Heaney stood up to speak to the fifty or so guests. After a few digressions, the Nobel laureate said, "Ladies and gentlemen, you will understand by now that I am approaching my subject by stealth, and I do so in order to imitate the methods by which the Atlantic Foundation has for years been doing its own legendary work of philanthropy." He was there, he said, "to acknowledge the magnificence of its activities and the reticence of its directors, the most legendary of whom, Mr. Chuck Feeney, will have to pardon me for overdoing things this evening to the point of mentioning his name." The intervention of the Atlantic Foundation in Ireland had been "epoch-making," Heaney went on, and came not just from the great traditions of philanthropy but "as a result of the great selflessness, the veritable Franciscan renunciation and Renaissance magnificence of one man in particular, Mr. Chuck Feeney." The poet finished with a reference to how "cease-fires, and Velvet Revolutions and the Atlantic Foundation are parts of a saving undersong within the music of what happens as our century comes to an end." He ended with some moving lines from his play *The Cure at Troy** that had been quoted in several speeches by President Bill Clinton on Ireland.

History says, don't hope
On this side of the grave,
But then, once in a lifetime
The longed-for tidal wave
Of justice can rise up
And hope and history rhyme.

It was a masterly performance. Chuck Feeney, normally most reluctant about receiving praise and thanks, was deeply moved. As the diners thundered out their applause, he was heard to say quietly, "My cup runneth over." Don Thornhill found Chuck Feeney to be a "very modest, very pleasant man." He felt that the placing was no accident, and that he was being

*Seamus Heaney, *The Cure at Troy: A Version of Sophocles' Philoctetes* (Field Day, 1990).

put under scrutiny. "I was flying blind," he recalled. "Like one of Elizabeth Taylor's later husbands, I had only a vague idea of what was expected from me."

Thornhill was correct in his assumption. "He *was* under scrutiny," said John Healy. "We were courting him." Chuck, Harvey, and John, in the subtle ways they had developed over years, were doing due diligence on the important bureaucrat, because they had sweeping new plans for education in Ireland, and they needed a reliable partner inside the government structures.

"Chuck was really keen to do really big things," said Healy. With Atlantic Philanthropies in a much stronger financial position, Feeney was looking to move beyond buildings and do something that would have a real impact on the growing tiger economy of Ireland. He wanted to shift gears, to move to a new level and fund postgraduate research on a scale unimagined by Ireland's government. Ireland's future prosperity depended on creating new knowledge, but the government had failed to invest public money in postgraduate research. The economy was heating up after decades of mismanagement and protectionism, while the research landscape remained bleak. Some noncommercial funding was coming from the European Union, but Ireland's spending on research was just 11 percent of the European average. On top of that, the university sector was disjointed, with little intercollegial cooperation.

For the first time in its history, Atlantic was aiming to enter direct negotiations with a sovereign government, to do a matching deal "where we put some money on the table, and force them to put some money on the table," said Healy.

Astonishingly, the secretary general of the Department of Education and Science was not really aware of the role Feeney had played in funding Irish universities during the previous ten years. After the dinner he asked one of his top officials, Paddy McDonagh, to make some inquiries about Atlantic Philanthropies. McDonagh spoke to contacts in the Department of Foreign Affairs and reported back, "It's highly secretive, and if you make any approach to them at all, that's it, all communications are finished, are dead."

It was a measure of the effectiveness of Harvey Dale's strictures that the education department was in the dark. It was, moreover, not in the interest of university presidents to let the world know anything about their friend Chuck, as they feared it could mean less funding from the Higher Education Authority. New libraries, science buildings, and student villages were going up on every campus, and there were jokes going around the system about the "edifice complex" of university presidents, but no one in the education department had connected the dots. Donations from wealthy Irish like Michael Smurfit, Anthony O'Reilly, Tim O'Mahony, Lochlan Quinn, and Tony Ryan had played a part, but their contributions didn't come close to what the universities were mysteriously raising elsewhere. University presidents seemed to have developed an extraordinary talent for raising money in America. Some complained with a straight face about the exhausting trips they had to make across the Atlantic to hustle up money, when in fact it was Feeney who came to them.

John Healy made the initial approach for what would become possibly the biggest single act of education philanthropy in modern Europe. Some weeks after the Heritage House dinner, he invited Don Thornhill, who had since then been made executive chairman of the Higher Education Authority, to join him for breakfast in the dining room of the Westbury Hotel, just off Grafton Street in Dublin. He also invited John Dennehy, Thornhill's successor as head of the Department of Education and Science, and Paddy McDonagh, adviser to the minister for education.

As they sipped their coffee, Healy told them, "You should understand our credibility because you know now through the grapevine what we are doing at a number of universities. We now think research capacity in Ireland is pathetically small and should be strengthened. You guys need to invest more. Why don't we do something together?"

How would they respond, he asked, if Atlantic put up IR£75 million (US$125 million)? Would the Irish government put up the same amount? There was a shocked silence. "They looked at me as if I were mad," recalled Healy.

"Think about it," Healy went on. "We don't have to spend our money in Ireland, we are working in lots of places, in the United States, Australia, Vietnam. In fact Colin McCrea, my collaborator, cannot be with me today because as we speak he is on his way to the airport to fly to Australia, where there is a very interesting opportunity in the University of Queensland."

Thornhill quickly recovered the initiative. "Right, OK, I'll do a paper," he said. Thornhill was naturally eager to get greater funding for research. "The economy was at that point beginning to turn from the situation where we were exporting our university graduates to one where shortages were developing in the information and communications technology area," he recalled.

When a new government had come into office in June 1997, he had persuaded the incoming minister for education, thirty-seven-year-old Micheál Martin, to "have a row" with the minister for finance over his department's recent veto of IR£50 million for information technology facilities in universities. But the sympathetic minister for education had come back shaken from an encounter with the finance minister. He had asked for IR£50 million and had got IR£5 million. The allocation was even then whittled down to IR£4 million.

Harvey Dale arrived in Ireland shortly after the high-drama breakfast, and he and Healy set up a formal meeting with officials at the Department of Education and Science headquarters on Marlborough Street. When they detailed their proposal, Dennehy asked them if Atlantic Philanthropies could be trusted to come up with the IR£75 million. "Look at our record," said Healy, as Dale fixed Dennehy with a cold stare. The foundation president in turn asked the civil servants how Atlantic could trust the Irish government. The foundation had never done a matching grant with a government: What would happen if there were a change of government? What would happen if someone asked the prime minister or minister for education a question about the anonymous donor? What if the Irish government failed to deliver on a pledge? "We can't sue the government, it is sovereign," Dale told them. Thornhill retorted, "You, too, are sovereign!" Thornhill understood that Atlantic's undertaking was just as revocable as the Irish government's and the foundation could not be sued for failing to deliver on a pledge. Dale came to admire and respect Thornhill. "But for him, we might not have done the deal," he said.

Thornhill became the key architect of the plan. It was fraught with problems. There had to be absolute secrecy. The seven universities in the Republic were fiercely independent and guarded their privileges and autonomy. Healy made it clear that the proposal depended on an open, genuine, competitive program for grants, to be reviewed by international experts. University presidents would not be able to rely on across-the-board handouts: The funding would only be for proposals that fit with the overall strategic plan of the institution.

Thornhill quietly slipped out of his office on a few occasions to meet Healy and his deputy Colin McCrea in the Atlantic Philanthropies office on a leafy Dublin boulevard. "I always made it my business to meet them there," said Thornhill, who became as secretive about his dealings with

Atlantic as any university president. "If people were coming into my office for a meeting there would be a record." He was also the keeper of the government's secrets and had to be careful what he told outsiders. Thornhill never kept notes of these meetings, nor did he make entries in his desk diary, as he might be forced one day to make them public under the Freedom of Information Act.

On a visit to Dublin, Chuck Feeney pushed the proposal along by dropping in to see Micheál Martin and telling him he believed Ireland should be spending more money on research. Thornhill heard about the encounter and mischievously remarked at the next departmental meeting with the seven university presidents, "Oh, by the way, the minister was talking recently to Chuck Feeney." The temperature in the room dropped by about twelve degrees, he recalled with a delighted laugh. "They were seriously uncomfortable with this notion of politicians and officialdom moving into their zone, and understandably."

The proposal was moved along inside the bureaucracy by senior education department official Paddy McDonagh, and the minister's political adviser, Peter McDonagh (no relation). Faced with an unprecedented, even outlandish, request for IR£75 million in matching funds, Department of Finance officials dragged their heels. As the delay lengthened, Feeney used an encounter with the new prime minister, Bertie Ahern, to get across the message that there was a very exciting proposal being developed but the Atlantic money wasn't going to sit around forever. "Basically we were unhappy with the fact that the government was not investing the kind of money that they should be investing," recalled Feeney. "We said, 'Look, frankly you've got to invest in research, and now we've put buildings in, you've got laboratories and classrooms.'" After this, said Thornhill, the Department of Finance officials became a good deal more amenable.

Still the interdepartmental negotiations dragged on. "It was excruciating," said Thornhill. Healy was getting more and more impatient. On Tuesday, November 10, 1998, he issued an ultimatum to the officials. He said he was going to South Africa on Saturday and had to leave for the airport at 1:00 PM. If there was no approval by then, there was no deal.

Paddy McDonagh informed the Finance Department what was at stake. At 4:30 on Friday, November 13, as people were preparing to leave their offices for the weekend, a document summarizing the proposal that McDonagh had sent to the Finance Department was returned with a scribbled amendment. The addendum turned out to be the authorization they were seeking. Seventy-five million pounds of taxpayers' money would be put up to match the anonymous IR£75 million from Atlantic. Bertie Ahern would announce the IR£150-million fund the following Thursday and would describe Feeney's half as private funding.

The university heads had to be told in confidence that Atlantic Philanthropies would be the source of the private money being put up, so they would not panic about having to raise it themselves. Don Thornhill invited Danny O'Hare, who was chairman of the Conference of Heads of Irish Universities, to meet him at his office in Ballsbridge on Saturday morning, November 14, and to keep quiet about it. When O'Hare saw John Healy with Thornhill, he knew it was something to do with Atlantic.

"There is agreement between Tara (Atlantic Philanthropies) and the government for £150-million research fund," Thornhill told him. "We want you to tell your university colleagues and nobody else." Danny O'Hare responded in awe. "Shit!" he said. As he left he wondered, "My God, did I hear right?"

"This was real cloak-and-dagger stuff," recalled Thornhill. "We were so concerned about secrecy that we wouldn't even use the telephone." When they wanted to talk about Chuck and Atlantic among themselves, they didn't dare say the names aloud. They referred to "our friends," or "our mutual friends." People in the know in education had become practiced at making sly references to Feeney. "They would say, 'I was talking to the person we are not supposed to talk about,'" said Danny O'Hare. When university presidents requested government funding, the civil servants would ask, "Do you think that secret crowd will come up with half of it?" O'Hare told Healy once, "For God's sake, John, will you break this anonymous thing because it is becoming a farce really!"

At a press conference the following Thursday in Dublin, Bertie Ahern announced a IR£150-million research program that would involve new laboratories, computer and study facilities, and research library development, to be called the Program for Research in Third Level Institutions (PRTLI). He made no mention of Atlantic, saying only that half would come from "matching private spending to be raised by the universities and institutes of technology."

Harvey Dale's worries about the danger of the government reneging on its promise proved justified. The program of funding was to be in three cycles over a number of years. After a general election in May 2002, Micheál Martin was replaced as education minister by Noel Dempsey. The collapse of the technology bubble in the United States threatened to curb economic growth, and Dempsey came under pressure to cut back. His priorities were with the disadvantaged. He was more inclined to see universities as bastions of privilege. Atlantic sought urgent reassurances that the third cycle of the PRTLI program would not be cut. They weren't forthcoming. Don Thornhill appealed to Dempsey not to take drastic action. But on November 14, 2002, the new minister announced a "pause" in all capital funding for research. For Thornhill, it was "one of the most miserable moments in my official career," though he took some comfort in the knowledge that a "pause" was not a "cancellation."

No one bothered to tell Atlantic Philanthropies. "To say I was upset about this was an understatement," recalled John Healy, who had moved to New York as chief executive of the foundation. Large-scale research programs around the country faced collapse, university contracts were threatened, and the confidence of the research community was shattered. "As far as I was concerned we had a partnership with the government, and this is not a way to deal with partners, and we immediately told the universities and the Higher Education Authority that if the money is not flowing from the government it is not flowing from us," said John Healy. "So we had a pause, too."

As the months went by and the pause lengthened, it was evident that only the intervention of the prime minister could end the impasse. The Atlantic directors came to Dublin. On October 1, 2003, Chuck Feeney, Frank Rhodes, John Healy, and Colin McCrea, who had succeeded Healy as head of the Dublin operation, set off for Bertie Ahern's office in the imposing Government Buildings complex on Upper Merrion Street. In the car, Feeney put on a tie, while they figured out who was to play the "hard man." The task fell to Healy.

Feeney, whose glasses were held together by a paper clip that stuck up like an aerial, sat quietly in Ahern's office as Healy laid it on the line. "I didn't make any friends in the Taoiseach's [prime minister's] office that day," recalled Healy. "I was quite direct. We told the Taoiseach we were pretty upset. We expressed disappointment that as partners we hadn't been informed. I said we didn't have to spend our money in Ireland, and 'if you're not going to continue in a serious way, then we'll pull out.'" Ahern replied, "This is something we can resolve."

The session was private and there was no announcement to the media. "But then something very interesting happened," recalled Healy. "The following day we read about the meeting in *The Irish Times*." The newspaper's education correspondent, Sean Flynn, wrote that "the reclusive Irish American billionaire, Mr. Charles (Chuck) Feeney," had met Bertie Ahern and warned him that private funding for the universities was in jeopardy "unless the government eases cutbacks in third-level research."

The leak could only have come from the prime minister himself, realized Healy. He figured this was Ahern's way of putting pressure on Dempsey. Five weeks later, the "pause" was ended.

The program Atlantic inspired brought about a massive step-change in research funding in Ireland, and the Irish research sector was truly transformed, reflected Thornhill later. Danny O'Hare said it had a "brilliant effect on the research support system in Ireland and blew everything else off the map." The president of University College Dublin, Hugh Brady, said Atlantic was a catalyst in transforming the Irish research landscape.

The Program for Research in Third Level Institutions "is the single most successful thing that Atlantic has done anywhere in the world," said Colin McCrea. "Chuck had this idea that a good higher education system would lift most boats in the country. We transformed the government support for research in universities. The amount of money the government has given has increased manyfold as a result of it."

All told, Atlantic put up 178 million euros of the 605 million euros ($800 million) that the first three cycles of the program cost, before easing itself out. (The euro replaced the Irish pound in 1999.) Forty-six research institutes or programs were created, the capacity for world-class research in Ireland was substantially increased, and the brain drain of the best research talent in Ireland was reversed. In 2006, Minister for Finance Brian Cowan announced a 1.25-billion-euro investment in postgraduate education over the following five years. It wasn't Ireland's low-tax policy that was the key driver of the Celtic Tiger, he said, but the education system and its ability to turn out high-quality people.

"It was Chuck's biggest legacy," reflected Tom Mitchell, who joined the board of Atlantic Philanthropies at Feeney's invitation in 2002, after stepping down as head of Trinity College Dublin. "It revolutionized research in Ireland. It was the perfect example of leverage. They put money on the table and said to the government—you have got to perform. It was a model of how a foundation can combine with government and use its leverage with government to change policy. This was social change in a very significant way." Frank Rhodes said Feeney "brought Irish universities into conversation with one another; he enabled them to dream greater dreams; he lifted research to a new level."

The model was replicated in Northern Ireland, where Atlantic Philanthropies and the Northern Ireland government each provided £47 million for a £94 million (approximately $150 million) program called the Support Program for University Research (SPUR).

Yet Atlantic's greatest triumph was followed in Ireland by its most embarrassing misstep. This resulted from a controversial effort to establish an organization in Ireland modeled on the Center for Public Integrity in Washington, D.C., a highly reputable nonprofit organization run by former TV producer Charles Lewis. With the help of grants from Atlantic and other major U.S. foundations, the Center for Public Integrity in the United States had, since 1990, issued scores of investigative reports and successfully exposed political and corporate corruption in the United States.

Ireland was one of the few advanced democracies that did not have such an independent watchdog. Feeney was concerned about the level of corruption being reported in the Irish media among politicians and businessmen. He had been granted Irish citizenship some fifteen years previously—he qualified by having one grandparent born in Ireland—and held dual Irish-U.S. nationality. He had reason to feel he had a stake in civil governance in Ireland.

In June 2004, he invited Frank Connolly, a forty-nine-year-old investigative journalist whom he had gotten to know personally through his involvement in the Irish peace process, to draw up a proposal for a similar center in Ireland. Two months later, the journalist produced a five-year plan for an agency to be called the Centre for Public Inquiry (CPI), of which he would be chief executive. He showed it to Chuck Feeney, John Healy, and Colin Mc-Crea at a meeting at Castletroy Park Hotel in Limerick in September 2004.

Connolly, a serious, methodical investigator, seemed an ideal choice. Seven years earlier, his reporting had been largely responsible for forcing the government to set up a tribunal of inquiry under High Court Judge Feargus Flood into corruption in high places. He had found evidence that Ray Burke, a minister from the majority Fianna Fail Party, had taken bribes from a real estate developer to have land rezoned for development. Burke was eventually found to be corrupt and sentenced to six months in jail.

Feeney and Connolly shared a left-of-center view on Irish and international politics and had dined together a few times. Connolly claimed that political corruption in Ireland went far deeper than most people were aware, and he recalled that Feeney was "quite mystified" at the way some Irish politicians had escaped proper scrutiny over the years.

In December 2004, Connolly reported to Atlantic directors in New York that he had been able to recruit Feargus Flood, then seventy-six and retired, as chairman of the board of CPI. The other directors would be theologian Father Enda McDonagh, lawyer Greg O'Neill, former newspaper editor Damien Kiberd, and Alice Leahy, a cofounder of Trust, an organization for the homeless. The Atlantic Philanthropies that same day approved funding of 4 million euros ($5 million) over five years and a launch was set for Dublin in January 2005.

Meanwhile, Connolly invited Charles Lewis of the Center for Public Integrity in Washington to come to Dublin and advise him on how the American model worked. Lewis declined. "What I read and heard about Connolly left me uncomfortable," he said later in a newspaper interview. "I had serious ethical concerns about him."

Lewis had been tipped off by another investigative Irish journalist whom he knew, Sam Smyth, about allegations against Connolly. According to Colin McCrea, Atlantic Philanthropies had overlooked these claims. Two years previously, the *Sunday Independent* in Ireland had reported that Connolly was being investigated by the Irish police for allegedly traveling to Colombia on a false passport in April 2001. The implication was that his visit had something to do with the so-called Colombia Three, a trio of Provisional IRA members arrested in Colombia in August 2001 and sentenced to prison terms of seventeen years for allegedly training rebels from FARC (Fuerzas Armadas Revolucionarias de Colombia). One of them was Niall Connolly, Frank Connolly's brother. Frank Connolly had denied any wrongdoing. Feeney knew about Connolly's brother, and that Frank was sympathetic to the aims of the IRA's political wing, Sinn Fein, but had not allowed that to influence his assessment of the journalist.

The Irish Government was also tipped off about Connolly's watchdog body even before it became public. Sam Smyth, who worked for the *Independent* group of newspapers, had told the combative minister for justice, Michael McDowell, with whom he was friendly, about Lewis declining Connolly's invitation to visit Dublin.

There was consternation in the Irish government at the idea of Connolly heading an investigative body. Ministers regarded Feeney, in McDowell's words, as a "philanthropic, decent, good guy" who was doing fantastic things in Ireland, but was being "conned" by Connolly. Prime Minister Bertie Ahern decided to warn Feeney privately at the first opportunity whom he was dealing with. The matter was both personal and political for the prime minister: Connolly had years before publicized a claim by a businessman that he had given a substantial bribe to Ahern, which a judge found to be "utterly, completely and absolutely false and untrue."

The launch of the Centre for Public Inquiry went ahead in Dublin on January 31, with the declared aim of promoting "the highest standards of integrity, ethics and accountability" in Irish life. Connolly emphasized that it would not target individuals but would look at what was going on "at the interface between politics and business."

There was a furor from politicians claiming that Connolly's investigations would be politically slanted and would undermine the state. A few days later, the *Sunday Independent* republished its story of July 2002, splashing the claim that Connolly "is being probed by *gardai* [police] about allegations that he traveled to Colombia on a false passport in 2001." When reporters asked Judge Flood about the allegations against Connolly, he retorted angrily he would have "no hand, act or part in any McCarthyism."

The affair grew murky. In February an unknown person with an English accent phoned the U.K. office of Atlantic Philanthropies on Albemarle Street, London, to accuse Connolly of IRA links. Shortly afterward, Atlantic directors began receiving copies of an anonymous one-page document in the mail headed "Interim Report," which appeared to be an intelligence report, also associating Connolly with the IRA. A copy was later found lying around in the Irish parliament building.

Bertie Ahern believed his first opportunity to speak to Feeney privately about Connolly would come during a visit he was to make to the United States in March 2005, but the Irish American philanthropist was not available. McDowell himself then undertook to seek Feeney out when he was visiting the United States in May. "I said to officials in the department, find out where Chuck Feeney is," he recalled. "I am going around America. And I will go anywhere in America to see him." Feeney was traveling and again no meeting took place.

Meanwhile, more serious allegations about Connolly surfaced. Lord Laird of Artigarvin, a Northern Ireland unionist and fierce opponent of Sinn Fein, alleged in the British House of Lords on June 9 and 14 that Frank Connolly had gone to Colombia with a known IRA man to collect some $3 million "as part payment to the IRA by FARC terrorists for providing training and expertise on bomb making." The claims by Laird, who had acted as a public relations consultant for Anthony O'Reilly, chief executive of Independent News & Media PLC, were reported prominently in the group's Irish flagship, the *Sunday Independent*.

John Healy in New York was thoroughly alarmed to learn that the Irish minister for justice wanted to speak with Feeney so urgently. On a visit to Dublin in July, he called on the secretary general of the Department of Justice, Sean Aylward, to ask what was going on. Aylward told him only that it concerned Connolly and his alleged association with "subversives." He declined Healy's request to arrange a confidential police briefing to establish what evidence there was against Connolly. On Wednesday, July 27, Healy went to see Dermot Benn, a former Irish army intelligence officer and managing director of the private security firm Risk Management International, and asked him to use his police contacts to find out urgently what the police had on Connolly. Benn called Healy the next day and told him the police were not currently concerned with Connolly and that they believed the Centre for Public Inquiry was an "august body."

Feeney arrived back in Dublin in late August and the meeting the prime minister wanted was finally arranged. He and Colin McCrea went to see Bertie Ahern in Government Buildings on Wednesday, August 31. The prime minister told him that he was afraid that under Connolly, the CPI would indulge in a "witch hunt," but that he should see Michael McDowell, who would tell him more. They met the justice minister at his office on St. Stephen's Green two days later. McDowell, an outspoken critic of Sinn Fein, began by stressing his own nationalist credentials to Feeney, pointing to the fact that his grandfather Eoin MacNeill had played a role in the Irish struggle for independence, and telling Feeney that a large Irish flag with a black sash across it displayed on his office wall was the funeral flag of his uncle Brian MacNeill, shot in the civil war on the Republican side. McDowell then read from a briefing note listing events in Connolly's background. As a student, Connolly had been associated with an extreme organization, Revolutionary Struggle at Trinity College Dublin, that had shot and wounded a visiting Englishman, following which Connolly was arrested "but maintained silence during a lengthy interrogation." Connolly had been convicted of riotous behavior on September 28, 1982, and given a two-year suspended sentence by the Special Criminal Court. On April 10, 2001, Connolly went to Colombia and visited the FARC zone controlled by Communist narco-terrorists, using a false passport in the name of John Francis Johnston of Andersonstown, Belfast, in the company of a top member of the Provisional IRA, Padraig Wilson and his brother Niall Connolly, both also using false passports.

Frank Connolly was part of a plot to exchange IRA technology for cash, concluded McDowell. Funding him was a serious matter, he said, adding, "He'll close you, not you him." McDowell gave Feeney a copy of a photograph on the alleged false passport used by Frank Connolly, which he said had been supplied to him by the Colombian authorities.

Feeney listened carefully and said little. "He was measuring me up to see if I was just blackening Connolly or did I have the goodies," concluded McDowell.

Feeney was in a dilemma. He had encouraged Connolly to set up the Centre for Public Inquiry. He strongly believed it was worth funding. He was loyal to friends, and he liked Connolly. McDowell had no hard conclusive evidence against him. Back in the Tara office, he and McCrea studied the photocopy: It looked like Connolly's profile, but the features were not distinguishable. They tossed around possible agendas people might have to blacken Connolly's name. Was the government worried about Connolly as a subversive, or as someone who could damage them, or both? Were Irish politicians genuinely fearful he would use the center to undermine the established political parties and enhance the electoral prospects of Sinn Fein, a peripheral force in Irish politics? Was Anthony O'Reilly concerned about Connolly and his team making allegations about his business affairs? Was the *Sunday Independent*, a strong critic of Sinn Fein, pursuing Connolly on ideological grounds?

The problem was now one of credibility, however. The CPI had to uphold the same standards of accountability that it sought to promote. Frank Connolly had never said where he was during the week he was alleged to be in Colombia on a false passport, and he continued to insist he would only address that question if he were charged with an offense. Colin McCrea compiled a list of questions for the journalist about the Colombia allegations to try to clear the air. He and Chuck Feeney met him the following Wednesday evening. But with his dislike of confrontation, and his preference for mulling things over, Feeney didn't put the questions. He just told Connolly to "get on with the job."

"Chuck was quite calm in a lot of this and to me privately he was saying, 'Listen, we have got to try and deal with this problem but let's move on, I think the work you do is very important, we knew there was going to be a storm,'" said Connolly. Later Connolly gave them, in writing, a statement that he was not involved in what he was alleged to have done, while still declining to answer specific questions about his travels.

The affair took a heavy toll on Feeney. He slept badly, worrying if he was doing the right thing. He feared that the reputation of Atlantic Philanthropies, which liked to work quietly, was being publicly undermined. The controversy was taking up a huge amount of his time. It was difficult for him to focus on other priorities.

Feeney soon afterward left Ireland to attend a board meeting of Atlantic Philanthropies in Cape Town, South Africa. The board asked Colin McCrea and Tom Mitchell to suggest to Connolly that he stand down so that the center could survive. Connolly was upset at the suggestion that his position had become untenable but undertook to put the matter to his board. They refused to ask him to quit. "As I anticipated, the reaction of the board members was pretty general—if you step down we are all going, in other words, the whole project will collapse," recalled Connolly.

The Atlantic directors then concluded that the CPI board was failing in its duty. It had to be a model of openness and high standards. "It's the primary responsibility of any board to protect the institution it has been entrusted with," said Tom Mitchell. "This board failed to do that."

McDowell was dismissive of the directors' role in his recall of the affair. "All of these people were stage furniture for 'your man' [Connolly]," he said.

Feeney returned to Ireland in November for what turned out to be a "fractious" meeting between Atlantic and the CPI, at which nothing was resolved. When Connolly's board members argued that a person was innocent until found guilty, Mitchell told them that they were "not in a court of law here, you are in the court of public opinion." The former Trinity president felt, however, that despite everything, Connolly behaved with decorum throughout.

Around this time, Connolly gave Feeney an advance copy of an eighty-three-page report by the Centre for Public Inquiry on a controversial plan by Shell to lay a pipeline carrying unprocessed gas from the ocean bed close to houses in the rural west of Ireland. Feeney read the report and phoned Connolly an hour later to congratulate him. Connolly said he called it "absolutely brilliant," and that this was the reason the CPI had been set up, and he wanted to see it continue.

The Shell pipeline was a subject of much agitation in County Mayo. Five men from the village of Rossport had refused to allow engineers access to their land and had been jailed earlier in 2006 under an injunction obtained by the oil and gas company. Feeney felt great empathy with the protesters and had told Ahern that jailing them was a disgrace. In early September, Connolly had taken him to Clover Hill prison in west Dublin to visit one of the Rossport Five, a retired schoolteacher named Micheál O'Seighin. Feeney told O'Seighin, "I have a few favors to call in from the government, I'll do my best." The men were released after ninety-four days in prison, when Shell dropped the injunction.

The CPI report contained evidence that the gas pipeline could not be made safe. It noted that Bertie Ahern was "closely associated" with the project to bring gas ashore at Rossport and that the senior executives of the Corrib consortium—Shell, Statoil, and Marathon—had been given "unusual access" to the national planning board. It claimed that the corrupt minister Ray Burke had been responsible for initial revision of offshore licensing terms favorable to the energy companies. It also noted that Anthony O'Reilly had financial interests in the Atlantic fields, and that the Flood Tribunal, sitting under a different judge and now known as the Mahon Tribunal, was scheduled to investigate a payment in 1989 of GB£30,000 (US$45,000) to Burke as a political donation by a director of a company owned by the Fitzwilton Group that was controlled by O'Reilly.

Coincidentally, around this time Feeney and O'Reilly were both involved in funding a new £45-million ($90-million) state-of-the-art library at Queen's University, Belfast. Of the £37-million total given by Atlantic Philanthropies to the university since 2001, Feeney directed £10 million toward the library, without public recognition. When completed in 2009, the building will be known as the Sir Anthony O'Reilly Library on the basis of a £4-million contribution from O'Reilly for the naming rights, half of which was provided by him and half by his Independent

News & Media Group and the Ireland Funds he cofounded to support worthy causes.

In November, Connolly learned through his solicitor that the director of public prosecutions did not plan to lay any charges against him regarding Colombia, due to lack of evidence. But McDowell did not let the matter rest. At Sam Smyth's request, McDowell provided him with information on Connolly from the police file. On Saturday, November 26, Smyth published in the *Irish Independent* a copy of Connolly's alleged application for a passport in a false name with the forged signature of a Belfast priest. In a subsequent edition, the newspaper also reproduced the alleged passport photograph alongside a recent photograph of Connolly to show a similar outline in profiles. Amid an outcry about a government minister leaking police documents, McDowell was forced to admit on Irish radio that he personally had leaked the material to Smyth.

Feeney and his directors gathered in New York on Tuesday, December 6, for a board meeting at which the controversy dominated the agenda. Just before getting down to business, they received a fax from Dublin with a written statement McDowell had made in the Irish parliament. In it he claimed—for the first time on the public record—that the Colombian authorities had established that Connolly had traveled to Colombia under an assumed identity with a known senior IRA member and that on the basis of "intelligence reports," it appeared the visits concerned a deal whereby the IRA provided know-how in the use of explosives in return for "a large amount of money" from FARC. McDowell claimed that Connolly posed a threat to the security of the state and accused the CPI board of not making an "adequate and sustained attempt" to address these genuine issues of public concern.

With the Irish justice minister now on record in parliament saying the head of CPI was involved with a terrorist organization, and with Connolly still refusing to say where he was during the time he was alleged to be in Colombia, the Atlantic directors had little choice but to pull the 800,000-euro-a-year grant for the CPI, after just one year. They did it "because the board of the center seemed totally unresponsive to the concerns the foundation had," said Atlantic Philanthropies chairman Frank Rhodes. "The feeling was that they have not given the sort of leadership the [Atlantic] board had hoped for."

Connolly complained bitterly about "the fairly savage campaign against the Centre for Public Inquiry in the *Sunday Independent*, and against me in particular, but also against all of our board members." The decision was a blow to Judge Flood, who was close to tears when contacted by reporters. He accused McDowell of "a private and public blackening of Connolly's character." The affair briefly caused uproar in the Irish media, with some law experts criticizing McDowell's leaking of police documents as in itself subversion of the state. Author Nuala O'Faolain wrote in the *Sunday Tribune* that McDowell had "behaved disgracefully" and that "the way he got rid of an extrapolitical power centre by shafting Frank Connolly shows the need for an extrapolitical power centre."

Atlantic directors were angered by the tenor of some public comments that questioned Feeney's motives in setting up the center. *Irish Times* columnist John Waters wrote, "The idea of a foreign 'philanthropist' sticking his nose and his dollars into the affairs of a sovereign nation, as Chuck Feeney has done in funding the centre, is to my mind deeply unhealthy." Mary Harney, then deputy prime minister and head of McDowell's party, made no friends in the foundation when she said that "the idea of some group of citizens setting themselves up with absolutely no justification to the wider public is absolutely sinister and inappropriate." "I found Mary Harney's remarks incredibly objectionable," said one Atlantic executive. "I find it hard to believe she said it."

Looking back, McDowell said that he did *not* in fact regard as "sinister" the idea of an investigative body like the CPI being set up in Ireland, even if funded by someone from outside Ireland. "The big thing was it was Connolly," he said. "There was no trouble with the concept at all. I don't believe Chuck Feeney thought for one minute he was helping a Provo [Provisional IRA] front. If he were, he could have just told me to get lost, and he would fund whoever he wanted and good night Michael. What could I have done? It was my intention to warn him off before the whole thing got going and to do it privately, just to say, 'You are dealing with someone who is not what he appears to be.' I deeply regret that he was upset because I am sure he is a private man and I am sure he doesn't like being dragged into a controversy when all he is trying to do is be philanthropic. It's a bum deal from his point of view, but the Irish government doesn't think worse of him for it. He has emerged as entirely honorable as far as we are concerned. He was faced with denials by Connolly, and Connolly is a plausible person. He wondered genuinely whether we were just trying to foot-trip Frank Connolly for political reasons, and that was a hard judgment call for him to make."

"Chuck Feeney made a judgment about Frank, and it was hard for him to let go of it," said Tom Mitchell. "That is his way. He is very loyal. And the disillusionment was correspondingly great."

Atlantic Philanthropies reached a settlement with Connolly, following which the Centre for Public Inquiry ceased its existence. Some 100 files of potential investigations went out the window, said Connolly. The whole episode was unfortunate, remarked John Healy, in that it concentrated on one unsuccessful initiative of the Atlantic Philanthropies. Feeney had by this stage overseen gifts totaling more than $1 billion for good causes on the island of Ireland, but his philanthropy had mostly been anonymous and many Irish people now associated him only with the controversy over Connolly.

"I think we have made 3,000 grants, so I suppose there is a scope for one of them to go sour," Feeney mused in his apartment in San Francisco one rainy day the following January. Connolly failed to convince him that he was not "the guy down in Colombia . . . there for no good purposes." He reflected that he might have gone further into the situation when Charles Lewis of the Washington Center for Public Integrity refused to meet Connolly, and looked at the allegations being made before starting up the Irish center. "We certainly won't venture into that area again," he said. As for the negative political and media comments, he said, "I'm a tough nut. I can put those things aside."

Charity Begins at Home

By the start of the twenty-first century, Chuck Feeney had made a measurable impact on several countries. He and his secret giving were becoming known in ever-widening circles abroad. He was less well known in the United States, the country where he devoted most of his giving, despite the surge of publicity in 1997 when he was unveiled as a big-time secret philanthropist. By 2006, Feeney had given more money to American causes—$1.7 billion—than to all other countries combined, the biggest portion to higher education and research. The sheer size of the United States meant that the impact of his foundation's giving was proportionately less on a national scale than in smaller countries. But the impact on one single institution was enormous. From the time he started his philanthropy, Chuck Feeney directed over $600 million to Cornell University. No other American university has ever received such a sum from a single alumnus.

Up to the early 2000s, Feeney was always referred to at Cornell University as the Anonymous Donor, or AD. Cornell, however, was the one place in America where AD's identity was an open secret. If someone gave anonymously to Cornell, people not supposed to be in the know would say, "Oh! Chuck Feeney!" "As time went on it was done with a nudge and a wink," said Frank Rhodes. "That became a little bit uncomfortable, a little bit absurd for some people, but to begin with it was taken very seriously. The nudge and wink meant that the "anonymous donor" became a kind of formula in the foundation world for Atlantic Philanthropies, and yet with a perfectly straight face you had to be careful to say that you didn't know who it was."

Feeney's request for anonymity set him apart from other big donors to Cornell, such as Class of '55 alumnus Sanford I. Weill, the former chairman and CEO of Citigroup, who made donations to the medical school and hospital approaching $200 million and for which he is commemorated by the Weill Cornell Medical College. Duffield Hall at Cornell is named after software millionaire David A. Duffield of California, who made a gift of $20 million to build a laboratory complex. Feeney's name did not appear on any of the many buildings he funded at Cornell, though he did once honor his old friend Bob Beck by funding the $16-million state-of-the-art Robert A. and Jan M. Beck Center at the Hotel School.

Ernie Stern, the fund-raiser for the Cornell Class of '56, believes that there is a connection between Feeney's drive to increase alumni giving at the start of his philanthropic work in the early 1980s and the enormity of subsequent gifts like that from Sandy Weill. "Sandy Weill was Class of '55," said Stern. "They were a nowhere class. Who the hell cares that the Class of '56 gave X million dollars? Well, the Class of '55 cares. And the Class of '57 cares. Competition is a wonderful motivator. It's completely stupid when you think about it. It's nuts. But it works. Everybody looked at our class, said, well they can do it, we can do it. I know it sounds kind of immature or nonsensical but I take it seriously. Cornell has now reached a level of giving by its alumni never before achieved. Last year [2004] Cornell raised $350 million and it was No. 3 in the U.S., and No. 1 among alumni givers in the nation, and I attribute that in some measure to this gradual year-after-year thing started by our class."

Feeney's insistence on anonymity was highly unusual. Only 1 percent of American givers ask to remain anonymous. Many rich Americans compete to make the most money, like the technology entrepreneur Jim Clark, who once aspired, unsuccessfully, to have more money than anyone else in the world. Feeney got involved with Clark in one of the biggest gifts ever made to Stanford University in California. In October 1999, Clark, the founder of Netscape, Silicon Graphics, and Healtheon, announced that he would donate $150 million to Stanford University for a new research hub to be called the James H. Clark Center. It was the largest single gift pledged to Stanford since its founding in 1891. The inventor said he felt indebted to the university for what it had given him: As a professor at Stanford in the early 1980s, he had been allowed to explore the technologies that he would later develop so profitably in the private sector. The university had made him rich, and he wanted to return the favor.

The San Jose *Mercury News* enthused that Jim Clark "eroded the stereotype of stingy Silicon Valley tycoons" with his "jaw-dropping" $150-million contribution for the center, which would be at the heart of a biomedical engineering and sciences project known as Bio-X.

Amid the flurry of glowing media testimonials, no one was aware that Chuck Feeney had agreed quietly to contribute $60 million to the project. Feeney had been an anonymous donor to Stanford since 1996—his son Patrick was a student there, and Chuck had been contacted in 1994 as a parent by Stanford's vice president for development, John Ford, who had no idea at the time whom he was asking for money—and he had already made two gifts totaling $65 million for Stanford research projects. Feeney met Clark at a lunch at the home of Stanford's president, John Hennessy, in March 2001. Chuck found him strange. He got a feeling that Clark was a one-time contributor, making a splash. "We like the project you are doing, and we would be happy to contribute to it," he told Clark, who responded, "Fine, as long as I can retain the rights to my name." Feeney replied, "Be our guest."

Six months later, after Clark had paid $60 million of his $150 million pledge, he dropped a bombshell on Stanford. He told Hennessy and Ford that he wanted to "suspend" payment of the remaining $90 million to protest the way President George W. Bush was limiting human embryonic stem-cell research, part of the intended purpose of the center. President Bush had said on August 9, 2001, that federal funding would only be available for stem-cell research using cell cultures established before that date. Hennessy was bewildered. Why would Clark want to punish the university—which had taken the lead in stem-cell research—for President Bush's controversial decision? They pleaded with him to reconsider. Clark relented a little. He told them he would pay $30 million of the $90 million outstanding, but he was adamant he would not pay any more.

The university had no legal redress. It preferred to trust donors to honor their promises rather than make them sign binding pledges. Stanford had to scramble to get the last $60 million to complete the Bio-X Center's development.

The Bio-X Center was opened in October 2003 to widespread acclaim for its architectural merits. Despite reneging on $60 million of his $150-million commitment, the inventor retained the naming rights. The visiting public is today informed that the James H. Clark Center was completed "thanks to the enormous generosity of Jim Clark and Atlantic Philanthropies."

Feeney's total giving to Stanford at the time Clark pulled out amounted to $125 million, $35 million more than Clark gave, making him one of the top five givers in Stanford's history, but nothing is named after him, as he wished. It equaled the Annenberg Foundation's record 2001 gift of $125 million to the University of Pennsylvania, which was hailed by the *Chronicle of Philanthropy* as the largest sum given by a private foundation to a single American university. At the time, Feeney's even greater giving to Cornell was still a secret.

Impetuous withdrawals of funding are rare but not unknown in philanthropy. In June 2005, Larry Ellison, the CEO of Oracle and Clark's onetime rival, pledged $115 million to Harvard to fund the Ellison Institute for World Health. It was to be the biggest gift ever to the Ivy League university, far outweighing the largest previous donation of $70.5 million from John Loeb, the former U.S. ambassador to Denmark. One year later, Ellison, with a net worth of $16 billion and fifteenth place on the *Forbes* rich list, announced that he had changed his mind, because of the departure of Harvard president Larry Summers, whose concept the project was. Twenty researchers, three top academics, and managerial staff, who had already been hired, were told to find other work.

Many of Atlantic Foundations' gifts in the United States arose from the initiatives, in the early years, of Ray Handlan, president of the Atlantic Service Company, and after 1993 of his successor, Joel Fleishman. But on his frequent commutes between New York and San Francisco, Feeney was always on the lookout for his own "new new thing." When spending a few weeks in San Francisco in 2004, he learned of a problem faced by the University of California at San Francisco (UCSF). In 2003, it had received a $35-million gift from property developer Sanford Diller for the construction of the Helen Diller Family Cancer Research Building at UCSF–Mission Bay. The university had to raise a balance of $40 million, and for over a year struggled to find it. Feeney sat down with the development officer and asked for the list of wealthy San Francisco people. He pointed to the name of venture capitalist Arthur Rock. What about him? Rock had just given $25 million to Harvard, he was told. "That just proves he has $25 million to give," said Feeney. "Why not offer him a challenge grant? If Rock puts up $20 million, Atlantic will match it with $20 million." Not only did Rock agree, he put his gift up to $25 million when the cost rose $5 million because of the delay. "That's what happens if you screw around a couple of years," said Feeney. "You get inflation." In March 2007, Atlantic gave the university its biggest cash gift ever—$50 million for a cardiovascular research center and clinic.

Feeney also relied on a network of contacts to identify good and worthy causes in the United States, and he was constantly reading local newspapers, listening to news, and studying reports. A major grant was as likely to flow from a page Feeney tore from a magazine as from a consultation with a research institute director. Few magazines survived Chuck's attention intact, and no university president was immune from the prospect that a nondescript man in blazer and aloha shirt, carrying his papers in a plastic bag, would one day walk into their office and ask how they were doing. Sometimes small academic institutions got as much, or more, of his attention and time as Ivy League universities. This was the case with Chaminade University, a tiny Catholic college nestled on the slopes of Kalaepohauku overlooking the Pacific Ocean just outside Honolulu in Hawaii.

When Dr. Mary Civille (Sue) Wesselkamper became the first woman president of Chaminade in 1997, she found the university was run down and that the undergraduate population, many from the original Hawaiian population and from the Pacific Islands, had declined to about 660. "The financial situation was much worse than I or the board imagined," she said. "We were very close to bankruptcy." When she appealed for help to the founding Marianist Order based at the University of Dayton, Ohio, they sent Brother Bernard Ploeger to be her vice president and to sort out the finances. He told her, "Your worst fears are realized, the institution is unraveling." Dayton paid $4.3 million to eliminate operating debt, but the fundamental problems of outdated facilities and substandard student accommodation remained unsolved.

A few months later, a taxi drove up the steep driveway that curved between the neglected campus buildings. "The most unassuming man stepped out and wanted to know everything about the university," said Wesselkamper. "I took him on the tour. He even wanted to see the bathrooms in the residence hall. He said, 'I'll be back to you.'"

Feeney had been on one of his periodic business trips to Honolulu and had heard about Chaminade's woes from a friend. After his tour of the campus, he invited Sue Wesselkamper to New York to meet Harvey Dale. "We have a general rule we don't do religious giving, and Harvey is always strong on those kind of things," said Feeney—who had already bent the rule with a $2-million gift to a Benedictine monastery in Ireland for library development. In New York, Wesselkamper explained that they had a two-tier system of a lay governing board and religious corporate board. Dale asked for a clearer separation from the religious side. "She came away from the meeting thinking, "We are small potatoes! I couldn't go to the Marianists and say we wanted to separate from them."

Feeney asked Wesselkamper to compile a strategic plan for the university, which she and Brother Bernard did. They sent Feeney the plan. "Most people would just take it and leaf through it," she said. "Chuck actually read the whole thing, and it was a hefty document."

"All of a sudden, later in 1998, Chuck comes into the office again—we had much older furniture then, and he sat on this bumpy couch—and he said, 'I really like what you are doing for students here. I want to help you get started.' I brought up the separation issue and he said, 'I think we can work this out.' He said, 'I'm going to give you a check for $3 million.' I asked him: 'Could you say that again?' Then he handed me a check for $3 million."

The standard letter arrived from Harvey Dale, telling her she would have to give the money back if anyone found out where it had come from. She recalled thinking, "This is Hawaii, it is a small island: There are no secrets here." But she dutifully told the board, "I can't tell you where the gift came from." She reckoned some guessed that it was Feeney—he was well known in Hawaii—but kept quiet.

Feeney became a regular visitor and took a close interest in the provision of new buildings and modular units to solve the accommodation shortage. Wesselkamper believes that what got Chuck's attention was the poor condition of the buildings—something that could readily be fixed—and the fact that the students were up against it, compared to those in other universities. Most were from low-income families and disadvantaged groups. Many were judged to have the potential for university study but were not quite "prepared." Some from the Philippines, Samoa, or Guam did not have English as a first language.

"His gifts were truly transformational," said Wesselkamper, on a walk around the campus in January 2006. "His giving is now close to $14 million." A new library was erected with $5 million from Atlantic and $5 million from

Jenai Sullivan Wall, daughter of a friend of Chuck's from early DFS days, called Maurice (Sully) Sullivan, an Irishman who secured the McDonald's franchise in Hawaii and founded the largest grocery chain on the islands, called Foodland, and who died in 1998.

In keeping with his practice of bringing universities into conversation with each other, Feeney brought Sue Wesselkamper to Vietnam and sponsored a Vietnamese student for her university.

Hawaii, though part of the United States, was an extension of Chuck's giving to a new geographical zone. His ability to seek out and identify major worthy projects for the cash-rich foundation was the key to Atlantic Philanthropies' success. But it was difficult for Atlantic directors and staff to keep up with him. Doing serious and thoughtful philanthropy in several countries required staffing and management.

With Feeney showing no sign of slowing down, directors expressed doubts about the wisdom of "opening up any new geography." Thomas J. Tierney, founder of the Boston-based Bridgespan management consulting company, summed up their apprehensions at a private seminar he conducted for Atlantic in 2000, by writing on a flip chart: "No Incremental Geographical Creep." "There was kind of laughter at that and it went into some document or other as "No geographical creep," said Harvey Dale, "and that was intended to constrain Chuck from opening up another geography."

Chuck Feeney's moral authority in the organization was, however, so great, and the board members held him in such reverence, that they would have deferred to his wishes should he have opted to open up another territory. When asked what would happen if Feeney wanted to get involved in directing large grants to a new country, for example, Zimbabwe, Harvey Dale replied, "In my view if Chuck decided there was something important to do in Zimbabwe, that may be smart or not smart, but if he really, really wanted to do it, I say—we can deal with that. And let's help him instead of trying to stop him."

CHAPTER 31

Geographical Creep

In 2003, Harvey Dale's reservations notwithstanding, Chuck Feeney started planning to go to a new country. It was perhaps inevitable that Cuba should attract his attention. He had become involved in Communist Vietnam and that had worked extremely well. Like Vietnam, Cuba had gotten a raw deal from the United States, he believed. Cuba and Vietnam came from the idea of righting an American wrong, said his daughter Juliette.

For most Americans, helping Vietnam was not a problem. Under the Clinton administration, America's relations with Vietnam had sharply improved. The wounds from the Vietnam War were beginning to heal. The U.S. economic embargo on Vietnam was lifted in 1994 and relations normalized in 1995.

Cuba was different. Hundreds of thousands of Cuban exiles in Florida were passionately opposed to any engagement while Fidel Castro was alive. They had bipartisan support in Washington. In 1996, President Bill Clinton signed into law the Helms-Burton Act, which made a punitive U.S. trade embargo permanent. There were no diplomatic relations between Washington and Havana. U.S. citizens were subject to heavy fines if they entered Cuba without Washington's permission.

The political risk of Atlantic's going into Cuba was therefore much higher than with Vietnam. "We haven't yet got to the reconciliation step with Cuba, whereas we had with Vietnam," said Chris Oechsli. "We are allowed to rebuild Vietnam, but we are not yet allowed to rebuild Cuba."

The Atlantic directors acquiesced in, rather than endorsed, Chuck's plan to explore giving in Cuba. "I would not personally do it, but I don't think it's the end of the world if Chuck chooses to do it," said chairman Frank Rhodes. Many of Chuck's American admirers were taken aback, however. "I don't know where this thinking comes from," said his old friend Fred Antil. "He is a good man with a Catholic upbringing and blue-collar Catholic background." Lawyers for Atlantic Philanthropies advised the American directors they should not even discuss giving funds to Cuba (and they didn't). John Healy, who had become chief executive of Atlantic and moved to New York in 2001, was an Irish national but would not even talk about Cuba in interviews because he was based in New York. As an American citizen, Chuck could not direct the foundation's operation in Cuba. However, he could *inspire* it.

To enable Atlantic Philanthropies to help projects in Cuba, an organization called Atlantic Charitable Trust was registered in London with the Charity Commission of England and Wales, to which funds were allocated from Bermuda for transfer on to Havana. No U.S. board member or American employee of Atlantic Philanthropies was associated with it. Irish national Colin McCrea, head of the international branch in Dublin and senior vice president of Atlantic Philanthropies, was made its executive director. "We were very careful that the laws of the U.S. be protected, in spirit as well as in practice," said McCrea. Its other members included director Tom Mitchell, also based in Ireland, and two English appointees. Mitchell had no qualms about his role. "I think what the United States is doing in Cuba is unconscionable," he said. He could see the reason for it before the end of the Cold War, but since then, Cuba represented no credible threat to the United States. "The main thing is that the foundation plays it straight. If Atlantic Philanthropies is going to give a significant gift to Cuba, it gets a license to do so. It is not trying to do anything through a back door."

Chris Oechsli made several initial trips to Cuba to identify projects that could legally be supported and to ensure that Havana knew enough to take the philanthropist seriously. Cuban officials often got inquiries from sympathetic Americans that never came to anything, mainly because of the American embargo. Oechsli detected an element of "not-unfounded paranoia" in the Cuban administration about the secretive Feeney operation. One of the directors of Atlantic Philanthropies was Fritz Schwarz, who had served as chief counsel on the Senate intelligence subcommittee investigating CIA excesses that former Senator Frank Church chaired in 1975: Half the publication was devoted to CIA attempts to kill Fidel Castro.

In November 2004, Feeney went to Cuba, flying directly from Paris to Havana, accompanied by a group that included board member Tom Mitchell, and Roger Downer, president of the University of Limerick. It actually wasn't Feeney's first time in the country. While still single and selling cars around the world, he had flown into Havana in January 1959, a week after the revolution. "Fidel and his camp followers had taken over the Hilton," he recalled. Feeney was able to travel uninterrupted to the U.S. military base at Guantanamo Bay, where he sold two cars and appointed a salesman for Cars International.

On the last evening of his weeklong trip in 2004, a Cuban official advised Feeney and his group to be at the Havana Conference Center in late afternoon. At 5:30 PM, two black Mercedes limousines approached along the driveway through the surrounding lawns. The first one slowed down and then zoomed off. The second one did the same. Having completed their security maneuver, the limos circled and came back.

Fidel Castro strode through the door, bearded and gaunt, dressed in military green fatigues. He greeted Feeney and led the way into a conference room. He seemed as if he had recently been asleep. The Cuban president had with him his physician, Dr. Eugenio Selman-Housein—famous for his prediction that Castro would live to be 140 years old—and his first vice minister for foreign affairs, Fernando Remírez de Estenoz Barciela, who had been the head of the Cuban Interests Section in Washington, D.C., at the time of the repatriation from Florida of the Cuban schoolboy Elian Gonzales.

Once he started to talk, however, Castro came to life and monopolized the conversation. His monologue went on almost unbroken for over six hours, ending just before midnight. He displayed a phenomenal memory and attention to detail. "He starts very inaudible and quiet and draws you in, and hours later you realize you are at another level of discourse and energy, and you have been engaged, you have been hooked," said Oechsli. "For me there was not one minute of dullness. It was quite engaging." At one point, Castro engaged Tom Mitchell on a discourse about Greek philosophy, and Feeney interjected to say, "If you guys go on like this, all we will be able to discuss is baseball." Castro replied, "No, we have much more important things to discuss," and launched into a debate on global warming and world health. During that time the guests were served fruit and fruit drinks.

Feeney drank little, aware from the start that they were in for a long night. At last Castro said, "I really apologize, I can't help myself, I go on, and I don't stop, and I've been very rude." Chuck was relieved in every sense—no one had dared interrupt the monologue to go to the bathroom. He agreed it was time to wrap up, saying it was so late "that my wife will think I am with another woman!" The Cuban leader made a show of being mortified. "Oh! I didn't realize your wife is here with you. I will have to give her flowers." "If you send her flowers she will *know* I am with another woman," replied Feeney, at which Castro laughed uproariously.

The next day, just before Chuck and Helga were to leave, Castro appeared again, this time accompanied only by his interpreter. He presented Helga with a bouquet of flowers and proffered a box of cigars to Feeney. "Do you smoke?" he asked. Feeney said, "No." "Well, do your friends smoke?" "No." "Better yet, give them to your enemies," said Castro, who himself gave up smoking in 1985. This time the meeting went on for two hours in a smaller room. Castro was very solicitous of Helga. Oechsli, who was also present, found that in the more intimate setting, Castro had a real grace and was very personable. The Cuban leader also sought out Roger Downer separately for a discussion on education, saying, "Last night I lectured you, now you inform me."

Under U.S. rules, Atlantic Philanthropies was allowed to support an important health study, known as the Isle of Youth Study, identifying risk markers for chronic kidney disease, which affects hundreds of millions of people worldwide. It was also permitted to provide medical backpacks for the Latin American School of Medicine, established by Castro in Havana in 1998 to train doctors from other countries without charge. Castro explained to Feeney that this was an opportunity to build human resources in health in the region.

By 2007, Atlantic had contributed some $11 million to Cuba, mainly to medical education cooperation. However, the U.S. embargo frustrated Feeney from doing what he did best, identifying the capital needs of colleges and universities, and providing funds for new buildings and facilities to raise the national level of educational achievement.

Feeney was enthusiastic, however, about helping the Cuban health program, which was based on prevention rather than cure and which succeeded in giving Cuba a greater average life expectancy than the United States. On one visit he asked Gail Reed, an American journalist based in Cuba, why so few people knew about the achievement of Cuban physicians. When she replied that a book was being written, he retorted, "Nobody reads anymore, make a movie." Atlantic Charitable Trust subsequently provided $1 million for a ninety-minute documentary called *Salud,* produced by Gail Reed and Academy Award–nominee Connie Field in 2006, and pledged resources for worldwide distribution.

Feeney remained determined to do all he could within U.S. law. On another visit to Cuba in January 2007, he told Ricardo Alarcon, president of the Cuban National Assembly, over dinner in the elegant Café del Oriente in Old Havana, "You haven't seen the back of me."

In the meantime, Feeney had "discovered" the Republic of South Africa. He went there in the autumn of 2005. But it wasn't a case of geographical creep. The Atlantic Foundation had been active in South Africa since 1994, largely on the initiative of Harvey Dale, who asked John Healy to find opportunities after the end of apartheid in 1991. In the following decade, it had committed some $100 million to education, reconciliation, human rights, and health, with significant funding for the fight against AIDS, and was ranked one of the country's top five foreign donors. Healy had become, as he put it, "an absolutely unabashed enthusiast for South Africa," but he could never get Chuck really interested. At a meeting of the Atlantic Philanthropies board in Brisbane in 2004 when Healy announced that the next board meeting would be held in South Africa, Feeney retorted, "Well, I won't be there."

"Every time I spoke to Chuck about South Africa to try and interest him in it, he just closed his mind," said Healy. "He didn't want to go there. He thought the problems were too great. And in recent years, perfectly understandably, his confidence waned even further because of the AIDS denialism of the president and because of the huge outflow of trained health professionals, and because of the less than smart way the South Africans are dealing with the Zimbabwe crisis. So all those things turned him off completely."

Feeney had a different explanation. "I am never daunted by the depth of a problem because if you are signing up to help you have to assume there are problems," he said. "I didn't go before because I only go to places on the track where I am going." South Africa was a major physical as well as psychological diversion. His travels took him around the world, but it was a fixed elliptical route that he traversed over and over, from New York to San Francisco, Hawaii, Japan, Australia, Thailand, Vietnam, the United Kingdom, Ireland, and back to New York, or else the other way around, the itinerary always recorded in ballpoint pen in a school exercise book that Feeney, who disdains computers, likes to call his "Jesuit's lap-top" and takes with him everywhere.

Feeney changed his mind, however, and went to South Africa some days in advance of the board meeting, giving Healy an opportunity to set up meetings with people who might influence his opinions. One of these was ex-African National Congress general secretary Cyril Ramaphosa, the powerful union leader who helped negotiate a peaceful end to apartheid. They met for lunch in Johannesburg's Sandton district in the private room of a restaurant that was once a famous brothel. They found a common interest in the Northern Ireland peace process. Ramaphosa and former Finnish president Martti Ahtisaari had been invited by the IRA to verify the decommissioning of its secret stores of weapons. He regaled Feeney with cloak-and-dagger stories of how the IRA made contact with him. "I was told to go to a pub in Paris and read the *Financial Times* and to be inconspicuous," he said. "Me? A black man?" An IRA man in dark glasses sidled up, and he was spirited to Ireland, where he ended up standing in Irish bogs, still trying to look inconspicuous, as caches of weapons were opened up and counted. Feeney had his own stories of adventures on the back streets of Belfast when making contact with Gerry Adams.

"The point of meeting Cyril Ramaphosa was to try and demonstrate to Chuck Feeney that this is not a 'basket-case' country, that there are terrific people here who are going to secure its future, and that it is a place where philanthropy can invest its money and be reasonably sure of getting a return," said Healy. It succeeded. As they parted, Feeney grasped Ramaphosa by both hands and told him, "Our work in South Africa has only just begun."

Feeney also sat riveted while Alistair Sparks, South Africa's best-known journalist, gave the Atlantic directors an overview of the country's history in the eleven years since it moved from pariah status to a fast-growing stable democracy, and again when retired chief justice of South Africa, Arthur Chaskalson, one of the heroes of modern South Africa, spoke about the shift into constitutionalism in South Africa at a dinner for grantees held at the Howard Hotel. The evening ended with a group of students from the Music School of the University of KwaZulu-Natal, singing arias by Puccini and Verdi.

Atlantic Philanthropies directed the bulk of its funding in South Africa toward higher education, donating substantial sums to major universities such as Witwatersrand in Johannesburg and KwaZulu-Natal in Natal province. Operating with a staff of five in Johannesburg under the direction of Gerald Kraak, a writer whose novel *Ice in the Lungs* won the European Union Literary Award in 2006, it has also given funding to organizations ranging from the Pietermaritzburg Gay and Lesbian Network to the museum at Robbens Island where Nelson Mandela was imprisoned, and it has paid for activists in Northern Ireland to come to South Africa to discuss conflict resolution.

Always on the lookout for university heads with vision and energy, Feeney told Brian O'Connell, the rector (president) of the University of the Western Cape, "We have come to the right place," after O'Connell explained over lunch, with considerable passion, what the mission of the university was. At a dinner at the Vineyard Hotel in Cape Town the next night, Mamphela Ramphele, who along with the murdered student leader Steve Biko was one of the founders of South Africa's Black Consciousness movement in 1969, spoke about why people should invest in South Africa. Urged on by John Healy's wife, Yvonne, Feeney made a short speech, the bottom line of which was that there was more work for Atlantic Philanthropies to do in South Africa.

"As the board visit proper progressed, you could see almost on a daily basis his mind changing because he kept encountering the most wonderful people, who are heroic in what they have done or are doing and have enormous obstacles to overcome, and he realized that this is a special country not just because of what it had shown to the world in the last few years in terms of moving from tyranny to democracy but because of the potential to lead Africa out of its present mess into a better future," said Healy.

Feeney duly recruited South African academics into his worldwide network of university leaders. At his suggestion, Brian O'Connell brought a delegation from the University of the Western Cape to Australia to start building links with universities there. John Hay, president of the University of Queensland, began a collaboration with O'Connell on public health, AIDS research, and language acquisition. Students from South Africa were given the means to study in Brisbane and upgrade their qualifications.

In late 2006, asked if he would consider another geography, Feeney, then seventy-five, replied, "I wish I was younger."

CHAPTER

The Old Turks

The four founding shareholders of DFS, who started with nothing and became fabulously wealthy, were by the turn of the century leading very different lives. Today they have little or no contact with each other, though Bob Miller, Alan Parker, and Tony Pilaro own chalets on the same wooded hillside at the tony ski resort of Gstaad in Switzerland. Feeney and Miller have not spoken since their last meeting before the sale. Nor have Miller and Pilaro. Feeney and Pilaro have met just once. Only Alan Parker continues to have cordial relations with the other three, though he himself did not see Miller or Pilaro for five years after the split.

On one thing Feeney's partners agree. They were extremely fortunate that the Irish American entrepreneur came into their lives, and they are happy to acknowledge his role in making them rich. Chuck Feeney "is a very special human being, there is no question about it," said Bob Miller. "There is absolutely no doubt Chuck was the visionary and the driving force in DFS," stated Alan Parker. "Feeney is a peripatetic, brilliant, goal-driven, visionary . . . he had success written all over him," reflected Tony Pilaro.

Bob Miller treats his wealth in conventional ways. He and his wife, Chantal, have become members of global high society. The *South China Morning Post*, Hong Kong's English-language daily, once described his and Feeney's opposite lives as "the story of the billionaire prince and the billionaire pauper." Miller resides most of the year in a magnificent house on the Peak in Hong Kong, where he is the richest Western resident. From early August to the end of January—the grouse-shooting season—he can be found in England at Gunnerside, a shooting lodge on his private estate in Upper Swaledale, Yorkshire, which includes the largest grouse moor in England.

The elegant stone-walled lodge is set in an amphitheater of meadows, blanket bog, and heathlands. An adjacent enclosure contains free-range pheasants. Fit and tanned, and with a full head of silver hair, the seventy-two-year-old billionaire was wearing a zip-up jacket bearing the logo of his yacht, Mari-Cha IV when he reminisced one November evening in 2005 about his relationship with Feeney and his own attitude toward great wealth. Over dinner, in a room hung with large oil paintings of dogs and hunting scenes, Miller talked with some regret about the breakdown in his relationship with the partner who helped propel him to billionaire status. They were never really close, he said, but in the early days they were the "Young Turks," and those were the best days.

As his butler, Andrew, formerly first footman to the Queen Mother and dressed in regulation black waistcoat and striped trousers, poured Chateau Gruaud Larose 1998, Miller reflected on how his attitudes to wealth were shaped by his childhood experiences, which were not dissimilar to those of Chuck Feeney but had very different effect. "I was born in 1933 and grew up in the Depression," he said. "I can remember my father wouldn't get paid until Saturday morning, and the Friday night dinner was always rather meager because my mother would have run out of her house money by then. It would be baked beans and brown bread. My father was very good at managing what little money he had, and I guess I learned all that from him. I could always make money. As a kid I was always delivering newspapers and usually had cash in my pocket. I worked as a short-order cook at nights while a student at Cornell. I waited on tables in the fraternity house and got my food free. I went right from high school into college and got a small scholarship that helped. My parents had to pay about half, and I could make the other half."

His Scots-Irish mother used to tell him, he said, "Money is like manure, spread it around and fertilize things and make things grow and happen—in other words you should enjoy it." That was her philosophy, and "I think a very good one." As DFS dividends grew, he noticed Feeney being more troubled about whether they really deserved that kind of success, but "making more money never did seem to bother me; you take where it comes and enjoy it, you know."

The Millers' lifestyle changed when they became wealthy. They spent on a grand scale, throwing multi-million-dollar parties and mixing with the crowned heads of Europe. In New York, they bought Bill Cosby's townhouse on the Upper East Side for $18 million in the mid-1980s and filled it with expensive art and antiques. In addition to elegant homes in Hong Kong, Paris, and London, they acquired a chalet in Gstaad and a holiday home on Harbour Island in the Bahamas, a hideaway for celebrities like Keith Richards and Julia Roberts.

In 1994, the Millers paid $13 million for Earl Peel's 32,000-acre Gunnerside estate—now expanded to 40,000 acres—and Chantal Miller spent several million more upgrading the hunting lodge, installing antique furniture and artwork and outfitting the guest bedrooms with fabric wallpaper and Fabergé alarm clocks. Miller employed a gamekeeper to organize the burning and draining of the moor every year to provide ideal conditions for the traditional sport of the aristocracy, breeding and shooting pheasants.

From the time he started accumulating money, Bob Miller indulged his passion for boats. He and Chantal spent much time sailing on Mari-Cha III, an oceangoing yacht replete with artwork, marble surfaces, and Honduran mahogany paneling. His $10-million, 140-foot, super yacht Mari-Cha IV, became the fastest yacht ever to cross the Atlantic. "This is what life's all about. The only reason you make money is that you can do something like this," Miller told a *South China Morning Post* reporter, after first breaking the Atlantic record in 1998. He and his twenty-three-member crew shattered the west-to-east transatlantic speed record by more than two days in 2003 in the sailboat emblazoned with a red dragon logo. Like Feeney, Miller does not put his name on things. He once remarked dismissively that if Donald Trump owned Mari-Cha IV, "he'd have his name written all over it."

Miller sent his three daughters—Pia, Marie-Chantal, and Alexandra—to the Institut Le Rosay finishing school in Switzerland, and as they emerged into society, they were feted in *Vanity Fair* as the "Three Graces." "Not since the Gilded Age have three heiresses been so well betrothed," proclaimed *W,* the American fashion magazine, which reported that for Alexandra's twenty-first birthday, Miller had the Rainbow Room at Rockefeller Plaza, New York, transformed into a 1920s speakeasy for a white-tie dinner costing more than $500,000. The three sisters were regularly included by style writers among the fifty best-dressed women in the world.

They all had fabulous marriages. In 1992, Pia wed Christopher Getty, a grandson of oil billionaire J. P. Getty, at a lavish ceremony in Bali, where hundreds of Indonesian children showered them with rose petals.

Marie-Chantal married exiled Crown Prince Pavlos of Greece, prince of Denmark, in London in 1995, bringing a dowry of £130 million from her parents, according to *Majesty*, the British royal magazine. Miller paid for a vast reception and dinner at Hampton Court, home of King Henry VIII, which witnessed the biggest gathering of European royalty since the wedding of Prince Charles and Lady Diana Spencer in 1981.

"We had the Queen of England and the Queen Mother, plus members of the royal families of Greece, Spain, Denmark, Sweden, Norway, Belgium, Luxembourg, Liechtenstein, Italy, Holland, Bulgaria, and Jordan," Miller recounted with a chuckle over the crème brûlée. "When I made my father-of-the-bride speech, I had to say, 'Your Majesties, Your Royal Highnesses, Your Highnesses, Your Holiness, Your Excellency, My Lords, Ladies and Gentlemen. . . .' Quite a mouthful!"

Three months later, his youngest daughter, Alexandra, married Prince Alexandre von Furstenburg, son of Prince Egon and fashion designer Diane von Furstenburg. Miller paid for a sumptuous black-tie ball for 650 guests, including singer Dolly Parton, socialite Bianca Jagger, and TV celebrity Barbara Walters, in a vast tent resembling a Chinese pavilion in New York's Battery Park.

Wealth and the marriages propelled the Millers into the exalted ranks of European high society. Bob Miller's shooting guests in August for the first drive of *Lagopus scoticus*, the red grouse that is indigenous to the British Isles, often included European royalty. He had so many friends in different royal families that when Cornell alumnus Fred Antil, after meeting Prince Egon, told Miller that he had met "the Prince," Miller replied, "Which one?"

Bob Miller established his own investment vehicle, the Search Investment Group, in 1970 and based it in Hong Kong. Search manages third-party capital and has invested over the years in a home shopping network in China, casinos in Italy and Greece, and real estate in the United States. The Miller family also created two charitable foundations, concentrating on scholarships for the needy, health and welfare for underprivileged children, environmental conservation, youth, arts programs, and the Asia Society, said Miller. But he keeps his affairs very private. There is no public record of the extent of his giving. He made it clear that most of his fortune will be passed on to his family.

"Maybe too much wealth can be a burden, but not if you know how to deal with it—and I think I am quite comfortable with it," he said. "In one way you want to do good works with your money. By the same token you have to plan for a succession and transfer the responsibility to the next generation. And obviously you have to train your children on how to govern wealth management and to do something productive with it. This is one of the most important things that you can do in your lifetime, passing it on constructively and productively. You have to leave instructions to your children and grandchildren and establish standards for them which they live up to and make their life productive so that they can enjoy themselves and enjoy the wealth."

One could of course give it all away like Chuck Feeney, said Miller, but he planned to give more responsibility to his three children and ten grandchildren to let them get more involved in charitable work. "Making money is difficult enough, but keeping it after you have made it can be even more difficult. I think making it and trying to give it away at the same time is almost impossible. You either have to do one thing or the other. Obviously if you are giving away huge sums of money, you have to do a great deal of due diligence to make sure that the money is being used properly and that takes a lot of time and you need people to help you. You want to make sure that it's put to good use, and that somebody is not fucking you."

Miller believes that Feeney had a "guilt complex" about making so much money. He said he told him once that he would have been a good Catholic priest because making money seemed to bother him so much.

Of the four DFS owners, Alan Parker currently has the most wealth and maintains the lowest profile. Tall and courtly, the former accountant is one of the richest people in the world, but he has not been written up in glossy magazines or celebrity columns and his lifestyle is notably lacking in ostentation. Little has appeared about him in print anywhere. He was described by the London *Times* as an "ultra-secretive" multimillionaire, worth some $2 billion in 2006. The wealth held in his family trusts and philanthropic foundation is in fact almost certainly more than three times that. Parker built up his fortune by carefully compounding his money, including the $840 million for his 20 percent of DFS, and he has made a lot more in the investment world than from DFS.

The Parkers live in a historic mansion overlooking Lake Geneva in Switzerland. Here he proudly produced from a box some of the hundreds of "thank-you" letters he received for the gifts he and Chuck Feeney sent to DFS employees after they sold their shares.

When he embarked on his career as an accountant, Alan Parker never expected to make a million dollars, much less a billion. He was born a British national in Zimbabwe, then known as Rhodesia, the son of a colonial civil servant of modest means. He was always tight with money, he conceded. He pointed out that like Feeney, he flew economy class for his first ten years with DFS, even when he had become a multimillionaire. He didn't fly first class until 1976, and then only because the lawyer accompanying him from London to the Bahamas on a legal matter said, "If you want to talk to me you will have to travel first class: We lawyers only travel first class."

Chuck Feeney impressed upon him by his example that philanthropy was something to take account of in one's life, and his views on giving evolved as he saw how big a role philanthropy played in the culture of the United States. He and his wife, Jette, created one of Europe's big charitable foundations, the Oak Foundation, with headquarters on the sixth floor of a nondescript office building on Geneva's Rue de Leon and offices in London, Boston, and Harare, Zimbabwe. Jette Parker chairs the five-member trust that governs the foundation, Alan Parker is vice chairman, and the other three trust members are their children: Caroline, Natalie, and Kristian. Parker admitted that he sometimes felt weighed down by the responsibilities of great wealth, and his obligation to the charitable foundation can take precedence at times over a round of golf. Being a billionaire has its limitations, too—he waited more than ten years to get membership in a golf club near his home.

The Oak Foundation focuses on the environment, homelessness, human rights, women's issues, learning disabilities, and philanthropy in Denmark and Zimbabwe. Jette Parker, who is from Denmark, has directed funds to the International Rehabilitation Council for Torture Victims, based in Copenhagen. After would-be philanthropist Alberto Vilar was arrested in New York in 2005 on fraud charges, Jette Parker took over his sponsorship of the Royal Opera House's young artists' program in London.

While his family name is not associated with the 200 or so grants a year varying from $25,000 to $10 million paid by the Oak Foundation, Parker doesn't work anonymously, nor does the Oak Foundation impose strict confidentiality. In May 2006, he and Jette accepted honorary Doctor of Law degrees from Colby College Maine, where in 1998 they established the Oak Institute for the Study of International Human Rights and endowed the Oak Chair in Biological Sciences. Here the Parkers also founded the Parker Institute and Muscle Laboratory.

Unlike Feeney's Atlantic Philanthropies, Parker's philanthropic foundation is structured to continue indefinitely as a family concern. Joel Fleishman, whom Parker has consulted, said it was considered to be one of the most successful family-run charitable foundations. For his part, Alan Parker said he believed that Chuck Feeney was mistaken in excluding his children from running his foundation.

Just as in the duty-free business, where Parker held the middle ground between Feeney and Miller, his views on inheritance fall somewhere between those of his erstwhile partners.

"There has to be a balance, because I don't think you can ever get yourself into a situation where your children resent the fact that all your money, or a large percentage of your money, has gone to charity," he said. A large proportion of his family wealth "is irrevocably in a charitable foundation and the rest is in a trust which is both charitable and family." His children, he said, would still be wealthy by any standard. At the same time, he believes that too much money "ruins more children than it saves."

"I guess I start from the basis that nobody really needs more than $10 million," he said as he sifted through letters and photographs from DFS days, adding with a wry smile, "I say that in a house that cost more than $10 million." He also thinks Feeney's policy of almost total secrecy was unnecessary. When the story first came out that Parker himself was very rich, he received only fourteen phone calls, mostly from cranks.

Tony Pilaro, who got $110 million for his 2.5 percent of DFS, today lives much of the time in his spacious wooden chalet on the slopes above Gstaad in the Swiss Alps. He also has homes in New York and Southampton on Long Island, and his investment company, CAP Advisers, is based in Dublin, Ireland. Like Miller, Pilaro has given up his U.S. citizenship. He got Irish—and thereby European Union—citizenship in 1993 under an Irish government "investment for passport" scheme. He walked into the U.S. embassy in Dublin the next day and turned in his American passport to a disapproving official. The dark wood of the chalet walls in Gstaad are hung with his extensive collection of contemporary art, chronicled in a hefty private volume called *CAP Collection*. Pilaro created the CAP Charitable Foundation, dedicated to "education, the arts and the environment," and conceived and established the Ron Brown Scholar Program in 1996 for the "next generation of African American leaders." It is named after the former U.S. secretary of commerce, Ron Brown, who died in a plane crash in the Balkans.

Although he had the smallest shareholding, Tony Pilaro played an important role in making the DFS owners rich. As the tax expert in the company, he ensured that none of the multi-million-dollar cash dividends were taxed before distribution to the shareholders. Feeney always said Pilaro was the smartest of the four. His own attitude to wealth, Pilaro explained, was that if a person could earn income free of tax, that person could invest it at a higher rate than the government, and then if the object of his largesse were his family and his charities, there would be more to distribute to the family and the charities.

"Chuck's attitude to tax is not dissimilar to my attitude to tax," he said in a living room of his chalet, where the framed photographs on the shelves included snapshots of himself with Paul Newman, the film actor and patron of the Hole in the Wall Gang camps, the residential summer camps for seriously ill children, with which Pilaro is also associated. "I think there are two approaches. An entity can pay tax to the government and then the government can spend the money. I think Chuck's view and mine was that the U.S. government is probably the most inefficient expenditure of these monies. So therefore if you could give it to yourself and spend it the way you want on your own charitable endeavors, and invest it at a higher rate of return than the government would get, you could do more for the world." It was a point Chuck Rolles also made about Feeney. "Chuck hates taxes," he said. "He believes people can do more with money than governments."

In the early 1960s, Pilaro joined Butler's Bank in Nassau for a time and this brought him into contact with Robert Vesco, one of the most notorious corporate villains in history. Allan Butler provided Vesco with the $5-million loan in 1970 that enabled him to take over Bernie Cornfeld's Investors Overseas Services in Geneva. Pilaro became a tax consultant to Vesco after his buyout of the mutual fund, from which the crooked financier extracted $242 million. While this is often mentioned in media references to Pilaro, he pointed out that he was also a tax consultant to the Dalai Lama and other highly reputable figures. In 1996, Pilaro bought a majority shareholding in an American company called BriteSmile, which has a chain of clinics promoting BriteSmile as a professional teeth-whitening solution.

Was he now or was he ever a billionaire? He didn't answer, but the next morning he said, "I reflected last night on the 'B' word. God knows how much I have made in life, but I have had a wonderful lifestyle, fantastic. If I wake up and want to do something that day, I do it. The freedom, the power to do, is enormous. I lead a good life." He cheerfully acknowledged that a disproportionate amount of his income generated by his assets goes to "living" and "giving," so he never did become a billionaire.

Pilaro expressed regret at the idea that there was any "direct causal connection" between the lawsuit that he and Miller brought to stop the DFS sale and the unveiling of Feeney's secret philanthropy. "I was shocked when our relationship became fragile because this was attributed to me," he said. Feeney's giving wasn't exposed by the legal action, he said, but through the letter Harvey Dale sent to dozens of people in January 1997 revealing everything about Chuck's philanthropy. "Why the hell did Harvey tell the story?" he asked with some agitation.

In 2003, a mutual friend of Feeney and Pilaro, Irish film producer Noel Pearson, invited both to lunch, but Feeney declined. Pilaro remembers being told that Chuck said, "I'd love to have lunch with Tony but tell him to say sorry, and he knows what he has to say sorry for." Pilaro wrote to Feeney, saying, "'If that's the case, Chuck, then I apologize profusely.'" Feeney said, with a cackle, "I'm Irish, I hold a grudge to the end." But he didn't. Late in 2005, Feeney and Pilaro met for lunch at a Dublin restaurant, Les Frères Jacques, and they agreed to let bygones be bygones.

No Pockets in
a Shroud

Anonymous giving, the hallmark of Feeney's philanthropy, was finally abandoned by Atlantic Philanthropies as the new century began. It was Feeney's wish from the beginning not to "blow his horn," but many of his other reasons for secrecy, to do with business and his children, had passed with time. Moreover, friends and beneficiaries found it a bit ridiculous adhering to a code of *omerta* when everyone *knew*. "The idea of anonymous giving was good, but eventually we became synonymous with anonymous," said Feeney. "It became evident that we were kidding ourselves." He also could not promote his example of giving while living, if nobody knew about it.

As the anonymity policy unraveled, Harvey Dale and foundation director Fritz Schwarz drew up a list of the pros and cons of continued secrecy and in June 2001 recommended that Atlantic Philanthropies drop its policy of enforcing absolute confidentiality. All grantees that year were told they were no longer bound by secrecy. Those who got gifts earlier than 2001 were informed they were free to identify Atlantic Philanthropies as the source of the grant, but "as we imposed these conditions on you we are not ourselves going to identify you as our grantee."

In September 2002, under John Healy, who took over as CEO when Harvey Dale retired in September 2001, Atlantic Philanthropies went further and launched a Web site for the first time. "Understanding that a policy of public access to our grant-making work would extend significant benefits to our grantees, we are no longer pursuing a policy of anonymity," it announced. "However, we remain committed to keeping a low profile and not seeking publicity for our organization." It announced that up to that point, the fund had secretly awarded approximately 2,900 grants totaling $2.5 billion. In future it would list every grant it made. From being the most secretive of philanthropies, it was now one of the most transparent, though not subject to U.S. disclosure laws, so that its salary structure stayed confidential.

One of the reasons for dropping anonymity related to the future of the foundation. Greater transparency would be needed for Atlantic to promote collaboration if it decided to wind down and go out of business. Feeney had deliberated on this question of "to be or not to be" with Hamlet-like uncertainty for years. His consigliere had favored a perpetual foundation. In a key report to the board in 1993, Harvey Dale had stated: "I think we should aim at creating our own institution as a perpetual source of funds for charitable purposes, rather than choosing to spend it out of existence." Spending down, he warned, would require turning over considerable resources to donees who might not do as good a job as those running a permanent foundation.

He and Feeney talked it over dozens of times over the years, at directors' meetings, on plane trips to Bermuda, and over lunch at P. J. Clarke's in Manhattan. "Having a conversation with Chuck is sort of like 'Brownian movement,' like some kind of random stream of consciousness," said Dale, referring to the phenomenon that minute particles, immersed in a fluid, move about randomly. "It doesn't go in a linear fashion. A sample conversation would include: 'What we did in the Vietnam War was really terrible, we've got to help those people in Vietnam, and you know the Ford Foundation has an office there but they are old and crusty, and that's the problem with foundations getting old and crusty, we shouldn't let that happen.'"

Feeney was not persuaded by the case for a perpetual foundation. Carnegie had written in *Wealth* that the millionaire was but a trustee for the poor and that the man who died leaving behind millions would pass away "unwept, unhonored and unsung," no matter what he said should be done with "the dross which he cannot take with him." Feeney made clear that he was leaning toward giving *everything* away and shutting down the foundation when he was forced to go public at the time of the DFS sale in January 1997. He wrote on the margins of a draft of the press release at that time, "I believe that people of substantial wealth potentially create problems for future generations unless they themselves accept responsibility to use their wealth during their lifetime to help worthwhile causes."

There were compelling arguments for doing so. Organizations grew more sclerotic as they got older. Perpetual foundations could never be as flexible, fluid, opportunistic, or entrepreneurial as Atlantic had been under his guidance. If Atlantic opted for perpetuity, it would have to spend less, and there would come a time when Feeney would not be around, and the foundation would be doing things he might or might not like. Harvey Dale conceded, "Henry Ford might or might not like what the Ford Foundation is doing, wherever he happens to be, but he is not in charge."

As the debate evolved in the months after the DFS sale, Dale advised the directors in a confidential memo what Feeney's final decision might be. "We are not confined by any requirement that Atlantic Foundation and Atlantic Trust continue in perpetuity," he wrote. Giving could therefore be conducted at a rate higher than the 5-percent benchmark required to maintain the endowment of a foundation while guarding against inflation.

Atlantic chairman Frank Rhodes was wholly in favor of giving everything in a fixed time span, on the basis that "deferred giving is really denied giving for those who go out of reach in the meantime." The danger with any long-life foundations, he felt, was that staff and directors might come to feel they *owned* the money. At a board meeting in Bermuda in 1998, he had broached the issue with Feeney. "What will the legacy of Atlantic Philanthropies be?" he asked him. "I'll think about that," said Feeney.

Feeney sketched out his response on October 13, 1999, at a board meeting held in a wood-paneled library room of the Cornell Club in New York. He handed directors a 200-word memorandum on the subject of legacy that he had written in pencil and had asked Dale's secretary to type up the day before.

He posed two questions. What should be the expected life span of Atlantic Philanthropies? And could grant making be expanded to reach the desired spending level? He pointed out that most foundations were making gifts of a fraction of their assets, and this might be the reason for the slow pace in the fight against cancer, diabetes, Alzheimer's, and other major diseases. Should they increase their level of funding to help achieve the desired goal of spending down, or would this be wasteful? He pointed out that annual giving had already increased to $400 million that year alone, which put them on the spend-down track. He proposed that this be increased to $450 million a year. This would be well over 10 percent of assets a year, double the yardstick for perpetual foundations. He concluded with a recommendation that they consider a life span for Atlantic Philanthropies of twenty to thirty years.

The board agreed "in broad principle." "My sense is that the board would do whatever Chuck Feeney wanted it to do," said Joel Fleishman, but most were genuinely in favor.

It was an historic document, one of Feeney's first attempts to write down on a piece of paper some of his thoughts, said Harvey Dale. "It was more catalytic than seminal. It catalyzed the conversation in the right direction."

When John Healy took over as chief executive officer of Atlantic Philanthropies in 2001, he found that there was a "common understanding," though no formal resolution, that the foundation would spend down in approximately fifteen years. Healy convened a strategic workshop to focus the minds of the directors—including Chuck Feeney—on the implications. Spending down a huge philanthropy required careful long-term planning, especially for one as unique as Atlantic, which owned illiquid assets in the form of property and businesses. He brought in foundation adviser Tom Tierney to conduct a workshop on Tuesday, January 29, 2002, in Atlantic Philanthropies' twenty-first-floor offices on Park Avenue. Chuck was there along with all the board members, with the exception of Harvey Dale. Healy felt that directors would speak more freely in the absence of the formidable former president, and Feeney had agreed.

Healy made the point that the staff—now numbering about 100—could do the numbers and figure out for themselves that the foundation could not sustain itself at the rate it was going. It was damaging morale. The directors should be straight and tell them what the future held. If they were indeed spending down in fifteen years, given expected returns on capital and investments, Atlantic would have to donate between $7.2 billion and $7.5 billion—the endowment plus interest—in that time frame, and this would require careful budgeting and planning.

The endowment of Atlantic Philanthropies was meanwhile soaring, in line with the Wall Street bull market in technology stocks. When Healy took over, Atlantic Philanthropies had assets worth $3.5 billion. In 1999, unrealized gains from investments had soared to $1.675 billion on a base of $400 million. This was more than Chuck Feeney's proceeds from the sale of the ownership in DFS two years before. In April the following year, the value of its $14.4 million investment in E*Trade rose to $500 million. General Atlantic Partners had gotten into information technology stocks early, and these showed a rate of return of 51 percent, three times higher than the 17-percent average return over twenty years for venture capital firms, according to *Venture Economics*. Out of eighty investments, General Atlantic Partners had only three losses. From 1980 to 2000, the investments showed a 29-percent rate of annual return before investment fees and commission, a staggering success rate.

Feeney and his investors had the Midas touch—everything they touched seemed to turn to gold. Which posed similar problems encountered by the Greek king Midas: What does one do with so much gold? The directors came to a firm conclusion—though again with no formal resolution—to go out of business at the earliest by 2016. "But I have to tell you, the last person to sign up to the decision, the last person, was Chuck Feeney," said John Healy. "Why? Not because he didn't agree with the decision. But because he never wants to be in a corner from which he cannot escape. He is the quintessential entrepreneur. Entrepreneurs often value above all flexibility." Once the decision was made, however, Chuck became "enormously enthusiastic" about it.

"Money is more worthwhile to the people in need when things are tough rather than when things are good," Feeney explained in the New York foundation office one day, wearing a cardigan with a hole in the sleeve. "If I have $10 in my pocket, and I do something with it today, it's already producing ten dollars' worth of good. The dollar you give today can be doing good tomorrow, giving 5 percent of it doesn't do so much good." He identified, he said, with the old Gaelic saying, "There are no pockets in a shroud."

At their workshop the directors reviewed what the foundation had achieved. They were unanimous that the Irish university grants and research funding were Feeney's most successful initiatives: They reshaped the institutions, created the potential to reshape the country, were successful in leveraging further funds, and overall had a transforming effect. It was, said one, a "home run." But some uncomfortable questions were aired. Chuck's support for higher education could be seen in a negative light—as elitist giving, especially in the United States. In the United States and Ireland, Atlantic had supported the haves over the have-nots, by 70 to 30 percent. On the other hand, in Vietnam, it was entirely a case of helping the have-nots.

Having agreed to a specific "sell by" date for the foundation, a number of questions arose. Where should they focus in the future for a disciplined spend-down? Where could they have the most impact? The discussion ranged over issues from aging and disadvantaged children to human rights and legalizing drugs. Feeney said little. But on each of the three occasions where he did have something to say, he mentioned biomedical research. At the end of the workshop, the eight directors at the meeting held a ballot on the issues they believed Atlantic should focus on while spending down.

On March 22, 2003, Atlantic Philanthropies shifted direction to accommodate the new reality. Chuck Feeney and John Healy jointly presented to the board a "Legacy and Purpose" paper. The outcome of the strategic review was the closure of sixteen areas in which Atlantic had been active. There would no longer be unlimited funds for higher education, the nonprofit sector, or philanthropy groups. In the future they would focus on four strategic areas: aging, disadvantaged children and youth, population health, and reconciliation and human rights.

"What makes a foundation successful," Healy believed, "is focus, and heavy and sustained investment in those things that you have chosen to focus on." The "Legacy and Purpose" paper confirmed for staff that they were going out of business so they could prepare their CVs in good time. "The spend-down train has left the station," said Healy.

The document reflected the liberalism of Atlantic Foundation's founder. It warned that in the political environment of the United States—this was the month that the U.S.-led forces invaded Iraq—there was hostility to the notion of foundations' pursuing progressive agendas, and it was only a matter of time before they attracted "unwelcome attention."

As time went by, Feeney had become more drawn to support progressive organizations that strengthened civil society. The "Legacy and Purpose" paper declared that Atlantic Philanthropies should aim "to initiate social change, not just make grants." Feeney had made private donations to the Democratic Party in the 1990s but did not allocate large sums to party political campaigns, as did some billionaires like George Soros. Atlantic gave money to organizations such as Amnesty International, Human Rights First and Human Rights Watch, and its contribution of $1 million was key to winning a campaign to persuade the U.S. Supreme Court in March 2005 that the death penalty for those who committed crimes when under the age of eighteen was cruel and unusual punishment and hence barred by the

Constitution. In the same year, Atlantic gave $3 million to *The NewsHour with Jim Lehrer* to support nonprofit public broadcasting.

A political junkie who reads the *Financial Times*, the *Guardian*, the London *Times*, the *International Herald Tribune, The Economist*, and *Newsweek* everywhere he travels, Feeney strongly opposed the war in Iraq and the reelection of U.S. president George Bush in 2004. The year before, on the eve of the U.S.-led invasion of Iraq, he joined a massive protest in London organized by the Stop the War Coalition, walking unnoticed among the throngs of demonstrators from Mayfair to Hyde Park.

Winding down a foundation is rare, but there were earlier examples from which Atlantic drew lessons. Julius Rosenwald, architect of the Sears, Roebuck empire, spent $63 million of his fortune—$700 million in today's dollars—before his death in 1932, mainly in setting up 5,400 schools for African Americans in Southern states; in accordance with his wishes, his trustees spent down the rest of his endowment by 1948. Rosenwald warned that "our immediate needs are too plain and too urgent to allow us to do the work of future generations." It was the first major U.S. fund to deliberately spend itself out of existence. The $300-million foundation set up by real estate developer Aaron Diamond was wound down by his wife, Irene, from 1987 to 1996, after establishing the largest private AIDS research facility in the United States. Its former executive director, Vincent McGee, said the idea was to find things that could make a major impact and stick with them, rather than waste the money in a big bureaucracy. The danger, he said, was that "all foundations tended to become arrogant and intellectually corrupt." Among other foundations, the Richard and Rhonda Goldman Fund, with over $400 million in assets, has raised grant levels to 10 percent so that it can go out of business within a decade of the death of Mr. Goldman, whose wife died in 1996. Richard Goldman told NBC television that foundations should stop acting like dinosaurs worried about their own extinction, and focus on the good they can do today.

"I'm pretty sure we will close the doors," said Healy, who retired in April 2007 after six years as chief executive. "It is increasingly unlikely that Chuck will change his mind. I don't see the present board not being faithful to his wishes, and by and large they are all enthusiastic about spending down."

Feeney himself felt a growing sense of urgency and moments of doubt. "I don't know if I will be alive in ten or twelve years," he said. "I don't think it's possible for us to spend down, because when you think about it, you can't give big chunks of money unless you do bricks-and-mortar. We are wandering around the world trying to find opportunities—the problem is we identify opportunities, and they are good but they are too small. And each time I see a project delayed it frustrates me."

"What worries him now is that we are not giving it away quickly enough," said Frank Rhodes. He doubted that Feeney or the board would "bet the whole store" on any one project. There was scope, however, for major initiatives. Said Feeney, "There is nothing wrong with a big bet, if a big bet is a good bet."

The new strategy did not exclude Feeney from finding more of his own projects. But the spend-down decision required budgets fixed in advance, rather than just adding up all the gifts pledged at the end of the year. Healy felt his task was balancing Feeney's enthusiasm for new projects with the orderly winding down of the foundation. He added a fifth program, the Founding Chairman's Program, in the form of a "pot of money" available to Feeney to pursue entrepreneurial philanthropy outside the four programs. In 2004, the amount set aside for the founding chairman's pot was some $35 million. If he needed more, there would be more, within reason. In fact, in 2004 Feeney personally recommended, and the board approved, five grants totaling $41 million.

The directors never lost sight of the fact that it was "Feeney's money," even though he had given it irrevocably to the foundation. At a board meeting in Bermuda early in 2005, Harvey Dale, who remained as a director, said, "As far as I'm concerned, and I'm sure I'm speaking for the board, if Chuck wants to spend more or commit more than $35 million, we should be accepting of that and consider the proposal." There was a response of "Hear! Hear!"

The problem confronting them, Dale reflected, however, was not just finding enough good opportunities to give away money, but managing a predictable portfolio. "If the return on the portfolio is really stunning, much more than 10 percent, you come to the end, and all of a sudden you have got $10 billion and you have got to give it all away that year, which is absurd, or the portfolio underperforms, you hit a bad patch, and you run out of money before you hit the date. In the meantime, the program staff don't know what their budget is because it fluctuates too much."

Paradoxically, during this period of internal debate on spending down, the endowment kept rising at a faster rate than spending. By early 2007, when Atlantic Philanthropies appointed a new chief executive, fifty-two-year-old Gara LaMarche, the endowment stood at $4 billion—despite the fact that total giving had risen since 2002 from $2.5 billion to $4 billion. LaMarche, a human rights advocate and director of U.S. Programs of the Open Society Institute, was given precisely nine years to complete Atlantic Philanthropies' active grant making by 2016. His task was complicated by the fact that half a billion dollars was still tied up in hotels, resorts, health clubs, and retailers across the world.

Like a big ship, the philanthropy slowed as it changed direction. Giving declined from a high point of $595 million in 2000 to $289 million in 2005. Feeney's entrepreneurial instincts were frustrated. He reckoned that annual giving would have to be ramped up to something around $350 million a year if his goal of giving while living was to be fulfilled in the allotted span. By the end of 2006, things began to fall into place and grant commitments that year exceeded $450 million.

In order to facilitate an orderly spend-down and to avoid its investments hitting "some extraordinary pay dirt and generating a huger amount of cash," as Healy put it, about half of Atlantic Philanthropies' liquid assets were moved in 2005 into absolute return strategies, a diversified portfolio with a low correlation to the public markets and the ability to perform well in any economic environment. It was a pioneering move for a major philanthropy.

The disposal of the "state" side of the assets of Atlantic Philanthropies, held by General Atlantic Group Ltd., and its subsidiary, InterPacific, had gotten under way in the mid-1990s. This was sometimes a painful process for Feeney. The constituent parts were never impersonal assets. They were "people" businesses in which he was personally involved, to which he had given some of himself. He ran them like a welfare state, said a colleague. The hardest wrench was selling off Castletroy Park Hotel in Limerick, Ireland. Feeney had personally overseen its design and construction and nursed it through its teething stages. He used it as a gathering place for family and friends and here, more than anywhere, he let his hair down and had fun in his later years. Once, he brought about 100 GAGL staff and families for a weekend, and when the band struck up, Feeney and fellow executives appeared in boxer shorts and did a dance routine. In 1998, he organized a trip by 154 former students from St. Mary's High School in Elizabeth, New Jersey, to the hotel for a fiftieth reunion of the Classes of '46, '47, and '48.

Many of the alumni, living all across the United States, had to get passports for the first time. Each paid $1,000 inclusive for the flight from JFK airport in New York to Shannon in Ireland and a week in Castletroy. Feeney provided everything else, including three buses to collect them from the airport. They were led into the foyer by a piper in traditional Irish costume. They were overwhelmingly of Irish descent, and many were in tears. "It was the best week of our lives," said his childhood pal Bob Cogan, a retired federal government representative. "Charlie never left his roots. These were his real, true friends." Feeney organized the reunion trip again in June 2003, though with fewer people, as time had taken its toll. On July 16, 2004, the last weekend before the hotel went on the market, he brought staff from Atlantic Philanthropies and General Atlantic and family members from around the world to commemorate the break with the hotel he built and loved. Typical of this most frugal of philanthropists, he laid on champagne for his guests, who included many of the friends he had acquired in Limerick such as Ed Walsh, Brendan O'Regan, and the Benedictine monk Mark Patrick Hederman.

By August 2004, Feeney had divested himself of his interests in Ireland, including Heritage House in Dublin, the Kilternan Hotel south of the city, the Trade Management Institute building in Blackrock, and Castletroy Park Hotel. All the properties made sizable profits: the Celtic Tiger economy, which Feeney had helped fuel, had sent property prices soaring. Winding down InterPacific was more complex. By the end of the 1990s, it was employing more than 2,000 people, generating annual sales in excess of $350 million, and holding investments valued at $650 million. The stores in the Hawaiian Retail Group that had caused the bitter split between Feeney and his DFS partners were closed or sold off by January 2003. Feeney came to Honolulu and took a function room at the Sheraton to throw a party for the staff. By early 2007, the Pacific Island Club Hotel in Saipan was still on the books, as was Couran Cove Island Resort and the Runaway Bay Sports Super Centre in Australia, and Western Athletic Clubs in the United States. "There will be no distress selling," said Feeney, dismissing prospects of a fire sale. "We will sell when the market is rising." InterPacific also continued to hold a half share in the Laguna Beach Resort in Phuket, where he and Helga would sometimes take short breaks from their travel. They were there when the tsunami hit on December 26, 2004. "Helga and I were having a his-and-hers massage," he said. "We heard screams and saw fear in the eyes of the staff, who shouted, 'Get out!'" The hotel escaped with minor damage. Feeney ensured that there were no layoffs, despite the fall in tourism.

In January 2005, Feeney stepped down as chairman of GAGL and handed over to Mike Windsor, with Jim Downey as deputy chairman and Chris Oechsli, Harvey Dale, and Cummings Zuill making up the board. By then the businesses had dwindled to just over 10 percent of Atlantic Philanthropies' total assets, a reversal of the situation two decades earlier when the ratio of "church" to "state" was one to ten.

"Chuck walked out of the meeting in San Francisco with his plastic carrier bag and said, 'Well, I'm off!'" said Windsor, describing Feeney's last day as chairman. "But all this is Chuck's, and I never lose sight of that. Anything we do strategically, he will still make the final call."

PART FIVE
LATE LIFE
CRISIS

CHAPTER 34

American Original

If home is where one pays one's personal taxes, then it could be said that Chuck Feeney's residence is in the United States. The truth is, however, he doesn't really live anywhere. He and Helga have never had a permanent home—just the small apartments in different cities where they stay for weeks at a time, with piles of books and newspapers but none of the trophies on the sideboard to commemorate the life of a successful man. He never aspired to live in a mansion. "I wouldn't be comfortable in an 8,000-square-foot home," he once said. "You couldn't find anybody in it."

Even in his old age, it is hard to establish where Chuck Feeney is going to be at any given time. He is constantly on the move. He told me one day in 2006 in his apartment in San Francisco, with its framed family pictures, including a photograph of Helga with Fidel Castro, "I just did a count: This is the first time in our lifetime we are spending three months anywhere." But he and Helga were soon off again on another odyssey, to New York, Dublin, London, Brisbane, Bangkok, Ho Chi Minh City, Paris, and back to San Francisco. He and Helga practically live at 30,000 feet. And right up to his midseventies the couple traveled economy class, often sitting at the back of the plane for journeys of more than ten hours. He always claimed it was a money-saving measure. "It would be different if it got me there quicker," he would quip. "A lot of bad-mouths say about me that I want to stretch out on two economy seats." Perhaps subconsciously he felt that by traveling business class he would be turning his back on the blue-collar culture from which he came. Perhaps he preferred to be in the company of the people who flew economy. Perhaps he felt he was not *entitled.* It certainly allowed him to travel unnoticed. Whatever the reason or reasons, it was one of the rules by which he led his life, and no amount of pleading from friends and relatives ever made a difference until he conceded, well into his eighties, that it was bad for his health. On an eleven-hour flight from Paris to Cuba in 2004, when his daughter Juliette and her husband, Jean Timsit, were bumped up to business class, she beseeched her father, who was with Helga in economy, "with the usual three plastic bags full of books and papers," to please change places. He responded, "No, no, no. It's the luck of the draw." He never demanded the same sacrifice from his associates, some of whom had the uncomfortable experience of being escorted to first class past Feeney standing in line for economy with his little wheeled Samsonite case and plastic bag of papers. Colin McCrea and Tom Mitchell were once flying business class to an Atlantic Philanthropies board meeting in Bermuda when they found Chuck among the milling crowds in the Paris airport terminal and persuaded him to at least join them in the business lounge. The receptionist didn't want to let him in. Finally she said, "He can go in provided he doesn't eat anything." By then Feeney was inside, sipping a complimentary glass of Chardonnay.

"Since my earliest days I have been frugal, but I am a frugal person in that I hate waste, at any level," explained Feeney, who always wears off-the-peg clothes, a cheap plastic watch, and reading glasses of the type sold in bookstores. "If I can get a watch for $15 that keeps perfect time, what am I doing messing around with a Rolex?" Helga shares his frugal nature, though she dresses with style, and the couple enjoy getting bargains when shopping. On the ground, Feeney always takes buses and taxis rather than limousines. "I cannot rationalize someone driving me around in a six-door Cadillac," he said. "The seats are the same in a cab. And you may live longer if you walk." When visiting the family in New Jersey over the years, Feeney would routinely take the train from New York. His nephew once told Jim Dwyer how he would pick him up at Elizabeth station, "and there's Uncle Chuck, waiting on a train platform near the junkies and the hookers." His brother-in-law Jim Fitzpatrick pleaded, to no avail, "Chuck, you've got to be careful. It's dangerous to be going back to New York at night in a bus."

Feeney avoids black-tie functions at which donors are the recipients of mellifluous expressions of gratitude. "I'm just not the kind of guy who gets any kick out of attending these mutual admiration society dinners." He has no tuxedo in his wardrobe. In fact, he has no wardrobe. He once turned up for a formal dinner in Dublin wearing a sweater and was only persuaded to borrow a bow tie and jacket from a waiter when told he would otherwise draw attention to himself.

He dislikes asking the staff in Atlantic offices to do anything personal for him. "I've worked for people who would have me go to pick up their dry-cleaning, their lunch, things like that," said Gail Vincenzi Bianchi at the San Francisco office of InterPacific. "He would never. He once mentioned to me that he had some dry-cleaning to pick up downtown, and it was a Friday afternoon, and I said, 'Chuck, give me the receipt and I will drive downtown and pick up the dry-cleaning.' And he said, 'No, no, I would appreciate if you would give me a ride down there, and I'll go pick it up.'" He does not think it beneath him to pick up rubbish in the street and put it in a trash can. "If everybody picked up trash, there would be no trash on the streets," he explained.

While frugal to the point of eccentricity, Feeney likes to give people thoughtful presents, often pictures he commissions from his friend Desmond Kinney, an Irish artist. Kinney and his partner, Esmeralda, have occasionally joined Feeney and Helga on their travels. In restaurants, Feeney would always insist on paying. And far from being reclusive, he has friends and acquaintances all over the world whom he and Helga meet for lunches and dinners, always with white wine, characterized by his wisecracks and his cackling laugh. He often gathers eclectic groups together, people from diverse backgrounds whose only common thread is that he has met them and befriended them. "Thus, artists, politicians, entrepreneurs, corporate executives, university presidents, writers, lawyers, and sometimes his own family members mixed freely," said his friend Niall O'Dowd. The publisher recalled that when spending weekends at the Feeney house in Connecticut in the 1980s, he would come into contact with other visitors without knowing what role they played in Feeney's life. "There were all these different layers being peeled away every time you heard something new about him." O'Dowd learned how parsimonious Feeney could be when his host one day took him for a long walk to the post office in Salisbury, where Feeney rummaged through a used magazine collection in a box in the corner. "Next thing, this multimillionaire comes up with 'Great!'—an old issue of *Time* or something." "If you see a magazine with pages torn out," Feeney would joke, "that means I've been reading it." His habit has served a purpose: The pages provide a means of communication. He often hands a friend or associate a cutting that has caught his attention, to show what is on his mind.

His life is full of paradoxes. He bought some of the finest mansions for his family but wouldn't live in them or do them up; in later life he owns neither a house nor even an apartment. At one time, he was the biggest retailer of cigarettes in the world, yet he has always abhorred smoking. He sold luxury goods, but would not be seen dead with a Louis Vuitton briefcase. He made his fortune pushing high-end consumer goods, yet dislikes Christmas because of its consumerism. The greatest paradox of his life arose from his relationship with money. He has loved making money, but not having it. In the early days, he never talked with Danielle about getting rich. His goal, she recalled, was to make a success of his business ventures, and he told her more than once, "My work comes first; my family is second." Wealth was a measure of success to Feeney, who explained, "I like the thrill of the chase." In later years he would measure success by the speed and efficiency with which he could give that wealth away to empower others.

Those who get close to Chuck Feeney believe him to be a person apart, a true American original. The common perception is that he has no ego whatsoever. Frank Rhodes maintained that Feeney "is saintly in the best sense, not in the literal sense," and that university presidents around the world should get down on their knees every day "and thank God for Chuck Feeney." Michael Sovern compared him to St. Francis, who gave everything to the poor (and was also a linguist and wine drinker). Sue Wesselkamper believed Feeney was really "profoundly religious." In the opinion of Michael Mann, "he made the lives of millions of people in this world so much better for him being on this earth, that if anyone can say on their death bed they have done 1 percent of what Chuck Feeney has done, they would be a very special person." His Cornell friend Ernie Stern said of his frugality, "I think he's nuts, crazy, but it's in keeping with his philosophy; I love Chuck, I believe he is a Good Man."

Feeney has never seen himself as a religious person, nor has he ever been a churchgoer. What drives him, he always said, is simply a sense that his wealth is surplus to his needs. "I had one idea that never changed in my mind—that you should use your wealth to help people. I try to live a normal life, the way I grew up. I think there's something in the makeup of people from the way they are brought up. I set out to work hard, not to get rich. My parents worked hard and they didn't get rich, but there was always the effort to find out who needed some help." Had some of that rubbed off on him? "For sure." Bonnie Suchet, who worked for Feeney for some twenty years, used similar words to explain his giving. "It came from his parents, I think. They helped shape his psychology. He gave it all away because of the way he was brought up."

Feeney's five grown children made clear in conversation that they believe their father's act of giving is something to acknowledge and celebrate. They resent it when people ask them if there is something wrong with their dad that he gives away all his money instead of leaving it to them. They do not feel disinherited. "We don't see it that way," said Diane. "We never have wanted to live an extravagant lifestyle. None of us are like that." They will not inherit billions, but their father set up modest trusts for them, "with enough money for what they should, and will, need in life," and their mother is endowed with a considerable portion of the family fortune. When people tell them they are lucky to have a lifestyle that involves nice homes and international travel, they reply that, yes, they are lucky, but they are truly lucky in their parents. "We have huge respect for our parents," said Caroleen Feeney. "I always liked my parents. I took it for granted. It was a shock when I got to school in New York, and other kids didn't like their parents. I loved my parents."

Juliette recalled that their father "was desperately scared that his children would be surrounded and wooed by fortune hunters," but they always had friends who were not interested in money. They lacked the sense of entitlement common to rich kids. "In my opinion," said Diane, "he felt guilty about making so much money and having so much ease in his life. Somehow he needed to redeem himself. It ascended to us, too. I think the responsibility of having so much weighed on him—that and trying to change the world." Caroleen felt her father has been motivated to respond to the unhappiness and problems in the world because he is more conscious of suffering. Everyone has circles of intimacy, she explained: The first circle exists around oneself; the second encompasses intimate relationships; the third, friends and confidants; the fourth, acquaintances; the fifth, people in one's neighborhood; and the sixth, the wider world. When there is a news item about terrible things happening in the wider world, people think it is terrible, "but for my dad, it would be in his immediate circle." "My father has amazing humanity, which leads him to get depressed about the condition of our life," said his daughter Leslie. "He has incredible empathy with people, which has its roots in his Irish Catholic background. He is a real child of his time. One needs to understand those Irish American neighborhoods during and after the war, how they worked, how they helped each other. That's a big part of his life. He saw his mother and father take people off the street, helping people. He always had a mischievous sense of humor which made him simple and accessible." "To this day we are all a bit uncomfortable with what we have," said Patrick. "He has this tremendous weight. He passed some of it on to us. Everything was always very serious. The world is a heavy place, not a place to enjoy."

Despite the constant travel and absences and the divorce, he always tried to be involved in their lives, especially when they were younger. He once flew from Hong Kong to Los Angeles to see Caroleen act in *Amadeus* at a little theater in Woodland Hills and flew back the next day. "The truth is, my father is very happy," said Caroleen over lunch in Paris one day in 2006. "He lives the way he wants to live. He likes to read his books, he likes to read the newspapers, he likes getting the news, he likes a good bottle of wine, he likes good food. I think he actually has greater access to happiness than most. We are so measured today in society with accumulating and coveting symbols of wealth and happiness, like being on the cover of a magazine, or driving a big fancy car. My father has his own idea of what happiness is for him and what makes him happy."

By the time he reached seventy-five, it seemed Chuck Feeney's lifework had been accomplished. He had made his billions and given them to his foundation. He had brought about transformative change on five continents. His wealth would all be disbursed to good causes within a decade, in keeping with his goal of giving while living. Feeney had realized by then that it was the right time to end his anonymity and have his story told to provide a template for future philanthropists.

When the first edition of this biography appeared, Chuck Feeney's friend Niall O'Dowd and Tom Moran, president and chief executive officer of Mutual of America, jointly hosted a book party on the top floor of Mutual headquarters on Park Avenue in New York. Knowing well his distaste for self-publicity, they did not expect Feeney to show up. However, not only did he decide to come, but he brought one hundred of his classmates from St. Mary's of the Assumption High School in Elizabeth, New Jersey. They arrived along with an extended clan of Feeney-Fitzpatricks in two hired buses. The mostly retired Irish Americans clearly adored the neighborhood kid from Elmora, whom they knew as Charlie. In crumpled blue blazer, baggy pants, and well-worn Mephisto shoes, Feeney was about the only male present not wearing a tie. He spent much of the evening greeting and signing books for old friends while perched beside the wheelchair of his twenty-one-year-old great-nephew, Dennis Fitzpatrick, who has cerebral palsy. "I used to be Charlie's girlfriend," one little old lady sighed. "Boy, did I make a mistake!" Family members related stories of Feeney's frugality. "He'd send my parents $50,000 for our college educations," his nephew Daniel Fitzpatrick told Margaret Roosevelt of the *Los Angeles Times*, "but if you went out to have a beer with him, he'd check the bar bill."

Having his life story published was a logical step for Feeney in establishing his legacy of "giving while living" as a template for others. If he remained anonymous, no one could learn from his example. In the days after the book launch, he subjected himself to a succession of interviews with newspapers and television and radio networks in the United States and overseas—no easy chore for a person who prefers to express himself through handing out magazine cuttings. Always his message was the same: The wealthy should give while they are alive, and they will get a lot of fun from doing so. On National Public Radio, he told James Hattori how he had watched a little girl in a Vietnam hospital cover her mouth because she had a facial deformation. "I saw that girl after she went through surgery, and she was smiling. And I thought: *My God, if we could take kids who were ashamed of something that they didn't cause and put them in a position to resolve it, then that's a great source of satisfaction.*" On RTE Radio in Ireland, he told broadcaster Eamon Dunphy, "As you know, I've been relatively unwilling to tell people what they should do, but I guess my attitude today is—try it, you'll like it. Secondly, giving while living has got to be better than giving while dead."

Feeney even agreed, reluctantly, to accept an invitation to deliver a graduation speech at the RMIT campus in Ho Chi Minh City in November 2007. Never a gifted orator, he spoke only a few sentences before an expectant audience. But his message to the students was succinct: They should strive to improve the lives of others and never stop learning.

Feeney, the "billionaire who wasn't," became a minor celebrity on a multiplicity of Web sites, with bloggers praising his unselfish largesse and asking each other for his private mailing address. His name was bandied about on religious sites as a Good Samaritan. In Chesterfield, Missouri, Francis E. O'Donnell, managing partner of a private equity fund, was so inspired by the story that he sent a check for $50,000 to Atlantic Philanthropies. "I thought, 'Boy, this is great,'" he told me in a telephone call. "Individual donors like myself can't achieve what Atlantic does." A copy of the book signed by Chuck Feeney and Brendan O'Regan, the father of duty free, fetched $23,000 for the New York–based cleft charity, The Smile Train, when it was auctioned at a travel retail conference in Hong Kong, the final bid coming from a representative of Duty Free Shoppers (DFS).

Atlantic Philanthropies and Feeney got a lot of extra mail, but the policy of not accepting unsolicited applications remained unchanged. So, too, did the practice of declining all offers from beneficiaries all over the world to name buildings after Feeney or Atlantic Philanthropies.

Feeney's next step was agreeing to participate in a television documentary, *Secret Billionaire: The Chuck Feeney Story*, made by New Decade TV & Film Company in Dublin, Ireland. Several of those whose lives had intersected with his were asked on camera to describe him in a few words. "Compassionate. He will know more about you in twenty minutes than you will ever know about him," said his sister, Ursula. "Spiritual," said Gerry Adams. "Paradoxical," said John Healy. "I think the man is a saint," said Bob Matousek. "Odd. A conversation with Chuck Feeney is unlike any other you will ever have," said Niall O'Dowd. "Astonishing. I have never encountered such an extraordinary individual," said Ed Walsh, who likened Feeney to a Benedictine monk.

"Complex. He certainly always wanted to play fair, but he wanted to fight tough," said Harvey Dale, described on-screen as Feeney's "lawyer and friend."

Despite his advancing years, Feeney remained relentlessly focused on his philanthropy, which meant constantly searching for new opportunities and checking the progress of projects around the world as the clock ticked toward the end of the foundation's life span. As always, he preferred to conduct business over a latte and a glass of water at a Formica-topped table in a café or in one of his small rented apartments.

However, at the very time when he could have been looking back at a record of great achievements and anticipating doing big things with what was left, Chuck Feeney entered the most stressful period of his philanthropic life. He became engaged in a bitter struggle with his board of directors over control of the remaining funds in the foundation. The conflict almost killed him, and it would severely compromise his long and complex relationship with Harvey Dale.

No Good Deed
Goes Unpunished

The crisis in Atlantic Philanthropies began simmering in the spring of 2009. At its core was the question of how best to dispose of the remainder of Chuck Feeney's endowment, then standing at $3 billion, of which $800 million was committed to cover previous grants.

Three years earlier, the then-chairman of Atlantic Philanthropies, Frank Rhodes, told staff that the foundation had to spend $1 million a day if it was to meet its target and limit its life span. To illustrate the point, he related an anecdote about a French general who ordered a sergeant to plant a tree. The sergeant said it would take one hundred years to grow. "Then plant it before lunch," said the general. "There isn't a moment to lose." The heart of the matter was deciding how the remaining funds should be spent—what kind of trees to plant.

For many years Atlantic had funded organizations and projects in the fields of aging, children, health, and human rights. Feeney fully supported progressive causes but was always more enthusiastic about transformational philanthropy—typically the provision of seed money for medical research centers and hospital and university buildings that would continue to benefit lives far into the future. Only a foundation like Atlantic Philanthropies, with its huge resources and limited life span, and with a leader of the caliber and vision and global reach of Chuck Feeney, could make the big bets this required.

However, the strategy of the chief executive officer and the board of directors at Atlantic Philanthropies evolved to a point where Feeney feared the foundation was losing sight of his vision and would jeopardize his ability to make large gifts for bricks-and-mortar projects.

Gara LaMarche had been appointed chief executive and president of Atlantic Philanthropies in April 2007, after John Healy moved back to Ireland. He was chosen over Chris Oechsli, the AP staff nominee. Spencer Stuart & Associates, a global executive search firm contracted by Atlantic to recommend a successor, short-listed LaMarche and two women candidates. At a board meeting, Feeney ruled out the two female contenders.

A wiry fifty-two-year-old native of Rhode Island and graduate of Columbia College, LaMarche had made his name in progressive circles in the United States as director of programs for the Open Society Institute of George Soros (now Open Society Foundations), which promoted democratic governance and human rights; during his decade-long tenure, OSI had become the leading funder of criminal justice reform in the United States. Before his selection, LaMarche had told the board that he wanted Atlantic to become a sizable backer of community organizing. "It was clear to the search committee and to the board, which included Chuck, what kind of approach I had to philanthropy," said LaMarche in an email interview years later. "Everyone knew what they were getting with me." His focus on advocacy and social justice at Atlantic was not a shift of mission, "just a further definition of the mission statement Chuck himself had drafted before I got there." To LaMarche, the "Legacy and Purpose" document of 2003—which committed Atlantic "to initiate social change," he pointed out—was a green light.

Helga sensed trouble ahead. "You will live to regret this," she said after Chuck gave his approval. Feeney would say later he signed off on LaMarche's appointment because of his record. "There was nothing wrong with the information at the time." The organization had always somehow managed to balance Feeney's transformational infrastructure projects and social justice giving, and he saw no reason this could not continue.

At first Feeney was supportive of LaMarche's activities. In March 2009, he made a point of acknowledging Gara's "two years of hard work." Feeney had no problems with promoting social justice. He would only have an issue if this goal in any way compromised the flexibility so critical to the work of an entrepreneurial philanthropist. The year LaMarche came on board, Feeney authorized a $75 million grant, on top of $50 million donated the previous year, for construction by the University of California at San Francisco (UCSF) Medical Center of a new building dedicated to cardiovascular research and clinical treatment in the Mission Bay district of San Francisco. It was designed to enable UCSF to bring together a scattered community of basic research scientists and clinicians to study the cardiovascular diseases underlying medical emergencies such as heart attack and stroke. In typical Chuck Feeney fashion, he held many of the strategic meetings with university and building officials around the corner from his apartment in the Crossroads Café on San Francisco's Delancey Street, where the kitchen was staffed by former drug users and the cheerful head waitress was a reformed prostitute. His vision was to transform a waste site not far from Fisherman's Wharf into a world-class medical center.

LaMarche did not entirely share Feeney's enthusiasm for such big-ticket concrete-and-glass projects. When I mentioned the San Francisco grant to LaMarche over dinner one evening, he commented, "And rising!" It was. In 2008 Feeney authorized another $125 million to the UCSF Medical Center for its women's, children's, and cancer hospital complex. It was the largest gift ever received by UCSF. The total in grants for 2008 alone reached $180 million, and Feeney's commitment to the Mission Bay campus would eventually top $292 million. The funding came with a condition, typical of Feeney, that it should be matched by donations from other sources. His involvement brought in Salesforce.com CEO Marc Benioff and his wife Lynne, who pledged $100 million toward the children's hospital.

In 2009 Feeney made another big bet, this time in Australia. In a reapplication of the formula he had used to revolutionize research funding in Ireland in the 1990s, he made a deal with the federal government in Canberra: Atlantic Philanthropies would provide half of the AU$205 million (US$132 million) required for three major medical research buildings in Brisbane, Queensland, if the government would provide the other half. The government agreed, and Atlantic provided the AU$102.5 million promised. This brought Feeney's giving for medical research facilities in Australia to half a billion Australian dollars, the largest by a philanthropist for higher education and medical research in the country's history. Later, in Brisbane, a taxi driver recognized Chuck as the city's benefactor and insisted on giving him a free ride. "Maybe I should have come out of the closet sooner," Feeney joked to his associate, David Kennedy.

Funding big projects while maintaining a grant stream for worthy causes had always created difficulties in forward planning at Atlantic Philanthropies. When he was chief executive in 2003, John Healy had brought some order to Atlantic's giving by identifying four areas for grant-making—aging, children and youth, population health, and reconciliation and human rights—while maintaining a separate founding chairman's fund, or "chairman's pot," for Feeney to pursue his initiatives. The problem was deciding what size the pot should be. It was arbitrarily set at $35 million in 2004 and later at $50 million. Feeney never took it seriously, and the Mission Bay and Brisbane grants made nonsense of it. The Atlantic Philanthropies board couldn't say no to Feeney's initiatives. But large bricks-and-mortar investments ran counter to LaMarche's strategy of creating multiple programs for social justice and advocacy, which inevitably meant a committed grants tail of several hundred million dollars at any one time. Feeney's large and unpredictable grant-making was taking chunks out of the remaining endowment. Who knew when Chuck would come along with another nine-figure pledge!

LaMarche was strongly supported in his grant-making focus by three of the longest-serving directors of Atlantic Philanthropies: Frederick A. O. "Fritz" Schwarz Jr., a top-class New York lawyer; Elizabeth McCormack, a doyen of the philanthropic world; and Michael "Mike" Sovern, a former president of Columbia University. The three had been recruited by Harvey Dale before the 1996 DFS sale, mainly to give Atlantic respectability. Before that, the secretive foundation had only had four directors—Harvey Dale, Chuck Feeney, Frank Mutch, and Cummings Zuill—and Dale feared the foundation might be forced to go public and face critical public scrutiny in the United States; it might even be suspected of fronting for the mafia. Schwarz, McCormack, and Sovern had satisfied three criteria set by Dale: They had impeccable reputations, they could guarantee discretion, and they were comfortable with the idea of being part of an unorthodox and ultrasecretive foundation based in Bermuda.

A great-grandson of F.A.O. Schwarz, the founder of the famous Manhattan toy store, Fritz Schwarz had known Chuck Feeney since 1991: At the time of Feeney's divorce, Harvey Dale had recruited Schwarz to represent the foundation after Danielle hired lawyer Milton Gould to challenge the finality of the 1984 transfer of assets that had been in her name. He also acted for Feeney in the sale of Feeney's DFS holdings. A patrician and well-liked liberal, Schwarz had become an outspoken opponent of the Bush administration's "war on terror" and co-authored a 2007 book, *Unchecked and Unbalanced: Presidential Power in a Time of Terror.* He chaired a number of other prestigious boards, including the Fund for the City of New York, and was chief counsel to the William J. Brennan Center for Justice at New York University School of Law, a leftist think tank and public interest law firm. He was a recipient of the New York State Bar Association's Gold Medal for distinguished service in the law.

Elizabeth McCormack was a formidable figure in New York's social and philanthropic circles. Having started her working life as a nun, she became president of the top-tier Manhattanville College outside New York City and an adviser on philanthropy to Rockefeller Family & Associates. Now in her eighties, she was a member of numerous charitable boards and had a chair in humanities named after her at Cambridge College.

Likable and funny, Mike Sovern had a reputation as a brilliant legal scholar. He was chairman of Sotheby's Holdings, Inc., president of the Shubert Foundation, and a director of the Shubert Organization and Comcast Corporation. He had been chairman of the American Academy in Rome, the Japan Society, and the National Advisory Council for the Freedom Forum Media Studies Center as well as a member of the boards of the NAACP Legal Defense and Educational Fund, the Kaiser Family Foundation, the Pulitzer Prizes, AT&T, Pfizer, Inc., and Warner-Lambert Company, among others. He also served as a trustee of President Clinton's Legal Defense Fund.

Feeney's relationships with all the foundation's directors, numbering a dozen, were normally businesslike and cordial. They would enjoy a good-humored dinner together during the quarterly board meetings in New York or Bermuda. Feeney, who liked to leave functions early, would always get up from the table as the coffee arrived and quip that he should go because Elizabeth McCormack, who was older than him, would want to retire to bed. Feeney was always treated with respect. He and Harvey Dale consulted together regularly. Chairman Frank Rhodes called him almost daily.

Over time, however, some directors had become more independent-minded and less attuned to the founding donor's grant-making priorities. When Rhodes stepped down as board chairman in 2008, he was succeeded by Fritz Schwarz, who did not maintain the same regular contact with

Feeney; nor did he entirely share Feeney's enthusiasm for bricks-and-mortar over social justice causes. Gara LaMarche did not liaise with Feeney as much as his predecessors. LaMarche also did not always defer to Feeney's schedule, as so many other people automatically did when they were in the same town as the roving philanthropist and would drop everything to accept his short-notice invitations to coffee, lunch, or dinner. Feeney was offended when LaMarche flew into San Francisco one morning and left the same afternoon without spending time to share his enthusiasm for what was then the single biggest investment for the foundation.

As he took me on a tour of the Mission Bay site one day in January 2010, Feeney complained, "Gara and others should be initiating bricks-and-mortar projects like this." Mission Bay in San Francisco was, in Feeney's opinion, the most important medical project in the United States; it would tackle America's number-one and number-two killers, heart disease and cancer, and optimize the length and quality of life. "The Mission Bay campus in its present form might not have existed without Chuck's foresight," said Regis Kelly, former executive vice chancellor of UCSF, who believed Feeney's genius lay in spotting the opportunity presented by a once-empty field. Feeney attended the groundbreaking ceremony at Mission Bay on October 26, 2010. He listened intently as eleven-year-old Paddy O'Brien, who had a rare form of bone cancer, read his own composition, "Needles," about how the doctors at the center gave him injections to keep his immune system working and kept him alive. "Needles, my worst enemy . . . [but] needles are curing me of cancer. Needles, they turn out to be my best friend." To Feeney, this was what philanthropy was all about.

The election of Barack Obama as U.S. president in 2008 created opportunities for LaMarche to increase the involvement of Atlantic Philanthropies in advocacy and social justice causes. The foundation contributed $135,000 to co-sponsor the Huffington Post eve-of-inaugural ball in the Newseum in Washington on January 19, 2009, with the theme "Countdown to a New Day." LaMarche mingled with celebrity guests Ben Affleck, Larry David, Jamie Lee Curtis, and Sharon Stone as they were serenaded by Sheryl Crow and Sting. "In many, many areas of concern to us there are opportunities for progressive policy action [and] as a foundation that is very engaged in advocacy, we are anxious to push the ball forward," he explained to Jennifer Moore of the *Chronicle of Philanthropy*, who was covering the event. On his personal blog, LaMarche wrote: "I've never been to, say, the

Vanity Fair Oscar Night party, but this was probably a close approximation, with the likes of Tim Geithner and Larry Summers mingling with Will.i.am, Sharon Stone, and Larry David. Or as *The Washington Post* put it this morning, 'Hollywood for Ugly People meets . . . Hollywood.'"

LaMarche's support for Obama was soon translated into significant funding for the White House's political initiatives. On March 9, 2009, at LaMarche's instigation, the board of Atlantic Philanthropies convened in the five-star Willard Hotel across from the White House for briefings on President Obama's health care reform bill, then going through Congress. Senior administration opinion-makers addressed the directors over dinner, including Valerie Jarrett, White House senior adviser and assistant to the president, and John Podesta, President Clinton's former chief of staff and now president of the Center for American Progress, a progressive think tank to which LaMarche directed $3 million in funding from 2008 to 2010. Richard Kirsch, a leading health care advocate, was flown to Washington to make a presentation. He noted Feeney's modest demeanor. "Everyone else in the elegant room was dressed as you'd expect for a business meeting of a multi-billion dollar foundation, held at a prestigious venue," Kirsch wrote in his 2012 book *Fighting for Our Health*. By contrast, "Chuck Feeney was wearing a faded white and black checked flannel shirt."

Feeney did not stay overnight with the other directors at the Willard. He checked into the more modest Embassy Suites Hotel, an eight-story brown-brick block on Twenty-second Street NW, a short taxi ride away. Fritz Schwarz and fellow director Tom Mitchell dropped by the Embassy Suites to find out what was on the founding chairman's mind, as Feeney sometimes disconcerted directors by springing things at board sessions. Schwarz asked him why he didn't come and stay with them at the Willard. The choice of a more modest hotel was typical of the founding donor. In Bermuda, he never lodged with other directors at the five-star Fairmont Hamilton Princess, where board meetings were customarily held, preferring to stay in a three-star hotel nearby.

Feeney was initially supportive of LaMarche's prioritizing of health care reform. Of all the things they could do to help people, he said, "health care was the right one." The United States was the only wealthy, industrialized nation that failed to ensure that all of its citizens had some kind of private or public health insurance. LaMarche eventually made Atlantic the major donor to Health Care for America Now (HCAN), a nationwide coalition of progressive organizations campaigning for health care reform founded by Kirsch in 2008. HCAN became the counterweight to Tea Party rallies protesting against President Obama's prescription for "socialized medicine." It ran television advertisements across the United States proclaiming: "If the insurance companies win, you lose." LaMarche recommended, and the board approved, an initial grant of $10 million to the campaign group even before Obama was elected in November 2008. In time the grant rose to $26.5 million—more than half of HCAN's total budget.

A year after the Willard Hotel board meeting, Congress approved Obama's Patient Protection and Affordable Care Act requiring most Americans to get insurance by 2014 or pay a financial penalty. Asked to evaluate Atlantic Philanthropies' role in getting the health care reform measure to this point, Kirsch opined, "Without Gara and Atlantic, the United States would not have enacted legislation making affordable health care a right for most of its citizens." An independent report commissioned by Atlantic concluded that, though it was difficult to gauge HCAN's impact, it was a major contributor to the success of the reform.

LaMarche's priorities began to attract the hostile attention of conservative commentators, some of which rubbed off on Feeney. Bob Bauman, on the Florida-based Web site The Sovereign Investor, complained in May 2011 that "money-bags" Feeney was able to freely fund the American left because his foundation was based in the tax haven of Bermuda.

Because of an aspect of U.S. tax laws, Atlantic Philanthropies could indeed more freely finance groups that lobbied for legislation and participated in political campaigns and elections. These groups were known as 501(c)(4) organizations. Contributions to 501(c)(4) social welfare organizations were not deductible by U.S.-based donors as charitable contributions for U.S. income tax. Ben Smith in *Politico* noted in May 2011 that through a quirk of the tax law, Feeney and Atlantic "could freely finance the 501(c)(4) organizations that play in politics, which American family foundations can't do." Atlantic Philanthropies "has emerged in recent years as a key, quiet funder of the institutional left, providing the money behind, among other groups, the health care outfit Health Care for America Now."

From 2007 to 2011, under LaMarche's management, Atlantic Philanthropies would make over one hundred contributions to 501(c)(4) organizations such as Freedom to Travel to Cuba Activities, Campaign to Defend Women's Health and Rights, Media Matters Health Care Initiative, and

The Advocacy Fund (for its campaign against the death penalty). Typically, grants ranged from $100,000 to $2 million.

LaMarche's prominent role in promoting health care reform did not go unnoticed in Washington. He was invited along with Congress members and health care reform advocates to the East Room of the White House on March 23, 2010, to witness President Obama sign the Patient Protection and Affordable Care Act, which made health care reform law in the United States. "I can't tell you what a thrill it was," he recalled.

Never keen to "blow his own trumpet," Chuck Feeney was uneasy with the high profile that Atlantic and its leadership were now gaining in the political and social justice arena. Before this, Feeney himself had been the thinker and spirit of the foundation. LaMarche, the anti–Chuck Feeney, was becoming a rival ideologue. Where Chuck was inept at small talk, Gara was a wordsmith. Chuck was intuitive, hyperactive, reticent, and shy, whereas Gara was charismatic, measured, articulate, and prolific. Feeney never used a computer or a cell phone or email, whereas LaMarche had his own blog, updated his Facebook page regularly, and obsessively checked his cell-phone messages. Feeney never articulated his thoughts in the media; LaMarche was an occasional columnist for the Huffington Post and *The Nation*, the leading chronicles of liberal America. Unlike his predecessors who ran Atlantic Philanthropies, LaMarche also put himself out in the public arena. He didn't just accept requests to speak to audiences—he sought out such invitations.

Feeney first voiced his unhappiness with LaMarche's leadership in a letter to his fellow directors prior to a board meeting in Bermuda on June 23–24, 2009. He expressed doubts about the direction the foundation was taking and the rising costs involved. He told the directors that it was time to take a breather, that the foundation was doing lots of things, some good, some mediocre, and some bad. He pointed to the proliferating number of causes that were being supported under the emphasis on advocacy and social justice. This support required hiring more staff to manage a multiplicity of programs. The practice of making multi-year commitments had produced liabilities in the form of a grants-payable tail of $800 million. This was far too much, argued Feeney. He asked about the impact of the large amount of cash for health care spending—$17 million at that point—on their capital. He had plans for spending assets, he said, and he did not want to be constrained. In fact, he asserted, there should be a halt to grant-making by management.

Harvey Dale offered his support for slowing down future grant-making. Since they were based in Bermuda, he pointed out, existing pledges were not legally enforceable in the United States.

However, Feeney's proposal cut little ice with the majority of the directors. The letter was very persuasive, but "all wrong," Elizabeth McCormack told the board. They had to say no to it. Atlantic was committed to four program areas, and "we can fail by default if we go too far and get too interested in building buildings, research centers, etc." They had to make sure that allocating funds to Feeney's initiatives did not harm their ability to carry out the work of the four program areas.

Billy Hall, a newly appointed director, was taken aback. A native of Northern Ireland and director of the Centre for Research in Infectious Diseases at University College Dublin, he pointed out that there was another program area—the founding chairman's fund—to which they were also committed.

As current chairman, Schwarz saw his role as supporting the staff of the foundation in their work. He admired LaMarche immensely for his record and ideals. Atlantic was doing great things by investing in advocacy and social justice, which everyone, including Chuck, supported, he said. Atlantic was encouraging reconciliation in Northern Ireland, campaigning against the death penalty in the United States, changing the perception of HIV/AIDS in South Africa, enhancing health care practices and the wearing of crash helmets in Vietnam, and transforming end-of-life care in the Republic of Ireland. Schwarz got a consensus from the directors that they were proud of the general strategic direction of the organization and the leadership of LaMarche and his team.

Feeney was rebuffed. He could do nothing. He might be the moral leader and source of all the foundation's assets, but he had only one vote on an independent board. "I will have more to say after I have mulled my thoughts," he warned.

Feeney's concern about the rising costs of running the foundation was shared by some in the ranks of the Atlantic staff. After LaMarche became chief executive, there was a significant turnover of employees, and there also evolved what, as one manager described, was a culture of fear and dependency at the prospect of losing a job with a large salary and generous expenses. A senior employee chose to resign rather than continue working in a "toxic" environment. As time went by, staff members began to express their feelings on an anonymous internal blog "so strongly," claimed this employee, "that it had to be closed down."

One of the biggest costs resulted from LaMarche's transfer of Atlantic Philanthropies' New York headquarters in 2009 from Park Avenue in midtown Manhattan to Varick Street in the SoHo district downtown. There were a number of reasons for this move, LaMarche would explain later. There was no additional office space in Park Avenue; the conference room was too small and some staff were doubling up in rooms. He needed accommodation for eight extra new staff approved by the board. "We also wanted to save costs of external meetings and convenings by bringing all those, including the quarterly board meetings, in-house, and to have the capacity for periodic, more public convenings." The two penthouse floors into which Atlantic Philanthropies relocated almost doubled the floor space, from 24,000 to 44,000 square feet, which was a remarkable expansion for a foundation planning to go out of existence. LaMarche moved into a large office with wide balconies overlooking the Hudson River and doors paneled with strips of antique wood. Harvey Dale left his office at 950 Third Avenue and moved into a room on the floor below.

The directors originally thought it was a good thing to have better facilities for meetings and video-conferencing. In time, however, they would conclude that the move was not such a wise investment. It cost $18.9 million, partly owing to the investment loss on the Park Avenue lease and a shortfall in subletting income of almost $5 million because of a collapse in the real estate market. Though Feeney hadn't shouted "stop" when the transfer downtown was proposed, it became a big issue in the growing schism in Atlantic. In hindsight, Harvey Dale, Fritz Schwarz, and others regretted not voting against the move.

The board's snub at the Bermuda meeting had a depressing effect on Feeney, which some directors failed to fully appreciate. Although he was the visionary and driving force of the foundation, as he had been of DFS, Feeney felt increasingly that he was not being treated with respect by those running it. The rejection of his letter and the way he was rebuffed contributed to that feeling.

It took special care, interpretive skills, and patience to work with Chuck Feeney. Like many persons of creative genius, he had an idiosyncratic way of conducting his affairs. He worked things out in his mind rather than in committees. He was on a different wavelength. His movements were unpredictable. He might get up and leave a board meeting while it was going on.

"When he showed up at meetings, he could be very articulate and focused, but other times, especially when he got push-back, he could be gruff, critical, intense, elliptic," said an Atlantic insider and fan of Feeney's. "People sometimes weren't quite sure what he wanted. He didn't attend meetings where decisions were made, and then he was angry about the decisions. He perceived that he was working harder and knew more than most of the people around the table. You combine that and you get other people reacting badly." Feeney also spent a lot of time out of the United States and felt that Atlantic directors and management staff were losing Atlantic's uniquely global perspective.

His children noticed a change in their father on the infrequent occasions they linked up with him on his global gyrations. Leslie felt that he had become more depressed and negative. Catching up myself with Chuck and Helga in Dublin, New York, or San Francisco, I saw his mood grow darker. He was suffering from the usual pains and frustrations of old age, which didn't help. His knees were the main problem. Gone were the days of fast walking and talking. He shuffled rather than walked, taking short steps and often stopping to grasp a railing or a friendly arm for support. He couldn't handle the couple of glasses of white wine he liked to have with dinner as easily as before. After collapsing a couple of times from stress, he discovered the delights of accident and emergency departments in various hospitals.

As his frustration grew, Feeney turned to the person who had been at his side in earlier difficult periods but who had failed to be short-listed for the job of Atlantic chief executive two years earlier. Chris Oechsli had left the organization in 2007 after working with Feeney on several initiatives in Australia, Vietnam, and Cuba, and he served for a time as counsel to Democratic Senator Russ Feingold of Wisconsin. He had since moved on to become project director at the Institute for Policy Studies, a multi-issue think tank based in Washington. Early in 2009, Feeney asked Oechsli to come and see him. He told Oechsli of his apprehensions about the foundation's strategy and spending. The then-fifty-five-year-old, quiet-spoken former executive agreed to keep in touch. When they met again in New York in late September, Oechsli found Feeney in a state of some agitation. He was more concerned than ever that no one was listening to him at Atlantic. Feeney urgently needed Oechsli's full-time help as mediator. In January 2010, Oechsli agreed to get professionally involved.

Chris Oechsli had a rare gift among Feeney's associates. Trained as a lawyer, he could interpret Feeney and articulate his thoughts and concerns in precise, clear language. He renewed an alliance with Feeney's longtime associate Jim Downey, which had been forged in the heat of the DFS sale. Based in Dublin, Downey was Feeney's numbers man. Like Oechsli, he was calm and unassuming and could figure out what Feeney was thinking and put it into sophisticated language. They were a well-matched pair when working together: Downey did the numbers and Oechsli the legal stuff, and both were at ease with Feeney.

David Smith, chairman of the foundation's subsidiary, General Atlantic Group, was the third person in a triumvirate of key advisers now dedicated to Chuck Feeney. Based in San Francisco, Smith would spend time with Feeney during his sojourns on the West Coast and often took the transcontinental red-eye flight to be at his back during important board meetings in New York and Bermuda. He and Downey, also a director of General Atlantic, were involved in determining the fate of the remaining foundation properties—including the Couran Cove eco-resort in Australia, Feeney's misguided venture that had been put into liquidation after operating for years at a huge trading loss, and the Bayside Village apartment complex in San Francisco, which was 47.5 percent owned by General Atlantic and where Feeney had his small West Coast residence.

The atmosphere at the quarterly board meetings grew more strained as Feeney continued to express his doubts about LaMarche's strategy. At the June 2010 meeting in Hamilton, Bermuda, he challenged the funding of the health care campaign and inquired pointedly how the new pattern of payouts on social justice and advocacy impacted on the foundation's capital. Asked by director Christine V. Downton if he would be proud of HCAN's work if it led to many lives being improved, he replied that the government provided health care and "we can't judge or really measure how our action impacted on this."

Chuck wasn't alone in his reservations about supporting President Obama's reforms. Harvey Dale was also leery about the investment in health care spending, taking the view that the president used up a lot of "green stamps" to get his initiative through and that it would perhaps be dismantled over time. Like some other directors, Tom Mitchell, who commuted to board meetings from Dublin, Ireland, wondered how far Atlantic Philanthropies should turn toward political activism and whether the foundation was designed for that, even though Obama's election had provided an unusual opportunity for making a difference.

Fritz Schwarz and Mike Sovern came to LaMarche's defense. Schwarz pointed out that the Obama administration was saying that their grantees' work was making a huge difference. Sovern said that there was a real probability the health care legislation would not have passed without Atlantic's support and that the reform would save hundreds of thousands of lives.

Feeney raised the question of expenses at a September 2010 gathering of directors in New York. In the previous four years, Atlantic's endowment had declined by $1.4 billion, yet annual operating costs had escalated by $17 million to $57 million—"an increase of over 40 percent during a period of economic distress." The number of staff had grown by 20 to 123 in the same period, he said. All this reflected problematic issues in grant-making strategy and operating values.

His intervention again was to no avail. In exasperation, Feeney voted against every grant proposal (except one for a charity in Bermuda). When asked at the board meeting why he did that, he retorted angrily, "All the work is garbage." It was his way of throwing down the gauntlet.

Harvey Dale grew very concerned about the way Feeney was hitting out. He took it upon himself to advise the other directors on how to cope with the situation, once counseling three of them, as they rode the Acela Express from Washington to New York, to go with the flow, warning that if they tried to restrain Chuck, he would just get angry and disappear around a corner. He traveled to Boston to explain to fellow director Sara Lawrence-Lightfoot how to deal with Chuck's methods and to urge her to understand that it was not a rational process. Lawrence-Lightfoot was another prestigious member of the Atlantic board. A professor at the Harvard Graduate School of Education and the author of eight academic books, she was the first African American woman in Harvard's history to have an endowed professorship named in her honor.

Then came a bombshell. Feeney asked Dale to meet him privately. He instructed his longtime ally to tell Fritz Schwarz, Elizabeth McCormack, and Mike Sovern that they should step down from the board and end their service to Atlantic Philanthropies. Dale had brought the three in at a time when they needed directors who had experience and respectability. Now Feeney wanted him to get them to leave. He saw them as obstructionist and—because of their strong support of LaMarche's strategy, which was creating a large grants tail—an impediment to his freedom to undertake new initiatives close to his heart. The board was in any event too large, he said, and its functioning too unwieldy and costly.

Because of the way the board had evolved, Feeney's request for resignations could be ignored unless it had the backing of a majority of directors, who could not be shifted as there were no term limits. A few years earlier, John Healy, as chief executive, had proposed a mechanism to bring new blood into Atlantic Philanthropies. He suggested a system of three-year terms, with directors limited in the number of terms they could serve. Fritz Schwarz cautioned, however, against the potential loss of years of valuable experience. Healy eventually persuaded the board to adopt a policy of three-year "staggered terms," whereby each year one-third of the directors retired automatically but were permitted to present themselves for reelection for three-year terms. There might be no term limits, but there would be terms. The board agreed that one of three "classes" of four directors each would come up for reelection each year. The members of each class were decided by drawing names out of a bowl, a process that Harvey Dale regarded as a bit of a charade. However, over time, as terms expired, nothing happened. Collegiality ruled. The endorsement of directors by their fellows when up for reelection became automatic. But the mechanism was there, and it would prove critical if ever collegiality went out the window.

Directors at Atlantic provided a voluntary service for which they were well compensated. Each board member received a cash fee of $50,000 a year—not excessive according to a 2003 survey of large foundations by the Georgetown Public Policy Institute, but generous in an industry where several major philanthropies do not pay any compensation to their directors. Atlantic directors were also entitled to designate up to $100,000 a year to eligible charities of their choice. They could charge for hotels, meals, transportation, and out-of-pocket expenses they and their spouses incurred when attending board meetings in Bermuda, extending from two days before the start of a board meeting to one day after. Being a board member of a major foundation such as Atlantic Philanthropies also carried considerable prestige in philanthropic and social circles.

Harvey Dale tried to talk Feeney out of his demand that Schwarz, McCormack, and Sovern stand down as directors. He told Chuck that it was a bad idea because they would refuse and would become antagonized; moreover, perhaps not all of the three were standing in his way. He urged him both orally and in writing not to go forward: It was one of the most distinguished boards in philanthropy, and he could not have persuaded the three to join years earlier if they were simply going to be "agents." However, Feeney was adamant. There was no opportunity for fresh blood and new ideas, he replied, and renewal of directorships had "hardened into an unhealthy rule" and militated against independent thinking.

Dale bit the bullet and approached the three individually to convey Feeney's request that they resign. They refused, as he expected.

Feeney was furious. He told Dale, "You have failed!" Feeney later confronted Elizabeth McCormack just before a board meeting and told her she should step down. Her reply, he recalled, was: "You will have to carry me out on a stretcher." Schwarz made the point that it would look bad if a foundation that supported aging programs dumped the oldest directors. Feeney offered to lead by example and resign himself, then seek to continue his giving initiatives from outside the boardroom; his associates talked him out of it, however, saying that, if he thought he was not being listened to now, leaving the boardroom would ensure that his voice would *definitely* not be heard.

The episode brought about a deterioration in Feeney's relationship with Harvey Dale, whom he had declared only a few years previously to be the most influential person in his life. They had remained on reasonably civil terms after Dale stepped down as CEO in 2001. Dale continued, however, to wield considerable influence as a director and often spoke up for Feeney at board meetings. But as Feeney saw it, his longtime adviser had brought in the three directors and should be able to get them to leave. He suspected, with some justification, that Dale had conveyed the request without any conviction.

At stake was Feeney's role in his own foundation. It seemed no longer the case that the directors never lost sight of the fact that it was "Feeney's money." Some saw it now as a gift that had been multiplied through shrewd investments by professional advisers. Underlying everything was the question of whether the directors had the right and the duty to determine how it should be put to use, regardless of the donor's priorities.

Feeney feared that he would experience, while still alive, a phenomenon not unknown in the world of philanthropy—the neglect of donor intent. There had been a notable case of this in the United States just the year before. In 2008, Princeton University had to pay $90 million to settle a lawsuit brought by the Robertson family, who charged it with ignoring the mission of its benefactor, the Robertson Foundation, to benefit the university's output of students schooled in public and international affairs. Now Feeney worried that his philanthropic model of giving while living would be dispensed with in what he described to me as "sprinkle philanthropy." A family member was also worried: "We have seen the foundation go from a mom-and-pop kitchen table to a big machine where the directors don't really know him, and our concern is that if they get rid of him, they would not spend down."

The question was complicated by internal debate on how to end the life of the foundation by 2016, in keeping with Feeney's policy of giving while living. Harvey Dale had expressed interest at board meetings in calving off remaining portions of the endowment, along with program staff, to other foundations to carry on Atlantic's work after they shut their doors, arguing that they should be thinking outside the box—or as he put it, "exogenously." He also suggested that a higher value could be realized in the future from handing off to other institutions the hotels, resorts, health clubs, and retail stores that still accounted for 6 percent of the foundation's net assets than if Atlantic were to sell them off for cash at short notice.

Feeney had to change tactics. Confrontation and anger hadn't worked. He needed to bring a majority of the directors around to his way of thinking, to make a definitive statement of his philosophy and a cogent argument as to why the board should change course.

For several months, Feeney worked with Chris Oechsli and Jim Downey on a 2,000-word manifesto, "Reflections and Comments on Philanthropy and the Atlantic Philanthropies." Feeney presented it to the gathering of the directors in New York in September 2010.

He was content, he explained, with his decision in 1984 to transfer nearly all of his assets for eventual philanthropic use. It was a sensible means for directing to good purpose his large and increasing wealth, and granting this wealth to good causes "has been a rich source of joy and satisfaction for me, and for my family as well."

Beginning with little more than a few nascent ideas, Feeney went on, he had learned and come to appreciate the challenges and complexities of philanthropy. His fundamental guides had been those values that served him well in his business career—dynamism, vigilance, and the informed risk-taking inherent in entrepreneurial work—together with making good relationships and personal engagement a priority. In business, as in philanthropy, he had always sought an independent, strategic edge where potential was often greatest.

In his view, the most critical tasks in philanthropy were to identify and pursue effectively the "highest and best use" for the resources available—subject to the organization's circumstances and philanthropic interests—to achieve the most good and lasting benefit.

"While I often initially identified a direction, however embryonic, subsequent investigations, typically involving a number of staff and advisors and encouraged by other directors, progressed and frequently developed into exciting and successful grants," he declared. As Atlantic Philanthropies' founder and sole donor, he expected to retain tacit final say over the guiding direction for grant-making.

"I probably have been the leading proponent at AP over the years for grants in support of 'bricks and mortar' development projects—and I apparently remain so today." The many building projects funded by AP formed one of its successful grant-making areas. "Personally, I draw a lot of satisfaction from this type of grant-making: It is uplifting to see an intelligently-designed project executed well and to know that it will be available as an asset for many future years. The projects I recommend are carefully selected and of the highest standard, and they typically provide a platform for the conduct of important work and foster an environment of excellence."

He intended to continue pursuing development projects in areas such as medical research, facilities, and hospitals. These projects, he pointed out, capitalized on a role that large foundations could uniquely play in supporting major undertakings and lent themselves to partnerships and leverage, which enhanced the potential for Atlantic's involvement to be catalytic and to multiply the impact of its funding. These projects could be further leveraged by complementary initiatives and collaborative links with other centers of excellence or areas of need. The commitment of large grants to UCSF's development at Mission Bay and the Translational Research Institute in Brisbane, for example, enabled multifaceted projects of world-class standard and proportion in the medical and health science fields and could provide fertile ground for other AP initiatives.

But Atlantic had taken a wrong turn. It must recast its strategic approach, he wrote. "Today, I stand in disagreement with AP's recent strategic approach for grant making, which emerged over the past two-and-a-half years. As I voiced on a number of occasions, I do not believe that the 'social justice' approach, as now defined for AP's purpose, is a viable strategy to attain the highest and best use for our resources. Furthermore, I can confirm that this style of grant-making is not one that I would have supported to any significant extent when, or since, donating the corpus that evolved into the endowment which AP now enjoys."

After reading the documents, a board member remarked to me that the foundation was now facing a crisis that could tear it apart. At its heart, the director said, was a fundamental question—whose money is it anyway?

CHAPTER 36

Blood on the Floor

An incident that occurred during the September 2010 board meeting deep-ened the rift between Chuck Feeney and Fritz Schwarz. When in Ireland, Feeney had been ill and irritable and untypically had upset two staff members in the Dublin office who had complained to Colin McCrea, head of the Irish operation. McCrea and Gara LaMarche took Feeney into a space off the conference room at Atlantic's Manhattan headquarters and confronted him about this. Schwarz came with them. They told Feeney that such action was not like him and that it shouldn't happen again. Feeney was described as "white-hot angry" when he emerged from the room. (McCrea was taken aback that Schwarz had gotten involved and would later apologize to Feeney.) Feeney subsequently took a swipe at Schwarz in a memo on the role of the chairman. As exercised historically, the role was that of manager of board meetings, with no exceptional authority or responsibilities beyond that of a director; the chairman role should not be endowed, he argued, with "a quasi-management or exceptional substantive policy-making role."

When Feeney's lengthy manifesto was discussed at that board meeting, Harvey Dale said that Chuck's thoughts were worthy of discussion and action. Listening to him was important: Chuck did not believe in the social justice approach, and they should understand that they could not reiterate social justice as a framework in light of this. Schwarz argued pointedly, however, that "we have had enormous success in areas where we are working and the results are, by any measure, as lasting as a building."

Feeney went to Dublin shortly afterwards. He was dispirited and dejected. He brought me up to date with events over coffee in the Boulevard Café near his apartment on Lower Baggot Street. "Do you think Gara should resign?" I asked. "Yes," he replied. He thought his foundation was not doing what he had intended. He quoted Hippocrates's advice to physicians, "Do no harm," as his guiding principle in his philanthropy and his life, adding enigmatically, "No good deed goes unpunished." Smaller organizations can do smaller things, he said, and bigger organizations like Atlantic Philanthropies can do bigger things, as well as develop deeper relationships.

Fritz Schwarz submitted a formal response to Feeney on November 17, 2010, in a letter co-signed by directors Tom Mitchell and Sara Lawrence-Lightfoot.

"In recent times the foundation has used the term social justice to characterize the heart of the mission," the chairman wrote. "You have reservations about the term. For some the phrase is another way of describing the motive that has always inspired your generosity, namely to help make progress towards a fairer deal in life for the less fortunate in society." He was proud of the many successes in advancing key objectives. "As a result AP is seen today as a courageous champion of the disadvantaged and vulnerable and as a bold innovator in identifying and finding practical solutions to a variety of social challenges." The board recognized "that infrastructure development can be a means to social change" and had supported Chuck's large-scale initiatives in Australia and at UCSF. However, he suggested that Chuck give up the idea of a separate founding chairman's program. "We believe that it would also be preferable if the projects you bring forward were integrated into the mainstream programs of the foundation rather than being viewed as additional or separate activities."

This was not what Feeney wanted to hear. "I do not find the letter a satisfying response," he replied on December 5, the eve of the next board meeting in New York. He had expressed deep concern and addressed serious, urgent matters he had been raising for more than a year. "I can only surmise that you underestimate, or perhaps wish not to engage with, my misgivings about, and objection to, Atlantic's current grant making focus, the structure of the board and certain of its practices, and a number of operational aspects, including ever-increasing staff numbers and elevated overhead costs." To say he had "reservations" about the term "social justice" was oversimplified and inaccurate. He didn't have any particular view about the term.

Rather, he did not believe that the social justice approach "is a worthy use of our resources."

Feeney attached to his reply a lengthy, twenty-three-point "Statement of Concerns." The grant-making focus of recent years had resulted in "mission creep, diffuse grant making and vague assessments of impact and value." As founder, he had consistently objected to the "overarching, amorphous social justice grant-making approach" that dominated all four program areas. Giving while living was coming to mean spending the donor's gift largely according to management's independent initiatives, appropriating the image and words of the founder in the process. The advocacy grant-making and public statements of Gara LaMarche had become increasingly political, Feeney went on, and had caused AP to be labeled a major force of the left for its support of HCAN. Advocacy grant-making crowded out rather than leveraged smaller donors. The 140 small grants that year had generated unwarranted administrative activity.

Feeney concluded: "It is the view of the founder that a change of leadership is necessary to achieve these outcomes."

To underline his contention that he was being marginalized by his own foundation, Feeney referred to an article in an internal journal, *Atlantic Reports*, which carried the imprimatur of Fritz Schwarz and Gara LaMarche and about which he had not been consulted. The article declared: "At Atlantic, we define giving while living as the decision by a donor to spend his or her philanthropic resources while alive, and generally, *but not necessarily* [Feeney's emphasis] with the donor's active participation in the giving program."

Later that day, Feeney asked Tom Mitchell to come and see him in his Upper East Side apartment. Recruited to the board by Feeney after ending his term as provost of Trinity College Dublin, the soft-spoken, white-haired professor of classics with a doctorate from Cornell was not wholly committed either way. Feeney told Mitchell that he wanted to take back control of the foundation. He wanted Gara out, and he wanted Fritz to step down. He wanted all grants put on hold, and he wanted nothing to be approved at the board meeting the following day. Mitchell warned him that the directors would not go along with that. Feeney also separately met with Billy Hall and asked him to second a motion stopping all grants. Hall agreed with Feeney's case, but he tried to convince Feeney that they didn't have the numbers and they couldn't just stop grant-making. Hall told him he couldn't support the motion for this reason.

The directors met on December 6 in the boardroom of the foundation's new headquarters on Varick Street, beneath framed posters illustrating Atlantic's good works. On the agenda was a motion from Feeney to cancel all grant proposals and have a special board meeting in January to discuss the "roles and appropriateness" of the company's leadership.

What was going on was a "folly and a travesty," Feeney argued. Gara had presented them with 850 pages of dense briefing material just seven days prior to the meeting, and they were now called upon to consider 78 grant proposals with an aggregate value of $120 million, while also being asked to approve grant and operations budgets for 2011, view presentations, and attend panel discussions and committee meetings—"and all this in just over a day and a half." The result was insufficient accountability by directors and undue deference to management proposals. They had to resolve critical, core issues with respect to Atlantic's leadership, direction, and operation.

Feeney put his motion to the board. There was no seconder.

The directors were nevertheless rattled. The man whose money had created Atlantic Philanthropies and who was now one of the world's most respected philanthropists had declared war by demanding that three board members and the chief executive leave the foundation and that all grant-making be halted. Relationships were fraying. There was a "horrible atmosphere," said one director, who recalled Schwarz at one point accusing the mild-mannered Mitchell of being a devotee of Chuck, to which the university don retorted that he was an independent thinker. In fact, Mitchell made it known that he agreed with practically every point Chuck made, but not that management should go: The document expressed disagreement with Gara and Fritz, but was not a convincing justification for kicking them out. Besides, Gara was widely respected in the civil rights community and could take the foundation to court, and that was an appalling vista.

Feeney took a taxi back uptown and spent the rest of the day brooding in his small apartment. Back in Varick Street, Schwarz proposed a vote of confidence in LaMarche. It was approved by all directors with the exception of Peter Smitham, who had been unable to travel from his home in London because of a family illness. Those who sympathized with Feeney knew that they were in a minority and that a counting of heads would serve nothing at that point.

Meanwhile, Schwarz made a decision that alienated Feeney even further. Feeney had asserted in his documentation that there was "a moral and fiduciary obligation that the interests, values, and passions of the living sole

donor be given central consideration in spending the fruits of his labor."
Schwarz contended that legal advice was needed to determine what their—
and Feeney's—rights were. Hall spoke up against the idea of using foundation money in a dispute with the founder. But without significant
objections, the board authorized the chairman to seek the advice of a law
firm experienced in corporate litigation.

The board subsequently hired Bernard Nussbaum, a partner at Wachtell,
Lipton, Rosen & Katz and a former classmate of Harvey Dale's at Cornell.
In the disputed DFS sale back in 1996, Nussbaum had been counsel for
Alan Parker while Schwarz represented Feeney. A fellow partner in the law
firm, Lawrence B. "Larry" Pedowitz—who was also a director of the Brennan Center, where Schwarz was legal counsel—was delegated to sit in on
meetings of directors in which they addressed how to respond to the crisis
and do the assessment work.

The directors did, however, accede to Feeney's request for a special meeting
in January to discuss the foundation's leadership. Billy Hall suggested that a
small group of directors be formed in the meantime to mediate with Feeney
and channel his thinking through to the board. Recent events showed how
unhappy Chuck was and how urgently they needed to listen to him. Schwarz
agreed. He needed an accommodation with Feeney to preserve the nature of
the work being done by LaMarche. He selected Hall, who was an ally of
Feeney's; Mike Sovern, who clearly wasn't; and Peter Smitham, who was
regarded as middle of the road and therefore the effective leader of the group.

Smitham, a board member since 2004, had considerable experience in
dealing with corporate upheavals. As a partner and former chairman of Per-
mira Partners, a leading global private equities fund manager, he had been
involved in 250 company takeovers. He was also head of Actis, a private
equity firm based in the United Kingdom and partly owned by the British
government. Smitham was respected by his fellow directors for the reasonable way in which he expressed his views in his soft Welsh accent.

Later that day, Schwarz sent Feeney a fax telling him that the board had
agreed to a special meeting in January. The proposal to stop all grants had
been unanimously rejected, he pointed out, so perhaps he might like to
withdraw it. Feeney agreed to edit out his demand to stop grant-making. He
had made his point.

The group of three directors met Chris Oechsli and Jim Downey on January 25 in the James Hotel in SoHo. Feeney's representatives almost didn't

make it in time, as traffic was snarled up after an overnight snowstorm. Oechsli outlined Feeney's concerns in detail. Sovern suggested that Oechsli become "vice president for Chuck" as a way of creating a conduit between Feeney and the board. Oechsli declined, but accepted the role as Feeney's official representative.

Around this time, each director received a copy of a 2,500-word anonymous letter, berating the board for its treatment of Feeney. Extraordinarily well-informed, the author claimed to represent a group of Chuck's friends who were not former, present, or future board members, or grantees or employees of Atlantic, but who wished to remain anonymous "to prevent strained personal relationships."

The writer warned that that they would make public the ill treatment of Chuck by his board if it did not stop. They had friends in the media, they were getting a Web site ready, and one of the group wanted to pay for ads in the *New York Times* and *USA Today*. How would the public react if "a talk show host like Oprah decides that some of you have lost your way?" They believed that Chuck had a moral obligation to go public so that those who might follow him could benefit from his mistakes as well as his successes. "What will potential philanthropists think if they find out that a foundation board doesn't listen to the wishes of the founder when he is alive and sitting in the room, never mind when he is dead?" It was imperative to tell the story of how Chuck Feeney's vision had been distorted by the present board, whose view was that Atlantic Philanthropies' money was not Chuck's money anymore, that the board knew better how to spend it, and that it was best to allocate a fraction of the giving budget to Chuck while he was alive and try to ignore him as best as possible. "Please do not take this letter as a threat," the author wrote, though it clearly was just that. Nor was it a "bluff"; rather, it was a "prediction of possible future events." They would go public despite possibly upsetting Chuck, whom they loved and supported "as an entrepreneurial legend if not a genius, one of the kindest and most generous human beings of our generation."

The letter listed a number of complaints about the board: spending millions to move office when the work of the foundation would be completed in five or six years; sponsoring an inaugural party in Washington with the Huffington Post; holding a board meeting at the five-star Willard Hotel in Washington; going to Bermuda with their spouses in winter (in the previous two years the Bermuda meetings had been held in June); and spending per-

haps half a million dollars to hold a worldwide staff meeting in Ireland—
"a real stunner." Hundreds of thousands of dollars were spent to record the
lifework of a fellow board member. "Noble for sure, but is this the highest
and best use of the foundation's limited resources?" (This was a reference to
a then-incomplete book project on Elizabeth McCormack, initiated by
Atlantic directors in 1999; it had involved three different authors and had
cost the foundation some $300,000. The book, *No Ordinary Life* by Charles
Kenney, was published the following year by PublicAffairs.)

The letter writer argued that it was legalistic posturing to protest that
Feeney gave his money away irrevocably and that it was up to the board to
direct strategy and operations. A board member who refused a request to
stand down was like Thrasymachus (the Ancient Greek sophist in Plato's *Republic* who argued that power trumps justice). "What happened to the one
who seeks what Plato called justice, capable of balancing one's own needs
against the greater good?" The writer continued: "Many of us are from the
wrong side of the tracks and some of us are even nostalgic for a good old-
fashioned street fight. Simply ask yourself this. How would YOU feel if you
made the billions, saved and invested the billions, eschewed the multiple
homes and innumerable consumer pleasures that billions could buy, asked
your wife and your children and grandchildren to also forgo the billions,
started and chaired a philanthropic foundation, gave away the billions, at 80
still worked and travelled nearly every day on behalf of the foundation, only
to have the majority of the board treat you the way you treat Chuck? Is
Chuck not still the most valuable human asset the organization has? And
Harvey the second most valuable?"

Gara had made some excellent reforms, the letter concluded. He was accomplished and well paid. If given a year to make course corrections, he
would either make the necessary changes or use the time to discreetly find
another position. "Either he will change for the sake of the organization or
he will change organizations. That is what professionals do."

Asked about the provenance of the letter, neither Chris Oechsli nor Jim
Downey had any answers. Nor had individual board members. Gara
LaMarche said, "I am not a big fan of anonymous attacks." In regard to the
contents, he later told me, the operating costs for Atlantic were always within
or under the budgets presented to and reviewed by the board, and under his
management Atlantic had remained a relatively lean operation in terms of
staff-to-grants ratio. "Whatever one says about how quick or slow the board,

or I, was to grasp the depths of Chuck's concerns about the foundation, I don't believe any fair observer could ever say Chuck was treated with disrespect, certainly not by me." Around this time a number of charitable organizations signed a letter to Atlantic praising LaMarche for his work and inspiration.

Directors who felt themselves singled out by the letter thought it was spiteful and petty. Others saw it as tuning into Feeney's anger. The issue, one said, was not who wrote it but whether the charges were serious. Fingers were being pointed and questions asked.

On January 27, 2011, the eve of the special board meeting, the Atlantic board members, without Feeney and with Larry Pedowitz sitting in, met informally in the Century Association Club, an Italian Renaissance–style palazzo at 7 West Forty-third Street, where Schwarz was a member. Some directors from out of town arrived late because of the snow, which delayed flights in and out of the city. They heard a report from the group of three board members on where things stood before retiring to the club dining room for dinner.

On Friday morning, the board met in the Cornell Club, on nearby East Forty-fourth street, with Feeney represented by Chris Oechsli. Oechsli told the directors that the upheaval was having a negative impact on Feeney's life: He was upset and rattled; he wasn't sleeping; he was waking up in the small hours of the night. He was an elderly man who needed rest, not stress, and he needed to be respected. This was literally and figuratively killing Chuck, Oechsli said. Chuck's distress was visible.

In contrast to the December meeting, the atmosphere was less fraught, one of "peace and love," as one attendee remembered it. No one wanted the crisis to get any worse. Oechsli treated the directors with respect and put Feeney's case in a nonconfrontational manner. Schwarz and LaMarche undertook addressing Feeney's concerns about spending and staff numbers.

The toll on Feeney's health had indeed become almost intolerable, and his restlessness was not helping. After the New York meetings, he and Helga flew to Dublin and the gloomy little apartment in Lower Baggot Street. "I am a guy who slept well all my life," Feeney told me over lunch in FX Buckley's. "I now started waking up at one o'clock and not getting back to sleep." He said he hadn't slept for four or five days before the board meeting in December.

Shortly after arriving in Ireland, Feeney took ill with a chest infection and was rushed to St. James's Hospital in Dublin, where he was treated in the accident and emergency department, while Helga sat in a bleak admission room with in-patients waiting interminably and a man wandering around the worse for drink. Feeney was admitted to the same hospital again when he took ill on another visit to Ireland not long afterwards. This was more serious. His heart had stopped briefly, and he had a pacemaker inserted. Later, in San Francisco, he had to have corrective surgery for the pacemaker. Friends and family feared that the crisis was destroying him and that there was no longer any joy in his life.

It wasn't long before Chuck and Helga were on the move once more. From Dublin they flew to London and then to Bangkok, where he was briefly hospitalized again, and then on to Australia. Feeney constantly mulled over the crisis when abroad and communicated regularly by fax with Oechsli in the United States. He composed another memorandum for submission to the board. Entitled "Founder's Request to AP Board Members," it stated that not only senior management but also board leadership should be removed. Nothing had changed, Feeney argued. Grants continued to be made with questionable effectiveness. The present leadership could not credibly achieve the necessary reforms. Moreover, "they have brought in lawyers, at significant cost to the endowment, to challenge my concerns and pursue a strategy of isolating me from the board."

Feeney was also prepared, "if push came to shove," to call in the lawyers himself, he told me. One senior Atlantic figure later recalled Chuck saying at a board meeting that he would fight "tooth and claw" if it came to a showdown.

The legal advice was proving costly. With fees of $1,300 an hour for the services of Wachtell, Lipton, Rosen & Katz, the total bill would rise to over half a million dollars, including a legal assessment for Harvey Dale of his duties and a substantial fee for one of America's top crisis communications consultants, George Sard of Sard Verbinnen, contracted by Wachtell to advise on the implications of the internal dispute becoming public. The advice from Sard was exclusive to the law firm and not made available to the board. But directors guessed that it boiled down to one thing: In any battle for public opinion, Chuck Feeney, the benefactor who gave away his fortune and transformed cities and countries for the better without seeking honors or accolades, would win, hands down, every time.

Supporters of Fritz Schwarz and Harvey Dale pointed out later that the lawyers were hired to ensure that the board acted properly and reached a mutually satisfactory solution to the conflict. But Feeney didn't see it that way. As far as he was concerned, half a million dollars of his money was being spent to take him on, and he was outraged.

Reinforcing Feeney's case was the impact of the "group of three," which created a dynamic that encouraged nine senior staff members to write to the board on March 17. They expressed operating concerns and unease with the discretion exercised in some grant-making. Also, LaMarche had accepted awards from a small number of organizations that had received or subsequently would receive grants from Atlantic. Atlantic Philanthropies' code of ethics stated that executives "will not accept gifts or awards or honors from a current or prospective grantee," but LaMarche's supporters on the board, including the chairman, contended that it was not a violation of Atlantic rules to accept an award if it was for lifetime service. In 2010, LaMarche accepted the Hubert H. Humphrey Civil and Human Rights Award for his lifetime record in promoting social and economic justice from the Leadership Conference on Civil Rights, which received $3.25 million in Atlantic Philanthropies grants from 2006 to 2010. The award was presented at a dinner where he took the stage alongside Democratic Senator Patrick Leahy and entertainer and activist Harry Belafonte. LaMarche's predecessor, John Healy, had barred staff members from accepting directorships in grantee organizations on the grounds that it was unwise and could give rise to conflicts of interest. This was no longer enforced. LaMarche was a director of StoryCorps, an oral history organization that received $1 million from AP in 2010, the year LaMarche joined, and of ProPublica, an independent newsroom for investigative journalism that received $250,000 from Atlantic Philanthropies in the same year.

The more Smitham heard, the more concerned he became. Staff had been let go with hefty packages and replaced; large amounts had been spent on consultants and travel; some of the grant-making was being outsourced; limousines were ferrying people to lunch; and lots of people were flying business class across America and around the world.

The staff complaints raised questions about the board's collective shortcomings. The directors should have known more about internal Atlantic matters.

Feeney returned to New York in late spring and Harvey Dale made a pilgrimage to his residence on May 3. Their long and close relationship had now almost completely unraveled. Calling in the lawyers had been the last straw. For months Feeney hadn't responded to communications from his former éminence grise. Papers sent by Dale that Feeney usually would have perused with interest piled up on his table unread. Chuck and Helga no longer went out for dinner with Harvey and his wife Debra LaMorte, a senior vice president for development and alumni affairs at New York University. Harvey had written recalling what they had done together over the years and saying that, if he had been the cause of the breach between them, he profoundly apologized. Chuck had not replied.

The encounter took place, with Jim Downey and Chris Oechsli present, in a tiny apartment adjoining the flat Feeney used on East Sixty-first Street. Feeney perched on a sofa facing Dale, who sat in an armchair drawn up in front of the television with the fireplace in between. Oechsli positioned himself at the other end of the sofa, and Downey sat at a round table. The exchanges were civil and sometimes personal, making it uncomfortable for the witnesses. At that point it was clear that LaMarche's time as chief executive was running out, and the two discussed who might be the new CEO, whether there would be board changes, and how directors might vote in a division. Dale said that he had always tried to support Feeney and always tried to serve his interests, but by being independent, active, and engaged rather than by acting as his voice.

Their ninety minute conversation did not soften Feeney's attitude toward his former confidant. Nothing changed.

With the foundation in turmoil, the dynamic on the board changed. There was a greater appreciation now of Chuck Feeney's role as the figurehead and spirit of the organization. Tom Mitchell was at last in favor of change—the letter from staff members had made up his mind. So, too, were Christine Downton, Cummings Zuill, and Billy Hall. It also did not go unnoticed that leadership change had the backing of Philip Coates, the chief investment officer of AP who was based in London with responsibility for managing the endowment.

The outcome for LaMarche was inevitable. On a business trip to London on May 16, 2011, he arranged to have dinner with Peter Smitham, who lived near the city center. They went to Le Caprice, a restaurant popular with politicians and actors in Arlington Street, just off Piccadilly. Atlantic directors learned afterwards what happened. LaMarche insisted that he was going to hang on, that he had never done anything that was a firing offense, and that he was going to win the battle against Feeney. Smitham reportedly asked what it was that he would win. Staff criticizing his management was not a win. An inability to make up with Feeney was not a win. It would be a Pyrrhic victory, a booby prize. At no point, friends said, did Smitham advise or tell LaMarche that he should leave. But after they had strolled up Piccadilly, past the Ritz, and LaMarche was about to get into a taxi, the AP chief executive, according to one account, turned back and said, "I'm going to resign." As he climbed into the back of the black cab, he added, "I'm going to tell Fritz." He did so on his cell phone minutes later.

Feeney wasted little time. Four days later, he sent an "urgent and confidential" memo to directors nominating Peter Smitham as chairman of a transition committee. Senior management, he said, should be instructed immediately to terminate all grant-making, cease public comments, and suspend all hiring. AP needed a fresh start.

There was no effective dissension this time. There was a consensus that it was better for the organization, and for LaMarche, that he should leave and a new beginning be made. No one could, at this stage, envisage Chuck and Gara ever making up.

LaMarche made his resignation official on June 3, 2011. It was an amicable separation in the end, with no suggestion that he had done anything wrong. He told colleagues in a letter that "it's time for a pause and a reset." He would take a post as senior fellow at New York University's Robert F. Wagner Graduate School of Public Service and write a book on reclaiming the moral life of philanthropy. He had achieved some memorable things. A year later, in June 2012, when the Supreme Court upheld Obama's Affordable Care Act, LaMarche informed his friends on Facebook, "Feeling more emotional about the health care victory than I expected to, having bet my Atlantic Presidency on a $26 million investment in advocacy. . . . "

The departure of LaMarche came as something of a shock to the American philanthropic community, where he was seen as a significant progressive figure. There was some dismay even within Feeney's family that it had come to this. His daughter Diane, who headed up the Feeney family foundation, the French American Charitable Trust (FACT), knew LaMarche well—both were active in the National Committee for Responsive Philanthropy and the George Soros–backed Democracy Alliance, which supported progressive organizations—and considered him to be a professional and a person of integrity. "He is smart, strategic, and got in over his head because of a weak board and a board chair that misread my dad and had his own agenda," she told me. "I do not fault Gara for wanting to put his own stamp on Atlantic Philanthropies. The ultimate resolution was quite hard on everyone." She thought her father had erred in initially creating a board of friends who eventually became a more professional board, and then straying too far himself from the board's mission, and that of AP, before coming back with a "heavy fist" that affected the reputation, integrity, and morale of Atlantic's staff. "I place the blame squarely in his corner," she said in an email. "My father is a bricks-and-mortar person. He should never have gotten away from those endeavors."

Reluctantly, Fritz Schwarz determined that the only prospect of preserving the social justice agenda he championed was to remove himself as an issue with Feeney and step down as chairman of the board. He had been mistaken in assuming the board would stay behind him and not swing toward Feeney. He had not been able to prevent the perception that he authorized expensive legal advice in order to challenge Feeney's position. The fact that he was now presiding over a divided board invited criticism of his handling of the disputes.

On the eve of the June quarterly board meeting, some three weeks after LaMarche's resignation, Schwarz told a gathering of directors in New York that, as they clearly felt Atlantic was drifting, he would relinquish the chair, while remaining on as a director. Peter Smitham was elected in his place to chart a new course. The board appointed Chris Oechsli as interim chief executive.

Feeney once again returned to Ireland, and as always he held court in the mornings in the Violà Café in Dublin or the Boulevard across the road. He told me he was sleeping at night now and felt better than he had in years, and for the first time was somewhat optimistic about the way things were going. He took a train trip to Limerick University and recounted with humor that it had broken down and the conductor had come through the carriage to announce cheerfully that "the engine's banjaxed." He had inspected his most recent projects in Limerick, which included a beautiful "Living Bridge" walkway over the Shannon and an Irish World Academy of Music and Dance to be run by his pal, Professor Mícheál Ó Súilleabháin. Feeney had commissioned his artist friend Desmond Kinney to create a magnificent $1.5 million mosaic representing the River Shannon as a woman, which took up two floors of the academy's entrance hall and could be seen lit up at night from outside. The Chuck Feeney that weekend in

Limerick was the old Chuck Feeney—friendly, benign, wisecracking, self-deprecating, surrounded by admirers and appreciative friends, and enjoying chicken and white wine in the Castletroy Park Hotel he had built two decades earlier.

Feeney returned to New York in late September for the next board meeting, at which directorships were up for renewal. Every year it was the turn of four of the twelve directors to be renominated and confirmed, and up to now confirmation had always been automatic. On this occasion, the cohort for renomination consisted of Chuck Feeney, Sara Lawrence-Lightfoot, Mike Sovern, and Fritz Schwarz. Each of the four directors in turn was asked to leave the boardroom at Atlantic headquarters as the renewal of their tenure was discussed. Feeney was the first to step outside. A few minutes later Smitham invited him back in and told him he had been reelected. Lawrence-Lightfoot and Sovern were approved with similar speed.

Then came Fritz Schwarz's turn. Tom Mitchell had privately advised Schwarz, whom he regarded as a good friend, to step down as a director rather than risk rejection by the board, on the grounds that he couldn't make war with the founder and still continue on the board. But Schwarz had seemed reluctant to accept that. After he left the room, Smitham went round the table. Everyone gave his or her opinion. Feeney was the first to speak: He wanted Schwarz out. Harvey Dale suggested that Schwarz be given a chance. Feeney responded angrily, saying words to the effect of: "You have let me down. I asked you to do things, and you didn't do them." He suggested that Dale himself should quit the board. Elizabeth McCormack and two others spoke up for Schwarz. But they were outnumbered.

Schwarz waited alone on a sofa in the adjoining room. Someone who glanced down from the executive floor above recalled him looking pensive and sad. Twenty minutes went by before Mike Sovern emerged to invite him back into the conference room. He was told that there was unanimous agreement that he should reflect on whether he should allow his name to go forward for reelection. Schwarz hesitated at first, saying he would think it over, then accepted the inevitable and agreed not to stand for another term.

It was an emotional and draining experience for everyone. Most of the directors were friends, and all were admirers of Fritz Schwarz, a high-caliber lawyer and a star in the world of legal advocacy. Feeney, however, did not speak to Schwarz afterwards, nor was there any further contact between the two.

The next day, the board ratified the permanent appointment of Chris Oechsli as president and chief executive officer. Advertisements for the position in the financial media had attracted 170 applications, but Oechsli was clearly best qualified. His patient and skillful diplomacy had earned him the respect of all sides. He understood what was wrong in Atlantic and what had to be corrected.

With the organization's need to be refreshed, 17 out of 127 Atlantic staff members were let go, including LaMarche's top aide, Marcia Smith. Under the terms of their contracts, LaMarche and Smith each received between $2 million and $3 million in compensation after their four years in Atlantic Philanthropies. By comparison, after eighteen years at the foundation, six of these as its chief executive, John Healy was granted a retirement package worth approximately $6.5 million gross to provide for his pension. Feeney constantly grumbled about the levels of remuneration in the foundation world, which he regarded as too generous, but he told me that he himself agreed to provide Harvey Dale—after Dale stepped down as chief executive in 2001 and was appointed University Professor of Philanthropy and the Law at New York University—with the sum of $10 million in recognition of his role as the architect of Atlantic Philanthropies and its leader for two decades. Plans were made to reduce full-time staff further and cut the annual operating budget by more than one-third by 2013. The directors agreed to end the practice of bringing spouses to annual board meetings in Bermuda with all expenses paid.

Looking back, a board member reflected that the formation of the group of three at the December board meeting was the turning point in the crisis. It was how Chuck won the war, said the director.

In a message to staff and colleagues on October 18, 2011, the new chief executive reaffirmed the foundation's long-term strategy to commit the remaining $2.5 billion endowment in grants by the end of 2016 and wind up its work by 2020. "This decision is driven by our Founding Chairman Chuck Feeney's belief in giving while living and his desire to encourage others with substantial means to engage themselves and devote their wealth to improving the human condition," Oechsli declared. He also promised a review of AP's grant-making strategies, with a commitment to the four core program areas *and* to the founding chairman's program.

The problem of how to manage the end game was now more urgent than ever. Ten years earlier, the board had voted to begin disbursing all of the institution's remaining assets, with final multi-year grant commitments to be made in 2016. By the time the crisis arose over AP's direction and strategy, a decade of planning had gone into ensuring the orderly winding down of the endowment. Atlantic had commissioned Tony Proscio, a former associate editor of the *Miami Herald* and one of America's leading philanthropy consultants, to analyze the foundation's sunset policy. Strategic changes become even harder when a foundation's life expectancy comes down to single digits, warned Proscio. At that point, the time for making adjustments is short, and the risk of a rushed or haphazard course correction rises steeply.

Chuck Feeney had unfinished business with the board. Harvey Dale, Mike Sovern, and Elizabeth McCormack, all of whom he wanted to leave, were still there. On April 26, 2012, he sent his fellow directors a letter in which he proposed a change in Atlantic bylaws to impose a term limit of fifteen years and the creation of a smaller board. This was important for good governance and would reflect peer organizations' practice, streamline procedures, and preserve fresh thinking and dynamism in putting the remaining funds to their highest and best use. With the foundation's life span coming to an end, the directors would have fewer duties. He himself would "step down with others similarly situated."

As chairman, Peter Smitham took soundings of the other directors by phone and found a majority in support of Feeney's latest proposal. Everyone knew that at the next board meeting there would be blood on the floor. Harvey Dale had served more than fifteen years, and his directorship was up for three-year renewal.

And so the final act in the internal drama of Atlantic Philanthropies took place in Bermuda on the last weekend of June 2012. The directors, now down to eleven with Fritz Schwarz's departure, checked in as usual to the Fairmont Hamilton Princess in Hamilton for the start of the three-day board meeting on Sunday, June 24, except for Feeney, who took a room in the Rosedon Hotel across the road. It was the first meeting under the new rule excluding spouses. On Sunday evening, they gathered along with senior managers for a thirtieth anniversary celebration dinner in the Café Lido in the oceanside Elbow Beach Hotel nearby. Oechsli gave a brief talk, looking back on the foundation's three decades of achievements. Chuck Feeney and Harvey Dale, who had founded the enterprise together and were once inseparable at such events, sat at different tables.

The next evening the directors met alone for dinner, this time around a single table, in a private room in the Port O Call Restaurant on Front Street. Feeney did not attend but sent Jim Downey to represent him. Everyone at this event recognized that it was a watershed moment for Atlantic. The vote on term limits would be taken the next morning, and the outcome was predetermined. Each of the directors said a few words. Dale appeared sad and reflective. The seventy-five-year-old lawyer had been personally involved in Chuck Feeney's foundation since the early days. He was its architect, its legal brain, the keeper of its secrets during the period of anonymity. He had an attachment and an interest in seeing the enterprise, about which he cared deeply, to its conclusion. He clearly felt it was incongruous to let people go so near the end. The new rule disregarded history and continuity. Anyone dismantling a building needs the wisdom of the original architect, who knows where the pipes and ducts are, and that man was Harvey Dale.

Before the executive session on Tuesday morning, held in a boardroom in the Hamilton Princess, Dale let Smitham know how he felt in no uncertain terms. He would not go quietly.

Feeney, sitting between Smitham and Oechsli, referred the board to his memo recommending an amendment to the bylaws on the grounds of good governance. Dale, who seemed "mad as hell" to one fellow director, argued that the change could not be justified on the grounds of good governance. He told Feeney that if prizes were given for bad governance practices, Feeney would win the gold medal. He pointed out that at the board meeting the previous December, Feeney had failed to tell directors of a commitment he had already made for a very large donation. How could Feeney say this change was motivated by good governance? Feeney retorted, "How do you know I didn't talk about this to other directors?"

Only Mike Sovern sided with Dale. By a majority of nine to two, the board agreed to amend the bylaws to limit the term of directors to fifteen years, effective from the end of each director's three-year term. All directors whose normal three-year term was up for renewal and who had served in aggregate more than fifteen years could not now put their name forward for reelection. These included Harvey Dale and Elizabeth McCormack. McCormack, who had just turned ninety, accepted her fate with grace. Though she had refused three years before to step down at Feeney's behest, she noted now that it should be Feeney's call and he deserved to get what he desired in reforming the board.

Four other directors had served more than fifteen years, but under the new bylaws could stay until their three-year term came up for renewal. These were Mike Sovern, Christine Downton, Cummings Zuill, and Feeney himself. Zuill opted to retire rather than wait for his term to expire. Feeney resigned, as he had promised, though he remained in the foundation as its only member, or shareholder. The board had thus been reduced almost by half in less than a year, from twelve to seven members.

In recognition of long service and to prevent the loss of access to institutional wisdom and memory, Oechsli said that contact would be maintained with, and advice sought from, outgoing board members in an informal way, which was a clear nod to Harvey Dale to ease the blow.

The meeting ended as soon as the decision was made. Dale got up and left the room. There were no words exchanged between him and Feeney, no final handshake.

Mike Sovern, isolated now on the board, had some soul-searching to do. On July 23, he wrote to Peter Smitham announcing that he, too, had decided to resign rather than wait until his term expired in 2014. He explained that he felt uncomfortable about seeming to go along with the removal of directors because they disagreed with the founding chairman. He admired Feeney's model, but accused him of a breach of faith with those directors who devoted years of service to the foundation on the understanding that the board was independent and not subject to the will and whim of a donor who wanted more control. And Feeney's wish to remove Harvey Dale, who had done more than anyone to build Atlantic and had much to contribute, was, he felt, "too cruel by half." To ease the transition, he declared that he would retire on December 31, 2012.

Feeney was unhappy with the idea of Sovern sitting in on board meetings until the end of the year after having said he was leaving. Other directors felt the same. They had not liked the tone of Sovern's letter and felt that he was unfair to Feeney. When Smitham wrote in September asking Mike to consider making his resignation effective immediately, Sovern acquiesced.

Harvey Dale's acquaintances were left in no doubt that he felt he had been treated cruelly. He would point out indignantly that Price Waterhouse had once listed the three most important financial contributions to the foundation as the transfer of the assets in 1984, the subsequent investments made by General Atlantic Partners, and the financial savings of $1.3 billion to $1.5 billion from the tax structures that he, Dale, had put in place. There were no tears shed among members of Feeney's family, however, when they learned of Harvey Dale's departure: Over the years they had nursed a resentment over his role in setting up the foundation in a way that involved their mother signing over all the assets in her name—at a time, as she remembers it, when she was confused and frightened.

Feeney later expressed few regrets about the split of one of the most unique and successful partnerships in American philanthropy. Harvey Dale's failure to persuade Schwarz, McCormack, and Sovern to quit as directors was in his mind unforgivable. He might have put his demand crudely, but he believed that Harvey Dale should have found a way. Dale had drawn up the constitution—he could propose changes. Instead, he sided with those who wanted to sideline the founding donor. Feeney attributed the end of the association to "lots of other things," including his sense that Dale had spoken critically about him a couple of times at board meetings. Commenting to me on the end of his relationship with the lawyer he once declared to be the most influential person in his life, Feeney made a revealing remark: "I guess it happens in business."

Dale had fallen foul of a characteristic of Feeney's that he himself had seen over the years. When a relationship ended with Feeney, there were no half-measures. It was over. One strike and you were out, especially if you were standing in the way of what Feeney felt passionate about doing; he needed people when they could do things for him to achieve his great and ambitious goals, and those who opposed him had to stand aside. "Chuck was intellectually intimidated by Harvey, but over the years Chuck needed his formidable skills as a first-class lawyer, and the partnership had worked effectively through the early days of making money and the first two decades of giving it away," said a friend of both. "Harvey benefited greatly from his association with Chuck, and had Chuck not had Harvey's tax advice and had he not gifted the fruits of his labor to a tax-effective structure, his personal checks would not have amounted, in dollars and impact, to that ultimately achieved by Atlantic Philanthropies."

"The golden days of the foundation were when Chuck and Harvey were working together, and if they had a disagreement, then they would find a way to work around it," noted someone close to Chuck. "But when a bunch of advisers became a board of outsiders, the dynamic changed. Chuck had got Harvey to help him set up the foundation on the assumption that he, Chuck, would always be in control, in the sense of being powerful and impactful. It hadn't worked that way."

No one believed that the role of Chuck Feeney, as the founding donor of Atlantic Philanthropies and its inspirational leader, would be drastically diminished with his own resignation as director. The elastic founding chairman's fund remained in existence, but because any major unplanned initiatives he favored would inevitably be constrained as the funds diminished, Feeney began to push for a speedy end to grant programs and a pruning of staff in the run-up to 2016.

Indeed, since regaining his footing in Atlantic Philanthropies with the departure of Fritz Schwarz as board chairman and Gara LaMarche as chief executive, Feeney had already reasserted himself in dramatic fashion as one of the most risk-taking, innovative entrepreneur-philanthropists in modern times with a bold stroke that shocked every member of the board of his foundation.

CHAPTER

Chuck Feeney's Christmas Present to New York

Chuck Feeney had kept in contact with Cornell presidents over the years. He made the acquaintance of the current holder of the office, Professor David Skorton, at the time of his inauguration in 2006. Skorton, the Wisconsin-born son of an immigrant from Soviet Belarus, shared with Feeney, the descendant of impoverished Irish immigrants in New Jersey, an interest in providing scholarships for low-income students. Tuition and fees for Cornell in 2011–2012 ran to $40,000, far beyond the reach of parents with modest means. Feeney had granted $15 million to the university in 2011 to support the Cornell Tradition fellowship program, bringing the historical aggregate for the program to almost $37 million.

The university president lived upstate in Ithaca but had a New York City residence, supplied by the university, five blocks from Feeney's Upper East Side apartment, and he would occasionally drop round when Chuck and Helga were in town.

To the surprise of those who knew Feeney well, Skorton persuaded him to agree to accept an accolade. The once-secret philanthropist had always declined invitations to accept recognition for his giving. This accolade would not be for his philanthropy, however, but for his business achievements.

Feeney had always been proud of his success as an entrepreneur and agreed to be recognized as Cornell's "Icon of Industry" for 2010.

The award ceremony was held in the American Museum of Natural History at Seventy-ninth Street and Central Park West in New York on June 8 that year. Family members, Cornell professors, and special guests arrived early for a pre-dinner reception with the honoree. They waited in vain for Feeney to appear. He was in a taxi stuck in traffic because of a street parade. He arrived almost two hours late, seeming not in the least put out. The hundreds of guests included several figures from Feeney's early business days. There was a designated table for veterans of Cars International, including Larry Smith, Joe Lyons, Bill Pappas, Charles Fishman, and Bob Matousek, and DFS veterans Peter Fithian and Phil Phong.

Ignoring Feeney's aversion to being lauded for his generosity, Skorton and former Cornell presidents lined up onstage to thank their benefactor profusely. President Emeritus Hunter R. Rawlings III described their favorite alumnus as a paragon of humility and generosity and presented him with a $13 watch, which Feeney accepted with glee, saying, "The award of this Casio is really appreciated because you can always sell these things on eBay."

Chuck's DFS partners Bob Miller, Alan Parker, and Tony Pilaro did not attend. They had gone their separate ways and were no longer the buddies who had made their fortune as "four men in a room," conquering the retail world. Miller held his own party four months later to celebrate the anniversary of the global giant retailer that he and Feeney had founded fifty years earlier. It was staged in Hong Kong's Kai Tak International Airport, the site of the original DFS store. Several hundred guests were entertained by the Haitian singer Wyclef Jean and treated to a short speech from the beaming host about the success of the enterprise he once called his "baby." "DFS has been through tumultuous times, but it has persevered and done well," Miller told the gathering.

To mark the occasion, DFS commissioned *The Moodie Report*, chronicler of the duty-free world, to produce a glossy book on DFS's history. It reported that in opening the first office in Hong Kong half a century before, Miller and Feeney "were writing the first page of what was to become one of the great stories in modern retailing." They had seized the opportunity presented by the emergence of the Japanese as a nation of travelers, and DFS was now targeting the Chinese. According to Toni Belloni, group managing director of the majority shareholder, LVMH, the duty-free company was thriving with a profit margin that fluctuated around 10 percent. (In a subsequent *Moodie Report*, Miller had "unexpectedly soft words" for Chuck Feeney and was said to be "deeply unimpressed" with his own portrayal in *The Billionaire Who Wasn't.*)

David Skorton dropped by Feeney's apartment again early in 2011, asking him to go one step further and deliver the annual Olin Lecture at Cornell on the occasion of the fifty-fifth reunion of the class of '56. The Cornell president knew that Feeney was not cut out to be a public speaker or to give lectures to an audience. Skorton explained that the event could be staged as an informal conversation. "That would be fine," replied Feeney. They agreed on a prearranged question-and-answer format.

On June 10, 2011, seated in easy chairs onstage before a packed Bailey Hall at Cornell, Skorton introduced his guest as the "Sandwich Man" who had become the world's most generous and modest donor. As he spoke, Feeney, wearing a dark blazer and open-neck gray shirt, began searching in his pockets for his glasses and bits of paper. The audience laughed, seeing it as part of an act. Asked by Skorton about what he did after Cornell, Feeney, reading from his notes, said, "I went on, according to this, to . . . " There was more laughter. How did he become rich? asked the university president. "I saw these guys selling everything from soup to nuts, I said, 'Shit, I can do that!'" replied Feeney. "A week later I was there with my sweets and candy, and before I knew it [*reading, deadpan*] I was a billionaire. Woof!" Feeney continued in this manner, sometimes glancing at his scripted dialogue. "The question to be asked by President Skorton here is—what would I have done if I had failed? The answer to that is—unthinkable. I was driven by success. We built a company which wound up with 4,000 employees. People who worked for us were treated fairly. That was part of the early learning game— be right with your staff and employees."

Skorton asked him, "What prompted your shift from making money to giving it away?" Feeney hammed up his reply by reading slowly, "Yes, that's a good question." He looked up and added, "One of the things I thought was that if we didn't have to make money anymore, then we wouldn't have any worries. We started out not making any money anymore, and boy, we had a lot of worries. So I said to myself, I got something wrong here. . . . There's a question here [*reading again*]: 'Did you even have any doubts?' and I can say to you in all honesty I never had anything but doubts. . . . " He concluded with the words he had used so many times before: "The theory of philanthropy is based on the highest and best use of the money you are try-ing to spend. I think we did a good job on that." A member of the audience asked Feeney about the personal risks he took dealing with dangerous para-militaries in Northern Ireland. "I just mentioned to these tough guys that I was from Elizabeth, New Jersey, and that scared the shit out of them," said Feeney. When the session ended, he got a prolonged standing ovation.

Cornell's Skorton at that time was playing for big stakes. He was involved in a once-in-a-generation opportunity to achieve two of his main goals: to estab-lish a campus in a major city and to increase Cornell's involvement in the all-important technology field. New York, a four-hour drive away, was the obvious location for the campus. Cornell already had a footprint there in the form of an important medical center. The city was also home to 50,000 of its graduates.

The opportunity came early in 2011 when Mayor Michael Bloomberg invited universities in the United States and around the world to bid for a contract to create a $2 billion applied sciences campus in New York. The proposed sites included Roosevelt Island, the two-mile strip of land in the East River that was once home to an insane asylum and smallpox hospital and was just a short subway ride or cable-car trip from midtown Manhat-tan. Mayor Bloomberg's ambition was to transform the Big Apple into a "beehive of innovation and discovery," a center of entrepreneurship and technology to rival Silicon Valley in California. Seth W. Pinsky, president of the New York City Economic Development Corporation, predicted that such a technology center would be as transformational for New York City as the opening of the Erie Canal that had connected the Hudson River to the Great Lakes nearly two centuries earlier and helped make New York a financial powerhouse. The deadline for proposals was set for October 28, 2011.

Strong bids were submitted by several of the top ten American universi-ties, including Harvard, Columbia, and Stanford. As the incubator for tech-nology innovation in Silicon Valley, and with an established entrepreneurial ecosystem, Stanford was the media favorite. Mayor Bloomberg expressed his delight that Stanford was competing and said publicly in Boston that the Silicon Valley university was "desperate" to win. Cornell, whose own engi-neering and computer science programs ranked in the nation's top ten, began lobbying intensively for the deal, but because of the high-grade com-petition, it seemed to face long odds.

Skorton told Feeney of his ambitions in one of his visits to the philanthropist's apartment early in 2011. "I liked to tell Chuck what's happening on campus," he told me later. "Chuck is a man of lively interests. He has the intelligence, insight, and impatience to get things moving. He seemed from the beginning positive about the proposal. He asked that I keep him up to date on it. I never thought that there was any chance he would be interested philanthropically. I was not thinking about him being a contributor. But each time we spoke he was interested in what was happening." The Cornell president also briefed the then-chairman of Atlantic Philanthropies, Fritz Schwarz, at his office at the Brennan Center on the Avenue of the Americas, about his plans.

In early summer, Skorton gave Feeney a summary paper of about twelve pages that Feeney copied and handed out to the usual suspects, such as Chris Oechsli and Jim Downey, as well as Dave Smith from the InterPacific office. It was his way of communicating to those closest to him what was occupying his thoughts. He was, by now, smitten with the concept.

In October, Cornell strengthened its case by announcing that it had secured a partner in the bid, Technion-Israel Institute of Technology in Haifa, Israel, with which it had been in months of secret negotiations. Known as Israel's MIT, Technion was at the center of a world-renowned high-tech business zone and had produced three Nobel Prize laureates since 2004. Under the agreement with Technion, Cornell would try to raise the money for initial construction work if it got the contract.

At the end of November, the leaders of five short-listed institutions, including Cornell, were invited to make detailed presentations at the New York City Economic Development Corporation office in downtown Manhattan. Skorton was scheduled to appear last, on December 2.

A few days beforehand, Skorton dropped by Feeney's apartment and told him that one of his concerns was informing the city officials how Cornell would finance the first phase of the project, in which the capital costs of buildings and operating funds would come to an estimated $350 million. Because of the extent of its existing leverage, Cornell had stopped borrowing money for bricks-and-mortar projects. It would have to raise the funds elsewhere.

By Skorton's account, Feeney said he would consider a gift to make the project happen.

"Chuck, it would be great if I could tell City Hall that someone anonymous will make a contribution," said Skorton.

"You can say that," replied Feeney.

Skorton did not feel, at this stage, that he should press the philanthropist for a figure. However, Skorton returned to Feeney's apartment on the evening of Thursday, December 1, just twelve hours before his presentation. He wanted this time to talk about the size of Feeney's commitment. He sat on the sofa in the small living room, with Chuck and Helga in easy chairs.

"Chuck, it would be really terrific if I could give [City Hall] some indication of the magnitude of the pledge," he said.

Feeney looked him in the eye. "Tell them we can support the effort up to $350 million."

"I want to ask you to give me that again!" said Skorton.

"That's what I said."

Skorton looked over at Helga. "Is that what he just said?"

"Yes, that's what he said," replied Helga in her slight German accent.

Overwhelmed with emotion, Skorton got up and gave the Feeneys a hug. He had all but secured the largest once-off grant from Chuck's foundation, and one of the largest donations in the history of higher education anywhere in the world. It would not just level the playing field but tip it sharply in Cornell's favor.

The next day, Skorton made his presentation to Seth Pinsky, Robert K. Steel, deputy mayor for economic development, and other municipal officials. He ended his submission by announcing, "I want to tell you all that we have a $350 million gift." There was a long silence in the room. This was a game-changer. Steel said afterwards, "It's pretty breathtaking when other schools are talking about the challenges of fund-raising, and one of your strongest competitors says on the first-phase financing: 'Done.'"

Skorton returned to Ithaca that Friday in high spirits. An accomplished jazz musician, he chilled out by accompanying Billy Joel on flute during Joel's rendition of "She's Always a Woman" at a sellout concert at Bailey Hall. "As far as I was concerned, Chuck's word was as good as a contract," said Skorton. Nevertheless, he telephoned Feeney to ask if he would sign a letter of confirmation. He would send him a draft. Feeney agreed to look at it. In New York the following Monday, the Cornell president faxed Feeney a copy of the proposed text to his Upper East Side apartment.

That same day, December 5, unaware of what was going on, Atlantic directors gathered in the conference room at Varick Street for a two-day quarterly board meeting with Peter Smitham in the chair. For Chris Oechsli, it was his first board meeting since being confirmed in his position as president and chief executive officer of Atlantic Philanthropies in succession to Gara LaMarche. Feeney attended but said nothing about his commitment to Cornell's president. It wasn't until the second day that Feeney brought up Cornell. "I'm interested in this," he remarked, holding up the Cornell-Technion prospectus, a ring-bound volume as hefty as a coffee-table book on proposals for the construction of the technology park on Roosevelt Island. That was all he said.

"Chuck did not convey that he had communicated to Skorton a willingness or even an intent to do something," recalled a director. "Everyone just thought, 'This sounds interesting, quite exciting, we'd be interested in hearing more.'"

The following day, Wednesday, December 7, Feeney's close adviser Jim Downey called Skorton on his cell phone. "Chuck would like to deliver that piece of paper," he said. He asked Skorton to meet Feeney in the lobby of the Cornell Club near Grand Central Terminal.

Skorton arrived at the club with Peter C. Meinig, outgoing chairman of the Cornell University Board of Trustees, and Charlie Phlegar, vice president for alumni affairs and development. They greeted Feeney and Downey and spread themselves around the divans and armchairs beneath the wood-paneled ceiling in the lobby. Feeney had signed the letter. It was a personal guarantee, from him, of up to $350 million of Atlantic Philanthropies' funds for Cornell, though the foundation was not specifically mentioned. He handed it over. Recalled Skorton, "I was again very emotional, as was everyone else."

Feeney was reinvigorated. This was like the old days, when he and his DFS partners were putting vast sums on the table for duty-free concessions. This was the biggest single amount he had ever wagered as a philanthropist. "The worst thing to do was lose," he once remarked about an excessive sum that DFS had paid for a franchise. Now Feeney "really wanted us to win the bid," Skorton would recall.

The next morning Downey and Feeney met Oechsli and Peter Smitham in the street-level coffee shop at the Atlantic building and gave them copies of the letter. They asked Feeney what the guarantee *up to* $350 million meant. He responded: "It means the full $350 million."

It was a fait accompli. Before the upheaval at Atlantic, the board had not been favorably disposed to Feeney's moods and suggestions. His internal critics might have pushed back against such a large pledge for Cornell. The crisis at Atlantic had been all about respecting and enabling Feeney's initiatives and that had been resolved in dramatic fashion. There could be no question of going back on Feeney's promise if Cornell-Technion won the bid. Everyone now held their breath to await City Hall's decision.

A week later, on Friday, December 16, Skorton was driving through the Pocono Mountains in northeastern Pennsylvania, en route from New York City to Ithaca with his wife Robin L. Davisson, when a call came to his cell phone through the car's Bluetooth connection. It was his office ringing to alert him that Stanford had made a stunning announcement: It was withdrawing its bid, as negotiations with New York City had broken down the day before. The Cornell president called Oechsli and got his go-ahead to announce publicly that his university had secured a major commitment from an unidentified donor. He explained that he did not want it to look as if Stanford had simply dropped out and that the contract, if Cornell got it, was going to go to the second-best. Within hours of Stanford's withdrawal, Cornell announced publicly the equally stunning news that it had received a $350 million gift from an anonymous donor to support its bid to build "Silicon Valley East" in New York.

That evening, Seth Pinsky and Bob Steel came on the phone to Skorton. They told him in confidence that Cornell-Technion had won and that Mayor Bloomberg would make the news public at a press conference at two o'clock on Monday.

On Saturday morning, Skorton called Feeney to tip him off about the news. He also got Technion-Israel's president, Peretz Lavie, on his cell phone in Haifa, Israel, where he was out walking. "Guess where you will be on Monday," he said. Lavie realized what was up. "I guess I will be with you in New York," he replied.

Oechsli urgently arranged a special board meeting, conducted by conference call early on Monday, to tell the directors of the momentous news that was about to break. That book that Feeney had held up was about to become a grant! One board member wondered aloud if Feeney had been railroaded by Skorton into making the pledge. There was some dismay that

Feeney had undermined his new chief executive by not taking Oechsli into his confidence before signing the letter to Skorton. At the same time, the directors recognized that the investment was a mold-breaker. With the City of New York behind it, the project was a good risk and the technology park would be a monument to Feeney. As one put it, "Chuck did the right thing the wrong way." An associate commented: "He was saying, 'Listen, this is the way I think money should be spent. This is the way Atlantic should be spending, and I am doing it,' and we all agreed it was fine." When a director later suggested to Feeney that it was a great thing he was doing, Feeney replied, "It's not a great thing. It's a great opportunity."

For Feeney, something very important had finally been acknowledged. "It's my money" is how he expressed it to me one morning in Dublin shortly afterwards, raising his arm high and pointing down at himself. Feeney's gift was the largest in Cornell University's history and the second-largest by any individual in the United States that year, trumped only by a massive $800 million pledge from Alice Walton to create an endowment for the Crystal Bridges Museum of American Art in Arkansas. The grant to Cornell brought Feeney's total donations to the university up to $1 billion.

That afternoon, in the Weill Cornell Medical College in Manhattan, flanked by David Skorton and Peretz Lavie, Mayor Bloomberg pronounced the Cornell-Technion consortium to be the victors. Cornell had been given the contract partly because they "wanted it the most," the mayor said. Theirs was also the largest proposal in terms of square footage, enrollment, and faculty population and had the most ambitious timeline. Over three decades, it would generate $23 billion in economic activity, 20,000 construction jobs, 8,000 permanent jobs, and 600 spin-off companies. And Cornell had cash for that first phase—from an unnamed donor.

The news that the enormous gift to Cornell came from a mysterious benefactor was a challenge to the New York media. It wasn't long before the phones at Varick Street were ringing. The origin of the funding was confirmed on Atlantic's Web site at 8:45 P.M. In a statement, Oechsli announced that the grant was a game-changing investment, "squarely rooted in the best traditions of Atlantic's support for bold investments in health, science, and education at select institutions." Within an hour, the *New York Times* and the *Wall Street Journal* broke the news of the donor's identity on their own Web sites.

Feeney's $350 million gift promoted some debate as to whether it did actually swing the contract for Cornell. Deputy Mayor Bob Steel told the *New*

York Times that in the final two weeks Cornell-Technion "kept putting on more and more attractive aspects to what was already quite a good proposal." Clearly the $350 million up front was the most attractive new aspect of all. One of Bloomberg's principal advisers in making the final choice, Charlie Kim, founder and CEO of the New York–based e-commerce company Next Jump, claimed that a plurality of the mayor's advisory committee recommended Cornell from the beginning. Stanford's proposal was overwhelmingly strong and rich in historic knowledge, past accomplishments, and detailed plans for the future, Kim told *Wired* magazine, but "Stanford was inherently conflicted from day one." New York City wished to be the best in the world, not second-best to California. "If you want to be number one, Silicon Valley has to be number two."

The media coverage of the donation was overwhelmingly positive, and several publications "discovered" Chuck Feeney. However, the *Non-Profit Quarterly,* while not finding fault with Feeney's "amazing generosity," pointed out that his gift to Cornell was larger than the endowments of almost every one of the 105 historically black colleges and universities in the United States, and "it still feels like even among institutions of higher education the one percent get richer and the 99 percent trail."

There was no hint in the reporting that the enormous grant came at the conclusion of a bitter struggle within Atlantic Philanthropies and that Chuck Feeney might not have been able to act with such freedom if the outcome of that struggle had been different. However, on January 3, 2012, the *Chronicle of Philanthropy* noted that, with Gara LaMarche gone and with Chris Oechsli as its new leader, "eyes are on Atlantic to see if the fund started by Charles Feeney . . . will continue to make big grants to progressive advocacy groups as it follows a path to spending all of its $2-billion endowment by 2016."

Feeney began to involve himself in the plans for the project that would transform the run-down, eleven-acre New York City site on the East River. This was what he liked doing best. "I think the Cornell–East Coast tech center is a perfect example of something my dad loves, and it will have a huge impact on New York and in the tech field," his daughter Diane commented approvingly.

Although Feeney was a changed person, and more content now with his life, he stubbornly declined to ease up and look after himself, and he continued to have health issues. During a visit to Ireland the following month, he was admitted to St. Vincent's Hospital in Dublin with threatened pneumonia. He spent the week in bed, where visitors found him studying Cornell-Technion's 220-page, plastic-backed, illustrated prospectus for the applied sciences campus on Roosevelt Island, checking out the spectacular designs for the complex created by Los Angeles–based architect Thom Mayne. As soon as he recovered he headed back to New York.

Giving Away
the Family Silver

It is their call what the rich do with their money," Chuck Feeney once said. "I would not want to impose my thoughts on any rich person—he can keep it all or spend it all. If he doesn't find anything wrong with buying big yachts, fine, more power to him." But Feeney believed that the rich should start giving early in life, when still full of energy and drive. "It's a lot of work when you are over sixty-five to start a giving program. It doesn't happen overnight. If you want to give it away, think about giving it away while you are alive, because you'll get a lot more satisfaction than if you wait until you're dead. Besides, it's a lot more fun."

When I asked him to elaborate, he produced a newspaper cutting about unhappy American billionaires, which concluded with the story of how the miserly Ebenezer Scrooge in Charles Dickens's *A Christmas Carol* found to his astonishment that giving money away is life's most pleasurable act. "Read it," he commanded.

Feeney had an opportunity to meet several dozen American billionaires to make these points after his role as a secret giver became known. He attracted the attention of Microsoft founder Bill Gates and Berkshire Hathaway investor Warren Buffett when they started looking for ways to persuade other holders of vast fortunes to become philanthropists like themselves. In early 2009, they invited Feeney to a private seminar and dinner with a dozen of America's top billionaires, hosted in New York by David Rockefeller, the ninety-four-year-old patriarch of the Rockefeller family. It was the start of what *Fortune* magazine called the biggest fund-raising drive in history. The meeting was held on Tuesday, May 5, in the secluded President's House at Rockefeller University, overlooking the East River. The seventy-eight-year-old Feeney found himself sitting around a table with Gates, Buffett, television host Oprah Winfrey, senior chairman of the Blackstone Group Peter G. Peterson, founder of Tiger Management Corp. Julian Robertson, CNN founder Ted Turner, Sun Life billionaire Eli Broad and his wife Edythe, John Morgridge of Cisco and his wife Tashia, New York Mayor Michael Bloomberg, investor George Soros, and David Rockefeller and his sixty-eight-year-old son David Rockefeller Jr. Their combined net worth was something in the region of $130 billion.

Like Chuck Feeney before him, Bill Gates had been impressed by the writings of Andrew Carnegie when making his transition from entrepreneur to philanthropist. The Bill & Melinda Gates Foundation had become the largest transparently operated charitable foundation in the world, with annual giving of about $3 billion, mainly to world health. Buffett, the world's richest man, had pledged to give most of his vast fortune to the Gates's foundation. Their letter of invitation emphasized the urgent need to plan for the future in a world facing recession. In the United States, the 18,000 U.S. taxpayers with adjusted gross income of $10 million or more reported giving less than 6 percent of their income to charity, according to *Fortune*'s senior editor-at-large, Carol Loomis, in an analysis of the Gates-Buffet project. Clearly there was much scope for improvement in American philanthropy.

Warren Buffet played master of ceremonies. Each of the assembled billionaires was asked to speak for fifteen minutes on their philosophy of giving and to tell stories of their philanthropic endeavor. It took three hours to go around the table. Several of the mega-rich guests expressed reservations about their ability to persuade other billionaires to part with the bulk of their wealth, worrying that their children would take exception to giving away the family silver.

Feeney was unique among the gathering: He had already given all his money away. When it was his turn to speak, he emphasized his favorite themes: Money should be put to the highest and best use, and doing so gives the donor much pleasure.

Shortly afterwards, Feeney met his publisher friend Niall O'Dowd in New York. On May 18, O'Dowd broke the story of the secret meeting on his Web site, IrishCentral.com. He accurately listed all the participants—except Feeney—leaving Gates and Buffet in little doubt about the identity of the leaker. As a result of the disclosure, they imposed a "cone of silence" on future dinners planned by the group to work out ways to persuade tight-fisted billionaires to open their wallets.

A year later, after two more private dinners without any leaks, the idea emerged of getting the mega-wealthy to sign a "Giving Pledge." Gates, Buffet, and Rockefeller began sending emails and letters to the wealthiest individuals in America, asking them and their families to sign a pledge committing the majority of their wealth to philanthropy—ideally 50 percent of their net worth—during their lifetimes. At the time, *Fortune* estimated the net worth of the Forbes 400 to be around $1.2 trillion: Giving half of their net worth while living or at death would amount to $600 billion. It was a big ask. In 2007, the 400 biggest taxpayers had given just 11 percent of their income to charity.

The dinner guests were all asked to sign the pledge. Feeney quite logically felt that he could not sign a pledge to give away his wealth when he had already done so. He asked Harvey Dale, with whom he was still on reasonably cordial terms at the time, to respond to Gates. On June 24, 2010, Dale talked to Gates, then wrote a formal reply. While Feeney supported the effort, Dale explained, he had long kept a fairly low profile. "In addition, as you know, he gave away virtually all his wealth more than twenty-five years ago, so it makes little sense for him now to sign a pledge to this effect." He hoped Bill Gates would understand Feeney's decision not to do so.

Gates was "devastated" when he received the rejection, according to one of his staff. The Microsoft billionaire told me subsequently that he had really enjoyed getting to know Chuck Feeney, and that he had really wanted Feeney's support. He was struck by Feeney's complete dedication to using his wealth to benefit others, and he and Melinda were inspired by his example. He had praised Feeney in a PBS interview with Charlie Rose. "People like Chuck Feeney have done amazing things," he told the talk show host. "If you look, there are models." Gates was most touched at the dinners by people like Chuck Feeney who had given almost everything away. "That's quite a phenomenal story." Buffet, who also appeared on the PBS program, said that they were hoping that people would pledge half of their wealth, though some people would commit more; as he pointed out, "Chuck Feeney already has."

Feeney was preoccupied at the time by the conflict in Atlantic Philanthropies and the harm it might cause in the world of philanthropy. Now he fretted about whether he had done the right thing with Gates. He suspected that the Gates-Buffet initiative would not achieve its goals, but the aim of persuading the wealthy to give while alive was good. He regretted the preemptory tone of Harvey Dale's letter and decided that he should go and talk to Gates himself. He asked for a private meeting, and it was set for January 11, 2011, in Seattle.

On the eve of the meeting, as I sat with him after lunch at a trestle table outside the Sonoma Estate Restaurant on a Sunday day trip to Napa Valley in northern California, Feeney expressed doubts about the sincerity of some of the billionaires who were signing the Giving Pledge. "It's only a promise, not a commitment," he said. He suspected that the fifty-eight mega-rich individuals who had signed the pledge up to then had lawyers tying up most of their wealth. Among them were billionaires already committed to giving but now receiving what a commentator in the *Wall Street Journal* called "billionaire P.R."—getting good media attention for what was already done. One of the pledgers, Wall Street icon Ted Forstmann, had commented that those not on the list were "both a billionaire and a jerk." Feeney's blue eyes registered concern about whether Gates and Buffett were going about things the right way. What would happen if a rich person got cancer or had a heart attack before committing his or her wealth irrevocably? The Gates Foundation was committed to spending all its money within fifty years of the death of the last member of the trio of Bill and Melinda Gates and Warren Buffett. How long did Bill Gates think he would live? In those fifty years, who would administer the estate? A board of directors? They might change their minds about what the original donors intended.

The next day Feeney and Chris Oechsli took the one-and-a-half-hour flight from San Francisco to Seattle. They met Bill Gates in his private office with a view over Lake Washington, with Oechsli and Olivia Leland, administrative manager for the Giving Pledge, sitting in. The billionaire and the billionaire who wasn't clearly liked and respected each other. Dressed casually in a pullover sports sweater, Gates explained to his guest that after the inaugural dinner in May 2009, he had focused on Feeney as the leader in the effort and wanted very much to have him sign on. "You set the best example of all," he said. "You were way, way ahead of all of us. It would be fantastic if you would join us." He expressed great admiration for what Feeney had done and the length of time he had remained anonymous. Feeney laughed. He was given credit for a lot of anonymous giving that wasn't necessarily coming from him, he said, because he became "synonymous with anonymous." Feeney explained that he had felt it was inappropriate to sign the Giving Pledge given that he had already made the commitment to philanthropy twenty-five years earlier. But he promised, "We'll do anything," to help the effort. As they spoke, Feeney reached into his plastic bag, took out a bottle of Robitussin cough medicine, and passed it to Oechsli, who was suffering from a cold.

Gates told Feeney that there would be a meeting of the principal participants in May at which they would begin to address general questions, such as the role of children in a family foundation, the life of the foundation, the size of staff and administrative expenses, and general areas of giving such as health and education. He speculated that there were three reasons why more prospective donors had not signed on: Some had inherited wealth and felt a moral obligation to pass on the body of their wealth to the next generation; very few of these people were signatories to the Pledge. Some wanted privacy and were concerned about being solicited for donations. A third category of prospective donors were undecided. He noted that, from the first meeting, other than Feeney, only George Soros and Oprah Winfrey had not signed on. Oprah had told him she wasn't sure she wanted to be grouped with a bunch of "old white guys." Gates asked Feeney to come to the meeting, which would be held at a resort in Arizona. It would be paid for by himself and Warren Buffett. Chuck replied with a chuckle that he had never been known to turn down a free meal.

Before leaving, and in the light of the ongoing interaction between Feeney and Atlantic's directors at the time, Oechsli asked Bill Gates if he had thoughts about the role of "outside advisers" in running a foundation. The Microsoft founder said that they had tried this with limited success. "We discovered they bring an agenda and ego of their own." He said he was aware of an article on the subject in the *Seattle Times*, written by philanthropy commentator Pablo Eisenberg, a senior fellow at the Georgetown Public Policy Institute. Eisenberg had argued that the Gates's foundation would be well-advised to have a board of four to eight outside directors to provide it with "that minimal measure of public accountability that taxpayers and the public deserve," given that what a U.S. foundation had in endowment was really tax dollars and should be directed to some degree by a more democratic decision-making process. Bill and Melinda Gates had no board, other than three trustees—Bill and Melinda Gates themselves and Warren Buffet—and only Bill and Melinda "shaped and approved" the overall direction and strategy.

Whether to have an outside board and whether to involve their children have been recurring questions for philanthropists and their descendants. In the aftermath of the crisis in Atlantic Philanthropies, Chuck Feeney's family wondered if being excluded had been such a good idea after all. Watching events unfold at Atlantic with increasing concern for the health and well-being of their father, they had thought about how they could have participated and supported him if one or two of them had been on the board. This possibility had, in fact, been left open at the time of the divorce proceedings with Danielle in a letter dated December 30, 1990, and signed by Feeney, Harvey Dale, Frank Mutch, and Cummings Zuill—then the only directors of the foundation—but it had largely been forgotten. The letter asserted that Feeney's descendants could be given a role in the foundation at a future date, though this was "not an obligation, rather an open door." His children had not sought to be directors then, believing themselves insufficiently experienced, but they now saw other foundations—like Alan Parker's Oak Foundation—doing some good things with only family members on the board.

There were, however, well-established drawbacks to family-only foundations. It was difficult to attract the most talented people to run them, as able executives would want a high degree of flexibility and responsibility. Other rich people had found unique ways to exercise control without involving either family or directors. George Soros gave his foundation a limited endowment that was funded along the way: He would finance a project for a period of time, but if he didn't want to continue it, he simply stopped. His method of ultimate control was to turn the tap on and off.

Feeney was now convinced that the best philanthropic model was one that allowed the founding donor to set strategy. In a submission to the Atlantic board, he noted pointedly that the number-one guiding principle of the Gates Foundation was: "This is a family foundation driven by the interests and passions of the Gates family." Noted a senior Atlantic executive, "On the big question of who gets to decide how to spend the money,

whether Chuck, the Atlantic board, Fritz, Gara, Bill Gates, it's so much eas-
ier to avoid involving others and to simply control decisions. The board
wrestled very seriously with the issue. Ultimately they decided that the living founder had important moral rights and some veto rights, but not on
everything, every time. Chris Oechsli's job consists of getting that balance
right."

Feeney had never thought it reasonable to ask his children to spend the
rest of their lives coping with immense wealth, and their children and
grandchildren after that. "Right from the very beginning, I felt this just
would give them a destination in life that they haven't earned per se, and
that I would be imposing on them," he commented. He saw how some
family-run foundations were abused by later generations. "He really believes
that wealth corrupts," remarked Cummings Zuill. "He believes it ruins families and individuals." In Juliette's words: "He realized that not all progeny
have the same values, interests, or capabilities."

Feeney nevertheless wanted to involve his children in giving. He had set
up a family philanthropic foundation in Bermuda in 1990 that got an
injection of $40 million at the time of his divorce from Danielle in 1991.
Called the French American Charitable Trust (FACT), it was run by Diane
and made grants promoting a more egalitarian society and aggressively persuading other foundations to give away more money. In 2004, the board of
directors—consisting of the five children; their mother, Danielle; Bruce
and Margaret Hern from Sterling Management in Bermuda, and family financial adviser Jean Karoubi—decided to distribute its endowment and
spend down as a one-generation philanthropy. With new foundations
being created for future needs, "we felt that we would have much more impact as a $4 million a year foundation than as a $2 million a year foundation," explained Diane. The trust issued its last grants in 2011, many of
which were aimed at strengthening grantee organizations' ability to raise
funds themselves.

Before leaving Seattle, Chuck Feeney promised Bill Gates that he could
offer much insight at the May meeting or along the way into "what we did
right, what we did wrong," at Atlantic, adding, "I have learned from experience that no good deed goes unpunished." He undertook to work on a letter that could be taken as his signing on to the Pledge project. "You are the
exemplar of all of this effort," Gates replied. "We would be super happy to
have your help."

With the aid of Chris Oechsli and Jim Downey, Feeney drafted a document that was sent to Bill Gates on February 3, 2011. He could not pledge to give what he had already given, he wrote, but he wanted now to add his personal challenge for Giving Pledge donors to fully engage in sustained philanthropic efforts during their lifetimes and not to postpone their giving or personal engagement. "I cannot think of a more personally rewarding and appropriate use of wealth than to give while one is living—to personally devote oneself to meaningful efforts to improve the human condition." Intelligent philanthropic support "can have greater value and impact today than if they are delayed when the needs are greater." He did not have the answers to the many challenges facing those who chose to contribute their wealth to philanthropic activities. But he had almost thirty years of personal and institutional experience engaging with the wide range of philanthropic issues and choices, and he would like to pass on his experience to the Giving Pledge effort.

"Fundamental to all philanthropic efforts are choices about grant-making focus and strategy, which naturally are strongly influenced by one's passions and interests, as well as one's perception of how best to achieve good value and lasting impact with the intended grant funds. This typically is a frequently-revisited process as one learns and gains perspective from experience and granting opportunities evolve. Another key element is the myriad of decisions associated with how to conduct grant-making, such as the nature, size and cost of support staff and operations.

"Critically, one must also navigate the complexities inherent in establishing an appropriate governance and long-term leadership structure to carry out one's philanthropic intentions. This incorporates many aspects, such as whether or not to institutionalize a set of guiding principles; the size, role and scope of authority of an outside board, if any; the involvement of children and other family members; and the participation and function of outside advisors—and the approach decided upon must stand the test of time.

"Thoughtful and effective philanthropy requires that the above issues, and more, be addressed with the same acumen, creativity and tenacity that many of us learned and applied in our business careers."

The letter was published in full on the Giving Pledge Web site. "Long before the Giving Pledge, Chuck Feeney was a role model for his fellow philanthropists," Gates told me in an email. "As others read his letter, he will have an even greater impact."

By April 2013, Bill and Melinda Gates and Warren Buffet had recruited 105 Giving Pledge members ranging in age from twenty-seven (Facebook cofounders Dustin Moskovitz and Mark Zuckerberg) to ninety-six (David Rockefeller).

Feeney attended the meeting at the Miraval Resort in Tucson, Arizona, in early May 2011, where about forty philanthropists spent a day and a half discussing their mistakes and methods of giving. Gates asked Chuck, as a role model, to lead a session for the group. "It was a unique opportunity for us to hear directly from him about why he decided to give it all away, his philosophy of giving, how he got started, and how he manages his giving," recalled Gates. "I know I learned a lot, and many of the other pledgers talked about how great it was to hear from someone who has a great passion for philanthropy and doesn't just talk about giving while living but has really put it into practice. Chuck Feeney's story is instructive for many reasons. Chuck has accomplished so much with Atlantic Philanthropies—in every-thing from education to medicine and in so many countries throughout the world. It is great to have such a tangible source for philanthropists to learn from his story and understand his philosophy of giving. As he points out, none of us have all the answers. But by being part of this group, we talk about common experiences, hear each other's stories, lessons learned. We are all smarter about giving because we are sharing with each other. Each of the pledgers is at different stages in their philanthropy—some have already given away the majority, while some are just getting started—it is especially important that we help each other and share our stories."

Warren Buffet described Feeney to the media afterwards as the spiritual leader of the group. "He wants his last check to bounce," said Buffet.

The James Bond
of Philanthropy

Chuck Feeney's face would light up with pleasure when he walked around a hospital and saw babies in incubators that actually worked, when he donned a surgical gown to watch an eye doctor restore a patient's sight, when he saw new hospital wards with one patient to a bed where there had been three, when he watched disadvantaged kids working on computer terminals, or when he looked out his hotel window in Vietnam and saw masses of motor scooter riders wearing crash helmets—the result of an Atlantic program to develop the manufacture of safety head gear in the country and advocate their use.

Countless people across the globe—in the United States, Europe, the Asia Pacific region, Australia, and Africa—owe Chuck Feeney their sight, their health, their education, or their life. He has made possible advances in cancer and other medical research and funded heart clinics and eye hospitals. Dozens of children's, aging, health, and human rights organizations thrive on programs aided by Feeney's wealth. Throughout the world, countless numbers of students spend part of every day in one of the scores of academic buildings, sports halls, or dormitories that his philanthropy has funded. Many of them are there because Feeney provided their scholarships.

The most treasured dividend from his giving has been the satisfaction of seeing people use a building he helped finance. He might drop into a library and simply watch students working late in the evening. "I just sit there and pick up a magazine to read." Friends tease him that he does this because it's free.

"Wealth brings responsibilities," said Feeney. "People have to determine themselves whether they feel an obligation to use some of their wealth to improve life for their fellow human beings rather than create problems for future generations."

Among history's notable businessmen and philanthropists, Chuck Feeney stands out for several reasons. Starting from nothing, he built a vast fortune, and then, in a single act, at the height of his powers, he transferred almost all of it, irrevocably, to his charitable foundation. Feeney's philanthropic model is unique in its combination of size, offshore location, freedom of action, flexibility, anonymity, limited life span, willingness to make big bets, and global impact. It is a philanthropic landmark of the new century.

Not only did he create one of the biggest and most successful philanthropies in the world, but he himself often found the countries, the institutions, and the people to support and then went out to "kick the tires," as he liked to say. It is a paradox that in a world afflicted by poverty and disease, a big problem facing philanthropists is finding causes where the money will make a difference. "Spending is not a big problem, but spending it meaningfully is," reflected Feeney. He brought his entrepreneurial acumen to the causes he felt passionate about and helped build organizations to become self-reliant. He leveraged money and favors and created networks of people across the world to support each other.

He always showed the greatest respect for his beneficiaries. He went to their premises. He never asked them to come to him. He meant it when he said thanks and almost resented being thanked himself. He would say to university presidents and hospital administrators, "It's you we have to thank for doing good things with the money." For example, when Feeney turned up at the opening in Brisbane in December 2012 of the Queensland Institute of Medical Research, which was partly funded by AP, he simply remarked, "I want to say thanks for the kindness I have received here." As always, he made a stab at humor to cover his shyness. According to the *Courier Mail* report of the event: "'My wife is mad at me because I forgot to wash my pants today,' the eighty-two-year-old quipped, wearing a pair of slightly-crumpled camel-coloured trousers." On reading this, an associate commented with a laugh, "He can change the world but he can't change his pants!"

By giving away his fortune, personally overseeing donations so that the money was put to the best use, and determining that Atlantic Philanthropies should spend itself out of existence, Chuck Feeney ensured his personal legacy as the champion of giving while living, at a point in history when individual wealth was soaring. "Chuck's gift to philanthropy is his challenge to high-net-worth individuals to apply both their wealth and their considerable personal skills to making a difference in people's lives now, in the donor's lifetime," said Chris Oechsli. "His legacy, and that of Atlantic, will be an example of how to do this effectively. Among his distinctive approaches is a willingness to invite collaborators to respond to ideas but to approach all such endeavors with high expectations. He initiates fluid, nimble, and intense collaborations to realize an entrepreneurial initiative—to bring it to life. He seeks, even demands, with Socratic rigor, engagement in the process, clarity about outcomes, and excellence in execution. His simple but powerful exhortation—"What do we have to show for it?"—embodies the philanthropy-speak of objectives, theories of change, impact, outcomes, metrics, and sustainability. It is an approach and experience that speaks to successful business entrepreneurs looking to apply their vigor and skills to helping improve the lives of others. Effective philanthropy—in Atlantic's case, achieving lasting changes in the lives of people who have been disadvantaged by circumstances that are not of their own making—is not easy. The dynamics between a formidable entrepreneur and the philanthropic vehicle he creates, with a staff seeking to discern and execute on an intense vision, are not successfully managed by those committed to rigid or singular plans or vague ideas, nor by the faint of heart. Chuck has raised the bar for philanthropy and philanthropists—and has made it clear by example that there is no greater personal reward in life than to fully engage in these endeavors during one's lifetime."

By the turn of the century, the New Jersey native, who in his twenties had set out to make his fortune with little more than a few hundred dollars from his GI scholarship, had far exceeded the giving of his philanthropic icon, Andrew Carnegie. The steel baron donated $350 million up to his death in 1919, equivalent to $3 billion in the year 2000, according to the *New York Times*. By mid-2012, Chuck Feeney's foundation had made donations to education, science, medical research, health care, aging, and civil society worth $6.2 billion, with the total likely to exceed $7.5 billion by the time the last check is written. (It won't bounce, Oechsli promises.) Like Gandhi, who said, "My life is my message," Feeney has lived up to Andrew Carnegie's advice that a man of wealth should not only leave nothing behind but set an example "of modest, unostentatious living, shunning display or extravagance."

The year 2016, when the foundation is due to close, will mark Feeney's eighty-fifth birthday, and he planned to live until then to see it all given away, he told me over lunch in FX Buckley's in Dublin in February 2012 as he splashed water into his customary glass of Chardonnay. He pushed a small cutting from the *Financial Times* across the table that had caught his eye. The headline said: "I can't imagine not working until I die, so my ambition is to live a long time." "I see my life in five-year segments," he said, "and I see myself living at least another five years." That would give him enough time to see the foundation close its doors and complete his goal of giving while living.

In April 2012, he accepted the Medal of the University of California at San Francisco as "a key visionary behind the creation of the UCSF Mission Bay campus, a magnet for the growing biotechnology industry in San Francisco." He arrived for the presentation at the campus wearing a dark jacket and open-neck blue-check shirt, accompanied by Helga, in an elegant gray suit and silk scarf, and his children Patrick and Caroleen and friend Bob Matousek. A video broadcast to guests showed Feeney paying an inspection visit to the UCSF Helen Diller Family Comprehensive Cancer Center. A commentator described the scene. "The gentleman on the right is at UCSF for a checkup. The security guard doesn't recognize him and so asks for an ID. . . . He's done it again. Chuck Feeney, the legendary secret billionaire, has avoided attention. You see, Chuck is checking up on the powerhouse he helped to create, USCF Mission Bay."

Feeney eventually agreed to accept an award in Ireland as well. He had always declined offers of honorary degrees from the universities he had helped build and develop. But in April the provost of Trinity College Dublin, Patrick Prendergast, wrote to the Irish prime minister, Enda Kenny, pointing out that Feeney, with his support for higher education and the peace process, had brought about a transformation on the entire island. Prendergast suggested that the governments of the Republic of Ireland and Northern Ireland should get together to recognize Feeney as a national hero.

Ireland had no system of national awards, so the prime minister endorsed a joint conferring of an honorary degree on Chuck Feeney by all seven universities in the Republic and the two in Northern Ireland, to mark his gifts to the island totaling by then $1.6 billion. (A further $23 million was subsequently gifted to Queen's University Belfast.) Nothing like this had ever been done before. The universities all enthusiastically backed the proposal.

Feeney agreed to accept the multiple honorary degrees. His giving to Ireland was just about over, and his cover had been blown. He was at last ready to receive an acknowledgment of his role. On September 6, 2012, an unusually warm sunny day, the nine university presidents, along with the chancellor of Trinity College Dublin and former Irish president Mary Robinson, two hundred robed academics, and a large audience of family members, friends, colleagues, beneficiaries, and the prime minister, gathered for the conferring ceremony in St. Patrick's Hall in Dublin Castle. Each university president individually stood to confer on Chuck Feeney, in Latin, the degree of laws. When called upon to respond, Feeney, looking uncomfortable in academic cap and gown, shuffled to the podium carrying his speech in a brown plastic bag. But he never opened it and simply said—using a phrase he had spoken fifteen years before when eulogized at a private dinner by the Irish poet Seamus Heaney—"My cup runneth over. Thank you one and all for your kindness and generosity." He added, "I feel embarrassed, as rightly I should be, by all this attention." Later, when teased that the degree from the nine universities meant he would now have to be addressed as "Dr. Feeney," he replied, "No, now I have to be called Dr., Dr., Dr., Dr., Dr., Dr., Dr., Dr., Dr. Feeney!"

Cornell University does not give honorary degrees but found ways to match the Irish initiative. On Sunday, May 26, 2012, Cornell President David Skorton, speaking at the annual commencement ceremony in Schoellkopf Stadium, acknowledged Feeney's almost $1 billion in unattributable gifts to the university. The 38,000 people in the sun-drenched arena rose to their feet as Skorton pointed out their benefactor sitting in the stands with Helga. Six months later, Feeney was inducted in his absence into the Cornell Athletics Hall of Fame for his financial contributions to the Athletics Department.

In September 2012, *Forbes* published a lengthy profile of Feeney in which associate editor Stephen Bertoni described him as "the James Bond of Philanthropy"—a secretive agent for good causes. Bertoni spent three days with

Feeney in Ireland and was taken with his modesty. He described arriving in Dublin after a train journey with Feeney to Limerick and back. "No commuter even glanced twice at the short New Jersey native, one hand holding a plastic bag of newspapers, the other grasping an iron fence for support. The man who arguably has done more for Ireland than anyone since Saint Patrick slowly limped out of the station completely unnoticed. And that's just how Feeney likes it."

Just after he was first listed in *Forbes* as a billionaire back in 1988, the journalist Buddy de Lazaro, like Feeney a native of Elizabeth, New Jersey, produced some recollections of Feeney's boyhood days in his regular column in the *Elizabeth Daily Journal*. He concluded that Feeney's achievement in becoming a billionaire was "not bad for an Elizabeth kid who started out hawking beach umbrellas and sandwiches." After reading it, Feeney contacted de Lazaro to tell him the article gave him more personal satisfaction than a cover story in *Business Week*. "We Elmora kids gotta stick togedder," he wrote. "There is an Oriental proverb," Feeney added. "Fortune doesn't change a man, it only unmasks him. I guess under the mask is a kid from Elmora wearing a baseball cap."

INDEX

ABC television (Australia), 265
Acela Express, 345
Actis, 355
Adams, Gerry, 186, 187–188, 189–190, 191, 193, 330
Adler, Harry, 26–27, 37, 238
Advertisements, 30, 32, 64
Advocacy, 333, 335, 337, 340, 341, 344, 353, 362, 364, 380
Affleck, Ben, 337
Affordable Care Act, 339, 340, 362
Age (Melbourne), 264
Ahern, Bertie, 181, 183, 272, 273, 274–275, 278, 279, 282
AIDS, 297, 341
Airport Chandlers Ltd. and Airport Chandlers Incorporated, 63, 65, 75
Airport magazine, 158
Akers-Jones, Sir David, 75
Alarcon, Ricardo, 297
Amadeus (play), 328
American Academy in Rome, 336
Americans for a New Irish Agenda, 186, 189, 190, 191
American Tourist and Trade Association, 47
Anchorage, Alaska, 77–79, 114
Andrade, 92, 161, 162, 163, 318
Annenberg Foundation, 289
Anonymous letter, 356–358
Antil, Fred, 12, 21, 238, 294
Army Exchange Service stores (PXs), 44
Arnault, Bernard, 199–204, 209, 210, 215, 216, 217–218, 219, 222, 223, 225, 226, 229, 239
Arnold, Fortas & Porter law firm, 46–48
Atlantic Charitable Trust, 294, 297
Atlantic Foundation, 105, 115, 116–119, 122, 127–132, 152, 166, 167, 170, 171, 175, 178, 197, 217, 241, 268, 289
Atlantic Foundation Service Company, 125, 130, 137, 289
board members, 104, 127, 236

secrecy/anonymity concerning, 120, 124, 126, 130, 131, 139, 141, 153, 154, 168, 169, 233–234, 240, 258, 309–310
See also Atlantic Philanthropies
Atlantic House, 175
Atlantic Philanthropies, 240, 241, 249, 253, 253, 269, 271, 273, 286, 294, 298, 309–310
board of directors crisis, 332, 350, 351–370
legacy of, 311, 314
endowment/spending down of, 312–313, 314, 315–316, 316–317
Atlantic Reports, 353
Atlantic Trust, 119–120, 168, 175, 217, 234, 240
AT&T, 336
Attebury, Ed, 90
Australia, 240, 256–266, 270, 299, 318
Council for the Encouragement of Philanthropy in Australia, 264, 265, 266
Aylward, Sean, 279

Bahamas, 62–63, 116
Bailey Hall, 373, 376
Bangkok, 323, 359
Bannister, Roger, 174
Baseball cap, 396
Bauman, Bob, 339
Bayside Village apartment complex, 344
Beattie, Peter, 258, 259, 266
Beauchamp, Marc, 151
Beck, Robert A. (Bob), 97, 104, 107, 127, 135
Belafonte, Harry, 360
Belarus, 371
Bellamy, Adrian, 114, 122, 143, 144, 146–147, 149, 163, 198–199, 228
Belloni, Toni, 372
Benedictine monk, 330
"Benefits and Burdens of Secrecy" (Hannon report), 122
Benioff, Marc and Lynne, 334
Benn, Dermot, 279
Bennett Jr., John G., 233
Berghofer, Clive, 259–260

**CONOR O'CLERY** is an award-winning journalist and author who served as foreign correspondent for *The Irish Times* in London, Moscow, Beijing, Washington, and New York. He has written and co-written several books on Russian, Irish, and American politics, including *Ireland in Quotes*; *Phrases Make History Here*; *Melting Snow: An Irishman in Moscow*; *Daring Diplomacy*; *Panic at the Bank*; *America, A Place Called Hope?*; *May You Live in Interesting Times*; and *Moscow, December 25, 1991, The Last Day of the Soviet Union*. He lives in Dublin, Ireland.

PublicAffairs is a publishing house founded in 1997. It is a tribute to the standards, values, and flair of three persons who have served as mentors to countless reporters, writers, editors, and book people of all kinds, including me.

I. F. STONE, proprietor of *I. F. Stone's Weekly*, combined a commitment to the First Amendment with entrepreneurial zeal and reporting skill and became one of the great independent journalists in American history. At the age of eighty, Izzy published *The Trial of Socrates*, which was a national bestseller. He wrote the book after he taught himself ancient Greek.

BENJAMIN C. BRADLEE was for nearly thirty years the charismatic editorial leader of *The Washington Post*. It was Ben who gave the *Post* the range and courage to pursue such historic issues as Watergate. He supported his reporters with a tenacity that made them fearless and it is no accident that so many became authors of influential, best-selling books.

ROBERT L. BERNSTEIN, the chief executive of Random House for more than a quarter century, guided one of the nation's premier publishing houses. Bob was personally responsible for many books of political dissent and argument that challenged tyranny around the globe. He is also the founder and longtime chair of Human Rights Watch, one of the most respected human rights organizations in the world.

•   •   •

For fifty years, the banner of Public Affairs Press was carried by its owner Morris B. Schnapper, who published Gandhi, Nasser, Toynbee, Truman, and about 1,500 other authors. In 1983, Schnapper was described by *The Washington Post* as "a redoubtable gadfly." His legacy will endure in the books to come.

Peter Osnos, *Founder and Editor-at-Large*